THUNDER BAY DISTRICT
1821-1892

ONTARIO SERIES

IX

THUNDER BAY DISTRICT

1821-1892

A Collection of Documents

Edited with an Introduction by

Elizabeth Arthur

THE CHAMPLAIN SOCIETY
FOR THE GOVERNMENT OF ONTARIO
UNIVERSITY OF TORONTO PRESS
1973

© University of Toronto Press 1973
Toronto and Buffalo

Printed in Canada

ISBN 0-8020-3281-8
MICROFICHE ISBN 0-8020-0179-3
LC 76-185698

FOREWORD

"FORT William on Lake Superior" is a phrase still capable of conjuring up a picture of colour and vigour, of doughty merchant adventurers and brave pioneer women. For several years the Thunder Bay region was an important funnel through which poured hundreds of men taking up the epic challenge of northern discovery.

But once the spectacular days of the Nor'wester were gone, the idea of industry and commerce blooming in northern barrens seemed to falter. The picture of Fort William, in southern Ontario eyes, became that of a place and social order belonging to the past. All the early associations with the north – the lucrative fur trade, the glittering lure of The Montreal Mining Company and the frontier-probing Canadian Pacific Railway – failed for a time to create the expected strong ties with the southern part of the province. The pace of history slowed with the big push west. Only in the late 1870s can one see the faint recurrence of real association with and participation in the life of the rest of Ontario.

It was necessary therefore that this volume extend nearly two decades closer to the present than any other in the series if the beginnings of real provincial history in Thunder Bay were to be glimpsed at all.

Professor Elizabeth Arthur, the editor of this volume, is the chairman of the Department of History at Lakehead University. She has lived in the District of Thunder Bay for more than twenty years, and her research is part of the effort of the District's new university to explore and analyse the area in which it is situated and to make its discoveries known to the rest of the province.

The purpose of the "Ontario Series" is to make readily available a selection from the extensive, and largely unpublished, sources which document the province's colourful and multi-faceted past. The editor's primary objective is to assemble and present a wide range of contemporary documents bearing on as many different aspects of a region or subject as possible. The documents are preceded by a general introduction in which the significance of each document and the interrelationship between various documents is brought out. Thus, a solid documentary foundation is provided upon which interpretive studies may be based and, at the same time, the general reader is given a comprehensive and meaningful picture of the entire subject. The editor is, of course, solely responsible for any opinions expressed.

The "Ontario Series" is the result of collaboration between the Government of Ontario and the Champlain Society which has been engaged in the production of historical documentary studies for more than sixty years. The Society selects and guides the editor of each volume while the Government defrays the costs of preparation and publication.

The eight previous volumes in the series, like the present one, document the historical development of a region or an urban community. In future some volumes will continue to be devoted to such themes; others will deal with specific subjects and individuals. Three volumes in the course of preparation at the moment are concerned with Ontario and the Great War, Colonel John Prince, and the city of London.

A knowledge of our past enables us better to appreciate the heritage that we hold in trust for future generations. It is with this in mind that I welcome the opportunity to thank Professor Arthur for her significant contribution to the history of Ontario.

WILLIAM G. DAVIS
Premier of Ontario

Queen's Park
Toronto
November 21, 1972

PREFACE

EARLY French explorers, drawing upon both their own experiences in summer storms and Ojibway legends recounted to them, wrote of the vast Baie du Tonnerre on the north short of Lake Superior. A century ago, "Thunder Bay" came to designate a district in the Province of Ontario. On January 1, 1970, with the amalgamation of the former cities of Fort William and Port Arthur and two adjacent townships, the name was also appropriated by the district capital. This book begins with another amalgamation: that of the North West and Hudson's Bay companies; it thus includes documents from the twilight period after 1821, and from the years in which new economic activities permitted the District to emerge in the late nineteenth century.

The geographical features of the north, and the transport routes in use at different periods, have imposed certain patterns and priorities upon the Thunder Bay District. Before the opening of the Sault Ste Marie Canal in 1855, for example, the entire north shore of Lake Superior formed one administrative unit within the Hudson's Bay Company organization; as a result, Michipicoten, outside the boundaries of the modern District, had a vital role to play in its history. Only in the case of documents after 1860 has it been possible to adhere very strictly to the limitations of the modern District boundaries.

If, after the amalgamation of the fur trading companies, 1855 may be taken as the first crucial date in Thunder Bay development, the next was not the year of Confederation, but rather the year of Wolseley's expedition to Red River. The Introduction and the Documents are arranged with the idea of stressing these peculiarities of Thunder Bay history, especially for the reader unacquainted with it. Section A deals with the problem of jurisdiction over the entire seven decades, 1821–92; sections B and C examine two aspects of development before 1855; section D concentrates upon the vitally important surveys of the country between 1855 and 1870; section E concerns itself with the construction of a transcontinental railway; in the last four sections are assembled documents pertaining to various topics in the years 1870–92. Within each section, the order of documents is chronological.

    The publication of this first excursion into the documentary his-
tory of a region north of the Great Lakes is made possible by the
co-operation of the Government of Ontario and the Champlain
Society. I am grateful to both for their support and encouragement.
Miss Edith Firth, who was the general editor of the Ontario Series
during the colection of the material in this volume, has given valued
advice, and has remedied many weaknesses in my presentation over
a number of years. Professor William Ormsby, the present general
editor, has been most helpful as the final date of publication drew
near. To them and to the editorial staff of the University of Toronto
Press I am deeply indebted.
    Archivists and librarians have been most gracious in permitting
access to the documents in their care, and most patient in answering
my queries. I wish to express my thanks to the staffs of the Public
Archives of Canada; the Department of Public Records and Archives
of Ontario; the Archives de la Société de Jésus du Canada Français;
the National Archives of the United States; the Archives of the United
Church, Victoria University, Toronto; the Metropolitan Toronto
Central Library; the University of Western Ontario Library; Lakehead University Library; the Corporation of the City of Thunder
Bay; and the Thunder Bay Historical Society. All these institutions
have generously given permission to include material from their
collections in this volume. Documents from the records of the
Hudson's Bay Company are published by permission of the Governor
and Committee of the Company. I am grateful also for permission to
publish extracts from certain documents in private possession, to
Miss Joan Featherstonhaugh for the diary of Captain Thomas G.
Anderson, to Mrs. Gordon McLaren for the diary of Peter McKellar,
and to Dr. Peter Ballantyne for the petition of the Fort William
Indians to Sir John A. Macdonald.
    Several people have provided me with essential and much appre-
ciated information. Father Léon Pouliot of the Archives de la Société
de Jésus du Canada Français very kindly read my translations of
documents from the "Lettres des Nouvelles Missions," and made
some amendments. Professor Morris Zaslow of the University of
Western Ontario read the first draft of the manuscript, and suggested
a number of important corrections and improvements. In a very
special sense, two long-time residents of Thunder Bay have contributed to this volume. Both Mrs John Dyke and Mr W. Russell
Brown have memories that extend to the period with which some of
these documents deal, and their recollections of people and events
have been invaluable.

Finally, I owe much to the encouragement and aid of my colleagues at Lakehead University – to those in the fields of anthropology, geography, geology, and history who are concerned in the development of northern area studies; to Mr Gerald Hashiguchi, who was responsible for much of the photography, and, above all, to Mrs Mary Humphrey who has typed and re-typed her way across a most unpromising terrain.

ELIZABETH ARTHUR

Thunder Bay, Ontario

CONTENTS

THUNDER BAY DISTRICT, 1821–1892

INTRODUCTION

A. THE UNDISTRIBUTED MIDDLE, 1821–92: A PROBLEM OF JURISDICTION

IF THE CANADIAN NATION exists in defiance of the rules of logic, the Thunder Bay area may be taken to represent the dubious middle term of a syllogism. The modern District of Thunder Bay is bounded by Lake Superior on the south and, for much of its extent, by the Albany River on the north. The surveys of the late nineteenth century established 91° longitude as the western boundary. On the east, the decisions concerning boundaries are less easily described. From Lake Superior north to a point just south of the 50th parallel of latitude, the line dividing Thunder Bay from the neighbouring District of Algoma was drawn slightly east of 85°30′. The projection of this line as far north as the Albany River established the eastern boundary of the Cochrane District. Its western boundary, and hence the eastern boundary of Thunder Bay above the 50th parallel, became 86°30′.

The mere recital of the details of the boundaries of the District illustrates the artificial nature of the creation, and a quick glance at its geographical features accentuates the point still further. The District includes the land which is drained into Lake Superior (in most places a narrow strip along the coast) and the vast region beyond the Height of Land. The first of these regions was always outside the chartered territory of the Hudson's Bay Company; the second was included by the terms of the 1670 charter. Yet the Height of Land has always been far more difficult to determine precisely than would occur to those unfamiliar with the terrain. Out of this circumstance arose disputes over jurisdiction. Even more important, out of this circumstance and the nature of the land itself, the communications available within it, and the use to which the land was put, arose in the mid-nineteenth century a very different pattern and pace of development in the northern and southern parts of the District. The coastal strip became familiar to Canadian interests decades before the territory between the Height of Land and the Albany received much of their attention.

The District of Thunder Bay did not become a recognized geographical entity, beyond legal question part of the province of Ontario, until the 1880s. For nearly seventy years its disparate regions had continued their slow and sporadic development, cut off from the rest of British North America, with little chance of identifying themselves strongly or permanently with any interest beyond their own. This experience tended to create a certain distrust of outside interests among any who remained long enough to be considered residents. But little sense of permanence or stability was apt to develop in the years of isolation.

The early links of the coastal area had been with the fur trading interests based in Montreal. In the North West Company operations the Thunder Bay area had been the vitally important meeting place for the Montreal partners and the winterers of the west. Then, when the Company was amalgamated with the Hudson's Bay Company in 1821 and the lake route virtually abandoned, the old ties with Montreal – jurisdictional, economic, and emotional – were abruptly cut off. The shock was one from which the region did not soon recover. It was the contrast between the actualities of the 1820s and 1830s and the significant role that Fort William had earlier played that underlay much frustration on the part of officials who had long experience in the area, much disappointment on the part of new clerks who came to the region expecting more than they found, and much confusion on the part of the Indians and half-breeds who formed the only permanent population.

In one sense the strip of land along Lake Superior was suffering from the fall of a commercial enterprise which, long before any adequate government surveys of the area or plans for permanent settlement were possible, had audaciously thrust into the wilderness. The amalgamation of the fur trading companies meant that Thunder Bay had to wait for decades before there was any possibility of aid from governments – imperial, provincial, or federal. The partial exploration required by one particular enterprise and the glamour associated with its brief career seem to have alternately inspired and infuriated those who understood anything about the area in the next forty years, and the past was seldom far from their thoughts.

In another sense the area around Thunder Bay was the victim of eighteenth century political developments. The British conquest of Canada might itself be taken as beginning the process of cutting off links between Lake Superior and the St Lawrence region; then the decision to create separate provinces of Upper and Lower Canada provided a political basis for the economic separation of 1821. The American Revolution and the Loyalist migration that followed it created a community on the lower lakes with a tradition alien to the Lake Superior region.

It was the Hudson's Bay Company that was to dominate Thunder

Bay for decades, providing the only real link with Great Britain, virtually isolating the region from Upper Canada of which it was presumed to be a part, and even perhaps accentuating the continentalist pulls inherent in the environment itself. Attachment to Great Britain might be strong on the part of individual Company officials; but the impermanence and varying strength of this influence, combined with the lack of fear of attack from the United States, left the Thunder Bay region without the emotional ties that existed elsewhere. The British government seldom enunciated any policy that impinged upon life in Thunder Bay. At the same time, contacts with the British colonies in America were infrequent and indirect. Upper Canada assumed that it possessed legal jurisdiction over the coastal area, although its knowledge of such a remote district was slight, and the administration of the district remained in the hands of the Hudson's Bay Company. Chief Trader Thomas McMurray at the Pic post in 1836 commented on the receipt of a copy of a new piece of Upper Canadian legislation of which he approved and which he intended to enforce.[1] Legally, there may have been no need for his approval; actually, the chances for enforcement without it would seem to have been minimal. When Upper Canada contemplated the problems of Indians within its borders in 1829, it included only those south of Sault Ste Marie,[2] and no reference to the Lake Superior Indians has been discovered in the correspondence of the Indian Department before the 1850s.

If the Thunder Bay area did identify itself with any empire in the pre-Confederation period it was the empire of the Hudson's Bay Company, not that of Great Britain. After the amalgamation of the fur trading companies in 1821, the operations of the Hudson's Bay Company were no longer restricted to the chartered territory, but included the coastal strip as well. The present District of Thunder Bay was for the first time united under one authority, in fact if not in law. It soon became evident, however, that the new arrangement served neither to draw together the two parts of the district nor to replace the sense of identity that had existed in one of them in the days of the North West Company. The most cursory examination of the Hudson's Bay Company records shows how powerful was the pull of Hudson Bay itself, how important became those rivers down which goods might be shipped to the Bay. The narrow strip along

[1]Public Archives of Canada (P.A.C.), Microfilm of Hudson's Bay Company Records, B-162-a, Pic Post Journal, Feb. 8, 1836.

[2]P.A.C., RG 10, Indian Affairs Department Papers, v. 23, Chief Superintendent's Office, Observations on the Civilization of the Indians in Upper Canada, 1829.

Lake Superior became less and less significant in Company policy, partly because of alterations in fur trade routes, partly because of the vast expansion of Company activities in other more westerly regions, partly because of the decline in the value of furs in the district.

Reorganization followed soon after the agreement of 1821. Fort William's role was at once drastically reduced, and an effort was made to cut down Company personnel at the various posts in the Lake Superior district (B 1). On rare occasions the annual Council did meet at Fort William, but the usual meeting place was Michipicoten where the portage route to James Bay began. It was at Michipicoten that the highest ranking Company officer on Lake Superior was customarily stationed, and from his headquarters came the reports from the area as a whole.

The volume of correspondence from the various posts may be taken as some index of their importance.[3] One can examine the letters written from various posts by the same men at different stages in their careers, and judge to some extent the nature of their responsibilities and the importance of their current posts in the general business of the Company. From Fort Garry and from Moose Factory came voluminous reports; from remote stations like Great Whale River and Esquimaux Bay came letters to be laid before the Governor and Committee; but from Fort William, Nipigon, Pic, and even Michipicoten, the reports were brief and infrequent. These posts must at least have received the general Company directives from headquarters which were filed with the post records in other areas, but, except for a few from Nipigon, such files do not seem to have been preserved. Similarly, the post journals, scrupulously kept in many remote locations, virtually ended in the Lake Superior District by 1840, and most of the detailed entries far earlier than that.[4] Can these lacunae be taken as the product of mere chance? Can they be interpreted as a reflection of the lack of importance of the area or the inefficiency of the clerks employed within it? Lack of importance and inefficiency may themselves have been related, and it is curious to note how much more detailed the reports became when a Company officer was transferred from the Lake Superior District to some other location.

[3]P.A.C., H.B. Co. Records, A-4, contains the Agenda Books for the meetings of the Governor and Committee; B-135-k, the Council Meetings for the Southern Department of which the Lake Superior District formed a part until 1863; B-135-b, Lake Superior District – Correspondence Outwards, has very few documents.

[4]Ibid., B-129-a, contains the Michipicoten Post Journals; B-162-a, Pic Post Journals; B-149-a, Nipigon House; B-231-a, Fort William.

A study of the prominent Company officials who worked in the area after 1821 and who remained even when the fur trade had become a diminished source of revenue makes very clear the economic effect of the amalgamation of the companies. A few former Nor'westers, already approaching retirement or else denied promotion in the new Company, did remain in the 1820s and 1830s, and then retired usually to Upper or Lower Canada. But those who achieved promotion after 1821 did so by leaving the Lake Superior District. By the 1860s the Company had decided that the coastal strip belonged as it had belonged forty years earlier with the Great Lakes rather than the Bay, and it was transferred to the Montreal Department.[5] Such a decision was in itself a rejection of any idea of the usefulness of the region in Company plans, and a preparation for the assumption of real power by the Province of Canada.

Yet it was the link with the Hudson's Bay Company throughout the pre-Confederation period that provided virtually the only basis for contact between the Thunder Bay area and the rest of the world. Sir George Simpson's nearly annual progresses through the area and his attendance at council meetings were taken as enhancing the importance of an area obviously fallen from its former position. The "little emperor" was usually diplomatic enough to flatter local pride by some reference to the past. When a town finally developed at Fort William, many of its streets received the names of Company officials who had little or no connection with the place. It would seem that any identification with the Hudson's Bay Company was a tenuous local creation, based on an unrealistic view of the interests of the Company in North America. Yet even that fragile link was to vanish by the end of the 1860s, and the Company's domination of the area in the previous decades had merely delayed jurisdictional disputes without providing the basis for local identification of interest with any of the contending parties.

Some questions of jurisdiction in the northwest involved an interpretation of the Quebec Act and its definition of the western boundary drawn from the confluence of the Ohio and Mississippi rivers.[6] If, as it came to be argued, that boundary was a line drawn due north from the junction of the rivers, it would cut the north shore of Lake Superior just east of the limits of the present city of Thunder Bay. The subsequent division of the province of Quebec into Upper

---

[5]*Ibid.*, B-135-k, Joint Meeting of the Southern and Montreal Departments held at Michipicoten, July 2, 1863.

[6]Adam Shortt and A.G. Doughty, eds., *Documents Relating to the Constitutional History of Canada, 1759–1791* (Ottawa, 1918), p. 571.

and Lower Canada was made by executive order at a time when the government of George III was much more concerned with the possibility of extending Upper Canada to the southwest than with any need for delineating its boundary on the northwest. Two related questions were thus apparent in the early nineteenth century. How far west did any Canadian authority extend? Did the area south of the Height of Land and east of a line drawn due north from the junction of the Ohio and Mississippi rivers belong to Upper Canada, or, in the absence of any specific statement to that effect, did it continue within the jurisdiction to which it had formerly belonged? These questions were raised in a Quebec court in 1818 when a charge of murder was brought against Charles de Reinhard, after the death of a Hudson's Bay Company employee in the Indian country. The testimony in the case (A 1) strikes a note familiar to any who deal with the history of Thunder Bay – the surveyor called upon to give evidence, the immediate references to the Quebec Act, and the brief intervention of men famous in their own right, knowledgeable in their own areas, but utterly innocent of any knowledge of the lands around Thunder Bay. Chief Justice Sewell and Attorney-General Uniacke, with their eastern seaboard backgrounds, their training in the American colonies and in Britain, attempted to unravel the case presented to them as so many others were to do in the future, but they were strangely alien to Thunder Bay.

The immediate problem of jurisdiction after 1821 was an international one, for the determination of the boundary under the Seventh Article of the Treaty of Ghent imposed particular problems. In 1783 the Treaty of Paris had stipulated that the boundary was to pass "through Lake Superior northward of the Isles Royale and Phelipeaux"[7] and thence west by way of a Long Lake waterway to the Lake of the Woods. Both Isle Phelipeaux and Long Lake were shown clearly on John Mitchell's map of 1755, upon which the 1783 Commissioners based their decisions, but it was generally known by 1821 that neither existed. All the eighteenth century maps were filled with errors. Anthony Barclay, the British commissioner in the 1820s, felt that no confidence could be placed in any of them and that what had to be decided forty years after the treaty was its intent.[8]

Both the British and American governments employed experi-

[7]*Ibid.*, p. 727.

[8]Robert McElroy and Thomas Riggs, eds., *The Unfortified Boundary: a diary of the first survey of the Canadian boundary line from St. Regis to the Lake of the Woods by Major Joseph Delafield* ... (New York, 1943), p. 9.

enced surveyors to report on the disputed territory. David Thompson was appointed by the British Commission, but his accounts dealing for the most part with the boundary in the Lake of the Woods region[9] are less informative for the Thunder Bay District than those of the American agent, Major Joseph Delafield (A 2–4), and his survey team. Delafield, speaking out of his first experience in the area and writing to the American Secretary of State, was more likely than was Thompson to include details that clarified the picture for an outsider. Besides his official concerns, Delafield commented upon the Hudson's Bay Company officials whom he met: "I have found these gentlemen with but one exception (Mr Stuart of Fort William) utterly indifferent to all the concerns of this world, save packs of furs."[10] About his French-Canadian voyageurs, he wrote: "They are, with few exceptions, prodigious gluttons, eating like Indians, and never satisfied with anything, at the same time the most careless & probably the most happy people. They will work the whole day without eating, and eat and sing the whole night without sleeping: are the best of canoe men & the worst to be managed without severity of any people I have had to deal with."[11]

Delafield repeatedly expressed his eagerness that a firm boundary line should be established in the wilderness, and his reasons were closely linked with a developing American nationalism sharply in contrast with the ambivalent attitudes of British authorities towards the centre of the continent. Delafield in 1823 saw little possibility that any business enterprise except the fur trade would succeed, but he was none the less anxious for a settlement. When the British suggested a line near the present city of Duluth, Delafield countered with a suggested boundary at Fort William, and there the matter remained for fifteen years. In 1842 the dividing line was placed where Delafield had at first proposed it ought to be.

The Hudson's Bay Company does not appear to have been deeply concerned over this failure to effect a settlement; no evidence has been found that it was urging the British government to take action on this or other issues affecting Thunder Bay. When Governor Simpson was asked his opinion concerning routes to the prairies, he made it clear that he considered the old route of the Nor'westers impractical by 1856 (D 1); and the fur trade returns as well as the

[9]Ontario, Department of Public Records and Archives (P.A.O.), Thompson Journals, 1823–5; Canada, Department of the Interior, *Report of International Boundary Commission* (Ottawa and Washington, 1931), Appendix III.
[10]McElroy and Riggs, *The Unfortified Boundary*, p. 456, diary entry of Sept. 8, 1823.
[11]*Ibid.*, p. 391, diary entry of June 21, 1823.

constant reorganization of the posts in the area suggest its lack of importance in the overall plans of the Company.

Even an experienced Chief Factor like George Keith, who had long service with the Nor'westers before 1821, was in considerable doubt about the extent of the territory he was in charge of – and not only because the United States boundary issue was unsettled. After earlier confessions of his ignorance of the boundaries, he tried to describe them in his 1834 report (A 5). His description is misleading in a number of respects, but the ambiguity can readily be explained. Not only was the Height of Land a far from clearly defined boundary, but also Company policy was constantly altering the limits of the Lake Superior District, so that a number of posts between the Height of Land and Lake Superior were detached from Keith's administrative district. Sturgeon Lake, about seventy miles west of Lake Nipigon; Arrow Lake, on what was ultimately to be the American boundary; New Brunswick (Missanabie); and Sault Ste Marie were cases in point. All of them had at one time lain within Keith's dwindling district.

A further division was brought about thirty years later when, acting on the entreaties of Peter Warren Bell, then in charge at Michipicoten,[12] the Company brought about a reorganization that had Fort William, and through it Nipigon, served directly from Montreal, without any connection with Michipicoten. Personality clashes may have been partially responsible for the division in this case, and the more rapid transportation by steamer in summer and by American railways in winter could be given as the official reason in the 1860s; but any notion of the economic unity of the north shore of Lake Superior was being abandoned. When Chief Trader Robert Crawford came to Nipigon in 1869 from southern Ontario, he was horrified at the effects of this decision.[13] To him Canadianism itself was being sacrificed. He found that the Fort William trade was by no means exclusively with eastern Canada, but to a considerable degree with the Americans as well, and was shocked to discover the continentalist attitudes of the interior of the continent.

Thomas McMurray, writing in the 1840s, had some of the same horror of American institutions as Crawford later expressed. He was concerned about the spread of republican ideas in general and, while discounting to some extent the importance of American competition from "a spiteful wasp," Pierre Coté at Grand Portage,[14] he tended

[12]P.A.C., H.B. Co. Records, B-134-c, Bell to E.M. Hopkins, March 24, 1867.
[13]*Ibid.*, Crawford to Donald Smith, Sept. 20, 1869.
[14]G.P. deT. Glazebrook, ed., *The Hargrave Correspondence* (Toronto, 1938), p. 431, McMurray to Hargrave, Pic, April 15, 1843.

to read signs of perfidy into every American action. When the Hudson's Bay Company schooner *Whitefish* went aground just off the mouth of the Pic River in 1837, he made this comment on the behaviour of an American captain who had promised to give assistance to the ship on its first voyage and had presumably failed to do so: "It is a dirty and shabby business, but like the generality of the Yankees."[15] Neither Crawford nor McMurray, however, can be taken as typical of Company personnel. Over the years most of the protests were directed against individual American competitors in trade, not against a system of government or a potential military threat. Incommoded Company agents mourned the defection of workmen (who transferred from one country to another with a fine insouciance) and frequently expressed the point of view that Indians and half-breeds ought not to be employed so close to the international border.

But the clearly drawn social distinction between the ranks in the Company's employ does not appear to have represented any fundamental difference in attitude toward the United States on the part of the two classes. At the official level the Company came to an agreement with the American Fur Company in 1833, and renewed it biennially until the mid-1840s. Sir George Simpson, in requesting an extension in 1842, observed: "It has been found to work so well in preventing all rivalry and competition and giving rise to the best feeling between both concerns."[16] As Sir George made clear, the agreement was as much an assurance of monopoly as it was a guarantee of international peace, for each company undertook to restrain free traders within its own territory. Each was quick to explain any apparent breach of the agreement (A 10); each was ready to accommodate the other when difficulties arose (A 11). The correspondence between Governor Simpson and Ramsay Crooks, president of the American Fur Company, was most cordial in tone, and Crooks' approach to the news of rebellion in Canada was by no means that of one eager to seize upon the discomfiture of a rival (A 9). A Scot by birth, a former Canadian resident who knew the fur trade both north and south of the Great Lakes, Crooks was fully aware of the mounting protests against monopolies, and suitably vague in identifying any "new power" that might assume control in the Thunder Bay area if the rebellions of 1837 were successful. Even more interesting than Crooks' caution, however, is the question posed by the American agent in London, Curtis Lampson (A 8).

[15]P.A.C., H.B. Co. Records, B-162-a, Pic Post Journal, Oct. 6, 1837.
[16]P.A.C., Microfilm of American Fur Company Records, Northern Outfit, Miscellaneous Papers, Simpson to Ramsay Crooks, June 11, 1841.

Lampson's business interests were to induce him to become a British subject in later years, and eventually to lead him into the inner councils of the Hudson's Bay Company itself. It would appear that the fur trade imposed its own form of loyalty, which had little to do with international boundaries.

The records of the American Fur Company contain a number of documents illustrating the way in which men with trading experience on one side of the border sought employment on the other – with no apparent consciousness of rejecting one jurisdiction in favour of another. A prospectus in April 1837, over the names of M. Wallace and A. McKay, urged the citizens of Buffalo and Detroit to organize a joint stock company to carry on Lake Superior fisheries within the limits of Upper Canada, ignoring the kind of legal question that Ramsay Crooks had appealed to Washington to clarify (A 6). Messrs Wallace and McKay introduced themselves to the American public as "possessing all the rights and privileges of British subjects, and having been engaged for several years in the Fur Trade and Fisheries ... in the services of the Hudson's Bay Company."[17]

One former Chief Trader in the Hudson's Bay Company, Captain Robert McVicar, applied to Ramsay Crooks for a position in 1839, and cited as a reference another Canadian trader by that time firmly established in the United States, Gabriel Franchère (C 9). McVicar was later to become one of the first permanent settlers in the Thunder Bay area, and his sons and daughters were to be closely associated with the early development of the communities of Port Arthur and Fort William. His offer of services to the American Fur Company was not accepted because, as Crooks put it, "though we doubt not your experience and responsible position would enable you to render a valuable service, we have not at present any situation where we can make them usable."[18]

At almost the same time another offer of services was accepted, that of James McKay.[19] He had been chief clerk in the Lachine headquarters of the Hudson's Bay Company and had left that post to enter private business in Michigan, only to go bankrupt in the 1837 bank failure. "Delicacy or a false pride," he explained, "prevented me applying to Governor Simpson for my former situation." McKay was sent to La Pointe on Lake Superior where he imported procedures from the Lachine office with the co-operation of the officials there, and bitterly criticized his superior, Dr Charles

[17]*Ibid.*, Prospectus, signed M. Wallace and A. McKay, April 1837.
[18]*Ibid.*, Letter Book 9, p. 451, Crooks to McVicar, May 4, 1839.
[19]*Ibid.*, Northern Outfit, Miscellaneous, McKay to Crooks, May 3, 1839.

Borup.[20] By the time he was dismissed from the American Fur Company's services and left La Pointe for Detroit and New York, John McKenzie, who had been his schoolmate in Dingwall, Scotland, and had joined the Hudson's Bay Company at about the same time, had become the officer in charge at Fort William. McKay retained his ties with Canada through his brother Duncan, a Kingston merchant, and there is at least a suggestion that he became a free trader on the north shore of Lake Superior.

It was from the United States also that the first missionaries moved into Thunder Bay. Roman Catholic missionaries were active on the south shore of Lake Superior in the 1830s, and Father Francis Pierz set up a mission at Grand Portage[21] from which he attemped to serve the Thunder Bay area. At a meeting at La Pointe in 1847 Father Pierz apparently agreed that the Jesuit order, recently re-established in Canada, should assume responsibilities for the far northwest on both sides of the international boarder. Two French-born Jesuit priests, Father Pierre Choné and Father Nicolas Frémiot, along with Brother de Pooter who was described as a "fortissimus Belga,"[22] arrived at Pigeon River in the spring of 1848. Later they decided upon a different site and built the Mission of the Immaculate Conception at Fort William.

Father Choné had previous experience on Manitoulin Island where he was most concerned over the activities of "the seductive Methodists of Owen Sound,"[23] but he found little competition for souls in Thunder Bay. The Methodists had shown some interest in the Michipicoten area and one of their missionaries, the Rev. Thomas Hurlburt, used the Pic post as his base between 1837 and 1842; but their penetration of the district from the east meant that only occasionally did one of the Methodists visit the western end of Lake Superior.

But Protestant laymen were soon concerned over the extent of Jesuit influence. When the demand for mining locations on Lake Superior raised the whole question of Indian title to the land, representatives of the Canadian government travelled to the Lake Superior region in 1849 and 1850. In the settling of this jurisdictional problem the Jesuits were vitally interested, and their influence with the Indians

[20]*Ibid.*, William Brewster of Detroit to Crooks, Jan. 1, 1841.

[21]Sister Mary Aquinas Norton, *Catholic Missionary Activities in the Northwest 1818–1864* (Washington, 1930), p. 46.

[22]Quebec, Archives de la Société de Jésus du Canada Français (A.S.J.C.F.), Lettres des nouvelles missions du Canada, v. 1, p. 397, Frémiot to the Provincial in Paris, Aug. 11, 1848.

[23]*Ibid.*, v. 1, p. 267, Choné to the Students at Brugelette College, Aug. 7, 1849.

might be of crucial importance. Captain Thomas G. Anderson, the superintendent of Indian affairs for Canada West, who visited Fort William in 1849, did not conceal his contempt for Father Frémiot (A 12), while W.B. Robinson, who negotiated the Indian treaty of the following year, referred to unnamed "interested parties" and "evil disposed persons" who were encouraging the Indians to demand more than the Canadian government wished to pay (A 16). Both Anderson and Robinson made use of an argument new in the northwest – the benefits to the Indians of living on British rather than American territory. Meanwhile, Father Frémiot was reporting to his Superior in New York upon the conference between the Canadian officials and the Fort William Indians (A 13) and keeping some notes of conversations with Chief Peau de Chat (A 14). By the Robinson Treaty the Indians surrendered the land between Lake Superior and the Height of Land in return for certain reservations and financial benefits (A 15). As this agreement with the Indians became the model for others in the west, the doubts and hopes expressed by those viewing the situation in the "undistributed middle" of British North America have more than local significance.

Cordial relations between Canadian and Hudson's Bay Company officials in 1849 and 1850 implied some acceptance of the Company's role in the north. In less than a decade Canadian businessmen (A 17), and the Canadian government itself, were challenging the Company's charter and questioning the Company's claim to jurisdiction in the Red River area: "Wherever they have any possession or occupancy there they are simply squatters, the same as they are at Fort William, La Cloche, Lake Nipissing, or any of their other posts in Canada" (A 18). The despatch of both a British and a Canadian exploring expedition from Lake Superior west was evidence of the new interest, yet it was soon clear that the interest was concentrated upon the potential wealth of the prairies, not Thunder Bay. Nevertheless, the idea of providing connections through territory no matter how inhospitable was bound to attract supporters as the idea of a Canadian confederation took shape. The recommendations and reports of these years pointed up the possibility that the Thunder Bay District would once more become a zone of east-west transit; but the tone of all these documents reveals how far apart were the attitudes of commercial and political leaders in Toronto and Ottawa and the few settlers in the newly surveyed townsite at Fort William. Neither the mining interest that had attracted some settlers from Bruce Mines on Lake Huron or the Ontonagon country in northern Michigan, nor the long-established fur trading interest

would be likely to inspire any confidence in transcontinental dominion. Ottawa and Toronto seemed very remote. The very concentration of interest that was beginning to focus on the chartered
territory of the Hudson's Bay Company and the enthusiasm in
Canada West for the development of an area loosely called the North-
west (but which apparently did not include Thunder Bay) increased
the sense of grievance and isolation.

If Confederation failed to provide a new sense of identity for the
people of Thunder Bay, the creation of the province of Manitoba
provoked further divisions among them. The old disputes over jurisdiction, which in the opinion of some had prevented the hanging of
De Reinhard in 1818, raised questions concerning the interprovincial boundary and, given the greater degree of settlement, discussion
among the residents of Thunder Bay as to which, if either, province
they would prefer. The idea of being separate from both, either as
a province at once or as a territory with provincial status to come
later, had obvious attraction. The report of the Boundary Commissioners (A 20) gave the entire "new territory" to Ontario, but when
the report came before the House of Commons Simon J. Dawson,
the M.P. for Algoma (which then included what was termed the
sub-district of Thunder Bay), moved that a select committee be set
up to invesigate the matter (A 21). As Dawson observed, the
Commissioners' report gave him a constituency larger than he had
dreamed of, equal, according to his computation, to the Maritime
provinces, Newfoundland, and the Gaspé Peninsula as well. In his
opposition to the Commissioners' report he argued that his constituency had powerful historical links with Quebec and Manitoba
and increasingly powerful economic links with Ontario, but few
historical or emotional ties with the latter.

The speech to the House of Commons on February 18, 1880,
was by no means the only time Dawson explored this theme. Earlier,
as a member of the Ontario House, he had urged an unsympathetic
audience to consider the impact of the North West Company on the
area he represented,[24] and it is even possible that concern over the
connection with Ontario was partially responsible for his decision
to contest the federal seat in 1878. Dawson's contention by 1880 was
one that his Prime Minister was willing to hear expressed: that the
recommendation of the Boundary Commission would give dispro-
portionate power to Ontario in the Dominion. Alexander Mackenzie,

[24]Ontario Debates, Feb. 9, 1876, as quoted in James Cleland Hamilton, *The
Prairie Provinces, sketches of travel from Lake Ontario to Lake Winnipeg ...*
(Toronto, 1876), p. 192.

Edward Blake, and David Mills argued that the Dawson motion was out of order and that the report of the Commissioners must be debated at once; but they were overruled by the Speaker and the House gave overwhelming support to the motion. The Dawson argument was an attractive one for members from the Maritimes and Quebec, and it also won the support of a former Premier of British Columbia, Amor de Cosmos, who served as a member of Dawson's committee.

In the ensuing hearings the select committee was told the difficulties of relying upon presumably unmistakable geographical features in determining boundary lines. Dr Robert Bell, assistant director of the Geological Survey of Canada, testified to the ambiguity of such phrases as the "Height of Land" or the "largest channel of the Albany River" (A 22). The committee also had laid before it the contradictory and ambiguous documents from the previous century concerning the boundary lines, and the cases in which disputes over jurisdiction had occurred. It was finally the duty of the Judicial Committee of the Privy Council to decide the issue, and again distinguished gentlemen far from the scene dealt earnestly with the intricacies of a local problem. Thunder Bay residents also pondered the problem and tried to make use of the dispute in their own interests. Counsel for a girl accused of manslaughter provided a unique argument that the trial could not take place before an Ontario judge since Prince Arthur's Landing (Port Arthur) was within the boundaries of the province of Quebec (A 24). Newspaper editorials weighed the advantages of belonging to Manitoba, which might be considerate of the interests of its only Great Lakes port, against the inflammatory remarks ascribed to Premier Norquay and the alleged conservatism of a purely agricultural province.[25] Occasionally, a cry of rejection of both provinces could be heard, usually followed, somewhat illogically, by a complaint that neither province seemed sufficiently eager to attach Thunder Bay to itself.

For a time there seemed a possibility of territorial and eventual provincial status for the north, but that dream was shattered by the Dominion government's decision in 1881 to extend the boundaries of Manitoba to meet those of Ontario. Most residents seemed to have reconciled themselves to their fate (A 23) even if the reasons given were sometimes less than gratifying to ardent supporters of the Ontario cause and the Mowat government. Sheriff John F. Clarke of Thunder Bay, for example, was eagerly pushing Ontario's claims in the Rat Portage region, urging prompt action, even if it were

[25]*Weekly Herald*, Port Arthur, May 27, 1882.

illegal, on the grounds that "right acts lead to legal ones."[26] Thunder Bay residents were excited and partisan spectators to the Rat Portage dispute over jurisdiction which only ended with the Privy Council decision of 1889 in the case of *St. Catherine's Milling and Lumber Company* v *The Queen*. But, like the rest of the province of Ontario, they *were* spectators. Questions of jurisdiction in Thunder Bay itself ended with the 1884 confirmation of the boundary recommended by the Commissioners six years earlier.

In the next years the Ontario government set in motion surveys to determine the boundaries of districts now unquestionably within the province, and Alexander Niven's definitive description of the Thunder Bay-Rainy River boundary (A 25) revealed to what extent clarity of description, if not the surveying itself, relied upon the presence of a completed line of the Canadian Pacific Railway. The middle of the continent had at last been assigned to one jurisdiction and the surveyors of 1890 were recording merely the limits of districts within a province, not supplying evidence to buttress one claim or another for possession of the land itself. Professor A.R.M. Lower has remarked that the building of Canada was an exercise in carpentry, in which dissimilar pieces were tacked together.[27] Perhaps the analogy might be altered somewhat for Thunder Bay, which seems to have become a community by virtue of triangulation.

[26]P.A.O., Sir Aemilius Irving Papers, Clarke to Hon. A.S. Hardy, Aug. 11, 1883.
[27]*Canadians in the Making* (Toronto, 1958), p. 289.

B. DREAMS OF POWER AND RICHES, 1821–55

IN THE GENERATION after the union of the fur trading companies the Lake Superior District was haunted by memories of its past, reminded constantly of its decline from the promise of Fort William's first decade, and, from time to time, aroused by hopes that wealth and influence might be recovered. It was all too easy for old Nor'westers and their sons to snatch at phantasmagoric dreams of the future. But the hard facts of the nineteenth century fur trade and the decline of existing transport routes offered little hope for the Thunder Bay area in the thirty years that followed the amalgamation of 1821. Even if valuable minerals were discovered, and there were rumours of such wealth from the 1820s on, difficulties in transportation were likely to prevent any extensive development until the route through the Great Lakes was opened in 1855.

The diminished importance of Fort William was made very clear by Nicholas Garry, the Hudson's Bay Company representative in the final negotiations between the fur trading companies. His distaste for his task was apparent from the outset. "Myself being the only single Man in the Direction," he wrote, "it became imperative on Me that I should not hesitate to undertake this long and tedious Journey."[1] Garry's account of his important meeting at Fort William (B 1) consists of only two pages of journal entries, almost entirely concerning the scenery, for the three weeks he spent at the Fort. In his account of the history of the Hudson's Bay Company, Douglas MacKay commented on what he considered the exasperating omissions in the journal;[2] but, for the Lake Superior District, both the items included and the omissions are revealing. For Garry, and for many who followed him in the direction of the Hudson's Bay Company, the region possessed nothing of importance beyond the scenery.

The chief spokesman for the North West Company who met Garry at Fort William was William McGillivray, after whom the place had been named. His letter to John Strachan (B 2) indicated how little hope he had for the fur trade of the Lake Superior area. It was only later that other old Nor'westers found reasons – real and imaginary – for hope. In the 1820s the prevailing mood was pessimistic. Major

[1]F.N.A. Garry, ed., "Diary of Nicholas Garry," in Royal Society of Canada, *Transactions*, 2nd series, 1900, v. 6, p. 75.
[2]*The Honourable Company* (Toronto, 1936), p. 169.

Delafield described (C 2) the impact of the 1821 decisions, visible within two years of the Garry-McGillivray meeting. Chief Factor John Haldane recorded in his official report for 1824 (B 3) what was happening to the fur trade upon which the district depended. The Governor of Michigan Territory gave a grim picture of the peace that followed the old battles between the fur trading companies. "The hustle and bustle of war have disappeared," wrote Lewis Cass in 1827, "and have been succeeded by the calm, still operations of trade. It is a silence that will not soon be interrupted. It is already becoming the silence of desolation. In these impassable regions, the oppressor and the oppressed are almost severed from the human family, and there are few now to disclose the deeds of the one or the sufferings of the other."[3]

The records of the Hudson's Bay Company do not reveal any abrupt lift in spirits from the pessimism of the 1820s. With the departure of Alexander Stewart and John Haldane from the Lake Superior District in 1823 and 1827 respectively, no man of the rank of Chief Factor was posted to Fort William. Even at Michipicoten, the new headquarters for the Lake Superior District, the officer in charge was often of lesser rank. George Keith and John Dugald Cameron were both former Nor'westers who became Chief Factors in 1821, but once they had left the district by the early 1840s Michipicoten was in the charge of Chief Traders like John Swanston, John McKenzie, and Peter Warren Bell, whose promotion to the next rank usually coincided with their posting elsewhere. At the same time, other posts in the Lake Superior District rarely rated a Chief Trader. A clerk was usually in charge or, in some cases, a post master (a rank below that of clerk) or an interpreter.[4]

Of the old Nor'westers who remained in the district until retire-

---

[3]*Remarks on the Policy and Practice of U.S. and Great Britain in the Treatment of the Indians*, reprinted from the *North American Review*, April 1827, p. 52.

[4]P.A.C., H.B. Co. Records, B-135-k-1, Council Meetings for the Southern Department. At the meeting at Fort William, June 14, 1832, Chief Factor Angus Bethune from Michipicoten was the ranking officer in the Lake Superior District, which also boasted three Chief Traders, McIntosh at Fort William, Alexander McTavish at Nipigon, and Thomas McMurray at the Pic. Meeting at Moose Factory, August 7, 1843, Chief Trader John Swanston of Michipicoten was the ranking officer in the Lake Superior District; Nipigon, Pic, and Fort William were in the charge of clerks, while Batchewana, Long Lake, and Lac L'Orignal had post masters or acting post masters. By the meeting at Michipicoten, July 20, 1855, John McKenzie, the only commissioned officer in the district at that time, had secured his promotion to the rank of Chief Factor; he was to depart for Moose Factory very shortly thereafter, leaving Michipicoten to Chief Trader J.S. Watt. At the Michipicoten joint meeting of the Southern and Montreal departments, July 2, 1863, which transferred the Lake Superior District to the Montreal Department, no Chief Factors or Chief Traders were listed for the district — clerks at Michipicoten and Fort William, post masters or interpreters elsewhere.

ment, Donald McIntosh provided an unhappy example (B 4). Jealous of the promotions others received, restive under the new regulations limiting the sale of liquor to the Indians, McIntosh was not highly regarded by the officials of the Company he joined in 1821 (B 6). There seems to be some reason to believe that his appointment as Chief Trader at that time came about partly in the belief that he was about to retire.[5] He changed his mind and was accordingly sent to Michipicoten, Nipigon, Pic, and Fort William, while the Company awaited his eventual retirement. Both Thomas McMurray's letters to James Hargrave (B 7) and his journal entries (B 8) reveal him as a very different type of "poor old N'wester." With McMurray, nostalgia existed but did not obscure the realities of the 1830s. The same might be said for young Dugald McTavish, who served as a clerk in Michipicoten in the 1830s, then rose in the Company service in areas as remote as the Columbia Valley and the Sandwich Islands. As a boy of nineteen he wrote realistically enough about the hardships of a posting to such a forlorn area (B 9). More than thirty years later he sent a clipping from a Washington newspaper for John Swanston. The clipping recorded the approval by the United States Senate of the appointment of one Donald McIntosh as second lieutenant, 7th Cavalry. McTavish commented: "The McIntosh mentioned is a grandson of Donald McIntosh – in his day a Chief Trader at Fort William on Lake Superior. Young McIntosh's father – John by name – was murdered by Indians in 1844 or 5 at Stuart's Lake in New Caledonia."[6] So had time cast some glamour over the man Governor Simpson had described thus: "Speaks Saulteaux, is qualified to cheat an Indian and can make a fishing net, which are his principal qualifications" (B 6).

Simpson's comments were written in 1832, and some of the judgments he made then were modified in the light of later experience. There was little opportunity for any such modification in the cases of McIntosh or the other officers described in B 6, however, for they were all nearing retirement. What Simpson had to say about them and, by inference at least, about the Lake Superior District in which they all had long experience, is important in any study of the land and the people employed in it. Although J.G. McTavish had been

[5]*Ibid.*, Minutes of Council, Moose Factory, Aug. 1, 1822, cites letter from McIntosh, dated June 23, 1822: "It was generally understood among you, that my intentions were to leave the country this season. I expressed a wish to that effect last summer to Mr. Garry at Fort William, but finding that no notice has been taken of it by the governor and Committee in London, I have determined to remain a few years longer in the country, although I was perfectly sincere in what I expressed last year." A motion that Donald McIntosh should retain his situation as Chief Trader was carried.

[6]*Ibid.*, 134-c-110, McTavish to Edward Clouston, Washington, D.C., June 27, 1868.

at York Factory and then at Moose Factory from 1821 on, Simpson's judgment of him has been included with the others, partly to show his views of the effect of long service in the north on a particular individual, partly to illustrate the point that former Nor'westers did not inevitably receive an unfavourable report, as McIntosh seems to have assumed. It would appear, instead, that it was the decline in the economic importance of the region rather than any Hudson's Bay prejudice against those who had served its former rival that created the contrast between the old and the new dispensations in Thunder Bay.

Out of the contrast between past and present arose more dangerous delusions on the part of a number of young men, sons of Nor'westers by Indian mothers. They felt themselves doubly dispossessed. A number of them received an excellent education; some of them had sought posts in the Hudson's Bay Company in which their fathers served, and had been refused. They assumed that the reason was their Indian ancestry, and Simpson's comments on some of the half-breed clerks inherited from the North West Company explain the assumption. In referring to the unhappy clerk, Roderick McKenzie (C 3), whom Haldane called "a promising young man,"[7] Simpson wrote "Tolerably steady for a half breed, manages a small post but has no right to look higher."[8] In 1836, a few of these young men joined in the fantastic scheme of "General" James Dickson to form an Indian liberating army, which was to cut through North America in a huge arc from the Great Lakes to Fort Garry to Texas, linking up Indians and métis, whether aggrieved by the policy of the Hudson's Bay Company or that of the United States or Mexican governments. John McLoughlin, Jr., Martin McLeod, John George McKenzie, and Charles McBean served as officers in Dickson's "liberating army." In the summer of 1836 the newspapers of Buffalo and Detroit and later Montreal gave some attention to what they termed "piracy on the lakes," and Hudson's Bay officials were aware of the potential danger. Governor Simpson was quick to offer positions in the Company service to McLoughlin and McLeod[9] and, when the latter vanished into Minnesota territory after the failure of the expedition, Simpson attempted to trace him on behalf of his relatives.[10]

Company personnel at Sault Ste Marie were encouraged to report

[7]*Ibid.*, B-231-e-3, Haldane's Report on Fort William District, 1824–5.

[8]*Ibid.*, A-34-2, Servants' Characters, 1832.

[9]P.A.C., Series G, v. 78, p. 507, Simpson to Judge McDonnell of Detroit, Sept. 7, 1836, encloses letters to both men offering them posts.

[10]P.A.C., American Fur Company Records, Miscellaneous Papers, Simpson to Crooks, Nov. 3, 1845.

all they could find out, and information concerning the actions of the young half-breeds was especially welcome since there was a possible danger of Dickson's adding more such recruits. The career of John George McKenzie, the secretary of war with the expedition, was a case in point. This young man, who had been born at Long Lac, was the son of Alexander McKenzie, nicknamed "Emperor," an old adversary of the Hudson's Bay Company who had never come to terms with it. Illness compelled John George to leave the expedition and, with his sister and her family, who lived at Sault Ste Marie, he travelled back to Montreal. James McKay, then a clerk at the Lachine office, reported on his activities: "Mr. McKenzie has come down ostensibly to recover his health, and join the expedition next spring which in the mean time proceeds on by Fond du Lac for Red River, where it is reported they are to found the capital of a new kingdom, composed entirely of half-breeds and Indians. They claim the whole of the Company's territory as their inheritance by birthright. Most contradictory statements are current, as regards the means of Dickson, some stating him to be equally bankrupt in means as in character, while others affirm him to be a man of large fortune."[11]

After studying his various sources of information Governor Simpson reported to the British Government on October 31, 1836 (B 10); and that government, by the end of the year, was discounting the importance of the whole incident except perhaps among "the Indians settled in the more remote districts of Upper Canada."[12] Hudson's Bay Company officials stationed in those remote districts were understandably concerned at the potential danger, even after the Dickson army had disintegrated. Thomas McMurray reported that Charles McBean came back from Red River to rejoin his father, a Chief Factor in the Lake Huron District, when the remnants of the army scattered.[13] Of the four "thoughtless young men" who served as officers in that army, McKenzie died near Montreal early in 1838; McBean vanished from the records with his return to his father's home; McLoughlin served the Hudson's Bay Company briefly and was murdered in the west in 1841.[14] Martin McLeod became a prominent businessman in Minnesota, and his diary provides the best source of information about the whole enterprise. Inscribed in the

[11]P.A.C., Series G, v. 78, p. 530, McKay to Simpson, Oct. 7, 1836 (enclosed in Simpson to Pelly, Oct. 31, 1836).
[12]Ibid., p. 471, Charles Grant, Baron Glenelg to Sir Francis Bond Head, Dec. 30, 1836.
[13]P.A.C., H.B. Co. Records, B-162-a, Pic Post Journal, entry of July 17, 1837.
[14]E.E. Rich, The History of the Hudson's Bay Company, 1670–1870 (London, 1959), II, 712.

diary of the twenty-three-year-old McLeod appears a most apposite quotation from *Childe Harold*:

> 'Twas as a dream – whose fine and tremulous joys
> Have being but in slumber – which a breath
> A touch of rude reality destroys ...[15]

Captain John H. Lefroy was only in his mid-twenties when he described the Thunder Bay region he traversed on his magnetic survey of British America, but Byronic influences were not in evidence. The rude reality he encountered convinced him that the environment destroyed those who lived in it (C 11, C 12). Shortly after his journey, however, the mining boom on the south shore of Lake Superior revived enthusiasm in some quarters at least. A feverish period of mining explorations on the north shore followed, and by the end of 1845 the government of Canada had received 160 applications for location along the Lake Superior shoreline. William Logan, the chief government geologist, was sent to report on the possibilities of the area and to recommend which, if any, of the locations should be granted. Logan's general remarks concerning the area (B 12) were made before his expedition set out and they illustrate the caution with which he approached his task. This caution contrasted with the exuberant reports being sent to interested individuals in Lower Canada and in the United States.[16]

While on Lake Superior in the summer of 1846, Logan reported on twenty-seven locations that were accordingly granted (B 16), injected another cautionary note concerning the possibilities for development of the area (B 14), and had his assistant, Alexander Murray, prepare descriptions of the valleys of two of the rivers flowing into Lake Superior – the Kaministikwia and the Michipicoten. The description of the former (B 15) was extremely detailed; of the latter, for reasons Murray explained in his report, very brief and incomplete. The Lake Superior District in the summer of 1846 thus had its first experience with "savants" (B 13) whom some old fur traders could watch with amusement. Two years later an American group headed by Louis Agassiz went north to report on the natural history of the region, and one of the members of the expedition, J. Elliot Cabot of Boston, provided a narrative of their experiences

[15]Grace Lee Nute, ed., "The Diary of Martin McLeod," in *Minnesota History*, Nov. 1922, p. 354.

[16]P.A.C., MG 24 I-8, Macdonell of Collachie Papers, Allan Macdonell, Mining Papers, J.F. Boynston (geologist) to Edward Ryan at Quebec, Aug. 22, 1846, indicated that Boynston was employed from June 1 on Ryan's behalf by C.H. Gratiot, formerly of the U.S. army.

to accompany the scientific reports published in 1850. Already there was evidence that the mining boom had been of short duration (B 13) and another dream was fading away. Again, as in the case of Major Delafield twenty-five years earlier, the trained and detached observer saw the realities of Thunder Bay in bleak terms.

For a brief period in the 1840s it appeared that commercial interests based on the St Lawrence would again focus their attention on Thunder Bay and recreate its past importance. Both the Quebec and Lake Superior Mining Association and the Montreal Mining Company were incorporated in 1847, and took over most of the grants made in the previous year to individual claimants, but the financial problems of the former and the deliberate policy of the latter soon removed both companies from effective influence on Lake Superior. Allan Macdonell of Toronto was one of the original shareholders of the Quebec and Lake Superior Mining Association and he kept copies of the initial glowing reports from the field as well as recording, about a decade later, what errors he felt had prevented the exploitation of potentially valuable property. Besides the complete and formal statement of his views, there were preliminary and fragmentary notes sometimes revealing more of the history of the Company (B 17). Macdonell was convinced that it was mismanagement rather than any lack of wealth in the district that had been responsible for failure. He was obviously at odds with many of the Quebec-based directors from the beginning, and claimed that their knowledge of the lumber trade did not equip them for their new task. He also claimed that their expenditures were exorbitant, and it seems clear that the comparative success of the Montreal Mining Company influenced his conclusions.

But Macdonell's comments ignored two rather important points in the contemporary development of the Montreal Mining Company. It was by no means so separate from the Quebec and Lake Superior Mining Association as his comparison of operation might suggest. There were early indications of interlocking directorates, and Thomas Ryan, later a president of the Montreal Mining Company, was extremely active in the interests of the other company in its early years.[17] Secondly, such success as the Montreal-based Company did achieve was on its Lake Huron, not its Lake Superior, locations. The Company had as its first president George Moffatt, an old Nor'wester, and both Hugh Allan and George Cartier were members of the

[17]Quebec and Lake Superior Mining Association, *Report to the Directors*, 1848; Montreal Mining Company, *Report*, 1851.

Board by 1851.[18] A Board guided by a veteran of old fur trading battles and the chief figures in the railway scandal of 1873 took a most realistic view. Neither sentiment for the past nor premature eagerness for transcontinental transport blinded them to the difficulties of mining in Thunder Bay in the mid-nineteenth century. They decided very early to cut unnecessary expenses by concentrating on Bruce Mines (B 19) and abandoning their locations on Lake Superior.

From the Hudson's Bay Company directors of 1821 to the Montreal Mining Company directors of the 1850s, the message was the same: immense optimism concerning the future of their holdings in areas other than Thunder Bay. The Hudson's Bay Company was prepared to discount the reports of restive old Nor'westers who dreamed of the past – a generation that had vanished by 1850. The Montreal Mining Company could dismiss stories of vast mineral wealth in Thunder Bay as the fantasies of diseased minds (B 20). Given the problems of transport from Lake Superior in the years before the opening of the canal at Sault Ste Marie, the directors of the companies were undoubtedly making decisions in the interests of the shareholders. But the history of Thunder Bay was more than the history of commercial enterprises operating within it. Those who lived in the area for considerable periods of time between the years 1821 and 1855 were constantly affected by the external view of their region, and the Company decisions resulting from that view, but they did not live without hope. Irrationally, perhaps, they snatched at every dream of improvement in their situation; they came to regard themselves as associated with the interests of a particular region. The social history of Thunder Bay – the development of customs and attitudes peculiar to the area – seems to have preceded economic development or the permanent settlement to which it gave rise.

[18]Montreal Mining Company, *Rules and By-Laws* (Montreal, 1847); *Report*, 1851.

C. TRAVELLERS AND RESIDENTS, 1821–55

IT WAS AN INESCAPABLE RESULT of the kind of economic activity that was carried on in the Thunder Bay area before 1855 that the people who lived there were transients rather than settlers. But there were degrees of transience. Travellers en route to the west, Hudson's Bay Company officials arriving only for annual council meetings, members of the Boundary Commission appointed under the terms of the Treaty of Ghent – these may be classified as genuinely transient. A second group was made up of Company employees and missionaries whose work kept them in the district for a number of years – representatives of institutions which continued in their influence even though individuals changed. In a third group were the Ojibways and some Company workmen, whether half-breed or not, who had married Indians and chose to remain associated with the district as a whole, appearing periodically at the various Company posts.

The travellers moved through the district, often commenting upon the social conditions they found there and presenting their own impressions of the life they saw. Both Dr Bigsby and Major Delafield (C 1, C 2) were members of the International Boundary Commission of the 1820s. Captain Lefroy had occasion to cross the continent twenty years later in connection with the magnetic survey of British North America (C 11, C 12). J. Elliot Cabot of Boston was a member of the scientific expedition led by Louis Agassiz in 1848 (C 16). Captain Thomas G. Anderson had much previous experience with the north and with the work of the Indian Department but his only journey to Lake Superior was a brief one in 1849 (C 17). All these men came to Thunder Bay for a specific purpose, remained only a short time in the area, and, in spite of a high degree of training in their particular fields of endeavour, could only record impressions hastily gleaned and dependent upon fragmentary or hearsay evidence. All these men either kept diaries in which they noted almost daily the events on their travels or, like Captain Lefroy, wrote voluminous letters to relatives. Of this group, only Dr Bigsby had occasion to revise his work. His journal was published in 1850, twenty-seven years after his experiences in Thunder Bay, and it is impossible to tell to what extent the events of the intervening years caused him to alter what he had originally written.

Hudson's Bay Company officers varied in their length of service in the district and varied in their attitudes toward the conditions of life there. Their reports contained much of economic importance to their superiors in London, but they also contained much of primarily local significance – the details of their trade with the Indians, the problems of securing and keeping trustworthy employees, the names of workmen who remained in the district, for example (C 6–8). The missionaries were in a unique position to record, from their particular point of view, both the customs of the Indians and the effect of Hudson's Bay Company operations upon them.

It is with the Indian residents of Thunder Bay that any consideration of potential settlement must begin. Every reference to the Ojibway of Lake Superior up to 1850 agrees upon the nomadic character of their life. When Thomas L. McKenney, the American Indian commissioner, visited Fond du Lac in 1826, he identified each of the Chiefs from the Lake Superior area who assembled to meet him with a particular region, usually the shores of some small lake, but he stressed their migratory habits. One of the few indications of any sign of permanence that he included was the case of the Chief Anacamigistica. When the North West Company headquarters was moved to Fort William, Anacamigistica had his grandfather's bones moved as well, although this did not ensure his own location near the place. McKenney identified him with the Rainy Lake area.[1]

The journals of the various posts recorded the appearance of various Indian Chiefs and their bands from time to time. At Fort William, for example, in the summer of 1831, entries read as follows: June 2 – "Illinois Chief and Band went off to Isle Royale where they intend to pass the summer"; June 27 – "The Spaniard with twelve other Indians arrived"; August 7 – "The Indian Chief Illinois here awaiting the arrival of Mr. C.T. McIntosh."[2] Both the Chiefs alluded to in these entries appeared frequently in the records, and each of them was described in some detail – the Spaniard by Governor Simpson (C 10) and the Illinois by Father Frémiot (A 13).

George Keith's report on the Lake Superior District indicated in 1833 an Indian population of 760 souls, about 200 of them fit to bear arms.[3] From his earlier more specific answers to queries concerning the Indian population, Keith made it clear that he was not counting Indian warriors with any idea of incipient revolt. He distinguished between warriors who might be mustered for a long or

---

[1]Thomas L. McKenney and James Hall, *History of the Indian Tribes of North America, with biographical sketches and anecdotes of the principal chiefs* (Philadelphia, 1836), I, no pagination.

[2]P.A.C., H.B. Co. Records, B-231-a, Fort William Post Journals, 1831.

[3]*Ibid.*, B-129-e, Reports on the Michipicoten District, 1833.

distant expedition – thirty or less – and those for defensive or temporary warfare – perhaps three times that number.[4] Roderick McKenzie's estimate (C 6) for the Fort William area alone was 195, and that number he considered too large for the region to support. The association of the Indians with the district as a whole if not with a particular place within it was strong and usually permanent. The only early reference that has been found to an Indian family's identifying itself with one post is that of the Fainiant family of Fort William who had "been brought up from their infancy at the Fort,"[5] but even they were to be found, sometimes reluctantly, at the Pic and Nipigon (C 4).

Many of the workmen the Hudson's Bay Company employed fitted into the same pattern as the Fainiant family – Louis Bouchard of Fort William, who married Charlotte Fainiant (C 5), the Collin family of Fort William, the innumerable McKay's, and so on. Some of these men had come from Scotland or Lower Canada; some were half-breeds; almost all married Indian girls. In addition, there were many workmen who were merely transient, working for the Company for a very few years and then departing. Lists of employees (C 7) reveal the changes among workmen and officers alike, but they also reveal a certain continuity of service among a few of the workmen. A number of the officers had Indian wives, but this did not mean they remained in the district. They either left the Indian wives behind, as Alexander Stewart chose to do (C 2), or, like Chief Trader Roderick McKenzie, they moved to new posts taking their wives and children with them. Captain Lefroy suggested a third alternative (C 12), that European "gentlemen" were cutting themselves off from civilization, and also presumably from promotion, because they had married Indians, but there is some reason to doubt Lefroy's evidence on this point.

Although Donald McIntosh and John Swanston both spent many years in the district, it is difficult to consider them as more than semi-permanent representatives of a continuing institution. The same could be said for Thomas Lamphier, the captain of the Hudson's Bay Company schooner, the *Whitefish*, who spent each winter from 1838 on in Fort William. Only occasionally and fleetingly do any references to the homes of these men appear – signs of permanence in a society of transients.

It is among the Bouchard, Laronde, Collin, and Deschamps

[4]*Ibid.*, B-129-b, Michipicoten Correspondence Outward, Keith's answers to queries concerning the Indians of the Lake Superior District, July 29, 1831.
[5]*Ibid.*, B-162-c, Pic Post Journal, McIntosh to Keith, Nov. 3, 1827.

families that one finds the longest established residents of a particular location. The Collins were in the Fort William area from the beginning of the nineteenth century.[6] Louis Laronde's name appeared on a list of North West Company clerks before 1821, and he was retained, with some reluctance, usually in the Long Lac region, for more than forty years. He died at Sault Ste Marie in 1868, and two of his sons continued in the local fur trade.[7] A daughter had married one of the Deschamps family, whose history in the area was almost as long, extending at least as far back as the 1820s. The Nipigon post journals record the continued presence of Louis Bouchard, and of his descendants. Bouchard and one of his brothers-in-law were working at Nipigon House in the spring of 1834; four years later Bouchard and one other workman, under the supervision of a clerk, constituted the summer staff at the post. One Louison Bouchard was working at the same post in the tenure of Chief Trader Robert Crawford in 1870,[8] while Nicholas Bouchard was in charge of one of the flying posts of the district in 1875, as was Charles Laronde (G 7).

It was the fur trade that explained the continuing presence of these families in the Thunder Bay District; the mining enthusiasm of the late 1840s did draw miners to such places as Prince's Location, but it appeared that they departed after a brief time. Richard Singleton was such a man and, when he was killed in 1883, the Thunder Bay *Sentinel* recorded the death of the district's first pioneer (C 24), ignoring the prior claims of those associated with the fur trade.

But if the mining boom did not produce permanent settlement in one respect, it helped to further it in another, because the concern over Indian claims to the lands north of Lake Superior led directly to the Robinson Treaty of 1850. In the fall of 1849 T.G. Anderson, the superintendent of Indian affairs for Canada West, with two assistants, entered the Thunder Bay District at Pigeon River and travelled along the shore attempting to discover information concerning the Indians living between the Height of Land and Lake Superior, and the conditions on which they might be willing to make a treaty with the Crown. The questions Anderson asked were not always as clear to the Indians as they appeared to the questioners and Chief

[6]*The Question of the Terminus of the Branch of the Pacific Railway North Shore of Lake Superior* (Toronto, 1874), pp. 12–13, deposition of Michel Collin.

[7]P.A.C., H.B. Co. Records, B-162-a, Pic Post Journal, 1830–1, Swanston to Keith, Aug. 25, 1830; B-129-b, Michipicoten Correspondence Book, Keith to Swanston, Sept. 18, 1830; B-134-c, Montreal Correspondence Inward, Laronde to Hopkins, Nipigon, June 16, 1867, Crawford to Clouston, Nipigon, Sept. 8, 1868; B-149-a, Nipigon Post Journal, Jan. 15, 1871.

[8]*Ibid.*, B-149-a, Nipigon Post Journals, April 30, 1834; June 16, 1838; Dec. 18, 1870.

Peau de Chat's version of the queries and the answers he gave to them is most revealing (A 14). Equally revealing is the content of Anderson's own journal (C 17). The north was not completely new to him, since he had previously lived at Michillimackinac and on Manitoulin Island, yet it was the scenery that received most of his attention. More important, he had been an officer in the Indian Department for more than thirty years, yet his comments upon the Indians might have sounded naïve from a visitor newly arrived from another continent. Of the actual conference with the Fort William Indians, Anderson included no details in his diary.

On the other hand, Father Nicholas Frémiot presented a very full report of the transactions of which he was a silent witness (A 13) and, although he had then been in the Lake Superior area only a little more than a year, he would seem to have learned a great deal more concerning the Indians than Anderson had been able to do. Frémiot felt no compulsion to treat decisions of the Hudson's Bay Company with respect and his observations concerning the selection of Indian Chiefs, the effect of monopoly in trade, and, later, the character of the treaty settlement were all far different from the official Canadian view at the time.

In one sense Father Frémiot (C 18) was pleased with the treaty of 1850. He wrote: "Nomadic life is the great obstacle which prevents our dealing with the majority of the Indians ..." He saw some hope of improvement in their condition, material and spiritual, as a result of the new incentive to take up permanent homes, and he regarded the Canadian treaty as preferable to American ones which pushed the Indians farther and farther west. But as early as December 3, 1851, Father Frémiot was blaming Chief Peau de Chat for "the indigence with which he endowed the Indians through the shameful treaty of Sault Ste Marie."[9] At least part of the condemnation arose out of the government practice, later changed after protests, to pay Indian annuities in goods rather than money. The argument which Captain Anderson had used in favour of such payment was repeated for several years, and Indian Affairs officials blamed petty traders on the Lakes for stirring up the Indians on this matter.[10] It is surprising that they did not specifically mention the missionaries in the same connection, since Anderson's general suspicion of their influence was many times repeated by other government officials. This was espe-

[9]A.S.J.C.F., Nouvelles missions, v. 2, p. 168, Frémiot to a Jesuit priest in France, Fort William, Dec. 3, 1851.

[10]P.A.C., RG 10 C-3, Indian Affairs Department Letter Books, v. 573, George Ironside to Viscount Bury, superintendent-general of Indian affairs, Manitowaning, March 3, 1855.

cially evident when Father John Blettner chose to question the legality of all Indian treaties.[11]

On one point, Father Frémiot's more detailed knowledge did support the opinion that Captain Anderson had derived second-hand – the character of the Nipigon Indians. Traders like Donald McIntosh had long contended that special problems existed in that area, and Frémiot acquired his knowledge from repeated trips to Lake Nipigon from 1850 to 1852. His last report, written from Isle Royale in mid-summer 1852, was prepared as he awaited passage to Sault Ste Marie and a new post. He included an account of the Easter services he had conducted for the first time at Nipigon that year, and he described the repeated appearances of fur canoes until his departure at the end of June. From a stay of several months he concluded that the Nipigon Indians far exceeded the Fort William ones in both superstition and in violence. Nevertheless, he reported with some satisfaction the baptism of thirteen adults and nine children, one marriage, one month of classes for the children, and singing classes almost every day. The Catholic population (excluding those at the Fort) had doubled to thirty. Two of the men had been baptized and married two years before at Michipicoten, and the seven children of the Chief had been baptized years before at Fort William by Father Pierz.[12] One can only conclude that, in the midst of this activity, the Bouchards who had agreed in 1828 to marry "on the first good opportunity" (C 5) can hardly have escaped.

His experiences at Nipigon and the contemplation of the Robinson Treaty occasionally produced in Father Frémiot an acute sense of depression. At other times his accounts show a sensitive appreciation of the land and its people, a gentle humour, and a feeling of accomplishment. Besides his description of the building of a chimney for the mission and of Fort William's first religious procession (C 18), there are many similar vignettes throughout his letters. While he was still at Pigeon River, for example, he spoke of his experiences as priest and schoolmaster: "The honour of celebrating mass devolved on me because Father Choné was needed in the orchestra. Accompanied by several Indians, he sang in their language the *Gloria in excelsis* and the *Credo* ... I have been repeating to satiety the a b c's to twenty-two Indian children."[13] His later letters regret the slowness in establishing a similar school at Fort William, but by 1851 there

[11]*Ibid.*, v. 574, pp. 39–41, Charles Dupont to William Spragge, Manitowaning, Jan. 18, 1864.

[12]A.S.J.C.F., Nouvelles missions, v. 2, p. 205, Frémiot to the Superior in America, Isle Royale, July 2, 1852.

[13]*Ibid.*, v. 1, p. 416, Frémiot to a Jesuit father, Pigeon River, Dec. 8, 1848.

were references to Father Choné meeting his pupils daily, at least in certain seasons.

Evidence of the existence of an Indian settlement at Fort William appears in a number of sources. The Fort William post journal for 1850–1 for the first time made reference to the mission and its influence. On August 15, 1850, the entry reads: "Being a Holiday among the Catholics, the Men at the post attended Mass, but after noon they were set to work on the Hay." On January 3, 1851, the journal reported: "All the people who are Catholics were sent today to chop cordwood for the church. The others were employed at various duties."[14] Some of the clearest, and presumably most disinterested, accounts of the "Indians living in their wigwams" (C 19) came from Methodist missionaries who visited Father Choné at Fort William in the early 1850s – Rev. Peter Jacobs, an Indian himself, who conceded that the Jesuit father spoke "tolerably good Indian," and Rev. John Ryerson, who marvelled at the "self-denying zeal ... worthy of a better cause" (C 20).

At the same time, Jesuits far removed from the little mission attempted to describe the qualities required in a worker at Fort William in that early stage of its development. They concluded that the success of Brother Leischner, who worked at the mission for more than a decade, was due to his being a "pioneer, Dan Boone type of man" (C 21). The qualities necessary for a missionary priest were more difficult to describe. Father Frémiot's career was too short to provide the basis for generalization. Father Dominique du Ranquet, who succeeded him in 1852, was commended for his zeal, but a fear was expressed that he would soon wear himself out in the service of his Order.[15] He proved indefatigable, however, and traversed the district again and again for more than twenty years. Both the strength and the weakness of Father Choné, who was identified with the Fort William mission for an even longer period, were clearly set out in the report of Father Nicholas Point, the visiting superior (C 23). At the same time, Father Point indicated how faint and tentative were the beginnings of Indian settlement.

The whole future of settlement offered little promise as long as the economic torpor of the previous decades continued. Many of the young Indians and virtually all the whites in the district were dependent upon the Hudson's Bay Company. When D. Young Leslie visited the region in 1860 he declared that, outside of Hudson's Bay Com-

---

[14]P.A.C., H.B. Co. Records, B-231-a, Fort William Post Journals, 1850–1.
[15]A.S.J.C.F., B-1-8, Report of Father Nicholas Point to the Superior of the Jesuits, Sept. 15, 1859.

pany personnel and their dependants, there were seven whites – two of them women – living on the north shore of Lake Superior (D 12). It is unlikely that his enumeration was correct, since according to Father Point's report of the same period there were five Jesuit missionaries in the region, and if these were included in Young's estimate he was denying the very real existence of free traders in the area.

Upon one point, however, all the travellers were agreed: white residents of Thunder Bay were few in number, living in isolated and usually deteriorating buildings in a hostile environment. J. Elliot Cabot described the Fort William post in 1848: "The old blockhouse ... is falling to pieces, and the banqueting hall has probably been burnt up for firewood, at least, we saw nothing there that looked like it. Even the little flower-garden opening out of the stone-paved courtyard was overgrown with weeds" (C 16). Captain Lefroy had been more concerned with the spiritual degeneration he felt resulted from life in such posts: "Rather than send a son of mine to become a clerk in the H.B. Company I would see him a day labourer at home. He would there be within the influence of civilization, would have society, would suffer (probably) less from privation, and enjoy as high an average of comfort. These boys lose all that, without a compensating prospect of acquiring wealth in the long run. They lose all religious influences and restraints, frequently marry squaws and return to civilized life as old men, if they do return, with habits that make it no longer enjoyment to them" (C 11).

D. THE COMMERCIAL REVOLUTION AND THUNDER BAY, 1855–70

THE OPENING OF THE American canal at Sault Ste Marie in 1855 transformed Lake Superior travel and, belatedly, brought the commercial revolution of the mid-nineteenth century to Thunder Bay. During the next decade came the surveyors and the prospectors. Individuals, companies, and governments pondered their reports, and made decisions of both economic and political consequence, for these were the years in which other parts of British North America were forced to reassess their position and ultimately to agree upon a political union. What gave the period a special kind of unity for Thunder Bay, however, was the concentration upon economic development and adjustments made possible or necessary by the new transport system, with little consideration of the political implications of the economic changes. Just as the physical isolation of the district was being broken down, the differences in social and political attitudes became more readily apparent.

The career of John McIntyre may be taken to illustrate the point of view of those who came to settle in Thunder Bay before 1870. He assumed control of the Hudson's Bay Company post at Fort William in 1855, and at first was as much immersed in the details of the fur trade as his predecessors had been (D 5, D 9). But gradually the changes he saw taking place about him captured his imagination, and he came to identify himself with the region on a permanent basis. Thus he, unlike any of the Company officers who had preceded him, can be reckoned a settler in Thunder Bay, where he spent forty-four years of his life. As he became involved in mining ventures and hopes of wealth, he became acquainted with a number of Canadian businessmen whose interests brought them occasionally to Thunder Bay. The relationship was at first a friendly one, as there was no perception, on McIntyre's part at least, of any conflict of interest. Sometimes, as in the case of John J. Vickers of Toronto, early acquaintance developed into life-long friendship. Association with distant commercial enterprises did not necessarily divide the absentee property holder from the settler, but involvement in Canadian politics was apt to do so. Simon Dawson as surveyor and property owner was welcome in the McIntyre home. Simon Dawson as brother of a member of Parliament might be useful on a specific question of interest to settlers in Fort William (D 11). But Simon Dawson as a Canadian with national concerns that eventually led him into politics himself could only briefly pursue interests that coincided with those of the early residents in Thunder Bay. In time, Dawson came to represent political power of a kind that McIntyre could never wield. McIntyre's influence, such as it was, was always exercised through Hudson's Bay Company officials, and through powerful men he knew because of his Company connection, but that particular kind of political pressure was becoming less and less significant. As the Canadian protest against monopoly mounted, it was unlikely that the Company or its officials could long influence policy for Thunder Bay. At the same time, there were few signs that governments in Britain or Canada were likely to be much affected by developing attitudes within a sparsely settled region.

When the Governor of the Hudson's Bay Company claimed in 1857 that there was no conflict of interest with the Canadian government, he also expressed concern that agitators from Canada might stir up Indian warfare at Red River and perhaps "on the adjoining frontier of Canada" (D 3). For this reason he was anxious for British military support. William Eyre, the commander-in-chief of the British forces in Canada and administrator of the province during the absence of Governor Head, revealed his own doubts about the wisdom of acceding to Company wishes. He also revealed how little the Thunder Bay region figured in the plans of either Company or government (D 11), and it was this fact that settlers at first ignored and later resented.

In 1857 the British-sponsored Palliser expedition to the prairie regions found little evidence of any kind of potential wealth in the Thunder Bay District.[1] The Gladman-Hind expedition, sponsored by the Canadian government, took only a slightly more sanguine view. Henry Youle Hind's narrative of his journey west from Fort William at least touched upon the possibilities of the development of shipping and of some agricultural settlement (D4). After his second trip to the area in 1858 he was prepared to advise the building of a road from Fort William to Arrow Lake, and then the use of the waterways west to Red River. Certainly the report he received from James Dickinson, an engineer with the expedition, supported this view (D 6). Yet the mere recital of the route, as Dickinson described it, is indication of the kind of transport problem facing anyone attempting to reach Red River from Lake Superior.

Simon Dawson, the chief surveyor on the Gladman-Hind expedi-

[1]Irene M. Spry, *The Palliser Expedition* (Toronto, 1963), pp. 20–4.

tion, was thinking on quite different lines. He declared the Pigeon River route could never be made practicable for larger craft than small canoes (D 8) and rejected the idea of a Kaministikwia River route for a similar reason. It was evident that he had in mind something quite different from the old canoe routes. His correspondence shows that he was already considering the future possibility of a railway, and of communication lines exclusively within British North America.[2] In the meantime, he wanted wagon roads to link waterways navigable for larger craft. Dawson's chainman, Lindsay Russell, a future surveyor-general of Canada, reported the discovery of a practical location for a road, beginning several miles north of the Hudson's Bay Company fort and proceeding to Dog Lake (D 7). This suggestion, which Dawson accepted at that time, became the raison d'être for the creation of a tiny hamlet at the beginning of the route – the future city of Port Arthur. The local historian, J.P. Bertrand, has suggested that it was Dawson who unwittingly began the rivalry of Fort William and Port Arthur that has enlivened the history of Thunder Bay in the past century.[3] Perhaps the distinction really belongs to Lindsay Russell. In any case, the demands of east-west transit were beginning to conflict with the desires of the first settlers.

By 1860 Dawson was attempting to raise capital for a new fur trading company, in competition with the Hudson's Bay Company, giving the so-called free traders an actual choice in the sale of their goods, and depending upon an all-Canadian route which he obviously believed the Hudson's Bay Company would never encourage.[4] The old North West Company operations appeared to him, as they were later to appear to Harold Innis,[5] as foreshadowing an international boundary line which could become an actuality only in the railway age.

At the same time, he and his brother, William McDonell Dawson, were obtaining titles to potentially valuable property in Thunder Bay. During the hearings of the Select Committee to examine the Hudson's Bay Company monopoly in 1857, William Dawson declared that he had no dealings with the Company and no animus against it.[6] The

---

2 P.A.O., Dawson Papers, S.J. Dawson to J.A. Nicolay, April 19, 1860; Dawson to A.T. Pennefather, July 24, 1860.

3 *Highway of Destiny* (New York, 1959), p. 173.

4 P.A.O., Dawson Papers, Dawson to Nicolay, April 19, 1860.

5 *The Fur Trade in Canada: An Introduction to Canadian Economic History* (rev. ed., Toronto, 1956), pp. 262, 392.

6 Canada, *Sessional Papers*, 1857, no 17, Testimony of William McD. Dawson before the Select Committee.

first part of the statement may have been literally true, but he had
already invested in enterprises that would be likely to appreciate in
value if the Company monopoly came to an end. In the following
year, after his election to represent Three Rivers in the Canadian
Parliament, he succeeded in pushing through his private bill to in-
corporate the North West Transportation and Land Company.[7] A
condition imposed on the new Company was that within five years of
the passing of the bill it should complete one hundred miles of railway
between Lake Superior and Red River, presumably on the line advocated in Simon Dawson's report. William Dawson became president
of the Company, and among the first directors were Thomas
Clarkson, Allan Macdonell, John McMurrich, George Monro, and
William McMaster. The very existence of the company was an illustration of the enthusiasm of Toronto businesmen for westward expansion. When Casimir Gzowski and his partner, David Macpherson,
already holders of timber licences for about a dozen pieces of
property at the eastern end of Lake Superior,[8] applied for one
hundred square miles on the banks of the Kaministikwia (D 2), they
were offering an additional example of the same enthusiasm. But
Gzowski apparently ignored the fact that a large part of the property
he described belonged to the Fort William Indians according to the
Robinson Treaty of 1850. The Crown Lands Department did not
grant the licences requested, and none of the surveys conducted in
these years gave much indication of timber wealth. William Dawson
and his friends possessed much more exact knowledge of the district
than did Gzowski, yet their achievements were scarcely more notable.

The North West Transportation and Land Company secured the
mail contract for Red River. It immediately became involved in
steam transport on Lake Superior, and set about acquiring land for
its future prospects. Once the steamer *Rescue* was purchased for the
mail service, the Company became popularly known as the Rescue
Company, and both names appear in the dreary, long drawn-out, and
unsuccessful lawsuits that marked its later history. The mail contract
was lost after a few years; the title to some of its lands was denied in
the courts; it did not find it possible to build the promised railway to
the west; but it did clear a few acres of land, erect two or three buildings, and begin a road from Lake Superior to Dog Lake. In 1863 the
Company was awarded $3350 as compensation for the cancellation

[7]Canada (Province of), *Journals*, 1st session, 6th Parliament, 1858.

[8]P.A.O., Crown Lands Papers, Applications for Timber Licences, May 20, 1857,
application by Gzowski *et al.* for renewal of limits #9, 10, 21, 22, 39, and 40 on
Michipicoten River, #20 at Goulais Point, #5, 6, 37, 38 at Whitefish River.

of its mail contract, but this was the last victory. Finally, in 1886, a committee of the Ontario Legislature rejected all claims for further compensation on the grounds that the Company had never held any title to the land involved, and squatters' rights could not apply in this instance.[9]

The acquisition of legal title to Thunder Bay land began with the first township surveys and, to a great extent, concessions of land went to men living hundreds of miles away. There is no record, for example, that James Morehead, who secured property in Neebing in 1861 (D 13), even visited the area. As early as 1865 a number of these early grants were registered in the names of new holders to whom they had been assigned, or else powers of attorney were granted to some individual on the scene. The Morehead lot passed into the hands of John J. Vickers, as did the land granted to John R. McVicar of Ottawa.[10] Vickers, the proprietor of the Northwestern Express Company, had first visited Thunder Bay in 1859, and continued to accumulate property there in the next two decades. Almost every report of mineral locations granted by the Crown Lands Department includes the Vickers name, usually for several hundred acres at the current price of one dollar an acre, but also for two-thirds of an acre on behalf of young Georgina, who thus became the owner of a tiny island at the mouth of the Kaministikwia, for which the Ontario government duly received 67 cents.[11] Seven Montreal residents who had each acquired about 400 acres of mining land north of Neebing decided to empower Simon J. Dawson to act on their behalf.[12] Another group, including some of the same businessmen, assigned their interest in 3200 acres in McIntyre Township to Benjamin Walker of Toronto, "subject to the rights and interests of Simon James Dawson and William MacD. Dawson to the undivided third part thereof in pursuance of certain agreements in writing dated the 20th day of November, 1867, and the 17th day of December, 1867."[13]

In his report on Neebing and Paipoonge townships (D 10) Thomas Wallis Herrick may be said to have launched the Fort

[9]Lakehead University Library (L.U.L.), J.P. Bertrand collection includes photostats of documents concerning the Rescue Company.

[10]P.A.O., Crown Lands Papers, Neebing Township, Assignment of McVicar property, Nov. 23, 1865; of Morehead property, Aug 23, 1866.

[11]Ontario Department of Crown Lands, *Report*, 1877, List of mining patents issued in Thunder Bay, Georgina E. Vickers, June 16, 1877, Mutton or Georgina Island ... $.67.

[12]P.A.O., Crown Lands Papers, Neebing Township, Dec. 17, 1867.

[13]*Ibid.*, McIntyre Township, March 8, 1872.

William counterattack on Dawson's contention that transcontinental transportation plans must focus on what was later called Port Arthur and the land and water routes from it. Herrick referred to the bar of sand at the mouth of the Kaministikwia as a "trifling difficulty," as John McIntyre assumed it to be. He thus prepared the way for an argument, repeated many times in the next three decades, in favour of dredging the river, permitting vessels to move upstream to the neighbourhood of Point de Meuron, and beginning wagon roads or railway lines west from that point, judged to be the head of navigation on Lake Superior. Before 1870, however, the rivalry of the two hamlets, like the rivalry of Dawson and McIntyre, remained incipient. It seems likely that James Dickson, recalling his experiences of 1868 (D 21) fifteen years later, placed an emphasis upon the machinations of Hudson's Bay Company employees and the Indians with whom they had constant dealings that did not occur to him at the time.

The surveys, the possibility of settlement, and, above all, the mining enthusiasm, affected Hudson's Bay Company personnel in the district in different ways. George Barnston at Michipicoten sounded one warning: the danger of American competition had very much increased with the greater degree of settlement on the south shore of Lake Superior (D 14). He made it clear that it was the northern posts within the chartered territory itself that might still be protected, while the southern ones were highly vulnerable. In a sense his letter is a further illustration of Sir George Simpson's description of the Lake Superior District years earlier "This is a frontier, and may be made a cover and protection to our own proper country."[14] But the tone of Barnston's communication was considerably less optimistic than Sir George's had been; he realized that an operation was about to be phased out.

The year 1863 seems to have been crucial in the Hudson's Bay Company's examination of its prospects in the Lake Superior area. Governor Dallas proceeded from Red River to Michipicoten where a joint meeting of the Southern and Montreal Departments was to be held, and carefully examined the region he traversed (D 16). He took careful note of the possibilities for settlement at various places along his route. He visited each of the posts and interviewed the officers, and there is some question that he may have accepted rather uncritically the evaluation of the situation offered him by John McIntyre at Fort William. At the very least, McIntyre seems to have

---

[14]E.E. Rich, *The History of the Hudson's Bay Company, 1670–1870* (London, 1959), II, 501.

made a greater impression upon him than he was often able to achieve in the 1860s.[15] The decision to join the Lake Superior District to the Montreal Department was followed by the separation of Fort William from the control of Michipicoten, to the pleasure of officers in charge at both posts. In summer, Fort William was now supplied direct from Montreal by steamer; in winter, the isolation continued to be extreme, since the nearest American railway was much more distant than residents desired it to be. It was clear that the new transport arrangements were a recognition of technological change, but it did not mean that either the Company or its Thunder Bay representatives were committed to the idea of east-west expansion that Canadian commercial interests supported. As E.E. Rich puts it, "The issue to be fought out in the last ten years of the Company's chartered history was precisely this, whether the old geographical allegiance to the Bay should be replaced by ties to the south or to the east."[16] The pull to the south remained noticeably the stronger in the Thunder Bay area.

It was evident that the changes taking place in Thunder Bay in the 1860s were the source of hope rather than despair for John McIntyre. He had acquired so much property in the district that he asked the Company not to move him elsewhere.[17] Still a clerk after more than twenty years in the service, he was turning his attention to other sources of wealth than the fur trade, and even promotion had apparently lost its attraction if it involved departure from Thunder Bay. Chief Factor John McKenzie had risen far higher in the Company service and he ridiculed McIntyre's enthusiasm for mining (D 17), yet he also was acquiring property in the hope that it would provide additional revenue for his forthcoming retirement.

By contrast, Chief Trader Robert Crawford, who arrived in the district after the decisions about administration and transport had already been made, was quite incapable of reading between the lines of the official reports. He could scarcely believe that the last thing anyone seemed to have any information about was "the paltry fur trade" (D 22), but his complaints fell on deaf ears. McIntyre agreed that the Nipigon post was in a ruinous state, that it was difficult to find reliable workmen, and added that the situation in the fur trade would probably get worse "as the influx of strangers and adventurers

[15]Canada, *Sessional Papers*, 1873, no 23, James Bissett to Wm. Spragge, Aug. 22, 1872, referred to him as William McIntyre, while many did not refer to him at all. P.A.C., H.B. Co. Records, B-134-c, Montreal Correspondence Inward, letters of P.W. Bell from Michipicoten, 1867–8.

[16]*The History of the Hudson's Bay Company*, p. 794.

[17]P.A.C., H.B. Co. Records, B-134-c, Montreal Correspondence Inward, McIntyre to Edward Hopkins, Feb. 25, 1869.

into the district goes on."[18] He seemed to view this melancholy prospect without being overwhelmed by it, for the newcomers who destroyed the fur trade might increase the value of his mining properties. He was equally prepared to make some adjustments in the conflict between economic necessity and the law. "The opposition," he observed, "commenced trading whiskey with the Indians and rather than lose the furs I let the Indians have it for nothing; it is likely we will be fined for giving liquor to the Indians – anyway we have the satisfaction of keeping the furs from petty traders."[19] Crawford continued to remonstrate against a situation that was tacitly accepted by others. He pointed out the weaknesses of Company management in the area, apparently unaware that the history of the Company in much of Thunder Bay was drawing to a close.

But in their acceptance of change, men like McIntyre ignored the the fact that the disappearance of Company control would leave the district subject to political decisions in London and Ottawa in which their interests were unlikely to be consulted. P.M. Vankoughnet listed with pride the plans made for the area by the Macdonald-Cartier government at the beginning of the 1860s (D 15) but failed to say how few of the measures actually taken applied to Thunder Bay. In 1866, when the judicial District of Algoma was set up, the Canadian government had little choice in determining who should be the first justices of the peace for the western part of the district. Two Hudson's Bay Company men, McIntyre of Fort William and Peter Warren Bell of Michipicoten, were to have an added distinction and to serve two masters. At the same time as mining excitement arose it became evident that the Canadian government must re-examine its policy toward the mining interests of the province, although its decisions might not be agreeable to the settlers of Thunder Bay.

As early as 1860 reports to the Commissioner of Crown Lands had stressed the need for rapid development on the north shore of Lake Superior (D 12); the chaos of earlier years had to give way to a new policy. The giant blocks of land granted in 1846 were subject to forfeiture if the terms were not met, yet all through the 1850s successive Canadian governments had been reluctant to take action. Individuals paying a licence fee were permitted to prospect for minerals on unconceded land after 1853, but any real significance in the new regulation depended upon the government's actions toward the defaulting mining companies which still controlled much of the

[18]*Ibid.*, McIntyre to Hopkins, May 15, 1869.
[19]*Ibid.*, McIntyre to Hopkins, March 14, 1867.

land.[20] By order-in-council in 1861 new grants would not exceed 400 acres, and the price was to be one dollar per acre, payable in advance. The patent could not be issued until two years after the date of purchase, and then only if evidence were provided of actual working on the location for at least a year. Such regulations were welcomed in Thunder Bay, and it was soon evident that they were being complied with. John McIntyre asked Edward Hopkins to place $400 in the Bank of Montreal "to the credit of the Hon. Commissioner of Crown Lands for a location I wish to secure in Black Bay. It is a good thing, and well worth securing."[21] A number of individuals and some companies that had held property since 1846 admitted that they had paid the minimum down payment, spent nothing on the locations in the intervening years, owed several thousand dollars in back payments, and accepted forfeiture in 1864. Another ten individuals had 400-acre locations more recently acquired. They were charged $1.50 an acre (the price charged between 1856 and 1861) plus accumulated interest. Some, like Chief Factor John McKenzie, chose to pay.

The "Statement of Mineral Lands Granted on the North Shore of Lake Superior" (D 18) was one of the documents asked for by the Legislative Assembly in an address to the Governor-General on May 30, 1864. It revealed the advantageous position in which the early locatees, especially the Montreal Mining Company, had been placed. That company still retained fourteen pieces of property, each 6400 acres in area, all acquired at forty cents an acre. The document also revealed the immense activity on the part of individuals searching out, claiming, and improving the smaller tracts. It marked the first appearance, for example, of the McKellar family in the history of Thunder Bay. Captain Duncan McKellar, Scottish by birth and for some years a resident of Middlesex County, Upper Canada, arrived in the area with two of his sons. They had come from the Ontonagon copper country in northern Michigan in 1863; five years later the rest of the family followed and quickly adopted a new allegiance to Thunder Bay. As early as 1864 Peter McKellar, the second son, was employed by a company in which both John McIntyre and T.W. Herrick, the surveyor, held interests, with the agreement that young McKellar would receive one third of the profits. Within the next three years he, with his brothers John and Donald who became

[20]P.A.C., MG 24 I-8, Macdonell Mining Papers, Regulations for sale of mineral lands.
[21]P.A.C., H.B. Co. Records, B-134-c, McIntyre to Hopkins (Private), June 3, 1865.

his partners, discovered deposits of galena, zinc, and copper in the Black Bay region (the Enterprise Mine) and deposits of silver near Current River (the Thunder Bay Mine).[22]

Local legend has it that it was these discoveries that led to the imposition of royalties to increase government revenues, and that Peter McKellar led the successful attack on the policy.[23] McKellar undoubtedly preferred the tax on privately owned mineral land which he had found applied in Michigan, and argued that the Canadian system discouraged investors. However, the experiment with a royalty of two and a half per cent on all ores extracted had antedated the appearance of the McKellars in Thunder Bay and the dramatic discoveries of the mid-1860s; the royalty had been decided upon in April 1862. The same resolution of the Legislative Assembly that called for all relevant documents and asked that the forfeiture regulations be finally adhered to, requested that the royalty be abolished in favour of a tax of one dollar a ton, payable on the removal of ores from the mine, commencing April 1, 1865.[24] Action was not taken on this matter on the eve of Confederation.

In the summer of 1867 a group of Ontario legislators headed by Hon. Stephen Richards, the commissioner of Crown lands, paid a visit to Thunder Bay, and Peter McKellar was able to argue on behalf of adopting American usage in a district which depended so largely upon American capital for the development of the mines[25] Richards was not immediately convinced, and the Ontario Mining Act of 1868 contained the provision for royalties that the local interests found objectionable. In the following year, however, an amendment to the act introduced the concept that McKellar had advocated: a tax of two cents per acre on all privately held land.[26] It seems probable that the 1867 visit was in part responsible for this change, as well as for the decision to survey new townships in Thunder Bay. Yet the concern of Ontario's legislators could only momentarily turn to the distant frontier of the province.

Also in the summer of 1867 Dominion officials of the Indian Affairs Department first visited Fort William to distribute annuities.[27]

[22]P.A.C., MG 29 B-10, Keefer Papers, Speech prepared for delivery by Thomas A. Keefer, pp. 54–5.

[23]*Historic Fort William – Canada's Diamond Jubilee 1867–1927* (Fort William, 1927), p. 23.

[24]P.A.C., MG 24 I-8, Macdonell Mining Papers, Return to an address by the Legislative Assembly to His Excellency the Governor General, May 30, 1864.

[25]Bertrand, *Highway of Destiny*, pp. 188–9.

[26]Ontario, *Statutes*, 1869, 32 Vict., c. 34, Amendment to Mining Act.

[27]P.A.C., RG 10 C-3, Indian Affairs Department Letter Books, v. 574, p. 530, Charles Dupont to Wm. Spragge, July 19, 1867.

Their concern was primarily with the transfer of authority from the Hudson's Bay Company to the Canadian government, and the particular problems in enforcing any regulations in such a remote area (D19, D 20). Unlike the members of the Ontario Assembly, these officials would visit the region annually from 1867 on, but only one department of government in Ottawa maintained even this tenuous link with Thunder Bay before 1870.

Relatively prompt governmental action on questions of immediate concern concealed from the residents of Thunder Bay both the weakness of their own political influence and the significance that Confederation might have for them. A rather careful examination of letters emanating from the district during 1867 has revealed no reference to the union of British North America. Even Simon Dawson, who was most concerned with this union, made no mention of any significance in the date he inscribed on a memorandum to the Superintendent of Colonization Roads, July 1, 1867.[28] His theme on that occasion was the appropriate method of deploying his limited forces in road building; and just how limited those forces had been was made clear in the report on achievements at the end of the summer: six miles of road constructed, one storehouse built, labour force returned to the east at the end of the season with the exception of one man left in charge of the storehouse, and two men who deserted to join a mining party.[29] Yet Dawson's correspondence of 1867 did at least deal with a project which depended for its success upon Confederation, while the miners and prospectors of Thunder Bay, no less than the Hudson's Bay Company of earlier decades were still thinking in terms of north-south communication. For them, the connections with the south shore of Lake Superior and with Lake Michigan were the powerful and obvious ones. Neither the dreams of a Canadian political union nor a transcontinental transportation system to tie it together would be likely to stir their souls. For them the only route for ore shipments was by way of the Great Lakes, often to American ports. For them, the commercial revolution just completed offered hopes of progress; with Great Lakes transport a dream just realized, they were not yet ready for the visions of the businessmen who came from the east.

Represented at both Ottawa and Toronto by men with only tenuous links with Thunder Bay, the tiny community that existed before 1870 was politically powerless and politically unaware. Around

[28]P.A.O., Colonization Roads Papers, Dawson to J.W. Bridgland, July 1, 1867.
[29]*Ibid.*, Report of Superintendent, Upper Canada Colonization Roads, Nov. 18, 1867.

John McIntyre and even the Hudson's Bay Company (as its authority vanished), around the McKellar brothers, and later around Simon Dawson developed a variety of myths as these men came to symbolize what different segments of a frontier community held dear – the link with the past and the picture of cultivated society in the wilderness that Fort William cherished; success in the frenzied search for minerals and the alteration in government mining policy, that seemed to offer promise to all; the dream of transcontinental communication which might be expected to exalt the "Station" into a new and vital community. It was the season of local myth-making.

E. THE ZONE OF TRANSIT, 1870–85

As RECENTLY as 1965 Arnold Toynbee generalized upon the significance of what he called "the zone of transit," which he described as
"a broad insulating zone of wilderness that comes down to the northern shore of Lake Ontario and stretches up from there to the Arctic
Circle."[1] For at least the District of Thunder Bay the Toynbee phrase
has always had particular significance. The transport arrangements
of the North West Company had focused attention upon the area,
and even in the years of diminished importance after 1821 the old
routes to the west had not been completely abandoned. Fort William
remained the point at which travellers and goods were transferred to
smaller craft for the journey west, and the demand varied only
slightly over the years. Six to ten North canoes were kept in readiness
for possible travellers. The prospect of a wagon road westward, elim-
inating the frequent portages, seemed little closer in 1869 than it
had been a decade before. Every description by those who tried to
use the few miles of road constructed confirmed the impression that
little had been accomplished. Hudson's Bay Company men might be
expected to ridicule Dawson's Folly (E 10), but more disinterested
sources repeated the same story.

It was the seizure of power by Louis Riel at Red River at the end
of 1869 and the decision to send a military force westward in the
spring of 1870 that made the question of an all-Canadian military
route more than academic. It was this series of events, rather than
Confederation itself, that marked the real dividing line in Thunder
Bay history between a virtually abandoned and a vitally important
transport line. The attitude of the United States government, which
refused passage to troops wishing to use the American canal at Sault
Ste Marie, and the accompanying Fenian scare that even had some
impact north of Lake Superior, did serve to convince many Canadians of the need for a route well removed from the United States
border. To them reliance upon lake transport would always be
hazardous, and the thought of a railway line far to the north of
Lake Superior was attractive. The Prime Minister was one of those
who was still clinging to such a plan more than a decade later

[1]*Globe and Mail*, Toronto, Aug. 11, 1965.

(E 16), although his argument was based far more on experience with southern Ontario than on knowledge of the north.

The military expedition of 1870 provided a number of reports, official and unofficial, of the Thunder Bay area and the problems of transporting men and supplies across it. The Denison diary (E 1) combines both the record of the duties required of an orderly officer and the reaction of a young Torontonian to a northern world where no military band had ever played before. Personal observations were even more clearly expressed by Hugh John Macdonald in his letters to a college friend (E 3, E 4). It was at Prince Arthur's Landing and on the Dawson Road that the Prime Minister's son, the future premier of Manitoba, had his first contact with the northwest. Colonel Garnet Wolseley's reports provide information of a different kind (E 2, E5). He described the laborious efforts to complete a wagon road to Lake Shebandowan. Officially he commended Simon Dawson's untiring efforts and absolved him from any blame for the unfinished state of the road; yet even in the formal despatches there is some hint of the greater usefulness to the expedition of the Hudson's Bay Company representative, John McIntyre. Wolseley considered that his decision to send many of the boats by way of the Kaministikwia River route was fundamental to the success of the expedition, and that gamble was taken on the advice of McIntyre in direct defiance of warnings from Dawson. When one reads the account of the preparation, manning, and equipping of these boats (E 6, E 7), as well as Wolseley's description of the problems incident to the transport of some of them over fifty miles of road, the eagerness to make use of a water route instead is understandable. When the effort proved successful, Wolseley chose to ignore all the risks that had been involved, risks which Dawson had anxiously pointed out. It can hardly be doubted that the tension that came to exist between McIntyre and Dawson stemmed in part from this incident.

There are also semi-official reports of the events of 1870, written by participants with access to the official documents who recorded their own impressions of the expedition shortly after the events they described. Captain G.L. Huyshe included in an appendix to his book certain official papers while his narrative loyally supported all the decisions Wolseley had made, including the highly controversial denial of rations of spirits. Huyshe concluded that the whole expedition had been "a most perfect triumph for tea" (E 8). Colonel Wolseley also made his own narrative available to the public, and it appeared in *Blackwood's Magazine* from December 1870 to February 1871. It was clear that he had absorbed an Ontario view of

the young Dominion. "The western province, now known as Ontario," he wrote, "has long been the go-ahead portion of British
North America, whilst that of the east, now called Quebec, was
always lethargic, progress being neither known nor desired there."[2]
It was thus natural that he should have preferred Macdonald to
Cartier, who was acting Prime Minister during the expedition and
who Wolseley was convinced was less than eager for its success. His
bias, however, does not entirely explain his decision to leave the
Quebec militia at Prince Arthur's Landing to guard against possible
Fenian raids.

Wolseley's particular prejudices might tend to embitter relations
with Simon Dawson, a Roman Catholic from Three Rivers. They
also have to be taken into account in his dealings with the Fort
William Indians. There can be little doubt that the Indians were
reluctant to assist in the expedition, and it was inevitable that Wolseley should ascribe this reluctance to the influence of the Jesuits (E 9).
At the same time, his unflattering view of the local Indians renders
doubtful a legend that he developed a lasting respect for their skills.
This legend is based on the fact that Wolseley was sufficiently impressed by the work of the voyageurs who had aided him in river
transport that he requested and received their assistance in his Nile
expedition nearly fifteen years later.[3] At that time, Simon Dawson,
M.P. for Algoma, reported that a number of young men from the
local Indian bands had volunteered to go to Egypt, but they had been
assembled so hastily that they failed to be ready for the transport
rushing the men east to Montreal.[4] No explanation was offered for
the lateness of the assembly. Thus the whole question of the actual
contribution of Fort William Indians to the 1870 expedition and the
role played by Simon Dawson remains in doubt. Local legend maintains that the contribution was crucial to success, and both Wolseley's
1884 request and the fact that Fort William Indians did volunteer
can be taken to show both the excellence of the earlier performance
and the amity that continued to exist. But Wolseley himself was by
no means clear on this point, and Huyshe's comments imply that it
was the Iroquois, not the Ojibways, that impressed the commander.
In any case, the Nile expedition did include fifty-six Caughnawagas
and no Ojibways from Lake Superior.

[2]Sir Garnet Wolseley, *Narrative of the Red River Expedition* (London, 1871),
p. 202. This is a reprint from *Blackwood's Magazine*, with the original pagination.
   [3]P.A.C., Series G 1, Correspondence of Governors-General, has many letters
on this subject during 1884 and 1885, for example, Derby to Landsdowne, March 1
and April 28, 1885.
   [4]P.A.C., RG 10, Indian Affairs Department Letter Books, v. 1086, p. 572, L. Vankoughnet to Dawson, Oct. 18, 1884.

top
"Fort William from South Side of Kaminitiquia River, Aug. 1857"
Sepia drawing by John Fleming, assistant surveyor, Canadian Red River Expedition
J. Ross Robertson Collection, Metropolitan Toronto Central Library

bottom
"Thunder Bay or Prince Arthurs Landing,
teams starting for Fort Garry, Aug. 4, 1873"
Pencil drawing by William A. Johnson
Metropolitan Toronto Central Library

top
"Roman Catholic Mission, Kaministiquia River, Fort William"
Lakehead University Library

bottom
"Fort William, C.W., 1861"
Watercolour by William Armstrong
J. Ross Robertson Collection, Metropolitan Toronto Central Library

top
Red River Expedition commanded by Col. G.J. Wolseley, 1870
Oil painting by Mrs F.A. Hopkins
Public Archives of Canada

bottom
Red River Expedition, 1870, on the Kaministiquia River
Watercolour by William Armstrong
J. Ross Robertson Collection, Metropolitan Toronto Central Library

top
Silver Islet
Lakehead University Library

bottom
"Sketch of Beaver Mountain Silver Mining Location, near Port Arthur,
looking west from magazine at foot of hill"
from Roland, *Algoma West*, 1887

top
C.P.R. bridge over the Nipigon River
Lakehead University Library

bottom
"Morrison's Cut, Ogilvie's Jackfish Contract, C.P.R."
Lakehead University Library

top
Queen's Hotel, Park and Water Streets, Port Arthur, 1884
Lakehead University Library

bottom
Port Arthur Docks, 1855
Lakehead University Library

top
Victoria Avenue, Fort William, 1885
Lakehead University Library

bottom
"Bird's eye view of Jackfish Bay, C.P.R., from the north"
Lakehead University Library

top left
SIMON J. DAWSON, from William Buckingham and George W. Ross,
The Hon. Alexander Mackenzie (Toronto, 1892)

top right
ADAM OLIVER, from *Historic Fort William* (Fort William, 1927)

bottom left
JOHN MCINTYRE, photograph in possession of Lakehead University Library

bottom right
PETER MCKELLAR, from Thunder Bay Historical Society *Papers*, 1911–12

The 1870 expedition, apart from its primary purpose of pacification in Manitoba, had shown that a force could move through Canadian territory, and had at last provided a road from Lake Superior to Lake Shebandowan. In the next decade, many urged the expansion and improvement of what already existed – the building of a railway virtually along the same route as that travelled by the expedition, the continued use of the waterways to the west, and the construction of dams and locks where necessary to improve the efficiency of the system. Others wished to see a complete railway line, no longer dependent on water transport, but differed about the best route for such a line.

Partly because of changing governments at Ottawa, partly because of the depression conditions of the later 1870s, partly because of the disastrous but almost inevitable reliance on expert and conflicting advice,[5] the plans for transcontinental transport were frequently altered. In the Thunder Bay area, only the plans for a telegraph connection with Red River proceeded without serious interruptions (E 13). In Sandford Fleming's *Exploratory Survey* of 1872 it was evident that a railway route north of Lake Superior, perhaps even to the north of Lake Nipigon, was envisaged. "It was deemed advisable," he wrote, "... to make the attempt of piercing through the interior at a considerable distance back from the Lake, in the hope of finding ground free from those serious obstacles which presented themselves on or near the coast."[6] Fleming's view was influenced by the experience of James Rowan, who had organized an elaborate series of surveys near Lake Superior (E 11). Parties G, H, I, J, and K were sent out to explore the Thunder Bay area from east to west, and each was dropped off at an appropriate location early in the summer of 1872. Rowan was conscientiously carrying through the task assigned to him. But he made it clear that, particularly in the Long Lake and Pic areas which he had occasion to visit just after a number of workmen had lost their lives, he could not advise the construction of a railway.

Any plans being formulated even tentatively were shelved when a new government took office in 1874. The Mackenzie administration then decided upon constructing the shortest possible railway line to link with the longest possible line of waterways. It accordingly let

[5]Examples of the conflicting advice are many. Both Harold Innis, *A History of the Canadian Pacific Railway* (Toronto, 1923), p. 91, and a contemporary local observer, John King, "C.P.R. Construction at Fort William," Thunder Bay Historical Society, *Papers*, 1909–10, pp. 46–7, come to the same conclusion concerning the causes of vacillation.

[6]*Progress Report on the Canadian Pacific Railway Exploratory Survey* (Ottawa, 1872), p. 5; P.A.C., MG 29 A-8, contains Fleming's letter books, 1871–90.

contracts[7] for a railway west from the Town Plot of Fort William, several miles up the Kaministikwia River from the Hudson's Bay Company fort. Such a plan assumed that the dredging of the river was a practical, and not a ruinously expensive, enterprise. As it turned out, the extent of building during the Mackenzie administration was slight. The slightness, along with the selection of the route, aroused local wrath; the expenditure per mile evoked an angry response elsewhere. In the motion to set up a committee to investigate these costs, Senator David Macpherson was expressing more than a party interest (E 14); both he and Senator McLelan were raising questions about the feasibility of the whole project, and they were sure to win a sympathetic hearing among Canadian taxpayers.

When a new syndicate was formed tin 1880 to build a transcontinental railway, a number of its members thought in terms of bypassing Thunder Bay by means of lines south from Red River to join American lines already in operation. In 1872 a group including both George Stephen and his cousin Donald Smith had applied for charters to construct railways from the vicinity of Prince Arthur's Landing to Fort Garry, as well as from Fort Garry to the American border.[8] Both these early requests had been refused on the grounds that they would compete with the Canadian Pacific Railway project at it was then envisaged. By 1880 Stephen and Smith were powerful members of a new Canadian Pacific Railway Company, and, in Thunder Bay, their motives were open to much suspicion. Stephen certainly began with the idea of a route from the Sault along the southern shore of Lake Superior, hence to St Paul and north to Winnipeg. He called this using American lines for the benefit of Canadian ones.[9] Yet it was soon evident that Stephen was at least willing to consider the northern route desired by the government,

[7]Canada, *Sessional Papers*, 1879, no 43h, C.P.R. Schedule of Contracts with statement of expenditure, June 30, 1877–June 30, 1878.

	Date of Contract	Expenditure in Fiscal Year
Oliver, Davidson & Co. (Telegraph)	Feb. 19, 1875	$ 89,059.16
Sifton & Ward (Fort William-Sunshine Creek)	April 3, 1875	$ 42,000.--
Purcell & Ryan (English River)	June 6, 1876	$687,600.--
James Isbester (Ten stall Engine House at Fort William	June 17, 1876	$ 18,831.--

[8]Heather Gilbert, *Awakening Continent – the life of Lord Mount Stephen, 1829–1891* (Aberdeen, 1965), p. 23, quotes *Canada Gazette*, Dec. 16, 1871, and Feb. 24, 1872.

[9]P.A.C., Macdonald Papers, v. 267, Stephen to Macdonald, July 9, 1880.

while the Grand Trunk remained adamant in its refusal to do so.[10] His company then was given the railway line built from Fort William west at government expense. Mrs Gilbert, Stephen's biographer, dismisses any earlier efforts at exploring a route through the eastern part of the Thunder Bay region as contemptuously as Stephen himself probably did. These earlier efforts, she observes, "had given employment to sundry naturalists and geologists whose professional jealousy appears to have been proof against their ever agreeing."[11]

The correspondence between Stephen and Sir John A. Macdonald in 1881 (E 15, E 16) makes it clear that a decision had at last been reached. Macdonald's final acceptance of the line chosen by the Company (E 17) and advocated by Toronto and Hamilton newspapers suggests a new alignment of forces between the residents of the shore area and southern Ontario, while the area north of the Height of Land could loftily measure its distance from Montreal and Winnipeg. The Macdonald Papers include a good deal of correspondence on the difficulties of railway building in Thunder Bay from a very selective point of view. Once the difficulties involved in the location of the line were over, the emphasis was almost always on the enormous expenses incurred in railway building. For one 200-mile strip, 12,000 men with 5000 horses laboured at a cost to the Company of $12 million, 10 per cent of which went to pay for the dynamite. The subsidy provided for in the contract was – for each mile – just over $15,000 and 9600 acres of land,[12] then of questionable value.[13] Moreover, the subsidy was to be paid only on the completion of each twenty-mile stretch.[14]

Men on the scene rarely left accounts of what this construction meant in other than financial terms. Roderick McLennan was in a position to do so, as he supervised the work of the various contractors in the Lake Superior section but, working in temporary headquarters

[10]Gilbert, *Awakening Continent*, p. 68.

[11]*Ibid.*, p. 83, cites the specific example of John Macoun, described by Henry Y. Hind, a fellow naturalist, as "more than a charlatan."

[12]*Ibid.*, p. 88.

[13]Information concerning the valuation of individual fairly small pieces of property in Thunder Bay is deceptive if applied to large tracts of land, such as those promised the C.P.R. The only documents that have been found to give some indication of the value placed on large tracts in varied locations are the exchange of letters between Oliver, Davidson & Co. and the Department of Public Works, Dec. 24, 1874, and Jan. 13, 1875, printed in Canada, *Sessional Papers*, 1878, no 52. The company valued its 10,000 acres at one dollar an acre, but the government was unwilling to accept this valuation.

[14]Canada, *Statutes*, 1881, I, 8–9, 44 Vict. c. 1, Canadian Pacific Railway Company Contract, Clause 9. Mrs Gilbert's estimates of the subsidy compare with the $13,333 and 16,666.66 acres per mile allowed on the original contract.

struggling to prepare his estimates for his superiors, he seldom re-corded in his diary anything but the briefest summary of his work. What he did provide (E 24) was some picture of the engineering difficulties as he saw them and the decisions he reached. These de-cisions were eventually to attract a good deal of unfavourable publi-city when the Company refused payment on work done from the Pic River eastward until the courts should decide on the cases (E 31). The lawsuit of particular interest in Thunder Bay was that involving James Conmee, the mayor of Port Arthur, and John D. McLennan, Roderick's son, but the controversy was only marginal to the history of Thunder Bay since it concerned construction in the White River area.

The newspaper accounts of the period of railway building were most fragmentary. During the entire period of construction on the north shore of Lake Superior, the Port Arthur newspapers seldom alluded to the work going on. The *Herald* did acquire a correspon-dent in some of the hamlets along the line but usually after construc-tion had ended. The theme was then the subsequent inactivity. From Peninsula Harbor, for example, the correspondent wrote:

The track of the c.p.r. is now completed between here and Heron Bay and in consequence but four men are employed now in Peninsula Harbor. Great activity is going on in building the immense trestles between Jackfish Bay and Heron Bay. The whole of the liquormen of the town were fined last week by Judge Hill, in all cases, the fines were $25. and costs. Several notorious women are here yet but neither the liquor men or they are meet-ing with much encouragement. Several narrow escapes from freezing to death are reported by men journeying between here and Port Arthur.[15]

From the memoirs and the private letters of men engaged in the con-struction have come a vast collection of anecdotes whose verity it is impossible to judge. From the accounts by men only briefly in the area, reporting to their friends far away, came some newspaper accounts in distant towns. The Stratford *Beacon*, for example, in-cluded some of the experiences of John Ross (E 30), and the Port Arthur *Herald*, in reprinting the story, found no reason to challenge its accuracy.

William Van Horne, the general manager of the Canadian Pacific Railway Company, had the widest view of what was happening in Thunder Bay 1883–5. Only occasionally did he have reason to reflect upon the problems of the labour force (E 26); only as the

[15]*Weekly Herald*, Jan. 21, 1885.

work neared completion and the financial situation compelled his
attention did he begin to stress the need for economy (E 25). Instead he concentrated on the administrative problems – the efficiency
and speed of operations (E 20, E 22), the meshing of the new railway system (complete from Thunder Bay to the Rockies in 1883)
with the passenger service on the Great Lakes (E 21), arrangements
for the hauling of wheat through Thunder Bay (E 20), the provision
of grain storing facilities, docks, coal supplies, and so forth. His
superhuman energy also led him into tourist promotion; on occasion
he helped plan an itinerary for distinguished visitors (E 32). Such
a list of some of his activities indicates both the importance of his
decisions for Thunder Bay and the possibility of overrating this
importance.

The encyclopædic knowledge and the lively style of the general
manager of the Company were likely to mean the adoption of the
policies he advocated. His enthusiasm for the transcontinental line
was such that he saw ample opportunities for development in both
of the Thunder Bay ports, and argued repeatedly for the expansion
of c.p.r. properties in both Fort William and Port Arthur. Most
lucidly, he put before the Board of Directors and the Canadian
government his particular vision of the development of the Thunder
Bay area, as entrepôt and divisional point in the Company operations. That his arguments would provide more satisfaction to Fort
William than to the much larger town of Port Arthur was inevitable,
and several years before the corporation of Port Arthur clashed with
the c.p.r. over its taxable property the peremptory note from the
Port Arthur Collector of Customs (E 28) might be taken to illustrate
the beginnings of disenchantment. Company plans might not always
take the direction local opinion desired.

But a careful examination of the Van Horne letters reveals how
marginal the Thunder Bay area actually was in many of the policies
he advocated. In the first place, his concentration upon the problems
of the area was inevitably short-lived and by 1886 his attention had
swung to the Maritimes and the Pacific coast. Secondly, when he
extolled the advantages of the northwest he was not referring to
northwestern Ontario but to the prairies from which would come the
wheat to which his Company looked for profit. This emphasis was
clearly brought out in a letter in which he rejected any idea of con-
trolling all eastbound wheat shipments from Thunder Bay. "We have
infinitely more to gain," he wrote, "from high prices for wheat in
the Northwest resulting from low rates from P.A. than our profits for

carrying the grain across the lakes."[16] Along with his concern for wheat being shipped from the west went his interest in attracting tourists and potential settlers from the east, again to move through Thunder Bay to other locations. If he did contribute to the first tourist literature of the c.p.r., there is no sign of his lively style or of his views concerning the development of Thunder Bay in the rather pedestrian description of Port Arthur in 1887.[17] It was at the local level rather than at the head offices in Montreal that the grim results of encouraging immigrants to move westward before adequate accommodation was available became apparent (E 23). The North West Rebellion of 1885 and the experiences of the men rushed westward to meet a military threat (E 27) focused national attention on the vital role a completed railway might play.

What was happening in the early 1880s was the creation of an early mid-Canada corridor through Thunder Bay, the consequent stimulation of the growth of towns where the railway decided they would be appropriate, individual settlements thus committed to the prosperity of the railway and the subsidiary industries to which it gave rise. At the same time, there was a vast increase in the significance of the transient rather than the settler. The old dichotomy of fur trade days was thus continued by the decisions of the c.p.r. and the federal government. Yet the emergence of any stable community in Thunder Bay once the railway line was in existence seemed to depend on the development of other aspects of the local economy – mining, lumbering, and farming – as well as the growth of municipal institutions, in all of which the role of the provincial government would be of prime significance.

[16]P.A.C., MG 28 III-20, Van Horne Letter Book 14, p. 88, Van Horne to Henry Beatty, Oct. 25, 1885.
[17]*Summer Tours by the Canadian Pacific Railway* (Montreal, 1887), pp. 68–71.

F. THE ECONOMIC DEVELOPMENT OF ONTARIO'S FRONTIER, 1870–92

As SOON AS CONFEDERATION had been accomplished there were signs that the new province of Ontario would promptly assert its authority over the distant region in which some of its businessmen were already interested. A number of decisions with respect to mineral lands' policy were debated in the first sessions of the Ontario Legislature. Surveyors were despatched to a series of new townships, beginning with McIntyre in 1869. Provincial legislation in 1873 grouped several of these townships and the village of Prince Arthur's Landing in the new municipality of Shuniah and, for the first time, the western part of Algoma District was referred to as the sub-district of Thunder Bay. In these years also, the province was assiduously pressing its claims for the northern and western boundaries it eventually achieved, for the Ontario government was determined that neither Manitoba nor a hypothetical new province should secure title to the lands so recently brought within its control.

From the information about Thunder Bay which was available in the early 1870s, it was mining activity that seemed to guarantee that the area would be an asset rather than a liability to the province. The report of Professor E.J. Chapman of Toronto on a mining property at Black Bay, owned by John McIntyre, T.W. Herrick, Peter McKellar, and John J. Vickers, was no more glowing than several others. "There is abundant water power for treating the ore in the immediate vicinity"; Chapman concluded, "and the location contains a large amount of good timber – suitable for mining purposes. The property may thus be confidently recommended to the notice of capitalists, as a location of more than ordinary promise."[1] Hopes for the Enterprise Mine, as this property was later called, and for other areas such as the one Simon Dawson described (F 2), naturally rose with the phenomenal success of Silver Islet. Silver was discovered on the Montreal Mining Company's property in the summer of 1868. The assays were promising, but the owners could not face the expenditures necessary to operate a mine on a tiny island in Lake Superior, an island which was completely submerged when heavy seas broke over it. An American syndicate headed by Major A.H. Sibley of Detroit and New York acquired the property and, with W.B. Frue

[1]P.A.C., MG 24 I-8, Mining Papers, Report of E.J. Chapman, April 1868.

as superintendent, constructed crib work around the entire islet and a stone and cement coffer dam to protect the area at the mouth of the mine shaft (F 3). In spite of delays and setbacks, Frue collected the $25,000 bonus he had been offered if the proceeds of the first year amounted to $250,000. Actually, the gross output for 1870–1 was nearly $1 million. A village sprang up on the shore opposite while the islet itself had machine shops, storehouses, boarding houses for workers, a lighthouse at the eastern angle, and docks on the sheltered site.[2]

The success of the mine in its first three years reputedly pushed the value of shares from $50 to $25,000, created fortunes for the American stockholders, and even secured a European title for a Detroit heiress, the Princess of Chimay, née Clara Ward.[3] It certainly created the possibility of American capital for other enterprises (F 9) and of pressure being exerted on behalf of that capital upon Ontario politics. A.H. Sibley pointed out the advantages his company offered and its willingness to deal with any government in power in Toronto (F 1), but Captain Frue's letters made it evident that the Company interests were not quite apolitical. Frue's association with a number of mining enterprises brought him closely in contact with the Blake and Mowat governments, and his relations with Adam Crooks, a cabinet member in both governments, were particularly friendly. It was to Crooks, as well as to the local member at Queen's Park and the Commissioner of Crown Lands, that Frue sent his complaints when the Indian Chief Blackstone stopped all work on the Jackfish Lake Mine (F 7) even though as Frue was well aware, Blackstone's actions resulted from the failure of the Dominion government to reach an agreement with the Indians beyond the Height of Land (F 6). Frue also chose to ignore the fact that Ontario's claim to the region in which the mine was situated was still in question; he was writing these letters six years before the award of the Boundary Commissioners was made public; but, in all matters

[2]A number of sources contain similar descriptions. Archibald Blue's "The Story of Silver Islet" (Ontario Bureau of Mines, 6th *Report*, 1896, pp. 123–57) is most valuable. Other accounts include: Janey C. Livingstone, *Historic Silver Islet – the story of a drowned mine* (Fort William, n.d.); Richard R. Haste, "The Lost Mine of Silver Islet," reprinted from the Dearborn (Michigan) *Independent* in Thunder Bay Historical Society, *Papers*, 1926–8, pp. 36–43; Gertrude H. Dyke, *Historic Silver Islet* (Fort Wiliam, 1964). "Silver Islet," printed in Thunder Bay Historical Society, *Papers*, 1911–12, pp. 31–42, is made up of extracts from a paper read at Montreal in September 1879 by Thomas Macfarlane, one of the discoverers of silver on the location in 1868.

[3]Livingstone, *Historic Silver Islet*, p.5.

that concerned his mining interests, he preferred to look to Toronto for redress.

On a number of occasions Frue's letters show how much he suspected the influence of Simon Dawson, and how closely he was allied with John McIntyre and the Hudson's Bay Company interests. There is at least an implication in his letters that it was Dawson who encouraged Blackstone to take his dramatic action; there is more than a hint of possible revenge in the reference to Dawson's use of funds allocated to the Red River Road. One can only regret that Frue left Silver Islet in 1874, just one year before Dawson became the representative of the district in the Ontario House and a supporter of the Mowat government. Adjustments in position would then have been necessary, since Frue also was a supporter of that government, but apparently because of its power over Crown lands, not for any ideological reason. He was most suspicious of Wemyss Simpson, the Dominion member from Algoma, and regarded E.B. Borron, who succeeded him, as a mere creature of Simpson's (F 12), yet both these men were Reformers in politics. It seems to have been the distinction between federal and provincial powers and the views of individuals with respect to American investors, not the opposing platforms of political parties in the 1870s, that determined Frue's alliances.

To the officials of the mining company the Dominion government appeared far less accommodating than the provincial one. That some difficulties should arise with the customs authorities was almost inevitable, because both the American president and superintendent of the mine were determined to secure equipment for the mine and for their own Silver Islet homes from the United States (F 10) and unwilling to pay customs duties on the imports. Peter Nicholson, the collector of customs at Prince Arthur's Landing, complained: "Major Sibley showed fight and contented [sic] that he had no right to pay duty on the congress water."[4] Sibley eventually gave way on this minor argument, but the contest with the Dominion authorities continued, even in the years before high protective tariffs were imposed.

As the first large employer of labour in the Thunder Bay area since 1821, the mining company at Silver Islet faced particular problems. Sibley claimed that the labour force was largely Canadian, and, after unhappy experiences with Norwegian miners and some of the Cornish ones (F 11) and an apparent failure to attract German and

4P.A.C., RG 16 A 5-7, Port Arthur Customs Records, v. 1, p. 30, Nicholson to Commissioner of Customs, Aug. 18, 1876.

American miners from Illinois (F 4), Captain Frue did search in eastern Canada for recruits. The four boarding houses were occupied respectively by Norwegians, Cornishmen, men of all other nationalities, and officers of the mine;[5] the division may offer some clue to the respective numbers of workmen of different nationalities. It was the diversity of nationalities as well as the success of the American company that impressed the Jesuit missionary, E.R., when he visited the "land of adventurers" in 1875 (G 8).

Besides the hazards of the occupation itself, and the distance workmen had to travel to the region, there was the continued possibility of the mine's closing down. Even in the period of highest dividends, the stockholders were nervously aware of the danger of loss, and Frue had constantly to reassure them. As early as 1877 work was actually suspended, and the labour force discharged. "To all appearances," Peter Nicholson reported to the Minister of Internal Revenue, "the outport of Silver Islet will be entirely abandoned in a couple of months."[6] The prediction proved inaccurate, but uneasiness continued, and the constitution and by-laws of the Silver Islet Employees Benefit Society, drawn up in 1880, took notice of the possibility of the mine's shutting down (F 13).

From its peak production in 1871 the mine's yield had fallen off gradually in the next four years, as the distance from the surface increased and the value of the ore diminished. Deficits by 1876 led to the organization of a new Company under the laws of the state of New York, the Silver Islet Consolidated Mining and Lands Company.[7] Reports to shareholders of this Company indicated a number of new efforts to realize profits, followed by a lack of success and mounting deficits. Those who had the greatest personal interest in keeping the project in operation were no longer in charge of the Company by the 1880s. Frue and Sibley were dead. Of the eleven directors, only three had been shareholders in the original Company. The only Canadian among the original group, Edward A. Prentice of Montreal, had vanished from the organization. When the waves of Lake Superior swept over the mine in the winter of 1884, the explanation for the disaster was the "non-arival of coal, unfortunately shipped in charge of an intemperate captain" (F 14), but no effort was made to revive the enterprise. It would appear that more than the story of an intemperate captain was involved.

[5]Blue, "The Story of Silver Islet," p. 150n, cites information supplied by James Cross.

[6]P.A.C., RG 16 A 5-7, p. 104, Nicholson to the Minister of Internal Revenue, May 16, 1877.

[7]Blue, "The Story of Silver Islet," p. 153.

The Silver Islet property was sold under foreclosure of mortgages, and two trustees tried to have it prospected for minerals, timber, farming, fisheries, water power – in any faint hopes of selling it in locations or in lots. Some of the buildings were moved to the villages of Prince Arthur's Landing and Fort William, suddenly overcrowded by the influx of islet residents. Others fell into disrepair. So ended the history of the only mine in Thunder Bay which had been "practically and successfully worked" before 1880.[8] But the very brilliance of the early years at Silver Islet had contributed to the mining craze in the district, and the *Reports* of the Crown Lands Department in the 1870s reveal how keen was the interest in acquiring mineral lands in Thunder Bay. The number of patents issued bears some relationship to the fortunes of the Silver Islet Mine, reaching a peak in 1874 and diminishing toward the end of the decade.

There were other indices, however, that needed to be considered after 1880. Finds such as the gold at Jackfish Lake were far from any existing means of transportation, and it was natural that mining should be delayed until the completion of the railway. The willingness of American capitalists to invest in the area was affected not only by what happened at Silver Islet but also by world economic conditions. With the discovery of the Rabbit Mountain Mine by Oliver Daunais (F 18), later the self-styled Silver King of Thunder Bay, the district entered into an even more frantic period of mining enthusiasm. A.L. Russell's report to the Crown Lands Department (F 16) indicated the number of mines that began operations in the years 1882–5, and the Port Arthur lawyer, Thomas A. Keefer, closely associated with several of these projects, saw a brilliant future, provided suitable arrangements could be made with the American interests who very soon acquired title to the properties. The Crown Lands *Reports* of the 1880s supported this optimistic view, yet, by the beginning of the 1890s, most of these new mines were closing down. The patents for mining lands became rare indeed and when the Ontario Bureau of Mines presented its first report in 1891 it devoted one page to silver mining in Thunder Bay – but almost as a summary of an era then passed. The collapse of world silver prices at the end of the 1880s had brought this era to an end. The Ontario frontier which had concentrated upon silver mining almost to the exclusion of other activities, had to reorganize itself, exploit more fully the resources it had so far devedoped merely as ancillary to mining.

[8] P.A.C., MG 29 B-10, Keefer Papers, Speech prepared for delivery by Thomas A. Keefer, p. 62.

The period between Confederation and 1892 did provide some indications of the lines that might be followed. All the early reports found little value in the timber resources, except in providing wood required in mining locations and, somewhat later, in railway construction. As a result, the surveying of vast timber berths in Thunder Bay only occurred in 1890, and the first sale of a Thunder Bay timber limit in 1892.[9] When the increasing scarcity of timber in the southern Ontario peninsula shifted attention to the possibilities of the north, it was the Rainy River and Kenora areas that received the earliest attention.[10] Yet there was limited activity in Thunder Bay lumbering in the previous two decades, even if it frequently passed unnoticed by Ontario authorities. The Commissioner of Crown Lands made a statement (F 22) that no timber licences had been granted west of Sault Ste Marie by the end of 1876 as he outlined the temporary and local regulations in operation at that time; yet an order-in-council of June 29, 1872, did authorize the sale of timber on lands on the north shore of Lake Superior at fifty cents an acre.

The firm of Oliver, Davidson & Co. established itself on an island opposite the Hudson's Bay Company post at Fort William in 1873, with the assurance of a contract to cut a right of way for the projected railway from Fort William to Savanne, and with the prospect of a licence to cut timber along the Carp River on the Fort William Indian Reserve. Their application to the Ontario government for a timber licence in Paipoonge Township seems, like the other nine received in 1872, to have been denied. No applications were made in 1873, and virtually none thereafter until a great rush of interest marked the early 1880s.[11] Again, however, there is a significant difference between the list of applicants, often specifically listed as requesting authority to cut timber for the Canadian Pacific Railway, and the records of ground rent collected. The only reference to the collection of ground rent in the 1870s that has been discovered is the $20 paid by Frank Moberly for four square miles of land in Paipoonge in 1876–7.[12] However, the inclusion of Thunder Bay in the Western Timber District covering western Ontario as well as the north shores of Lake Huron obscures many details of the local operation and makes it impossible to separate the value of the timber cut in one particular region. The first sawmill established by Oliver,

[9]P.A.O., Crown Lands Papers, Western Timber District Licentiates, 1890–2, Sale of Timber Berths by public auction held Oct. 13, 1891.

[10]Ontario, Bureau of Forestry, *Report*, 1886, p. 36.

[11]P.A.O., Crown Lands Papers, Applications for Timber Licences, 1872–87.

[12]Ontario, *Sessional Papers*, 1885, no 22, Report on applications for authority to cut timber in the Thunder Bay District, for the C.P.R.

Davidson & Co. ended operations by the late 1870s, and W.H. Carpenter attempted to repeat their early successes. Thomas Marks & Co. launched a similar enterprise in Prince Arthur's Landing and sold their interest to Vigers Bros. – a firm that lasted under constant threat of insolvency until the beginning of the twentieth century.[13] Graham & Horne had meanwhile entered the competition in Fort William. Their planing mill dated from 1883, but it was evident that the first mills could not provide the lumber for extensive construction then going on,[14] and that all of them continued a somewhat precarious existence based on their production of saw logs for the local market.

By 1882 Thunder Bay had its first Timber Agent. William Margach remained in the area until 1889 when he was moved to Rat Portage and replaced by Hugh Munro. By this period, also, appeared the reports of licences granted at approximately $2 per square mile along the C.P.R. line from Nipigon to Lac des Milles Lacs.[15] It was in 1886 that the Department of Crown Lands recognized the dangers of fire in an area where prospectors were at work, "some of whom wantonly start fire prior to setting out to explore, so that the debris may be cleared off the surface of the rock and the veins exposed."[16] Only in that year was a fire distrist proclaimed to extend to the western boundary of the province and to be administered like those already in existence in other areas. In 1892 and 1893 General Russell Alexander Alger, later to be McKinley's Secretary of War, acquired three large timber berths along the Canadian side of Pigeon River to add to his vast American operations. In October 1892 came the recommendation of Aubrey White, the newly appointed assistant commissioner of Crown lands, that pulpwood licences should be granted for lands not included in any timber berth.[17] The real history of lumbering in Thunder bay was about to begin.

In the years in which mining was the dominant industry and constant hope of the area, it was natural to find that provincial assistance in road and railway building bore a close relationship to the state of mining activity. At the time of Confederation the colonization road projects so important in other regions had had practically no effect on Thunder Bay. The completion of the Dawson Road and even the building of a transcontinental railway could not supply

[13]P.A.O., Woods and Forest Branch Report Book, v. 1, p. 292.
[14]P.A.C., RG 16 A 5-7, p. 93, Nicholson to Commissioner of Customs, April 4, 1877.
[15]P.A.O., Crown Lands Papers, Ground Rent Journals, Western District, 1883–6.
[16]Ontario, Department of Crown Lands, *Report*, 1886, p. vii.
[17]P.A.O., Woods and Forest Branch Report Book, v. 2, p. 197.

adequate transportation for the miners. The demands for winter communication with the United States (F 5) developed when the sudden increase in the volume of mail at Silver Islet caused the Duluth authorities to refuse further responsibility. In response to local demands, the first work on the Pigeon River Road was begun in 1872, and the completion of the route at a cost of about $24,000 was reported in the following year (F 20). Also in 1873 the Black Bay Road, of obvious importance for those holding mining locations in that area, was begun, as was a road from Prince Arthur's Landing to Fort William. Building on these projects continued through 1874; then, for several years, small contracts represented a very modest investment on the part of the province. The Silver Islet Road was completed in 1882, a little over a year before the mine closed down; the new silver mines were more promptly served with the building of the Rabbit Mountain and Whitefish Lake Road (F 16). Once the area had its first rail communications in 1882, local businessmen urged the building of a Thunder Bay Colonization Railway, again with the mining centres in mind. By 1887 this project had altered somewhat, and a reorganized company proceeded with the construction of the Port Arthur, Duluth, & Western Railway as far as the American boundary (F 24). The closing down of the mines made it impossible for this local enterprise to survive for long.

From the point of view of the Ontario government there seemed little urgency in the development of agriculture in Thunder Bay. Free grants were obtainable under the Homestead Act of 1868, and that seemed incentive enough. In urging the immediate settlement of Oliver Township, Surveyor J.J. Francis pointed out its nearness to Prince Arthur's Landing, the suitability of the land for agriculture, and the high costs in the region in 1873 – hay from $35 to $40 per ton, potatoes from $1.00 to $1.50 a bushel, beef from .15 to .20 a pound, and so on.[18] Both J.J. Francis and Hugh Wilson believed that the costs of labour, which they considered exorbitant, were directly related to the lack of agricultural settlement. Wilson saw great potential advantages in the Slate River Valley (F 19). His enthusiasm for the region was only equalled by Adam Oliver, M.P.P. for South Oxford. Oliver was a strong supporter of Edward Blake, after whom he seems to have suggested naming both a son and a township, but he was no more successful than Wilson in promoting settlement. He did not live to see the developments of a decade later.

Both Walpole Roland's description of abandoned locations (F 23)

---

[18]Department of Crown Lands, *Report*, 1873, pp. 30–1, Report of J.J. Francis on survey of the Township of Oliver.

and the records of early applications for free grants tell the same story of forlorn hopes.[19] In the early years there was little evidence of the kind of glowing reports the Department of Agriculture could select for inclusion in its pamphlet advertising the advantages of life in Thunder Bay in the 1890s (F 26). But the applications reveal more than the disappointments of the early settlers. They indicate the advantages that local people possessed in the land grants system. Most of the applicants who actually located on homestead grants in the townships of Oliver and Paipoonge after 1880 were men already resident in the district, presumably acquainted with its hazards and even with the particular piece of property they were applying for. But the local residents of the 1880s had been the newcomers of a decade before who had survived early disappointments and found a place for themselves in Thunder Bay.

The applications for free grants (F 21) also show from what regions settlers came, and in what numbers. Within less than two weeks in the fall of 1876, for example, there were about thirty applications from residents of the Township of Adjala, most of them from the tiny hamlet of Athlone, some sworn before the reeve of the township, John T. O'Connor, and some before the Justice of the Peace, James Sigsworth. (These gentlemen obligingly witnessed each other's applications.) With this early representation, Simcoe County might be expected to provide the largest contingent from outside Thunder Bay itself; eventually, its numbers were equalled by York County, the great majority of the applicants coming from the Markham area. No other county in Ontario was represented by more than two or three applicants, except Huron County from which a mass migration of six related McKenzies was recorded. Of the entire list, only two applicants were from outside Ontario, and very few came from east of York County. It appears that social and economic conditions within particular regions, as well as the contagion of example, accounted for many of these applications. The poverty of the Adjala soil and the difficulties between its Irish Roman Catholic population and the Irish Protestants of neighbouring townships contributed, it can hardly be doubted, to the migration from Athlone and to the ethnic and religious variety of Thunder Bay.

When the mining boom ended in the early 1890s Thunder Bay faced readjustment as it had in 1821 — but with a very great difference. Completion of the c.p.r. assured that it would remain a zone of transit even with the closing of the silver mines. Mining, as it turned out, faltered but did not vanish, and in any case other eco-

[19]P.A.O., Crown Lands Papers, Townships of Oliver and Paipoonge.

nomic activities already in existence helped to provide for the future. Most of the those who had been attracted to the area by dreams of fabulous wealth remained to cope with reality. For more than two decades before the collapse of the mining industry, citizens had been identifying themselves with some segment of this Ontario frontier, even though any sense of belonging to the district as a whole was slow in developing.

G. ON THE FRINGES OF SETTLEMENT, 1870–92

FOR ALL THE ECONOMIC ACTIVITY that marked the 1870s and the 1880s in Thunder Bay, settlements remained isolated from each other and often short-lived. A shifting and impermanent pattern of settlement in turn imposed special administrative problems and involved rather tentative and unsatisfactory results for those upon whom Ontario civilization impinged for the first time. What became arrestingly clear in these decades was the extent to which large parts of Thunder Bay continued in their old routine, virtually untouched by changes taking place in particular areas. The correspondence between Osnaburgh and Martin's Falls about the arrival of packets, the unreliability of Indian traders, the failure of the potato crop, and so forth (G 1) might as easily have dated from the 1840s as the 1870s.

Farther south than the area served by the Martin's Falls post, geological survey teams ventured for the first time beyond the Height of Land (G 2) in 1869 and 1870. A few years later E.B. Borron, stipendiary magistrate for the neighbouring District of Nipissing, was sent on a number of exploratory trips for the Ontario government.[1] His reports, which he preferred to submit in the form of journals, give striking illustrations of the unchanged character of life in the "new territory" Ontario was then claiming. When Borron travelled from Nipigon to Long Lake in 1883 (G 15) his whole arduous journey carried him only a few miles to the north of the locations where, at that very time, the transcontinental line was being constructed, but he seemed to move in a different century.

The Hudson's Bay Company continued its trade throughout these areas, north of the transcontinental railway, long after the Fort William post was closed in 1881. Travellers continued to comment on the limited nature of the Company operations; energetic outsiders would occasionally criticize the lack of initiative of gentlemen in charge of posts who failed to seize upon profits that might have accrued from railway construction workers, "all naturally averse to

[1]*Reports of the Stipendiary Magistrates with respect to the Northerly and Westerly Parts of the Province of Ontario* (Toronto, 1880) Introduction, Borron to Oliver Mowat, Dec. 31, 1879; P.A.C., RG 10, Indian Affairs Department Letter Books, v. 1102, p. 664, L. Vankoughnet to Colin Rankin, July 14, 1890.

purchasing from their employers."[2] The fisheries, long associated with the Hudson's Bay Company monopoly, and the tourist trade along old canoe routes, were still to some extent linked with the past. Newton Flanagan, the Company agent at Red Rock, reported to the Ontario Department of Crown Lands concerning fisheries (G 21) from 1887 until his retirement. In 1890 he departed for St Paul, for the old internationalism of fur traders continued. The Crown Lands Department appointed William McKirdy as fisheries overseer in Flanagan's place; thus, very slowly, was the old reliance of government on Company personnel beginning to disappear, even in an area opened up by the railway. Off this line, government's reliance on the officers continued even longer.

In these areas also, the role of the missionary remained unchanged. The Jesuits examined the extent to which they might rely on Company officials to co-operate with them (G 11, G 12), and described their journeys to still remote posts by bark canoes and snow-shoes (G 9). When the Rev. Robert Renison served at the Anglican mission on Lake Nipigon in the 1880s (G 20) he faced the same situation that his son, the future Bishop, described: "I entered a land of yesterday. The twilight of the Romance of the Hudson's Bay Company still hovered over Ontario's back door. The Dominion government sent down occasional surveyors. The Indians were left alone ... There were only two outside interests, the old Company that came for fur, and the Missionaries who remembered that Indians had souls."[3] This conflict, however, took on new significance in the vicinity of white settlements where the government agent, no longer necessarily a Company man, confronted the missionary.

Just where the important areas of settlement would be depended upon the mining activity and the route chosen for the transcontinental railway. The Ontario government had assumed that the land around Thunder Bay itself would attract most of the settlement, had accordingly despatched most of its northern surveyors into that region, and in 1873 created the municipality of Shuniah, composed of Thunder Cape, the townships of McGregor, Pardee, Crooks, McTavish, McIntyre, Paipoonge, Neebing (which included Fort William), and the village of Prince Arthur's Landing. Almost simultaneously, Chief Trader Robert Crawford and some of the C.P.R. engineers were advocating a plan quite opposed to the interests of

[2]P.A.O., Miscellaneous Papers, John S. Black to P.W. Bell, Dog Lake, Oct. 10, 1881.

[3]Thomas C. Boon, *The Anglican Church from the Bay to the Rockies* (Toronto, 1963), p. 144, cites Bishop R.J. Renison, "New Life in Moosonee," in *M.S.C.C. Quarterly Bulletin*, Dec. 1946, p. 2.

Shuniah. If Red Rock, near the mouth of the Nipigon River, should become the transhipment point for goods moving westward (G 5), the District of Thunder Bay would be provided with a potential metropolis more centrally located and possessing, according to Sandford Fleming's 1872 *Exploratory Survey*, far greater advantages for railway building. Against the pretensions of Nipigon Harbour, Shuniah residents united their forces (G 6). Peter McKellar, one of the municipality's spokesmen, claimed that it was eventually the influence of Adam Oliver, Liberal M.P.P. for South Oxford with the Mackenzie government, that foiled Nipigon's plans.[4] He described the evidence of Nipigon as fraudulent and explained his reasons for leaving it out of the pamphlet published on this occasion.[5] "I did not think it wise to put it in," he explained many years later, "as I knew that after the information given that they would not think of bringing it forward against the Thunder Bay evidence."[6]

The victory of Shuniah was decisive; the question of the economic centre or judicial capital being outside its limits never again arose. Instead, small settlements grew up after the completion of the railway line at such places as the C.P.R. decided upon (G 16) notably at Schreiber, which became the divisional point east of Shuniah. One particular incident at Jackfish, where the Lake Superior section was completed in May 1885, reported in the Port Arthur press (G 19), indicated the continuing existence of a community there; it also pointed up very clearly the problem of the administration of justice over a scattered population, with the district capital far from centrally located.

A decade earlier James Cleland Hamilton had tried to describe the essential character of a frontier settlement (I 1) – the mining craze, the varied and transient populaiton, an incipient lawlessness. It was only at the end of the 1870s that an attempt was made to administer justice in the district according to the pattern applied in settled areas, and then only slowly were changes introduced. The local magistrates handed down summary justice whenever cases were obvious enough or serious enough to command their attention. When a sheriff was appointed for Thunder Bay in 1879 and the first assizes were held at Prince Arthur's Landing in 1880,[7] at least the frame-

---

[4]"How Nepigon Bay Lost the C.P.R. Shipping Port on the Great Lakes," in Thunder Bay Historical Society, *Papers*, 1911–12, p. 25.

[5]*The Question of the Terminus of the Branch of the Pacific Railway North Shore of Lake Superior* (Ottawa, 1874).

[6]McKellar, "How Nepigon Bay Lost the C.P.R. Shipping Port," p. 27.

[7]Ontario, *Statutes*, 1880, 43 Vict., c. 12, An Act Respecting the Administration of Justice in the Districts of Algoma, Thunder Bay, and Nipissing.

work for a more traditional administration of justice was set up. The judicial district of Thunder Bay was created in 1884.[8] But these statutory changes were less significant than they might appear. The vast number of offences that came before the courts on the frontiers of settlement were not such as to command the attention of the assizes. After examining the evidence contained in the report of the Inspector of Prisons, the Thunder Bay *Sentinel* concluded: "Heinous crimes have been unknown in this particular district during the years covered by the Inspector's report, and the seasons of navigation were largely responsible for the incarceration of those who partook of the cup which cheers and inebriates also."[9] By 1892, however, the *Sentinel* was admitting that "heinous crimes" did sometimes take place in the district, and commented upon the difficulty of apprehending criminals in a country so thinly populated, with bush surrounding the few settlements, and with a railway line convenient for escape.[10] Moreover, the account of the proceedings at Jackfish also suggests that, unless the victim of assault seemed on the point of death, criminal charges against his assailant might not be pressed.

For white settlers on the frontier, the problems they faced had counterparts in every semi-wilderness region. They had chosen to move to a remote area and hoped to gain from that move; above all, they were still a part of the political unit and the society from which they had come. For Indians living near Lake Superior and coming into more frequent and more varied contacts with outside influences, the results were quite different. Father du Ranquet reported from Fort William on the deaths from measles among Indians and half-breeds (G 3). He did not comment upon the medical treatment they received (G 4) but Dr John F. Clarke continued his interest in the subject after he had given up any hope of being appointed "surgeon to the Indians." In 1882 he made public charges that the Indians were receiving inadequate treatment and Coroner T.S.T. Smellie replied through the columns of the *Herald*: "Sheriff Clarke has gone somewhat out of his way in dishing up to your readers in official form a most disgraceful story with only sufficient truth in it to give coloring to the tale ... If Dr Clarke could be induced on all occasions to mind his own business, professional as well as official, it would pay him and save him from getting into ridiculous positions."[11]

Most of the records make no reference to the question of medical treatment, but deal rather with the manifold complaints of Indians

---

[8]*Ibid.*, 1884, 47 Vict., c. 14, An Act Respecting the Districts of Algoma and Thunder Bay.
[9]March 16, 1888.   [10]Dec. 16, 1892.
[11]April 22, 1882.

against agents appointed by the federal government, or against their own chiefs elected, it was alleged, under undue pressure by agent or missionary. Behind the complaints against individual persons often lay the more generalized question of mining or cutting timber on Indian reserves, and numerous sources of resentment, expressed and unexpressed.

The unhappiness on the Fort William Reserve was closely linked with rising land values, and with the issue of licences to cut timber. The Indian Affairs Department came to the conclusion that injustice had been done on both these counts. When Chief Penassie protested the low prices paid for lots in 1882, he was told to take his case to court if he wished, and Amos Wright's tenure as Indian agent was brought to an end (G 13). The evidence concerning the means by which timber licences were originally made possible was even clearer. The Department concluded that the document on the basis of which it had been authorizing individuals to cut timber on the Fort William Reserve for more than a decade was "utterly spurious and invalid" (G 14), yet apparently continued to regard the licences themselves as valid (G 17). When Madame Farijana, who held the licence in 1883–4, complained that Father Hébert, on behalf of the Indians, was having timber cut on the Reserve, the Department advised compromise, but concluded: "... the best way will be to allow them to fight the thing out between themselves. We have got our money for the timber and that is all we need care for, and Madam Farijana has her own remedy at law in view of the license issued to her" (G 18). In the circumstances, it is perhaps not surprising that the documents concerning the protests of Fort William Indians should not have been available to lay before the House of Commons when Edward Blake was demanding an inquiry.[12]

Neither the Algoma representative in Ottawa nor the Indian agents of the Thunder Bay area were pressing the government for any investigation of the general Indian complaints. Simon Dawson faithfully relayed the specific complaints over limitations on Indian hunting during closed seasons[13] and requests for schools on the

---

[12]P.A.C., Macdonald Papers, v. 291, contains a series of letters from the Indian Affairs Department asking Joseph Pope to send back the files on the Fort William Indians. Finally, Pope reported (May 11, 1885) that Sir John did not want them to leave his office, and a marginal notation by Robert Sinclair of the Department indicated that he had shown Pope's letter to the Deputy Minister on the following day, and they had agreed that under these circumstances no return to the address of the Commons was possible. In RG 10, v. 1090, p. 71, Vankoughnet to Langevin, March 15, 1886, there is a further refusal to comply with the request of the Commons since Sir John still had the relevant files. Vankoughnet then wrote to Pope again, indicating that Edward Blake was pressing for their submission to the Commons.

[13]P.A.C., RG 10, v. 1102, p. 67, Vankoughnet to Dawson, May 7, 1890.

reservations,[14] but there is no indication that he wanted any changes in policy. Both Dawson and James P. Donnelly, the Indian agent, did forward requests by the Port Arthur Separate School for a grant to cover the cost of educating Indian children, but they seem to have been satisfied with the government response. The Deputy Minister wrote:

In the case of Indians who leave their Reserves and locate themselves in towns and villages or elsewhere, it has been customary for the local school authorities in such places to regard them in the same light as the other inhabitants of those places by allowing their children admission to the schools, and it would be a questionable policy on the part of the Government to encourage Indians to locate themselves in towns and villages by affording the children special school facilities, as you are aware that as a rule Indians when located in such places become very demoralized and it is therefore undesirable to lend the sanction of the Department in any substantial manner to their living in white centres. Mr. Donnelly should exert his influence to induce the Indians not to reside in Port Arthur but to return to their respective settlements.[15]

John McIntyre had become Indian Agent for the Savanne District in 1880 and when Amos Wright was induced to retire he almost assumed responsibility for Fort William District as well (G 13). The recommendation had already been made to the Council when it was withdrawn on the advice of Simon Dawson. Dawson had expressed doubts about the original McIntyre appointment, but too late to effect any change. This time his intervention was decisive.[16] The officials of the Department, perhaps because of Dawson's influence with them, were increasingly critical of McIntyre (G 22), but there is no indication that disagreements sprang from differing views of policy. When McIntyre reported his activities for 1888, for example, he included an idyllic description of a school on an Indian reservation, sure to gladden the heart of a Deputy Minister who desired to maintain segregation. "There were thirty-one children assembled, all clean and neatly dressed, the youngest was five years old and the eldest eighteen. They opened duties by singing 'Praise God from whom all blessings flow' ... At the close of the examination, I gave each of those more advanced and those who had attended regularly a little present to encourage them – they were very gratified and proceedings were closed by their singing 'God Save the Queen.' "[17]

14*Ibid.*, v. 1103, p. 365, Vankoughnet to Donnelly, Dec. 10, 1890; v. 1105, p. 602, Vankoughnet to Dawson, June 27, 1891.
15*Ibid.*, v. 1092, p. 72, Vankoughnet to Dawson, Nov. 10, 1886.
16*Ibid.*, v. 1081, p. 565, Vankoughnet to Macdonald, Sept. 27, 1882.
17Canada Department of Indian Affairs, *Annual Report*, 1888, p. 59.

The Indians on the reserve at Michipicoten asked to be transferred from the control of the Indian agent at Sault Ste Marie to that of James P. Donnelly of Port Arthur.[18] Distance seems to have lent him an attraction the Fort William Band did not always perceive. In urging Donnelly's appointment, Simon Dawson had pointed out that he was a Roman Catholic and fluent in both French and English,[19] but neither his religion nor his bilingualism prevented a series of disputes with Father Hébert, which reached a climax after the election of Thomas Boucher as Head Chief in 1886 (G 23). When Father Jones examined the causes of discontent (G 24) he concluded that strife became inevitable when "mere wards of the government, placed under the tutelage of an agent" were given the right to vote in federal elections. The agent, as a government appointee, desired their support for the party in office; the missionary might or might not agree.

Father Jones' observations might have applied with equal justice to Indians in many areas. The Fort William Indians were not unique in their disputes with the government, in their factions supporting agent and missionary. What was perhaps unique was the extraordinary experience and ability of the missionaries in charge at Fort William. Father John Blettner, who died in 1882, was a former professor of theology at Fordham University; he spoke French, English, and German, understood several Indian languages, knew Latin and Greek, but considered Sanskrit and Hebrew his specialties. Father Hébert, who succeeded him, had practised law in Quebec before he became a professor of theology at the Collège Ste Marie. The academic distinction of both men helped to explain why young priests in the 1870s and 1880s were sent to the Fort William mission to receive their training for posts among the Indians. Any government representative faced formidable opposition at the Fort William Reserve, yet it was unlikely that the Society of Jesus could mobilize sufficient strength to alter Dominion government policy in any significant way. The first residents of Thunder Bay were thus caught between political forces almost equally balanced, so that the result was continued strife on the reservations on the fringes of settlement with little of the compensating economic advances being experienced within those settlements themselves.

[18]P.A.C., RG 10, v. 1104, p. 743, Vankoughnet to Edgar Dewdney, May 4, 1891; v. 1110, p. 513, Vankoughnet to T.M. Daly, Dec. 3, 1892.
[19]P.A.C., Macdonald Papers, v. 289, Dawson to Vankoughnet, Jan. 10, 1883.

FROM THE MOMENT that Colonel Wolseley provided the name Prince Arthur's Landing (which the exigencies of ticket and sign printing caused the Canadian Pacific Railway to alter in 1883) it seemed apparent that this port would become the centre for a developing district. Tiny as the hamlet was, it could still claim the largest concentration of population in northern Ontario, and the influx of settlers during the 1870s raised its numbers to about fifteen hundred at a time when no other centre in Thunder Bay could boast more than a fifth of that number. The Dawson Road began at its waterfront and provided its main east-west thoroughfare. Through the "Silver Gateway" flowed the supplies for the mining areas; to it came merchants and hotel keepers and professional men. When Hugh Wilson conducted the surveys for the new village (H 1) he inquired about plans to reserve an area for Dominion and provincial buildings. By 1876 the first of these buildings, the new registry office, court house, and jail, was under construction. A district capital had been established.

By comparison, Fort William in 1870 seemed to offer no such promise. The old Hudson's Bay Company fort retained its small staff, but already plans for closing the post were being discussed. A few homes had been built; the first lumber mill, that of Oliver, Davidson & Co., situated on the island opposite the fort, began operations in 1872. Several miles upstream lay the Town Plot Herrick had surveyed in 1859 – the land upon which John McIntyre had then doubted that anyone would be persuaded to settle – still virtually uninhabited in the early 1870s. Across the river stood the buildings of the Indian mission. Yet the contest was by no means so one-sided as it appeared. The few who lived in Fort William possessed a knowledge of the country acquired through years of association, a special knowledge which the Landing's newly arrived citizens could not match, a special knowledge which enabled the Shuniah delegation to Ottawa to convince the government that Thunder Bay had a longer shipping season than Nipigon Bay. The Hudson's Bay Company, however small its Fort William operation, was identified with a fort whose name was already known as a centre of importance in earlier years; the very name Fort William on Lake Superior evoked a memory of a past in which the *parvenu* Landing

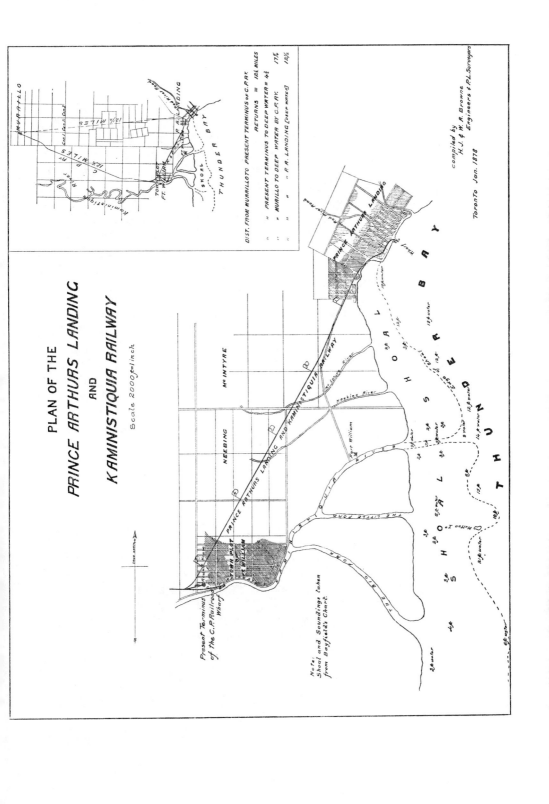

PLAN OF THE

PRINCE ARTHURS LANDING

AND

KAMINISTIQUIA RAILWAY

Scale 2000 = 1 inch

compiled by
H. J. & W. R. Browne
Engineers & P.L. Surveyors

Toronto Jan. 1878

DIST. FROM MURRILLOTO PRESENT TERMINUS OF C.P.RY. = 12¾ MILES

" RETURNS = 17¾

" PRESENT TERMINUS TO DEEP WATER = 4¾ 12½

" MURILLO TO DEEP WATER BY C.P.RY.

" " P.A. LANDING (DEEP WATER)

had no share. The Company also, as a holder of property and an institution with influence in governmental and financial circles, might exert pressure in its own interest and thus, indirectly, in that of Fort William. Although absentees held titles to land in both communities, it appeared that those owning the property along the Kaministikwia were in a slightly better position to influence the governments at Toronto and Ottawa to implement policies that would cause the value of their holdings to appreciate.

The conflicting interests of the Port and the Fort, then, were remarkably evenly balanced. As governments reacted to one interest or the other, ambitions were stirred and then periodically crushed. The result was suspicion and anger, directed not only against distant governments but also against whatever local interest was temporarily triumphant. In a sense, these white settlements at Thunder Bay could be compared to the Fort William Indian Band at the same time; they were caught between forces so equally matched that neither side could secure a continued or consistent policy. The Port and the Fort reacted the same way as did the Indian Band, wasting much of their energies on internal dissension and fruitless squabbles which often distracted attention from their genuine grievances, and made them appear ridiculous in the eyes of those whom they wished to convince of the justice of their cause.

The first chapter of the long conflict between the Port and the Fort opened with the Mackenzie government's decision that the Town Plot, several miles up the Kaministikwia River, was the head of navigation on Lake Superior. Accordingly, contracts were let for a railway westward from that point, about seven miles from the Landing. The village which had been destined for success, which had prided itself on its achievements and upon the amenities it offered where forests had so recently stood, now faced the prospect of being cut off from the main line of transcontinental transport. The mood of the disappointed citizenry of a village which had numerical advantage entirely on its side was expressed in a number of ways in the next five years. Peter Nicholson and about one hundred other residents signed a petition to the government stating their case (H 2) but their petition had no effect. The "Thunderbolt," a hand-written newspaper edited by George Thomas Marks, the young nephew of the Reeve of Shuniah, and G.F. Holland, sought to answer the rival publication, the "Perambulator," edited by Peter McKellar and Miss Groom, the Fort William school teacher. The "Thunderbolt" chose to take an optimistic view of the Landing's future prospects, and a derisive one of Fort William's pretensions (H 3). Individuals answering routine questions from government departments seemed more than usually prone to defend their actions. The mood of the Thunder Bay *Sentinel*, which began its weekly publication at the Landing in July 1875, was angry rather than merely scornful or defensive. Repeatedly, Michael Hagan, the editor for the first three years of the newspaper's existence, used the columns of the *Sentinel* to denounce the individuals whose interests in the Fort William Town Plot were presumably influencing the governments in Toronto and Ottawa.

The chief "Plotters," as they came to be called, were those who had benefited financially from the decisions of the Mackenzie government. When the *Sentinel* published the list of all those who had so benefited, the same list as that laid before the House of Commons,[1] it also made its own recapitulation of what it considered the significant purchases (H 4), omitting not only minor ones but some very large ones from individuals not at that time under special attack. The chief target was the firm of Oliver, Davidson & Co., and the symbol then calculated to rouse Landing residents was the Neebing Hotel in the Town Plot which that Company had sold to the railway for offices. Eventually the government investigation revealed the actual expenditure (H 8) and the Landing spokesmen admitted their choice of a symbol had been a poor one. Even if the $5029.36 paid for the property were added to the cost of renovations ($3456.85) something less than a new Pacific Scandal had been discovered. By 1878 the citizens of the Landing were calling this "a mere vulgar bit of sharp practice" and concluding that "it is but reasonable to suppose that the speculators are rather pleased than otherwise at the ceaseless din about a crumb, comparatively so small, for it serves to divert public attention from the larger schemes of profit which are being cunningly, surely and deeply laid."[2]

It would appear that the selection of Oliver, Davidson & Co. for the *Sentinel*'s attack resulted in part at least from their absentee status. Joseph Davidson of Toronto was never a resident of Thunder Bay; Peter Brown, the third partner, was a resident long enough to be elected to the first Shuniah Council in 1873, but not long enough to establish much of an attendance record at its meetings. Adam Oliver of Ingersoll did spent at least part of each year in the Thunder Bay area in the early 1870s, but his membership in the Ontario House and his influence in the political party then in power at both

---

[1]Canada, *Sessional Papers*, 1877, no 57, List of property bought for a terminus in the Town Plot, Fort William.

[2]*Prince Arthur's Landing and the Terminus of the C.P.R.* (Toronto, 1878), p. 8.

Toronto and Ottawa marked him out as the chief plotter against the interests of Prince Arthur's Landing. His public speeches were hardly reassuring and he was rumoured to have a map of Thunder Bay, as he wished it to develop, prominently displayed in the Ontario Legislature.[3] Oliver did try to combat the *Sentinel's* local influence by encouraging two young Ingersoll men, Colin Patience and Walter T. Burdick, to launch a counterattack. Their enterprise, the *Fort William Day-Book and Kaministiquia Advocate*, survived less than a year.[4] At the local level the Landing continued to triumph. But even after Oliver retired from politics and withdrew from business in Thunder Bay, the Landing interests were far from successful in influencing distant governments. The *Sentinel* then looked for other plotters to unmask, and "Governor" McIntyre soon received much unfavourable attention, especially when he gave interviews to newspapers in cities he visited, and secured the kind of publicity for his views that few frontiersmen had an opportunity to achieve (H 5).

A group of leading citizens of the Landing, while still disputing the wisdom of the government decision to build a railway west from the Plot, decided to act upon this decision and build a seven-mile railway to link the district capital with the end of steel. The entire municipality of Shuniah, including those areas that would hardly benefit from the project, gave financial support. Again, the weight of numbers gave the Landing power in the municipality. But again this power was ineffective in dealing with the Mackenzie government. When permission to connect the Prince Arthur's Landing and Kaministiquia Railway to the Canadian Pacific at the Town Plot was refused, the hopes of Landing interests were again dashed. The conviction that there was a conspiracy against them grew stronger than ever.

The citizens of Prince Arthur's Landing published a pamphlet in an effort to lay their claims before the Canadian public, and expressed in it most clearly their sense of injustice. They declared that "they were first trifled with and then denied the privilege of connecting their line with the Pacific Railway, at the instigation of parties interested in crushing their settlement and building up a town on the Kaministiquia ... Through the sinister influence of these parties, they have been subjected to the most cruel persecution, involved in litigation, and grossly misrepresented to and placed in a false light before the Government and the country."[5]

[3]Thunder Bay *Sentinel*, Feb. 24, 1876.
[4]F. Fregeau, "Reminiscences of Early Journalism in Fort William," Thunder Bay Historical Society, *Papers*, 1911–12, p. 20.
[5]*Prince Arthur's Landing and the Terminus*, p. 1.

With the change of government in Ottawa and the formation of the new Canadian Pacific Railway Company came a revival of the buoyant hopes of Prince Arthur's Landing. There was a new rush of settlers and land values and the cost of living again rose. There was now no question of being by-passed by transcontinental transportation lines, and the new town of Port Arthur set to work assuring its position. The ambitious building projects of the time, the volume of trade passing through the harbour, the prospects for a shipping industry, the descriptions by distinguished visitors, all seemed to indicate that the period of depression was past. The exuberance over the completion of the railway line to the west produced a whole series of headlines in the *Weekly Herald* of July 8, 1882 (E 18). But " 'Tis done! the great transaction's done" was unconsciously ironic. The writer seems to have forgotten the opening line of the hymn he quoted – "O happy day that fixed my choice" – and the choice of divisional point for the Canadian Pacific Railway was far from decided in 1882. A little more than a month after the *Herald*'s story, George Stephen was writing John McIntyre about the possibility of making Fort William the lake terminus (H 9). As soon as suspicion of such intentions grew in Port Arthur, the conspiracy theory was bound to be revived. This time, not only the Hudson's Bay Company but at least certain individuals within the Canadian Pacific Railway Company, particularly George Stephen and Donald Smith (H 29), were accused as Oliver, Davidson & Co. had been in their time.

If the Port Arthur press early selected the villains in the piece, it soon decided on its hero – Duncan McIntyre, who was presumed to have been the special supporter of Port Arthur interests, but retired from the Company in 1883 after a break with Stephen. It was somewhat awkward that the hero had the same surname as one of the villains. After the retirement of Duncan McIntyre, the Port Arthur press was able to rejoice that William Van Horne's ancestry was not Scottish like that of so many of the plotters. Only occasionally and under very great stress did the Port Arthur newspapers identify Van Horne with any Fort William conspiracy, and his letters make it very clear that he was no consistent supporter of any one group. He viewed the Thunder Bay harbour as a unit (H 10) and seems to have been an early proponent of amalgamation of the two communities. He was eager to take advantage of the interest in Hudson's Bay Company property which his Company had acquired in Fort William (H 14) but he was also fully aware of the advantages he could gain as different individuals and different communities sought to exert pressure. He was prepared to expropriate property from John McIntyre; he did not wish to accede to all the conditions the

McKellar family were proposing; and of Major Walsh of the Dominion Coal, Coke & Transportation Company he wrote: "... as he is intimate with the McKellars, I think you can use him to great advantage. His anxiety to help the Company may not be entirely disinterested, but knowing that you can use him just as well" (H 13).

Both Stephen and Van Horne had cause to regret the arrangements they had earlier made with the McVicar family. The Company had secured essential property at "Prince Arthur's Landing now called Port Arthur" from Christina, Victoria, and George McVicar (H 11). But to do so it had to agree to the construction of the railway station and freight sheds several blocks from the centre of the town, to the inconvenience of the Company and its passengers, as well as the town itself (H 19). After this experience, there was a noticeable effort to make sure that no other family was able to dictate Company policy.

Van Horne continued to urge the Department of Public Works to dredge the Kaministikwia River, and selected Fort William as the site of the second, and by far the larger, of the elevators constructed at Thunder Bay (H 16, H 17). It was not until 1887, however, that the Port Arthur Council began its efforts to secure additional tax revenue from the railway Company, and it was this dispute, reaching its climax with the seizure of C.P.R. property for arrears in taxes, that caused the Port Arthur press to include Van Horne temporarily among its villains. In 1887 the Clerk of Port Arthur had submitted a bill for $5144.62 in back taxes, but had also indicated that the Council of that year desired to make a number of concessions. It was willing to grant a bonus to the Company equal to one-half of the tax bill, and it was prepared to submit a by-law to the ratepayers to provide for further exemption (H 19). Van Horne's advice concerning this letter contained specific observations on every point raised by the town Clerk except the matter of taxes (H 20). One group in the Council considered the replies received to be unsatisfactory (H 21) but the majority at that time had no desire to provoke an outright confrontation. In the view of one Fort William observer, this policy of lenience toward the C.P.R. had its roots in the Conservative party affiliation of the Marks family.[6]

In any case, there was still hope in 1887 – provided some alteration in provincial legislation was made – that Port Arthur could reach agreement with the C.P.R. on the tax question. Two years later the town's mood was less ebullient, and it was less likely that the moder-

[6]Peter McKellar, "Incident in the History of the Canadian Pacific Railway," Thunder Bay Historical Society, *Papers*, 1925, pp. 10–11.

ates in Council would prevail. The Mayor of that year was Thomas Gorham, a lawyer who had formerly worked in the offices of the c.p.r. in Winnipeg, and a Liberal in politics. By 1889, also, the Council was faced with a refusal on the part of the Ontario government to alter its statutes. Moreover, the beginnings of construction on the Port Arthur, Duluth and Western railway created the illusion of an alternative to c.p.r. favour. At least its terminal buildings and workshops would be situated in Port Arthur (H 22). In 1889, then, there was a renewed effort to collect the c.p.r. taxes, now allegedly amounting to about $15,000 (H 24).

When no settlement had been reached by December 9, 1889, the tax collector, acting as his own bailiff, seized a c.p.r. yard engine and several cars standing in Port Arthur and offered them for sale. Mayor Gorham, with the support of the majority of Council, had proceeded with this dramatic action, and it did produce immediate results. William Whyte, the superintendent of the western division of the c.p.r., arrived from Winnipeg, met the Port Arthur Council, agreed to pay the taxes but not the accrued interest, and secured the release of Company property (H 28). Gorham and his supporters did not run for the new Council (H 26) and the careers of most of them in municipal politics were at an end. Within months the new c.p.r. works at Fort William, designed to employ five hundred men, were under construction. Buyers, many of them from Winnipeg, were quick to scent a new opportunity, and lots along Simpson Street, the main thoroughfare in the new Town Plot opening up near the site of the fort of earlier days, sold at prices ranging from $500 to $700.[7] In 1891 Fort William became the port of embarkation for c.p.r. steamers, and the bands were out to greet the *Athabaska* on her first arrival there.[8]

The decision of the Canadian Pacific Railway Company was clear; more difficult to determine was the extent to which the action of the Port Arthur Council had contributed to that decision. The *Sentinel* concluded that the seizure of Company property had not affected the issue, that the Company in general and Donald Smith in particular – with his important influence in both the c.p.r. and the Hudson's Bay Company – had long before decided in favour of Fort William (H 29). Rumours of the impending change had been circulating well before the engine and cars were seized[9] and it was reported that

[7]Fort William *Journal*, Aug. 9, 1890, included descriptions from the *Hamilton Spectator*, the London *Advertiser*, and the *Winnipeg Free Press*.
[8]*Ibid.*, May 9, 1891.
[9]*Sentinel*, May 9, 1884; *Journal*, June 15, 1889.

Mayor Gorham had tried to bargain with Van Horne on the basis of cancelling the tax bill in return for a guarantee that the Company would continue to run its steamers from Port Arthur.[10] A local legend promptly credited Van Horne with predicting that grass would grow in the streets of Port Arthur, just as, on other occasions, he was supposed to have made the same prophecy for Port Moody and Winnipeg. But the Van Horne letters reveal no particular preference for one community above the other. Nor is there evidence of any abrupt change in Company policy in reaction to the Port Arthur Council demands. The transfer of the divisional point to Fort William had been given serious consideration in the head offices of the c.p.r. for half a dozen years before the decision was reached.

In its bitterness over that decision, however, the acknowledged capital of Thunder Bay lashed out against its rival and sought means of survival. Port Arthur businessmen feared the collapse of their interests as a rapidly expanding Fort William threatened to draw workers from its neighbour. The building of the Electric Street Railway between the communities was one device to enable workers to continue to live in Port Arthur and work at the c.p.r. shops. "Port Arthur's manifest destiny," declared the *Sentinel* in a year of crisis, "is to be the city of Thunder Bay, and it is equally the manifest destiny of Fort William to be a bustling railway suburb of Port Arthur" (H 31). In spite of reverses, the weight of numbers still lay with the district capital, and there was accordingly a desire to snatch this opportunity to assure amalgamation, at least with the neighbouring Fort William wards in which the railway shops were located.

But amalgamation was unlikely to be an attractive idea in Fort William. The secession of Neebing from the municipality of Shuniah had only taken place in 1881, and the memory of the minority position held in the old united municipality was still fresh. The incorporation of the town of Port Arthur in 1884 had further diminished Shuniah's boundaries, but, more significant, it gave the Port Arthur Council a better bargaining position when issues like the extension of the Electric Street Railway beyond the town boundaries arose. Fort William as part of a township found that authorities in Toronto assumed a preponderance of influence in the existing town, whether or not it was the case in fact. The Fort William *Journal*, even before the 1889 crisis, had complained over the inclusion of Fort William elevators as part of the Port Arthur scenic attractions in tourist literature, and commented: "Port Arthur is like a clipped and

[10]*Sentinel*, Dec. 13, 1889.

plucked rooster trying to steal a few peacock feathers."[11] Its attitude toward any planned amalgamation was predictable (H 32). At the same time, Fort William secured incorporation as a town, and promptly decided upon a locomotive as its symbol (H 33), flaunting its recent triumph, and already looking forward to the day when it would outstrip its rival in population.

Neither united action nor symbols of unity existed in the Thunder Bay District in 1892. Any symbol connected with the fur trade might be cherished by one town, but it was likely to be regarded with suspicion by the other. Any symbol connected with transcontinental railways was bound to be divisive. The ghost of William McGillivray might brood over Fort William and infuse the very word "amalgamation" with sombre colours, but the Nor'westers belonged to a past in which Port Arthur had no share, and Port Arthur had no tutelary spirit of its own. Its very name had come by virtue of the British army and a railway company; Prince Arthur, Duke of Connaught, had no particular claim upon the affection of the residents, and the attempt to link the new town with Chester Arthur (who occupied the White House at the time of incorporation) was unlikely to evoke much enthusiasm. The protracted battle for power had, in a sense, weakened the claim of either town to represent the entire district, and the lack of a recognized focal point delayed the development of a wider sense of community.

[11]July 6, 1889.

I. A SENSE OF COMMUNITY

IN THE PRE-CONFEDERATION PERIOD it had been impossible for any sense of community to develop in Thunder Bay. The geographical barriers, the dominance of a fur trading Company in which the area was of secondary importance, the transient nature of the population, all served to divide rather than to unite. Sir George Simpson recognized this, but indicated also the possibilities of change, in a passage frequently quoted ever since by those urging development of the Lakehead area:

Compared with the adamantine deserts of Lake Superior, the Kaministaquoia presented a perfect paradise. One cannot pass through this fair valley without feeling that it is destined, sooner or later, to become the happy home of civilized men, with their bleating flocks and their lowing herds, with their schools and their churches, with their full garners and their social hearths. At the time of our visit [May 1841], the great obstacle in the way of so blessed a consummation was the hopeless wilderness to the eastward, which seemed to bar for ever the march of settlement and cultivation. But that very wilderness, now that it is to yield up its long-hidden stores, bids fair to remove the very impediments which hitherto it has presented. The mines of Lake Superior, besides establishing a continuity of route between the east and the west, will find their nearest and cheapest supply of agricultural produce in the valley of the Kaministaquoia.[1]

In the quarter century after Confederation a community did appear in the area Simpson had predicted it would develop. That community was agricultural only in a secondary sense; its economic base was silver mining and the requirements of transcontinental transport. A Torontonian visiting it in the early 1870s (I 1) was struck by the newness and crudity of life on a semi-civilized frontier, and by the exuberance and optimism of the inhabitants. This optimism manifested itself in many ways, surviving temporary setbacks and exulting in apparent successes. The boom years of the early

[1]*Narrative of a Journey round the World during the years 1841 and 1842* (London, 1847), I, 37. The book seems to have been ghost-written from the actual journal kept by Simpson (P.A.C., H.B. Co. Records, D-3-a). This passage was much expanded from the original observations after the mining developments of the mid-1840s and it was the expanded version that was frequently quoted. See Allan Macdonell, *The North-west Transportation, Navigation and Railway Company: Its Objects* (Toronto, 1858), p. 39.

1880s were reflected in the trade statistics (I 26, I 27), in the rapid expansion of dock facilities (I 18), and in shipping (I 22). Local enthusiasts delighted in these statistics and predicted successes for new business enterprises (I 23), successes that did not always materialize.

In the homes of Fort William and Port Arthur by the 1890s there lived many families who considered themselves long established in Thunder Bay, and firmly identified with its aspirations. A reading of the local press might suggest their violent opposition to each other, but the evidence of their diaries and letters modifies the picture considerably. Peter McKellar's diary for 1874–5 (I 5) began in October with an account of his visit to Toronto, seeking financial support for his new mining enterprise. On November 6 he returned to Thunder Bay, and in the almost daily entries from then until the end of the year many characteristics of the community as a whole emerge – the constant business dealings between the two feuding hamlets, the social connections as well between the McKellars and the Marks and McVicar families of Prince Arthur's Landing. In the less frequent entries after the new year, church activities received most of the attention; then, in the spring, preparations for a new expedition to Little Pic. Even the turning of the first sod for the Canadian Pacific and the outburst of local oratory that accompanied it were secondary to the main business of the year.

The almost contemporary diary of the Rev. Donald McKerracher (I 4) made no distinction between the two villages, except on the basis of numbers. It was to the much larger Prince Arthur's Landing that McKerracher went first as a summer supply in 1873 and then, after his ordination, as the first Presbyterian minister resident in Thunder Bay. The church's efforts, and its strictures, were divided according to numbers only; if anything, the Fort William contingent got slightly more favourable notice, at least until 1874 when another summer supply commented on the need for a church there "in more ways than one" (I 3). McKerracher's fairly detailed diary of his first few months in his new charge indicates an increasing preoccupation with the problem of getting a church built at the Landing, but also his efforts to maintain some kind of regular services in Fort William even though the worldliness of his congregation and the visits of a Governor-General might prevent it. Later, the battle with the hotel keepers occupied much of his time (I 9), and this focused his interest on the Landing where they were concentrated. But there was no evidence that the affection he expressed for one congregation was either stronger or different in character from his feelings for the other.

He seems to have perceived none of the deep divisions the *Sentinel* was dwelling upon.

At the same time, the Anglican Church was establishing itself first in the more populous centre where church bazaars and decorated sanctuaries were already possible (I 11). But, like the Presbyterians, Anglicans quickly reached out to the Town Plot. As the Rev. J.K. McMorine put it: "we worship in 'an upper room' and so are apostolic in this respect" (I 12).

When Dr T.S.T. Smellie decided to leave Fergus in 1879 he was unaware of any difference in the prospects of the two villages (I 14, I 15). Acting on McKerracher's advice he chose Prince Arthur's Landing, and his Board of Health Reports showed how closely he had identified himself with the interests of that place by the late 1880s (I 24). In 1890 he could see no future for the area and moved to Manitoba, yet within a year he had returned and established a practice in Fort William. Medical officers, church and school officials, could easily be drawn into the rivalry of the Port and the Fort and temporarily forget their community of interest, but it became obvious to them on reflection that their basic problems were the same. Smellie's decision to move to the north was taken by hundreds of Ontario residents in the 1880s and 1890s. When to their number was added the migration from Manitoba of those originally from Ontario, the very great impact of Ontario's cultural values upon a community hitherto without any real association with them, becomes evident. In time, the environment and the previous history of the area modified the inheritance and, in so doing, slowly created a sense of community.

The establishment of the first public schools in the municipality of Shuniah (I 2, I 6) in 1873 and 1874 gave evidence of the special problems confronted by the early trustees. Before that time the Hudson's Bay Company had provided space in which the children of its employees were taught; a private school had begun in Prince Arthur's Landing; and the Daughters of Mary had opened a school at the mission chiefly for Indians. Financial problems and the sometimes mystifying edicts from Queen's Park which resulted in thirty-two citizens all claiming to be school trustees in 1880 (I 16, I 17) roused local ire. But at the same time, in the newly erected classrooms, the children of Thunder Bay were following a curriculum devised for the whole province, and entertaining their elders on special occasions with the traditional Ontario school concert (I 8).

When Edward Biggings of Sault Ste Marie ran as the Conservative candidate in Algoma in the Ontario election of 1875, he tried to arouse interest in educational problems. "It will be one of my objects," he promised, "to have established in some central part of the District, a Grammar and Collegiate Institute, that our youth may not be compelled to go below at great expense to obtain the higher branches."[2] The sub-district of Thunder Bay did not respond to this appeal, either because the voters felt Mr Biggings' "central location" was not likely to benefit them, or because of a powerful sentiment in favour of the first candidate from Thunder Bay itself. The vote in Prince Arthur's Landing was 7 for Biggings to 172 for Simon Dawson, and in Fort William Biggings got 2 votes to 45 for Dawson.

The election of 1875 was a significant one in Thunder Bay history. Simon Dawson, although not a permanent resident of the district, had been associated with its interests for nearly twenty years, and could hardly be considered an absentee. Up to that time the district had been represented in the federal parliament by W.M. Simpson of Sault Ste Marie, J.B. Robinson of Toronto, and, as a result of the 1874 election, E.B. Borron, the former mining inspector and long time resident of Bruce Mines. In the Ontario House Dawson's only predecessor had been Colonel F.W. Cumberland of Toronto, who had won an easy victory in 1867 and been returned by acclamation in 1871. Cumberland and Robinson were Conservatives, Simpson and Borron Reformers. Their elections thus indicate no strong party bias on the part of the electorate. It was appropriate that Dawson should win his first electoral victory as an independent, although his support for the Mowat government during the next three years was so consistent as to make his independence largely illusory.

The battles over the location of the railway terminus during the Mackenzie administration had tended to make Prince Arthur's Landing voters at least temporary supporters of the Conservative party, while the rightness of Liberal thinking seemed obvious to Fort William. In these circumstances Dawson wisely contested the federal seat as an independent; only after the granting of the contract to the C.P.R. did he become a Conservative and, under that political label, successfully contest the elections of 1882 and 1887. The Thunder Bay *Sentinel* was strongly Conservative in its attitude and supported Dawson consistently throughout his career, urging his appointment to the Senate in 1891 when another Conservative candidate was nominated to contest the election. Neither Sir John A. Macdonald nor the Prime Ministers who succeeded him seemed to agree. The *Sentinel* tended to adopt extreme positions in defence of both Dawson and the interests of Port Arthur, yet the election results made it clear that Dawson's victories were not won by Port Arthur votes alone and

[2]P.A.C., MG 29 E-1, Algoma *Pioneer*, Extra, July 16, 1875.

that he had opponents also within the town he was alleged to favour. Fort William, and particularly Oliver Township (I 28), were considered to be Liberal strongholds, yet at least a sizable minority of votes from these areas helped keep Dawson in office. His position became increasingly precarious, however, in the elections of the 1880s and his last victory was achieved with a margin of eleven votes for the whole riding of Algoma.

Dawson's political longevity was based only partly upon the contemporary success of the party which he had decided to join. He was more thoroughly acquainted with the Thunder Bay District than his early opponents. He was aware of its history, of its economic potential, and of the ethnic and religious divisions among the voters. No Thunder Bay politician since his time was likely to urge the encouragement of settlement in such terms as he did in 1875: "The settlers now going in chiefly belong to the eastern provinces of the Dominion and are, of course, vastly superior to foreign immigrants."[3] But Dawson was well aware of the prejudices of the electorate, and in his day the influx of settlers from central and eastern Europe had not yet begun. As a Roman Catholic he was especially sensitive to criticism of his actions with respect to Orange Bills (I 13), yet he had every proof that the Thunder Bay electorate was unlikely to divide along religious lines. The successful Liberal candidate in provincial elections from 1885 on was James Conmee, also a Roman Catholic. One of Dawson's most publicized difficulties lay with Father Hébert who advised the Indians to vote for a Protestant candidate (G 24).

When the *Weekly Herald and Algoma Miner* began publication in Port Arthur, its announced intention was to support the Conservative party. Within a year it had veered in the direction of independence, and then, in its conviction that Simon Dawson was providing inadequate representation for the Thunder Bay region, it moved into personal attacks on the sitting member, while retaining some objectivity on national and provincial issues. By 1886 James Dickinson, formerly a night editor with the Toronto *Globe*, became editor of the *Herald* and announced support for the Liberals in all subsequent political battles.

The *Herald* criticized Dawson on three main counts: corrupt election practices (I 19), ineffectiveness as a member of Parliament, and blindness to the special interests of Ontario. The first charge was made repeatedly against members of any opposing party, particularly when that party formed the government, and the *Sentinel's* accounts of the Liberal tactics (I 20) merits attention in this connection. When

[3]*Ibid.*, Nov. 26, 1875.

the Fort William *Journal* began publication in 1887, it attempted a somewhat more dispassionate consideration of the narrow election victory of Dawson in that year (I 21) and revealed the extent of corruption indulged in by both parties. Dawson and his opponent each filed complaints on that occasion, and each chose to drop the matter when apprised of the strength of the case against him. In trying to substantiate the second charge, the *Herald* examined *Hansard* and produced a fairly accurate description that might have been applied to a number of representatives since Dawson's time:

You can speak about nothing but the vastness of the great northwest, and have shown your total incapability of addressing the house upon any other subject. It is nothing but timber lands, minerals, numerous islands, inland seas and ponds, big mountains, wood ravines, length and breadth of the great northwest, latitudes and longitudes, etc. etc. Enough then about your great talents and universality of knowledge. Mr. Dawson must ever take a back seat upon the topics and great questions of the times as he has never yet, in parliament, displayed any knowledge or familiarity with them.[4]

In all this, Dawson can be said to have mirrored the interests of those who repeatedly elected him. Against the third charge there could scarcely be a rebuttal. His attempts to set aside the boundary award made in favour of Ontario made it clear that he favoured separate status for the north. The *Herald* denounced him as "an agent of the Eastern Provinces, some of whose representatives unacquainted with the subject and jealous of Ontario's wealth and influence desired to weaken and humiliate her."[5] For committed Ontario Reformers of the 1880s, this conclusion seemed inescapable, but Thunder Bay contained many voters acutely aware of the differences in outlook between their region and the Toronto region, and these were traditionally Dawson supporters.

Yet in provincial elections the district continued to elect supporters of the Mowat government as it had done when Dawson first ran for office in 1875. Until the division of the provincial riding in 1885, R.A. Lyon of Manitoulin Island represented the district, and party organization was strong enough to overcome Dawson's aid to Lyon's opponents. In 1885 James Conmee was elected to the Ontario House for the newly created riding of West Algoma and continued to represent the area in Toronto and Ottawa for a quarter of a century. As a

[4]May 16, 1883.
[5]June 21, 1882; P.A.C., Macdonald Papers, v. 315, Copy enclosed in Dawson to Macdonald, Dec. 9, 1882, along with W.H. Plummer to Dawson, Oct. 4, 1882.

former Mayor of Port Arthur, he was still able to poll a heavy vote in rival Fort William. His numerous railway and lumbering enterprises coincided with some local interests and ran counter to others. J.A. Mathieu, for many years an important lumberman in the Rainy River District and Conservative member at Queen's Park after 1911, explained his choice of political parties on his arrival from the United States years before: "Conmee, the Liberal asked me for his support and I wouldn't give it to him. I was cutting on some Indian land at the time, and he had my contract cancelled. I didn't like that kind of liberalism, so I became a conservative."[6] The equally hostile Thunder Bay *Sentinel* pointed out the diversity of Conmee's interests (I 30), although in this case the conflict of interest was between Port Arthur and Fort William, not the welfare of the district and the personal advantage of the member. The Toronto *Globe* moved from fulsome praise for Conmee's maiden speech to rather modified enthusiasm in the 1890s to a reference to him by 1905 as "a notorious character."[7] But the voters of Thunder Bay continued to support him. The *Sentinel*, unable to explain his popularity on any other grounds, decided that he was a mere cipher, but that the all-powerful c.p.r. desired to keep the Mowat government in power (I 31). It accordingly opposed the idea of a division of the federal riding, in case the same melancholy result should ensue and the Liberal party represent the district at both Toronto and Ottawa.

The voters of Thunder Bay managed to be represented on the government side in both capitals consistently from 1875 to 1894, yet this circumstance did not seem to bring the sympathetic attention they felt they should receive. A common desire for economic advancement could not unite the district behind one political party, since there was too much confusion over the direction in which that development should lie. The volume of trade with the United States continued in the pattern established many years before, but local attitudes toward the United States trade policy were ambivalent. Liberals in 1891 could hardly give unquestioning support to a policy of unrestricted reciprocity and expect continued profits from the c.p.r. connection (I 29). Resentment against American tariffs mounted during the 1890s, especially when the Fort William saw mills lay idle in 1897, and the western lumbermen perceived the results brought about "by a country of pronounced antagonism to

[6]Ontario, Department of Lands and Forests, Timber Branch, Report of interview with Mathieu by L. Weisberg and V. Nelles, July 27, 1965.
[7]June 30, 1886; Feb. 16, 1894; March 30, 1905.

our lumber trade."[8] A new resentment of the southern neighbour had appeared without bringing any great measure of confidence in Canadian governments. A long series of complaints about government inaction had aroused resentment elsewhere. The *Winnipeg Tribune* included the following Ottawa despatch: "There is also here to-day a large delegation registered as from new Ontario, and which consists of many of the old exploiters living west of Lake Superior who have made the life of every government miserable for years, pressing for some scheme by which they can get their fingers in the treasury."[9]

In time even the Winnipeg papers that had been presumed to be sympathetic to the aspirations of Thunder Bay joined in the criticism of it. Yet the view from the west continued to differ in many respects from the view from the east. In the December 1892 edition of *Dominion Illustrated*, Captain Henry Woodside of Winnipeg, a representative of a pioneer Port Arthur family, could invoke for the whole district the memory of a past in which all of the Thunder Bay area had been involved, and take pride in a burst of economic activity from which Fort William benefited most (I 32).

Confederation itself, the building of the Canadian Pacific and the introduction of the National Policy, the victory of the Ontario government in its battle for the "disputed territory," all had created new associations and new tensions within the community of Thunder Bay. Behind much of the quarrelling and the ascription of blame for the evils encountered lay coinciding interests often obscured. What was apparent was negative rather than positive – a common sense of grievance against outside authorities ignorant of the local situation, unaware of the needs or even the geographical location of the area. But the rest of Canada at the end of the nineteenth century was likely to know little about a district still so sharply divided within itself, so thinly populated, so unaware of the common features of its heritage, still defining its identity in terms of what it was not.

[8]P.A.O., Lands and Forests Department Papers, Minutes of Association of Ontario Lumbermen, Copy of brief of western lumbermen to Prime Minister Laurier, March 21, 1898.
[9]L.U.L., D.F. Burk Papers, clipping enclosed in F.E. Trautman (Editor, Fort William *Daily Times-Journal*) to Burk, March 7, 1901.

THUNDER BAY DISTRICT, 1821–1892

DOCUMENTS

A. THE UNDISTRIBUTED MIDDLE, 1821–92: A PROBLEM OF JURISDICTION

A 1 TESTIMONY IN THE TRIAL OF CHARLES DE REINHARD, 1818[1]

[Canada, House of Commons, Select Committee on Boundaries of Ontario, Report, p. 185]

William Sax,[2] sworn. I am a surveyor. I am acquainted, according to a map which I have here, with the limits of Upper Canada, that is to say, of the old Province of Quebec; the western limit, the mouth of the River Ohio, is in longitude 88°50' west from Greenwich, and latitude 37°10' north. That appears by a map which I have made and have in my hand, to be the latitude and longitude of the junction of the Ohio River with the Mississippi.

Chief Justice Sewell.[3] – When you speak of the junction of the Ohio River with the Mississippi River, do you mean where the Ohio River empties itself into the banks of the Mississippi?

Mr. Sax. – That is my understanding, and the Statute provides also –
Chief Justice Sewell. – We do not require any information or assistance in the construction of the Statute; we require it as to the fact. The construction of the Statute, it is our province to decide on.

Attorney-General.[4] – Would a line running north from the junction of the Ohio and the Mississippi strike, in its passage to the Hudson's Bay Territory, the great lakes, and where would it strike Lake Superior? And where would it leave Fort William?

[1]Charles de Reinhard was charged with a murder committed in the Indian country, tried at Quebec in 1818, found guilty, but never executed. During his trial there was much dispute over what court had jurisdiction in such a case. Several of the points then at issue were clarified in 1821 with the passing of the Act for Regulating the Fur Trade and Establishing a Criminal and Civil Jurisdiction within Certain Parts of North America. The question of the location of the western boundary of Upper Canada, however, continued to be debated for years afterward. Argument centred on the direction the boundary line was to take from its established base, the confluence of the Ohio and Mississippi rivers. Of all possible interpretations, only drawing a line directly north from the base point would affect the District of Thunder Bay, leaving all land from Fort William west outside the limits of Upper Canada.
[2]William Saxe was a surveyor from 1797 to 1825. All his work was associated with the Montreal area, hence he had no direct knowledge of the area about which he was called to give expert testimony.
[3]Chief Justice Jonathan Sewell (1766–1829) had been born in Cambridge, Massachusetts, and received his early education in England. He came to Quebec in 1785 and by 1808 was Chief Justice of Lower Canada, a post he held for thirty years.
[4]Norman Fitzgerald Uniacke (1777–1846) belonged to the prominent Nova Scotia family. He served as Attorney-General of Lower Canada from 1809 to 1825.

Mr. Sax. – Such a line, drawn due north, would strike Lake Superior on its passage, and at or about a degree east of Fort William, or perhaps three quarters of a degree?

Attorney General. – That is to say, the west end of Lake Superior?

Mr. Sax. – Yes, nearly so; when I say that such a line would strike east of Fort William, I mean that it would leave Fort William about three-quarters of a degree to the west of it. It is so laid down in all the maps.

A 2   JOSEPH DELAFIELD[5] TO J.Q. ADAMS[6]
[United States, National Archives, Treaty of Ghent, Arts. VI and VII, Delafield Letters]

Washington, D.C.
July 24, 1822

In respect to the Seventh Article of the Treaty, great pains have been taken by the Commissioners[7] to effect its speedy execution. The American party now employed consists of a principal surveyor,[8] and one assistant,[9] who is also the draftsman, with a few batteau-men to conduct their boats and provisions ...

Although there is a reasonable prospect that the work may be perfected in another season, yet there may be obstacles which our imperfect knowledge of the country must keep concealed until our own investigations shall

[5]Major Joseph Delafield was a United States army officer who had graduated from Yale in 1808 and had been admitted to the bar in 1811. In 1820 he was appointed Agent to the American Boundary Commission under the Treaty of Ghent. His diary has been published under the title *The Unfortified Boundary*, edited by McElroy and Riggs.

[6]John Quincy Adams (1767–1848) was Secretary of State in the Monroe administration and was President of the United States when the final reports of the Boundary Commission were tabled in 1827. His father, the second President of the United States, had been one of the American Commissioners at the signing of the Treaty of Versailles in 1783 and, when he was consulted over one of the points concerning that agreement, wrote to Delafield giving his account of what had taken place forty years earlier.

[7]The Commissioners who were in charge of determining the boundary under the Seventh Article of the Treaty of Ghent – that is, the boundary through Lake Superior to the Lake of the Woods – were Peter Porter for the United States and Anthony Barclay for Great Britain.

[8]The principal surveyor for the Americans was James Ferguson who had been born in Scotland in 1797, had previously served as an engineer on the Erie Canal, then as assistant surveyor, and finally as astronomical surveyor with the Boundary Commission in 1822–7. With his assistant, he spent the winter of 1822–3 in Fort William.

[9]George Washington Whistler, father of the artist James McNeill Whistler, served as assistant-cum-draughtsman on this expedition shortly after his graduation from West Point. Thus early in its history the Thunder Bay region might have reason for complaint in that it knew only Whistler's father.

disclose them. From the line of trading posts, but little can be learned that is satisfactory of this part of the North West Territory; and it will sometimes occur that the surveyors must explore a section that is unknown, and even untrod but by the hunter ...

That the line under the Seventh Article should be soon designated is becoming daily of additional interest and importance. Our Indian relations, the competition of the fur trade, and the increase of a lawless population in that quarter, are amongst the claims for a definite limit of jurisdiction between the two countries, even if it was not a treaty obligation.

A 3 DIARY OF MAJOR JOSEPH DELAFIELD
[*Printed in McElroy and Riggs*, The Unfortified Boundary,
pp. 393–4, 396, 398]

Monday, June 30 [1823] Clear and pleasant. Embark[10] at half-past five o'clock. Wind s.e. The frost of last night was to be seen after sunrise. Run about 30 miles using both sails and paddles, passing one of the canoes that sailed in Co. yesterday. Breakfast in my canoe on cold pork with mustard and vinegar as a persuader, and some corn as dessert, which with my hard bread made as good a breakfast as I cared for.

The coast consists of the like rock formations as yesterday, and similar in all respects except that the cliffs were not quite so precipitous, the beaches more extended and consequently the landing places more frequent. Pass a very remarkable rock, called by the Indians the Otter's Head ... because it looks as if it darted perpendicularly from the mountains, as the otter does from the water, when he rises from below its surface. It is of great notoriety & considered by the voyageurs to be the half way point between the Sault Ste. Marie and Fort William.

Observe much of the lake water thro' this day's route to be stained by the streams that empty into it, and assuming various colors. Sometimes it had the black color of rain water pools that are deep, sometimes the light green of the lower lakes, which seemed to be a mixture of the river and lake water, and sometimes the turbid water of the rivers ...

Encamp at sunset in company with the canoe that had been frequently near us. It proved to be a party of free-men discharged by the Company and returning to their homes at the Red River of Lake Winnepec. A Mr. D'ease,[11] an individual trader, was returning with them to his home. They

[10]The party had spent the night on the shore opposite Michipicoten Island, near the mouth of the Pukaskwa River.

[11]John Warren Dease (1783–1829) was born at Niagara, one of the sons of Dr John Dease of the Indian Department (a nephew of Sir William Johnson). Both John Warren Dease and his brother Peter first served the North West Company, then became Chief Traders in the Hudson's Bay Company after 1821.

were a hardy looking crew, and the witches of Macbeth were never made a more outre group over their cauldron than these fellows did over theirs. Mr. D'ease takes tea with me, and seems much to enjoy it.

Engagees of the Hudson's Bay Co. when their term of service is expired are called free-men. During the engagements they are slaves in a sense that none but Canadians could endure. In short, the more I see of Canadian-French, their mode of life, and connection with the Indians, the more I feel assured that without this very race of men, the fur trade of the North could not be carried on. They are more hardy than the Indian, are far more capable in the canoe, and in Winter will soon break down the Indian if travelling on snow shoes or with trains ...

Wednesday, July 2. In the afternoon sail thro' groups of rocky islands. The country assumes a less rude aspect. The mountains begin to have greater slopes, and the islands become inclined instead of mural. They increase very much in number. We pass thro' a group of perhaps twenty that stretch across a deep bay, making a traverse of a long distance.

At sun set encamp in a miserable place, on the shore of a flat little island covered with scraggy pine & cedar and briars, so that the pebbles of the shore are the only carpet for my tent. Its front within two feet of the water & its rear as nigh the woods, leave me no chance to advance or retreat in case of trouble. A most unmilitary position, but most soldierly like maintained for want of a better. The lake being calm, pass a comfortable night.

This is called Pays Plat, which includes the group of islands lying in a great bay off the River Nipigon ...

Friday, July 4. At sun set are abreast of a very large island running nearly E. and W. that the men call Isle des Meule and say that it is the largest in the lake. Suspect it to be Isle Royal, and it afterwards proved to be so. I found experienced traders on the route, who had never heard of Isle Royal, & nobody seems to know any islands by the names of Phillipeaux, nor have I yet found any person that ever heard the mouth of the Pigeon River called Long Lake,[12] as it is laid down on Mitchell's Map of 1775.[13] That map (used by the treaty makers of 1783) seems to have had so limited a circulation that the names arbitrarily laid down upon it have not prevailed. In truth, to this day, the first French names given are in use, or more uniformly the Indian names.

[12]Delafield had already reason to doubt that any island called Philipeaux or any Long Lake existed. Investigation was to prove him right on both counts. The first problem was solved with relative ease since Isle Royale was located and was clearly indicated in the treaty as United States territory. The second problem resolved itself into this: since no Long Lake existed, which of the rivers flowing into Lake Superior from the west – the Kaministikwia at Fort William, the Pigeon at the present international boundary, or the St Louis at Duluth – might have been mistaken for a lake?

[13]The date here is in error. The map on which the Treaty of Versailles was based had been published in 1755 by Dr John Mitchell, a botanist who had at one time lived in Virginia.

A 4 DELAFIELD TO ADAMS
[*National Archives, Treaty of Ghent, Arts. VI and VII, Delafield Letters*]

New York
November 28, 1823

It having been ascertained that by the Long Lake, mentioned in the Treaty, was meant the mouth of the Pigeon River,[14] emptying into Lake Superior, our surveyors proceeded early in the season of '22 to enter the Indian territory by the old Grand Portage route. This portage is from Lake Superior to the Pigeon River, and intersects it above the great falls and rapids. The Grand Portage was formerly used by the British traders, and was their only passage to the interior. Twenty years ago it was abandoned by them, upon the supposition that it was within the limits of the United States, and they discovered[15] and adopted a more northern route, ascending the river Kamanistegua,[16] which empties into Lake Superior forty miles n.e. from the Grand Portage; and they then established their principal trading depot there, known as Fort William.

The American traders enter the Indian country by a more southern route, through the Fond du Lac[17] country ...

As to the nature of the country beyond Lake Superior, that part of it which is adjacent to the Boundary Line is most strongly characterized by a formation that is, I believe, quite peculiar, for its extent, to the North West Territory. I mean by mountains and valleys, or rocks and water, to the exclusion of plains and of earth ... In an agricultural sense, the country is of no possible value. In short, I do not foresee any inducements but the fur trade that can ever draw the people of the United States to this part of the Indian N.W. Territory. The climate would forbid, if its rocky wastes did not. It does not afford any means of subsistence for the voyager. The animals are too scarce to be depended upon, and the fish, the berries, and the wild rice that alone support its famishing inhabitants, are but a periodical supply, that leaves them destitute much of the year.

Notwithstanding this gloomy reality, the Indian trade carries a great number of people annually over the routes I have described. The American trader has a strong desire that the Line should be determined. The British

[14]Thus early it was clear that Delafield was prepared to accept the Pigeon River as the boundary, although later, when the British tried to argue for the most southerly of the three routes, Delafield produced an argument in favour of the most northerly.

[15]Delafield was in error here, since the Kaministikwia or Dog Lake route had been known in the late seventeenth century and had frequently been used in the French régime. It was the North West Company that developed the Grand Portage route and, when it was suspected that that route lay partly within the United States, reverted to the other route after 1803 and built Fort William to replace Grand Portage as its major depot.

[16]Kaministikwia is the official modern spelling, although Kaministiquia is often used. Delafield and others employed a wide variety of spellings.

[17]Fond du Lac is the most westerly bay of Lake Superior into which the St Louis River empties. At this stage Delafield did not seriously consider that the route from Fond du Lac to Rainy Lake and Lake of the Woods might be claimed as the international boundary, but that was precisely the claim which Barclay later made.

trader enjoys the use by a sort of prescriptive use [?] within the limits of the United States. A remedy is wished to such encroachments; but what perhaps is more essential to American citizens having any interests there, is their wish to be protected by the laws of their country (especially in cases of crime) and to enforce them to the limit to which we claim the sovereignty.

A 5   GEORGE KEITH'S[18] REPORT ON THE
LAKE SUPERIOR DISTRICT
[*Public Archives of Canada (P.A.C.), Hudson's Bay Company
Records, B-129-e, Report of 1833–4*]

Lake Superior district is boarded on one entire side by the northern shores of the lake extending from Sault Ste. Marie to beyond old Grand Portage,[19] a distance computed to be about 400 miles. It is limited by Goulait's Bay and Green Lake[20] (situated in the interior of Lake Huron district) to the southeastward; by New Brunswick and other sections of the Moose River district;[21] to the northwestward are the territories of Albany River and Lac La Pluie district. The greatest breadth of the district in a direct line does not exceed, I am fully confident, 80 miles.[22]

A 6   RAMSAY CROOKS[23] TO GENERAL GRATIOT[24]
(CONFIDENTIAL)
[*P.A.C., American Fur Company Records, Letter Book 1, pp. 60–1*]

New York
December 20, 1834

We have great hopes of adding to the usual returns of our trade a new and important item in the fisheries of Lake Superior. It however unfor-

[18]George Keith, who died in 1859, was a Nor'wester who had become a Chief Factor in the Hudson's Bay Company in 1821. In charge at Michipicoten from 1830 to 1835, he was the ranking official in the Lake Superior District. After leave, he returned to the district, retiring from the Company service in 1846 and returning to Scotland.

[19]The breakdown of negotiations over the Seventh Article of the Treaty of Ghent left the international boundary in doubt until 1842.

[20]Green Lake is one of the sources of the Spanish River and therefore within the Lake Huron District, but Goulais Bay, on Lake Superior itself, hardly fits the description given.

[21]New Brunswick in the Moose River District, north of Michipicoten, was later called Missanabie after the lake on which it is situated.

[22]Keith's estimate of the width of the district between the lake and the Height of Land is somewhat misleading since in most places the strip is so much narrower than was suggested here.

[23]Ramsay Crooks (1787–1859) was born in Scotland and emigrated to Canada in 1803. He joined the American Fur Company in 1816 as second in command to John Jacob Astor; when Astor retired in 1834 Crooks became President and held that position until the Company was dissolved in 1848.

[24]General Charles Gratiot (1786?–1855) was the son of a Swiss emigrant who

tunately happens (as far as we yet actually know) that the very best fishing grounds are *probably* on the British side of the boundary line running through Lake Superior, and we may in consequence be liable to pay duty upon all the fish caught beyond the limits of the United States. If such be the law, we shall lose one dollar upon every barrel, which is full one fourth of the value. This tax we are of course anxious to save if we can honestly do it, and in order to test the matter, we beg you will be so kind as to enquire of the Secretary of the Treasury whether fish *taken* and *cured* within the jurisdiction of Canada on Lake *Huron* by American citizens, cured with American salt, and henceforth wholly in American vessels, the entire capital being exclusively American, are, or are not, subject to duty. If dutiable, how much is the impost?

We do not at present wish it known that we have in contemplation to establish any fishery, and we have therefore used the scene of our operations on Lake *Huron,* as the decision of the Secretary will apply equally to all these lakes which are divided by the line of demarcation.

A 7 GEORGE SIMPSON[25] TO CROOKS
[*P.A.C., American Fur Company Records, Northern Outfit, Miscellaneous Papers*]

London
November 15, 1837

It is satisfactory to the Governor and Committee to learn that the American Fur Company are willing to extend the agreement entered into between Mr. Aiken[26] and me above noticed for a further term of two years from 1st June 1838 to which they assent; they can have no objections to your establishing Posts for the purpose of taking and curing Fish anywhere on the shores of Lake Superior, within the territorial limits of the United States, nor have they any objection to your trading Furs that

---

had entered the fur trade in Montreal in 1769 and later was associated with John Jacob Astor. In 1834 the General was the chief engineer of the u.s. army and inspector at West Point and influential enough to be Crooks' "man in Washington." His influence vanished in 1838 when he was dismissed after questions arose concerning the disbursement of government funds; but Gratiot's interest in Lake Superior continued and in the 1840s he was active in organizations seeking to exploit mineral resources in the Thunder Bay region.

[25]George Simpson (1792–1860) had been governor of the Northern Department of the Hudson's Bay Company since 1821. With the retirement of William Williams in 1826, he assumed control over all the Company lands in North America, chartered and leased. He was knighted in 1841.

[26]William Aitken was born in Scotland. He had been in the Indian country as early as 1802. By the 1830s he was ruling the Indian tribes near the headwaters of the Mississippi in semi-despotic fashion. He was in charge of the American Fur Company's post at Fond du Lac, until dismissed by Crooks for incompetence in the summer of 1838. The practice he initiated of biennial agreements between the two trading companies, however, continued throughout the next decade.

may be hunted by your Engaged servants employed in such fisheries, nor to your taking Furs at those fishing stations from Indians suffering under privation or a scarcity of food, in payment for Provisions only that may be given them.

A 8 CURTIS M. LAMPSON [27] TO CROOKS
[*P.A.C., American Fur Company Records, Miscellaneous*]

London
December 27, 1837

Will the quarrels in Canada, should the Canadians in the end succeed, either now or in two or three years hence, in establishing their independence, induce you to extend the business of the Company in the neighbourhood of the Lakes?

A 9 CROOKS TO LAMPSON
[*P.A.C., American Fur Company Records, Letter Book 7, p. 94*]

New York
March 8, 1838

The troubles in Canada may *in time* produce a separation from the mother country, and in that case no doubt the new Government's first step would be to destroy the influence of the Bay company, and their expulsion would follow as a matter of course, and the trade be thrown open to private competition among the citizens of the new Power.

A 10 DR CHARLES W. BORUP [28] TO THE GENTLEMAN IN CHARGE [29] [AT] FORT WILLIAM
[*P.A.C., American Fur Company Records, Northern Outfit, Letters, 1840*]

La Pointe
October 1, 1840

I have this day received a letter from the President of the Am. Fur Co. in which he in the strongest terms expressed his wish that the arrangement

[27]Curtis Miranda Lampson was a Vermonter by birth who became a prominent London merchant and served as agent there for the American Fur Company from 1837 to 1842. Later he became a British subject, was knighted, and in the 1870s was Deputy-Governor of the Hudson's Bay Company.

[28]Charles W. Borup was a medical doctor from Sorol, Denmark. He was in the Lake Superior country by the early 1830s and in 1837 became agent for the American Fur Company's Northern Outfit, with headquarters at La Pointe, on the largest of the Apostle Islands. He remained there until the mid-1840s, in spite of repeated quarrels with his staff. He was later a prominent businessman in St Paul.

[29]The vagueness of the address may suggest Borup's detailed knowledge of the organization at Fort William rather than any ignorance on his part, since the command changed so frequently. In 1840 the "gentleman in charge" seems to have been the clerk, John Swanston.

entered into between the Honble Hudson's Bay Company and the American Fur Company should be kept by everyone in the services of the Am. Fur Co. and with the most strict adherence to both the letter and the spirit of the agreement. It is with pleasure that I conform to such instructions and to prevent any possible misunderstanding I think it best to explain to you what might perhaps be construed wrongly. Last spring the chiefs of Grand Portage came here, and requested us to help them in gaining a livelihood and also begged us to furnish them with hunting material & to make us more willing to grant their wishes they told us that if we would assist them they would not ask our new opponents[30] for anything or even allow them to come here. The reason for all this they gave as simply a wish to remain on their own land which they believe will soon be demanded by the U.S. Government, and of which they are afraid that others who have no right might dispose of without their consent.

I assured them in terms not to be misunderstood that if they wished to fish, we might try to assist them, but as regarded hunting I could do nothing. I requested them to go home and promised to ask Mr. Crooks whether we could without violating the Agreement existing between the Companies give credit to such Indians as hunted in the United States land and made old Grand Portage their abode. Before I received Mr. Crooks' answer the Indians came back, and after refusing to do anything I was at last obliged either to give credit to one of the Indians who came and to one of his friends or else let them go to our opponents here who offered to furnish them and to send a small outfit on the north side. To prevent this, I choose to get rid of them at as cheap a rate as I could, not doubting but that, by explaining the whole affair, everything would appear in the right light. I shall keep a correct account of the goods given and furs received, of which I will furnish you next spring a statement in the sure expectation that in the meantime you will believe that nothing shall be done on our part either directly or indirectly to create any misunderstanding.

A 11 SIMPSON TO MESSRS SWANSTON,[31]
BALLENDEN,[32] AND H. MCKENZIE[33]
[*P.A.C., American Fur Company Records, Northern Outfit, Miscellaneous*]

London
December 24, 1844

An unfortunate accident last autumn having deprived the American Fur Company of the services of their brig for the transport business

[30]One of the terms in the biennial agreements between the two fur trading companies was that each would suppress private traders who might cross the international boundary and harass the other. The reference here seems to be to a private Cleveland-based company that plagued the American Fur Company in the early 1840s.

[31]John Swanston, b. 1802, had become a Chief Trader in 1843 after many years

between the Sault and La Pointe next spring, and it being impossible to provide another vessel in sufficient time to carry the supplies required at La Pointe early in June next, Mr. Crooks has applied to me to know whether we could allow the "Whitefish"[34] Schooner to carry up a load of provisions from the Sault to La Pointe ...

You will therefore understand that if the time the schooner would occupy in conveying a cargo to La Pointe would not materially interfere with our transport arrangement, she is to be dispatched from Fort William (or wherever she may have wintered) at the earliest possible date for the Sault, and upon arrival there, that she is to be placed at the disposal of the American Fur Company's agent for the purposes above mentioned.

A 12   JOURNAL OF THOMAS G. ANDERSON [35]
[Anderson Papers, copies in Metropolitan Toronto Central Library (M.T.C.L.), originals in possession of Miss Joan Featherstonhaugh, Richmond Hill]

Sept. 24th [1849] – Rose at 5,[36] got breakfast and started at 7. The morning was fine and passing along high mountains some of a 1000 feet high and at 1 o'clock arrived at Fort William. Mr. McKenzie[37] in charge

in the service of the Hudson's Bay Company in the Lake Superior District. Married to a daughter of George Keith, he became a Chief Factor in 1854 and retired in 1858. In 1844 he was in charge at Michipicoten.

[32]John Ballenden had served for several years as a clerk, and had just been promoted to Chief Trader in charge of the Sault Ste Marie post in 1844.

[33]Hector McKenzie (1817?–71), who was in charge at Fort William in 1844, was then a clerk. By 1846 he was a Chief Trader, and in 1851, the year in which he became a Chief Factor, he married the sister of R.M. Ballantyne, the chronicler of Hudson's Bay Company life in the nineteenth century. By 1863 McKenzie was Superintendent of the entire Montreal Department, to which the Lake Superior District was by then appended.

[34]Although the North West Company had maintained several vessels on Lake Superior and the American Fur Company also maintained a number, the Hudson's Bay Company's Whitefish was the only schooner supplying the posts along the north shore for many years. It wintered at Fort William.

[35]Thomas Gummersall Anderson (1789–1875) was born in Sorel, Quebec, and was engaged in the fur trade at Michilimackinac before the War of 1812. After service in that war he entered the employ of the Indian Department with the rank of Captain. He became Superintendent of Indian Affairs for Canada West in 1845, and retired in 1858.

[36]Anderson and his party were starting from Prince's Bay, near the American border, after travelling from Sault Ste Marie along the south shore of Lake Superior. They returned by the northern route.

[37]John McKenzie had been born in Scotland and had become an apprentice clerk in 1830. In his years as a clerk he was described as well educated but lacking in initiative. He had become a Chief Trader by the time he assumed control of the Fort William post in the mid-1840s. From there he moved to Michipicoten and became a Chief Factor in 1854, just before he moved to Moose Factory, the headquarters for the Southern Department. He retired to Lennoxville, Lower Canada, in 1866.

of the establishment who received us most cordially. We dined and tea-ed with him and at 10 went to bed in our tent. Mrs. McKenzie could not be seen because the infant was not very well. Gave some pork, flour and tobacco to the Indians and invited them to meet us at 10 o'clock in a room kindly appropriated by Mr. McKenzie for the purpose.

Sept 25th – Up and dressed by times – Breakfasted at 9 and shortly after the Indians began to assemble, about 25 were all that could be mustered. They were accompanied by a Jesuit named Frimeault[38] and finding he meddled with our business I could not forego the pleasure of informing him he had no business to interfere with them &c. but still he did not move his body though his tongue was less busy. Mrs. McK. dined with us – she is a very nice lady from Montreal. At 6 we closed our Indian Council for the day.

The Jesuit here, as well as elsewhere, tries to influence the Indians with his way of thinking not only as regards his erroneous creed, but also as regards the duties of our mission, not because he is familiar with our object but because he fancies he can direct the Indians and thus influence the Government into what he considers a good bargain for the natives and ultimately that he might get their cash to the exclusive benefit of his Priest craft, but of this the Government must be on their guard.

A 13 FATHER FRÉMIOT'S REPORT TO HIS SUPERIOR
IN NEW YORK
[*Archives de la Société de Jésus du Canada Français (A.S.J.C.F.),
Lettres des nouvelles missions du Canada, v. 1, pp. 448–53*]

Fort William,
October 18, 1849

I was present at the meetings merely as a spectator, and I accepted Mr. Mackenzie's invitation to dinner with the gentlemen. I was thus an eye-witness and can trace for you faithfully the character of the meeting. Mr. Vidal[39] was stationed in an arm chair in the centre of the room and wrote down everything that was said. Captain Anderson sat on his right. He speaks English, French, and Ojibway, while his colleagues speak only English. It was he who put the government questions to the Indians and translated their replies. Behind him sat one of his oarsmen, Peter Bell a young man from Sault Ste. Marie, whom he questioned about the meaning

[38]Father Nicholas Frémiot (1818–54) was a Jesuit missionary, born in France, who arrived in Canada in 1845. He was associated with the Thunder Bay area, Pigeon River, Fort William, Nipigon, and Isle Royale, for the years 1848–52, and wrote many detailed and perceptive letters during those years. He drowned in the Mississagi River near Sault Ste Marie in 1854.

[39]Anderson was accompanied by two assistants. A. Vidal was a surveyor at Sault Ste Marie in the late 1840s and, according to Frémiot, acted as secretary on this occasion. The role of Sommerville is left in some doubt.

of an Indian phrase whenever he was in doubt. Mr. Sommerville sat on Mr. Vidal's left with his desk a little to one side and scarcely seemed to be aware of what went on in the meeting.

Opposite these gentlemen sat our two chiefs, Joseph Peau de Chat[40] took the foremost position. He was dressed like the white men, as were most of the Indians. He is a man of about 40, tall and well built, with a vibrant, sonorous voice. His eloquent enthusiasm and vehement impetuosity have caused the Indians to elect him as their chief. All that he lacks is a spirit somewhat more imbued with Christian virtues. The other chief is an old man in his seventies whom they call the Illinois.[41] He is quite clearly one of those "fur chiefs" established in power by the Hudson Bay Company. Eash year he receives two outfits, and one of these is always red, with gold braid and metal buttons. That is why he has been given the name Miskouakkonaye – Red Coat. A few years ago he, with several members of his family, was plunged into the river by a Baptist minister at Sault Ste. Marie – but that seems to have been his only contact with religion. This old man – whom the Indians agree to recognize as a chief but who has not the principal authority – today wore, as you might guess, his full regalia. Mr. Sommerville spent the first part of the meeting making sketches of this ridiculous costume, further enhanced by an enormous pipe which he rested against his thigh, while propping it up with one hand. That poor pipe! What evils conspired against the lighting of it! For more than a quarter of an hour he kept fumbling with his tinder-box, to the silent amusement of the company. Behind the chiefs, all around the room, the Indians sat on the floor, their backs to the wall.

The meeting began with a roll call from the list prepared the evening before by Mr. Mackenzie. The half-breeds were passed by in silence, for they have not the right to speak at such gatherings. Is this wise? Do some people fear that they, better informed than the Indians themselves, might be in a better position to defend their rights ? ...

Then begins the long series of questions which the gentlemen wish to address to the Indians on behalf of the government. Where do you come from? What is your name? Are these your chiefs? Which is the principal one? ("Joseph Peau de Chat" replied the Indians) What is the shape and extent of your land? To what use can it be put? Do you wish to sell your lands? What price do you want for them?

"Besides a reserve on both banks of the river where we are living, we

[40]Peau de Chat seems to have been a name applied to more than one Indian chief. In the late 1820s and 1830s there are references to an old Peau de Chat, to his wife and sons coming to trade, often from the Grand Portage area. There are also references to a Peau de Chat who appeared at posts as far east as Michipicoten, in fact carrying the news of the Papineau rebellion to the post at the Pic. It is probable that this was Joseph Peau de Chat, chief of the Fort William Indians in 1849.

[41]References to this particular Chief appear in the Hudson's Bay post journals as early as the 1820s, but nowhere is there any indication of any preferred position which he may have enjoyed. Frémiot was convinced that any influence the Illinois ever enjoyed among the Indians was the result of Company policy.

ask for thirty dollars a head (including the women and children) every year to the end of the world, and this should be in gold, not in merchandise. Besides, we ask the Government to pay the expenses of a school master, a doctor, a blacksmith, a carpenter, an instructor in agriculture, and a magistrate."

Before closing the first day's session, Captain Anderson spoke to the Indians. "There are two things here that give me no pleasure and that will also, I think, be displeasing to our Father who is in Montreal [Lord Elgin]. The first one is that he has not ratified your selection of first chief. The second is that you ask too high a price for your lands. Look at what the United States is doing on the other side of the lake! The Indians there are only given payments for twenty-five years and, at that, they are to receive less each year than you ask. As for you, you want payment until the end of the world! and thirty dollars a head! Besides, once the term for payments expires, the American government is going to push the Indians beyond the Mississippi; you, on the other hand, will remain here for ever, in peaceful possession of your land. Finally, the money you would receive – would it not do you more harm than good? Think of what has happened at La Pointe.[42] The Indians give up their money, even their blankets, for a glass of water mixed with a little whiskey. The same thing would happen here. It would be far more to your advantage to get clothing for yourself instead of money payments. Reflect on these two points overnight and if, tomorrow, you still cling to the same views, they will be duly recorded. Now, it is as friends that we give you advice, for we do not think that the Great Chief who is at Montreal will accord you everything you are asking."

The next day, after mass, Joseph Peau de Chat came to tell me that the Englishman was afraid of him and wished to deprive him of his position, but he was going to have his name scratched off the list.[43]

"My child," I said to him, "the Englishman is not afraid of you; he fears no Indian. He has given up any wish to deprive you of your position; in any case, that is not in his power. It is the Indians who have chosen you as chief and you will retain the office as long as they choose to leave you in it. If they reply as they did yesterday, the matter will be finished, and there can be no more question about it. Only you are of a different religion than the Englishman; it is Red Coat who belongs to the Englishman's faith; that is why he would prefer to see Red Coat as the first Chief. Do

---

[42]Under the treaty of 1838, in which the American Ojibways had ceded some of their lands, La Pointe became the centre where payments were given out. However, the place received such a bad reputation among the Indians and whites that the new treaty of Fond du Lac, signed in 1847, moved the location farther west. In his trip along the American shore, Anderson had received very full reports of the La Pointe events and had included in his journal for September 21: "I hope our Indians may never be thus served."

[43]Peau de Chat appears to have reasoned that removing his name from the list would thwart English designs and preserve his own dignity. Father Frémiot was quick to suggest another course of action.

not be afraid and be sure that you allow your name to stand, or you will lose everything. If you do not wish to remain Chief, you can say so later, and the Indians will choose another – but this is no time to resign."

The Indians who witnessed this interview made preparations to elect another chief in case he did something rash in the general meeting. But apparently reflection altered his position for, without a word about resignation, he restrained himself to remarking very aptly on this subject – "Neither the Great Chief in Montreal nor the Queen can claim any right to change Indian elections or influence Indian deliberations in any way." This statement was recorded in the minutes. The question of the price to be paid for the lands was not discussed at this meeting ...

When we reassembled, Red Coat, the old chief, addressed the meeting for the first time. He began thus: "My Father, I do not quite know what to say; there is very little spirit left in me. Like you, I have become old." After this winning introduction, our Nestor of the wilderness traced his origins back – to the flood, I believe, or perhaps earlier – and then moving down through history step by step, he finally reached the appearance of the white man in these parts and the marvellous things that the Indians saw then for the first time.

"But it was not you, the English, who came first; we hardly knew you – it was those we call Ouemitikoje, the French, who visited us first."

As for the peroration of this discourse, I must admit that it has slipped my memory; I can only recapture isolated fragments of it. It was late and the Indians who were beginning to be very hungry were bored with a speech of such epic dimensions. One of the sons-in-law of the orator went up to him and told him he had spoken long enough. "Patience" replied Red Coat. "I do not want to ruin any of my effects."

Finally another son-in-law who was seated beside him and who sometimes had kindly helped him out when memory failed him, whispered quietly in his ear that he had spoken very well and at once the suggestible speaker, having pronounced his ritualistic conclusion "That is all I have to say" sat down and was silent.

Then Captain Anderson rose in his turn, and gave his closing speech ... He exhorted the Indians to accept the civilization of the white man, to devote themselves to agriculture ... "Listen to your priests, do not wrong the traders in your midst, for the Great Spirit sees all; but especially meditate often on eternal life."

After this edifying conclusion, everyone shook hands in farewell and left the best of friends ...

Such, Reverend Father, is the account of an event memorable for our mission. Witness our poor Indians about to receive – not a fortune so great that they need never work again, as some fondly imagine – but some feeble aid which at least will help them buy clothing. For in this area the difficulty is not so much in staying alive as in being properly dressed. Agriculture and fishing furnish an adequate diet but clothing costs more to procure, because the Hudson's Bay Company has the fur-trading monopoly and, as a result, a monopoly on all trade.

A 14   CHIEF PEAU DE CHAT'S REPORT[44] ON HIS
INTERROGATION BY VISITING INDIAN AGENTS
[*A.S.J.C.F., A-16-1*]

"Where do you people, who live here, come from?"

"I inhabit the body of a man; I was born" I replied. His question was ambiguous; my answer left no shadow of doubt.

He added: "Is the land good as far as Nipigon? Do you think people can live on it by farming?"

"Most certainly" I replied.

"What kinds of trees are there?" I listed for him all the species, except for maple, red oak, red pine and poplar.

He went on: "Who is your chief? Who is it that commands you."

They answered "It is Joseph."

"This old man" he said, "when have you elected him?"

"We elected him recently"

"He owes his election to you, but he is not still your chief. I will not ratify the election. All the same I recognize him as a wise man; I know him very well."

"I understand what you say" I told him, and then I added "I am the chief of the Catholic Indians. You wish to snatch away my power and give it to another, if you can – that is your purpose. You intend to make a dissolute savage chief of the Band. I tell you that you are usurping our authority. Neither the queen nor the chief in Montreal can ever alter what the Indians have enacted."

That is what I said to And.[erson]

He questioned me about our receiving payment in the United States. "What is it you wish to know" I asked him. "Would it be a crime for the Americans to give me money? Would it be a crime also for the English to pay me?"

"Of course not; it is our duty to pay you. Your question is trifling" But is it not my land that is in question in this deal? The English land is also my land.

A 15   THE ROBINSON SUPERIOR TREATY,[45] 1850
[*Printed in Morris,* The Treaties of Canada with the Indians, *pp. 302–4*]

THIS AGREEMENT, made and entered into on the seventh day of September, in the year of Our Lord one thousand eight hundred and fifty, at

[44]This document, like several others in the Archives de la Société de Jésus du Canada Français consists of a French transcript of an approximation of the Indian words Peau de Chat actually used in his conversation with the priests at the mission.

[45]This treaty is known variously as the Robinson Treaty, the Robinson Lake Superior Treaty, and the Treaty of Sault Ste Marie. It became the model for later treaties with Indians living north and west of the area ceded to the Province of Canada in 1850.

Sault Ste. Marie, in the Province of Canada, between the Honorable William Benjamin Robinson,[46] of the one part, on behalf of Her Majesty the Queen, and Joseph Peandechat, John Iuinway, Mishe-muckqua, Toto-mencie, Chiefs, and Jacob Warpela, Ahmutchiwagabou, Michel Shela-geshick, Manitoshainse, and Chiginans, principal men of the Ojibewa Indians inhabiting the Northern Shore of Lake Superior, in the said Province of Canada, from Batchewananng Bay to Pigeon River, at the western extremity of said lake, and inland throughout the extent to the height of land which separates the territory covered by the charter of the Honorable the Hudson's Bay Company from the said tract, and also the islands in the said lake within the boundaries of the British possessions therein, of the other part, witnesseth:

That for and in consideration of the sum of two thousand pounds of good and lawful money of Upper Canada, to them in hand paid, and for the further perpetual annuity of five hundred pounds, the same to be paid and delivered to the said Chiefs and their tribes at a convenient season of each summer, not later than the first day of August at the Honorable the Hudson's Bay Company's Posts of Michipicoton and Fort William, they the said Chiefs and principal men do freely, fully and volun-tarily surrender, cede, grant and convey unto Her Majesty, Her heirs and successors forever, all their right, title and interest in the whole of the territory above described, save and except the reservations set forth in the schedule hereunto annexed, which reservations shall be held and occupied by the said Chiefs and their tribes in common, for the purposes of residence and cultivation, – and should the said Chiefs and their re-spective tribes at any time desire to dispose of any mineral or other valu-able productions upon the said reservations, the same will be at their request sold by order of the Superintendent-General of the Indian Depart-ment for the time being, for their sole use and benefit, and to the best advantage.

And the said William Benjamin Robinson of the first part, on behalf of Her Majesty and the Government of this Province, hereby promises and agrees to make the payments as before mentioned; and further to allow the said Chiefs and their tribes the full and free privilege to hunt over the territory now ceded by them, and to fish in the waters thereof as they have heretofore been in the habit of doing, saving and excepting only such portions of the said territory as may from time to time be sold or leased to individuals, or companies of individuals, and occupied by them with the consent of the Provincial Government. The parties of the second part further promise and agree that they will not sell, lease, or

[46]W.B. Robinson (1797–1873) was the younger brother of John Beverly and Peter Robinson. He represented the County of Simcoe in the Legislative Assemblies of Upper Canada and then the united Province of Canada, and was briefly an Execu-tive Councillor in the 1840s. His nephew, J.B. Robinson, later represented the Dis-trict of Algoma in the Canadian House of Commons, 1872–4.

otherwise dispose of any portion of their reservations without the consent of the Superintendent-General of Indian Affairs being first had and obtained; nor will they at any time hinder or prevent persons from exploring or searching for minerals or other valuable productions in any part of the territory hereby ceded to Her Majesty as before mentioned. The parties of the second part also agree that in case the Government of this Province should before the date of this agreement have sold, or bargained to sell, any mining locations or other property on the portions of the territory hereby reserved for their use and benefit, then and in that case such sale, or promise of sale, shall be perfected, if the parties interested desire it, by the Government, and the amount accruing therefrom shall be paid to the tribe to whom the reservation belongs. The said William Benjamin Robinson on behalf of Her Majesty, who desires to deal liberally and justly with all her subjects, further promises and agrees that in case the territory hereby ceded by the parties of the second part shall at any future period produce an amount which will enable the Government of this Province without incurring loss to increase the annuity hereby secured to them, then, and in that case, the same shall be augmented from time to time, provided that the amount paid to each individual shall not exceed the sum of one pound provincial currency in any one year, or such further sum as Her Majesty may be graciously pleased to order; and provided further that the number of Indians entitled to the benefit of this treaty shall amount to two-thirds of their present numbers (which is twelve hundred and forty) to entitle them to claim the full benefit thereof, and should their numbers at any future period not amount to two-thirds of twelve hundred and forty, the annuity shall be diminished in proportion to their actual numbers.

Schedule of Reservations made by the above named and subscribing Chiefs and principal men.

First – Joseph Pean-de-chat and his tribe, the reserve to commence about two miles from Fort William (inland), on the right bank of the River Kiministiquia; thence westerly six miles, parallel to the shores of the lake; thence northerly five miles, thence easterly to the right bank of the said river, so as not to interfere with any acquired rights of the Honorable Hudson's Bay Company.

Second – Four miles square at Gros Cap, being a valley near the Honorable Hudson's Bay Company's post of Michipicoton, for Totominai and tribe.

Third – Four miles square on Gull River, near Lake Nipigon, on both sides of said river for the Chief Mishimuckqua and tribe.

A 16 WILLIAM B. ROBINSON TO THE
SUPERINTENDENT OF INDIAN AFFAIRS
[*Printed in Morris*, The Treaties of Canada with the Indians, *pp. 17–21*]

Toronto,
24th September, 1850

I have the honor herewith to transmit the Treaty which on the part of the government I was commissioned to negotiate with the tribes of Indians inhabiting the northern shore of Lakes Huron and Superior, and I trust that the terms on which I succeeded in obtaining the surrender of all the lands in question, with the exception of some small reservations made by the Indians, may be considered satisfactory. They were such as I thought it advisable to offer, in order that the matter might be finally settled, without having any just grounds of complaint on the part of the Indians.

The Indians had been advised by certain interested parties[47] to insist on such extravagant terms as I felt it quite impossible to grant; and from the fact that the American Government had paid very liberally for the land surrendered by their Indians on the south side of Lake Superior, and that our own in other parts of the country were in receipt of annuities much larger than I offered, I had some difficulty in obtaining the assent of a few of the chiefs to my proposition.

I explained to the chiefs the difference between the lands ceded heretofore in this Province, and those then under consideration, they were of good quality and sold readily at prices which enabled the Government to be more liberal, they were also occupied by the whites in such a manner as to preclude the possibility of the Indian hunting over or having access to them: whereas the lands now ceded were notoriously barren and sterile, and will in all probability never be settled except in a few localities by mining companies, whose establishments among the Indians, instead of being prejudicial, would prove a great benefit as they would afford a market for any things they may have to sell, and bring provisions and stores of all kinds among them at reasonable prices.

Neither did the British Government contemplate the removal of the Indians from their present haunts to some (to them) unknown region in the far West, as had been the case with their brethren on the American side ...

The chiefs from Lake Superior desired to treat separately for their territory and said at once in council that they accepted my offer. I told them I would have the treaty ready on the following morning, and I immediately proceeded to prepare it; and, as agreed upon, they signed it cheerfully at the time appointed ...

I trust his Excellency will approve of my having concluded the treaty

[47]Other sources make clear that these "interested parties," and the "evil disposed persons" referred to elsewhere in the letter, were free traders, challenging both the Hudson's Bay Company and the authority of the Canadian government, but there are sometimes suggestions that the Catholic missionaries were included as well.

on the basis of a small annuity and the immediate and final settlement of the matter, rather than paying the Indians the full amount of all moneys on hand, and a promise of accounting to them for future sales. The latter course would have entailed much trouble on the Government, besides giving an opportunity to evil disposed persons to make the Indians suspicious of any accounts that might be furnished.

Believing that His Excellency and the Government were desirous of leaving the Indians no just cause of complaint on their surrendering the extensive territory embraced in the treaty; and knowing that there were individuals who most assiduously endeavoured to create dissatisfaction among them, I inserted a clause securing to them certain prospective advantages should the lands in question prove sufficiently productive at any future period to enable the Government without loss to increase the annuity ...

I have much pleasure in acknowledging the valuable assistance afforded me by all the officers of the Honorable Hudson's Bay Company resident on the lakes; and the prompt manner in which their Governor, Sir George Simpson, kindly placed their services at my disposal.

The reports made last year by Messrs. Anderson and Vidal I found of much use to me, and the long services and experience of the former gentleman in Indian affairs enabled him to give me many valuable suggestions.

A 17 PETITION TO LEGISLATIVE ASSEMBLY OF CANADA BY TORONTO BOARD OF TRADE
[*P.A.C., MG 24 I-8, Macdonell of Collachie Papers, Allan Macdonell, Mining Papers*]

That an association of Traders under the title of the Hon. Hudson's Bay Company, during a long period of time, have claimed and exercised a sovereignty of the soil, together with the right of exclusive trade over a large portion of the province of Canada, and that the exercise of such claim is subversive of all those rights and privileges which were guaranteed to the inhabitants of Canada by Royal Proclamation immediately after the conquest of the country, and subsequently secured to them by those Acts of the British Parliament that gave Canada a Constitutional Government ...

Your Petitioners now especially pray the attention of Your Honorable House to that region of country designated as the Chartered Territory over which the said Company exercises a sovereignty in the soil, as well as a monopoly in the trade, and which said Company claims as a right that ensures to them in perpetuity in contradistinction to that portion of country over which they merely claim an exclusive right of trade but for a limited period only. Whilst your petitioners believe that this latter claim is founded upon a legal right, they humbly submit that a renewal of such license of exclusive trade is injurious to the interests of the country so monopolizing [*sic*] and in contravention of the rights of the inhabitants of Canada.

Your petitioners therefore humbly pray that your Honorable House will take into consideration the subject of how far the assumption of powers on the part of the Hudson's Bay Company interferes with Canadian rights and also the necessity of more particularly declaring the boundary of Canada on the westward and on the northward, and of extending throughout the protecting arm of Canadian laws, and the benefits of Canadian institutions.

Charles Robertson,[48]   Thomas Clarkson,[49]
Secretary   President
Toronto, April 2, 1857.

A 18   EVIDENCE OF WILLIAM McD. DAWSON [50]
BEFORE COMMITTEE OF LEGISLATIVE ASSEMBLY
[*Canada,* Sessional Papers, *1857, v. 15, no 17*]

I am the head of the Woods and Forests Branch of the Crown Land Department, and reside in Toronto; I never had any difficulty or quarrel with any one connected with the Hudson's Bay Company.

Q. – Have you particularly studied the titles under which the Hudson's Bay Company claim certain rights of soil, jurisdiction and trade, on this continent?

A. – I have made this subject a particular object of study for many years, and have omitted no opportunity of acquiring information upon it, and although with more time than I could devote to it, and a more extended research, much additional information could be obtained, I believe that it would only tend to fill up details, and strengthen and confirm the results of the investigation I have already made.

Q. – Will you state to the Committee the result of your investigation?

A. – The result of my investigation has been to demonstrate that in the Red River and Saskatchewan countries, the Hudson's Bay Company have

[48]Charles Robertson was immediately involved in the formation of a Toronto-based company to develop the northwest. He served as secretary to the Northwest Transportation and Land Company, later known also as the Northwest Transit Company and the Rescue Company, during the years 1858–68.

[49]Thomas Clarkson became in the following year one of the first Directors of the Northwest Transportation and Land Company, along with Allan Macdonell, John McMurrich, George Monro, and William McMaster. Clarkson and Macdonell, with the first President William McD. Dawson, were all vitally concerned with the development of the north shore of Lake Superior.

[50]William McDonell Dawson had been born in Scotland and had emigrated to Canada before 1840. He held a variety of civil service posts in the Timber Office, then in the Surveyor's Department in Bytown, before moving to the Toronto position he held in 1857. From 1858 to 1861 he represented Three Rivers and from 1861 to 1863 Ottawa County in the Assembly of the Province of Canada.

no right or title whatever, except what they have in common with other British subjects. Wherever they have any possession or occupancy there they are simply squatters, the same as they are at Fort William, La Cloche, Lake Nipissing, or any of their other posts in Canada.

The Governmental attributes they claim in that country are a fiction, and their exercise a palpable infraction of law.

A 19   ADDRESS OF THE CANADIAN PARLIAMENT TO
QUEEN VICTORIA, AUGUST 13, 1858
[*Canada, Legislative Assembly,* Journals *1858, p. 1028*]

We, Your Majesty's most dutiful and loyal subjects, the Legislative Council and Assembly of Canada, in Provincial Parliament assembled, humbly approach Your Majesty, for the purpose of representing –

That the approaching termination of the License of Trade granted by Your Majesty's Imperial Government to the Hudson's Bay Company over the Indian Territories, a portion of which, in our humble opinion, Canada has a right to claim as forming part of her territory, renders imperative the adoption of such measures as may be necessary to give effect to the rights of the Province, and presents a favourable opportunity for obtaining a final decision on the validity of the Charter of the Company, and the boundary of Canada on the north and west.

That Canada, whose rights stand affected by that Charter, to which she was not a party, and the validity of which has been questioned for more than a century and a half, has, in our humble opinion, a right to request from Your Majesty's Imperial Government a decision of this question, with a view of putting an end to discussions and questions of conflicting rights, prejudicial as well to Your Majesty's Imperial Government as to Canada, and which, while unsettled, must prevent the colonization of the country.

That the settlement of the boundary line is immediately required, and that therefore we humbly pray Your Majesty that the subject thereof may be forthwith submitted for the opinion of the Judicial Committee of Your Majesty's Privy Council, but without restriction as to any question Canada may deem it proper to present on the validity of the said Charter, or for the maintenance of her rights.

That any renewal of the license to trade over the Indian Territories should, in our humble opinion, be granted only upon the conditions that such portions thereof, or of the other territories claimed by the Company (even if their Charter be held valid), as may be required from time to time to be set apart by Canada, or by Your Majesty's Government, into settlements for colonization, should, as so required, be withdrawn from under any such license and the jurisdiction and control of the said Company; and that Your Majesty's Government, or the Governor-General in Council, should be permitted to grant licenses to trade in any portions of the said territories while held by or in occupation of the said Company, upon such conditions for the observance of law and the preservation of the peace, for the prohibition or restriction of the sale of ardent spirits, for the protection of Indian tribes from injury or imposition, and with such other provisions as to Your Majesty's Government, or to his Excellency in Council, may seem advisable.

That in our humble opinion Canada should not be called upon to compensate the said Company for any portion of such territory from which they may withdraw, or be compelled to withdraw, but that the said Company should be allowed to retain and dispose of any portion of the lands thereof on which they have built or improved.

All which we humbly pray Your Majesty to take into Your Majesty's gracious and favourable consideration.

A 20   AWARD OF THE BOUNDARY COMMISSIONERS
[*Canada, House of Commons, Select Committee on Boundaries of Ontario, Report, p. 480*]

The undersigned having been appointed by the Governments of Canada and Ontario as Arbitrators to Determine the Northerly and Westerly Boundaries of the Province of Ontario, do hereby Determine and Decide the following are and shall be such Boundaries, that is to say: –

Commencing at a point on the southern shore of Hudson Bay, commonly called James' Bay, where a line produced due north from the head of Lake Temiscaming, would strike the said south shore; thence along the said south shore westerly to the mouth of the Albany River; thence up the middle of the said Albany River, and of the lakes thereon, to the source of the said river at the head of Lake St. Joseph; thence by the nearest line to the easterly end of Lac Seul, being the head waters of the English River; thence westerly through the middle of Lac Seul and the said English River to a point where the same will be intersected by a true meridianal line[51] drawn northerly from the International Monument placed to mark the most north-westerly angle of the Lake of the Woods by the recent Boundary Commission; and thence due south, following the said meridianal line to the said International Monument; thence southerly and easterly, following the International Boundary Line, between the British Possessions and the United States of America, into Lake Superior ...

---

[51]The arbitrators were not nearly so sure of themselves as the wording of this paragraph suggests. In a later paragraph, omitted here, they indicated what the boundary was to be if it should happen that the true meridianal line here described should pass west of the point where the English River emptied into the Winnipeg River.

Given under our hands, at Ottawa, in the Province of Ontario, this Third day of August, Eighteen Hundred and Seventy-Eight.

(Signed) Robert A. Harrison[52]

Edwd. Thornton[53]

F. Hincks[54]

A 21 SIMON J. DAWSON'S[55] SPEECH ON THE BOUNDARY QUESTION, FEBRUARY 18, 1880 [*Canada, House of Commons*, Debates, *1880, v. 1, pp. 61–2*]

Another reason why the House should not be asked to confirm the award without investigation exists in the fact that the advocates opposing the Dominion have suggested no less than eleven different western boundaries for Ontario, and as many as ten northern boundaries, with not one of which does the award agree, so that, on the showing of the counsel for Ontario, the Arbitrators are decidedly in error. No one could be more anxious to advance the interests of Ontario than I am, but I doubt very much whether it would be to her advantage that this award should be confirmed. Ontario has no means of dealing adequately with these distant territories and whatever policy would lead to their most speedy development would be most in her interest. The land, until the Indian title was extinguished, belonged in fact to the Indians. The Dominion Government has purchased it from them, or at least a portion of it – some 50,000 square miles or so – in lieu of which the Indians had annuities paid to them which, with other allowances, amounted annually to about $25,000 or $30,000. The residue of the territory within the limits designated by the award

[52]Robert A. Harrison (1833–78) was Chief Justice of Ontario from 1875 until his death, three months after this award was made. Born in Montreal, he had been educated in Toronto, and had been a civil servant, then a practising lawyer, and from 1867 to 1872 member of the House of Commons for West Toronto.

[53]Sir Edward Thornton (1817–1906), after holding a number of diplomatic posts in Latin America, became the British minister to Washington in 1867. He held that position until 1881 when he became Ambassador at St Petersburg.

[54]Sir Francis Hincks (1809–85) had been a Prime Minister of the united Province of Canada, then had been appointed governor of Barbados and later of British Guiana. He had returned to Canadian politics as Minister of Finance in the Macdonald government 1869–73. By 1874 he had retired from politics.

[55]Simon James Dawson (1820–1902) was born in Banffshire, Scotland, and with his mother and brothers had emigrated to Canada by the early 1840s. He was a civil engineer in the Three Rivers area and, through his brother William McD. Dawson, had some links with the Ottawa timber trade. He was chief surveyor for the Gladman-Hind expedition 1857–8, and for the rest of his life was associated in various ways with the Thunder Bay area. He became the representative of the District of Algoma (which included Thunder Bay) in the provincial House in 1875, then resigned to contest the federal seat. He represented Algoma in Ottawa from 1878 to 1891, first as an Independent and then as a Conservative. He failed to win the nomination for the 1891 election, and, in spite of pleas of his loyal supporters in the editorial offices of the Thunder Bay *Sentinel*, he was not named to the Senate.

might cost as much more, so that it would eventually involve Indian payments of some $50,000 or $60,000 annually. Of course the payments to the Indians form in fact a lien on the land, and Ontario is in no position to assume such burdens, more especially as the opening up, organization, and development of these vast regions would cost her millions more. In this territory she would have a white elephant which might amuse the people at first but the older districts would soon become weary of so costly a pet. The true policy, in my opinion, would be to come to an arrangement with Ontario in which the whole of Algoma, including the new territory, should be formed into a separate province.[56] It is with the cities and settlements of Ontario that the trade of these regions must always be. As a province, their great natural resources would become sooner developed, and therefore it is in the interests of Ontario that a new province should be formed. It should never be forgotten that the claims of Quebec to, and interest in, all the territories of old Canada beyond the limits of the provinces were equal to those of Upper Canada.[57] Quebec and Upper Canada for a long time exercised concurrent jurisdiction in these areas and, previous to the Union, Quebec had issued writs for execution on Lake Superior, in the vicinity of Fort William, as Upper Canada had also done. There is one other question connected with this matter which I think deserving of the gravest consideration. It is this: when the scheme of Confederation, which was so happily carried out, was under consideration, the part of the then Province of Canada known as Canada West had certain well-defined limits. In general estimation, it was considered to have been bounded north and west by the Height of Land. Had it then been suggested that its area would, in the near future, be more than doubled by the addition of the fairest portion of the vast territories at that time claimed by, and afterwards purchased from, the Hudson's Bay Company, would the other Provinces have consented to an arrangement which they must have believed would ultimately give to Ontario a vast preponderating influence in the Confederacy.[58]

[56]Both in his speeches in Ottawa and earlier as a member of the Ontario House, Dawson had stressed this separate province theme. Sometimes he mentioned the possibility that, in view of the sparse nature of settlement in Algoma in the 1870s, it might be set up first as a territory, similar to those being established on the prairies and in the north.

[57]Dawson made frequent references to this association of Thunder Bay with Quebec. In the appendix to the *Report* of the Select Committee on Boundaries he included a number of documents illustrating this connection – the judgment in the De Reinhard case, and the commission to Lord Dorchester as Governor of the province of Quebec, clearly indicating his authority over the Lake Superior shoreline.

[58]Dawson's argument won considerable support from every province except Ontario and came under attack from the Ontario Liberal contingent – Alexander Mackenzie, Edward Blake, and David Mills, for example. His motion to set up a select committee passed 123 to 52, with strong French-Canadian support, although Laurier and a number of others obviously regarded the matter as a party issue and voted against it. The committee was made up of the following MP s: Dawson (Chairman), Robinson, Geoffrion, De Cosmos, Brecken, Royal, Trow, Mousseau, Caron, McDonald (Cape Breton), Weldon.

A 22   TESTIMONY OF ROBERT BELL[59] BEFORE THE
SELECT COMMITTEE ON BOUNDARIES, 1880
*[Canada, House of Commons, Select Committee on Boundaries of
Ontario, Report, pp. 42, 44]*

It has occurred to me, however, that if the height of land were to be defined as a boundary, it would be exceedingly difficult to find it. The country in its vicinity is almost always level, and the heads of the streams interlock so much that you cannot easily tell which way the water may tend to run ... If the country were rugged you could find a line dividing them [the streams] even if they did interlock, but along this line it is so level it would be difficult to do so. The water soaks through the moss and swamps and one cannot always tell on which side of the watershed he may be ...

The Albany River would make a very good boundary, if you could define what part to follow ... That river frequently splits up and flows in different channels. At one place it follows two widely separated channels for about twenty miles ... It is not always easy to say which is the largest channel.[60]

A 23   THE THUNDER BAY SENTINEL[61] ON THE
BOUNDARY QUESTION
[Thunder Bay Sentinel, March 25, 1881]

The latest phase of the question of boundary would indicate that we shall become either a part of the Province of Ontario or the Province of Manitoba.[62] Of two evils it is always advisable to choose the least but in the present instance it would appear difficult to say which is the least when both are of such magnitude. Our position is this: we are a simon pure

[59]Robert Bell (1841–1917) was born and educated in Toronto and for more than half a century was connected in some capacity with the Geological Survey of Canada, taking part in a number of expeditions in the Thunder Bay area. By 1877 he was Assistant Director of the Survey. He became chief geologist in 1890.

[60]This comment on the peculiarities of the Albany River, later selected as the northern boundary of the District of Thunder Bay, came in answer to a question from one of the committee, after Dr Bell had made the observation that he thought a natural boundary formed by some geographical feature was usually the best choice for an interprovincial boundary.

[61]The *Sentinel* began publication as a weekly in July 1875 and in 1882 began to produce a daily edition as well. Its first editor, Michael Hagan, claimed to support no political party, but was sympathetic to Simon Dawson. By the 1880s there was no doubt that Hagan's successors were supporters of the Conservative party.

[62]In previous editorials, that of December 10, 1880, for example, the *Sentinel* had strongly favoured the setting up of a territorial government. As recently as February 25, 1881, the argument had been against joining either a completely agricultural province (Manitoba) or one whose capital was so distant as Toronto.

mineral district and the Provinces in question are both more or less agri-cultural, so much so that the preponderance of legislation is favorable to agriculture and commerce and entirely neglectful of the interests and needs of mineral belts of country such as our own.

It has been decided that the eastern boundary of Manitoba shall be the western boundary of Ontario, wherever that is decided, and we are there-fore to be included in one or the other. Perhaps if there is any choice in the matter it should be made in favor of Ontario, as there are in the Ottawa and Kingston[63] districts large tracts of mineral country and if an attempt was made by the several districts interested to introduce such legislation as would aid the development of mining there would be more opportunity for expecting favorable results in Ontario than would be obtained in the district single-handed from Manitoba. In referring to the same subject a correspondent of the *North Shore Miner* hits the nail on the head, and his views coincide with ours so entirely that we reproduce them.

"Reading your article on the probability of Thunder Bay being set off from Ontario and attached to Manitoba, or organized into a territory by itself, I can heartily second your conclusion as to the importance of the territory not being attached to one that is purely agricultural. We of the upper peninsula of Michigan, which is strictly a mining territory, have felt the necessity of a separate organization for many years. While there was a disposition on the part of the state government to deal fairly with the interests of the upper peninsula, it was very difficult to make an agri-cultural legislator see our needs.

"The fact is a mining country wants a different class of legislation from an agricultural, much more broad and liberal. When asked to enact laws allowing corporations a capital of millions and to own large tracts of land, the agriculturalist imagines there must be something wrong – the amounts are too large for his wants or conception. For nearly thirty years has the mining interests of Michigan labored for such enactment as would secure capital to develop her mining resources and not until 1877 was it possible to secure such laws ... The North Shore of Lake Superior is strictly a mining country, and if it is to be developed it will have to be done with foreign capital which is slow to take the risk of mining unless the most liberal inducements are offered as to the mining property and liberal min-ing laws ... Open wide the door to capital and every hill top will be alive with the hardy explorer and resound with the echoes of the busy mine. Time may open the pockets of your people to develop the wealth hidden in your hills, but at present your main dependence for capital is from outside your country; to reach it you will have to make it an inducement to seek your shores – this done, success is sure to follow."

[63]The argument here, no matter how tenuous, was one that Dawson frequently made – that Algoma had far more in common with eastern Ontario than with the golden triangle.

A 24 THE TRIAL OF LIZZIE WASHINGTON[64]
[*Thunder Bay* Sentinel, *June 23, 1883*]

The Queen v. Washington. The grand jury having presented a true bill, this was the next case called, and the prisoner brought into court to plead on the indictment ... On the indictment being read, the prisoner's counsel, Mr. E.R. Cameron[65] read the following plea on the jurisdiction of the court before going into the merits of the case.

"And now the said Elizabeth Washington, called Lizzie Washington in her own proper person comes and having heard the indictment aforesaid read and protesting that she is not guilty of the premises charged in the said indictment or of any part thereof, for plea, nevertheless saith that she ought not to be compelled to answer to the said indictment because she saith that the place called Prince Arthur's Landing in a place called the District of Thunder Bay, said to be within the Provisional Judicial district of Algoma, is situated outside the province of Ontario and outside the jurisdiction of any courts of the said Province, but is within the jurisdiction of the courts of the Province of Quebec, and the said Elizabeth Washington, called Lizzie Washington, further saith that in the said province of Quebec there are now courts and jurisdictions therein ... competent and sufficient for the trial of all offences committed by the natives and inhabitants of the said place called Prince Arthur's Landing.

"And the said Elizabeth Washington, called Lizzie Washington, further saith that she was born in the said place called Prince Arthur's Landing and outside the province of Ontario ..."[66]

John Macpherson Hamilton,[67] who prosecutes for our lady, the Queen in this behalf, says that ... the felony charged by the said indictment was committed at Prince Arthur's Landing in the said District of Thunder

[64]Lizzie Washington was a Negro girl accused in the slaying of one William Winfield (recently arrived in Prince Arthur's Landing from Elora, Ontario) on December 16, 1882. The charge, originally murder, had been reduced to manslaughter before her trial opened in the following June.

[65]Edward Robert Cameron of Strathroy, with his partner T.A. Keefer, established a law practice at Prince Arthur's Landing in the spring of 1883. The Port Arthur *Herald* reported on May 23 that their office would soon open and on May 30 that they had been retained to defend Lizzie Washington. It was presumably their first case. Cameron did not long continue in his northern venture; he practised law in southern Ontario and became registrar to the Supreme Court of Canada in 1898.

[66]Lizzie Washington's age was given as seventeen at the time of the crime, and this makes her statement of place of birth highly dubious. Certainly the *name* Prince Arthur's Landing was not used before 1870, and there is no record of her birth there in 1865.

[67]J.M. Hamilton, Crown Counsel, of Sault Ste Marie, travelled to Prince Arthur's Landing with Judge McCrae for the Assizes. On October 21, 1884, Hamilton became the first judge in the Thunder Bay District, with residence in Port Arthur. The son of Senator John Hamilton of Kingston and the son-in-law of Chief Justice W.H. Draper, he ended his association with the north in 1894 when he became a judge in Halton County.

Bay, and is in the province of Ontario and not in the province of Quebec as is in said pleading alleged, or if P.A. Landing is not within the said province of Ontario, it is on the western or northwestern boundary thereof, and thus forms portion of the territory claimed by the government of the said province of Ontario as being within the said province of Ontario ...

Mr. A.L. Russell.[68] – I am a provincial Land Surveyor, also a Dominion Land Surveyor. I have maps showing the junction of the Ohio with the Mississippi Rivers. On reference to these maps I find a line drawn north from the junction of these rivers would strike the north shore of Lake Superior east of Prince Arthur's Landing. The map I refer to is one issued by the Crown Land Department of Toronto under the authority of the Ontario government. Map dated May 12, 1882. P.A. Landing is south and east of the Height of Land, dividing the waters of Hudson Bay and Lake Superior. P.A. Landing is northeast from the boundary line between Canada and the u.s., as shown at Pigeon River ... I have heard statements that the country described by me is in the province of Quebec. I would consider it to be within the disputed territory, and that it would be either in the province of Ontario or Manitoba. P.A. Landing is east of the boundary of Keewatin, and is not within the territory described as the district of Keewatin[69] ...

Mr. Cameron then addressed the court in support of the plea, and claimed that the jurisdiction given the old province of Quebec ... had never been taken from that Province as regards its power to deal with crimes committed in the Indian territory. It must be shown by the Crown that the offence was committed within the Province of Ontario or that the Ontario Courts were clothed with proper authority to take cognizance of the matter. Mr. Cameron proceeded to show that Prince Arthur's Landing was in a territory that even the Dominion Government had never received authority over; also that it was not in the Province of Ontario, neither was it in the territory described as within the District of Keewatin. It was certainly not within Manitoba ... The confederation of the Provinces embraced only the territories clearly within the Provinces. In the De Reinhardt case it was clearly shown that the Province of Quebec had jurisdiction over the Indian territories to the west of the old provinces ... P.A. Landing was therefore in that triangle or portion of territory known as the

[68]Alexander Lord Russell (1842–1922) was the son of Andrew Russell who, as Deputy Commissioner of Public Lands, had been extremely important in encouraging the early land surveys in Canada. Alexander Russell, who had settled in Prince Arthur's Landing in the 1870s and remained there about forty years, had before this time taken part in the special survey of the Athabaska region initiated in 1874.

[69]The District of Keewatin, formed in 1876, was to extend north of Manitoba and to occupy an ill-defined area then in dispute between the provinces of Manitoba and Ontario. The 1881 statute to extend the boundaries of Manitoba limited Keewatin on the south and east so that there was no longer any question of territorial status for Thunder Bay. In 1884 the confusion apparent in the argument in this case was ended in so far as the District of Thunder Bay was concerned, by the Privy Council decision confirming the boundary award advised by the Commissioners in 1878.

Indian territory, which had never been ceded by the British Government to the Dominion, nor was it included in the lands purchased from the merchants and adventurers of England trading into Hudson's Bay. The Dominion Government had therefore no authority to constitute courts having jurisdiction over this territory and unless the court was prepared to say that the western boundary of Ontario included P.A. Landing, then it could not be contended that the Ontario Government had any authority over the territory in which P.A. Landing was.[70]

A 25 ALEXANDER NIVEN[71] TO HON. A. S. HARDY[72]
[*Ontario, Department of Crown Lands*, Report, *1891, app. 34, p. 51*]

Haliburton,
December 20th, 1890

I proceeded to the work[73] on the 5th day of July last via Canadian Pacific Railway to Savanne and thence by canoes along the old Dawson route through "Lac des Milles Lacs" and other waters to Hunter's Island ...

The district line crosses the north rail of the Canadian Pacific railway at sixty miles, seventy-eight chains and seventy-five links[74] and thirty chains and twelve links easterly of the three hundred and fourteen mile post from Winnipeg – said post being opposite English River station.

[70]Judge McCrae rejected the defence plea against the competence of the court, and Lizzie Washington was found guilty of manslaughter and sentenced to five years in prison. While she was serving her sentence in Kingston penitentiary, her brother James was convicted of armed robbery, and observed that "He would as leave go and keep Lizzie company as not" (*Sentinel*, March 14, 1884).

[71]Alexander Niven (1836–1911) of Haliburton was a qualified and experienced surveyor. He had been an employee of the Canadian Land Emigration Company until 1879.

[72]Hon. Arthur S. Hardy, later premier of Ontario, held several posts in the Mowat government. In 1890 he was Commissioner of Crown Lands.

[73]That is, the survey of the boundary line between the districts of Thunder Bay and Rainy River.

[74]The unpunctuated and mystifying description becomes clearer when it is realized that the first measurement refers to the distance north of Niven's starting point – Hunter's Island.

B. DREAMS OF POWER AND RICHES, 1821–55

B 1 NICHOLAS GARRY'S[1] VIEW OF THUNDER BAY
[*Printed in Royal Society of Canada,* Transactions, *2nd series, 1900, v. 6, pp. 116, 178, 118*]

Sunday, 1st July [1821] At 12 we came to the great Traverse of Thunder Bay and at 3 o'clock arrived at Fort William where we were received by Mr. Norman McCloud,[2] Mr. Rocheblave,[3] and Mr. McTavish.[4] We were received with the firing of Guns, and the shouts of the Indians, Canadians, etc.!!! 'Timeo Danaos et dona ferentes.' Fort William is in Lat 48.15 Lon. 89.30w ...

Fort William,
July 5, 1821[5]

The North West Company having made Fort William the principal Depot of their Trade have a very large Supply of Goods in Store and as from the Manner in which the Trade under the new Arrangement will be conducted, the keeping up of so considerable a Depot would be useless and would only incur great Expense and Risk, it is in Contemplation to send forward as large a Proportion as may be practicable and thus it is probable it will be found expedient to supply from hence the Posts of the Athapascan, Saskatchewan, English River, Cumberland House, Fort Dauphin, and the Red River.

The Canadians in the Service of the Hudson Bay Company exceeding so much the Number which will be required, it will be expedient not to

[1]Nicholas Garry (1782?–1856) had been a Director of the Hudson's Bay Company for a number of years and was Deputy-Governor from 1822 to 1835, when he was forced to retire because of mental illness.

[2]Archibald Norman McLeod had been with the North West Company as early as 1796, and had been involved in many clashes with Hudson's Bay Company personnel. A partner of McTavish and the McGillivray Bros., he retired from the fur trade in 1821 and returned to Britain where he died about 1838.

[3]Pierre Rastel de Rocheblave (1764?–1840) was first associated with the XY Company and then with the North West Company. He retired from the trade in 1821, and subsequently was a member of the Legislative Assembly of Lower Canada (1824–7) and a member of the Legislative and Executive Councils.

[4]John George McTavish (1778–1847) was the commander of the Fort William post for the North West Company in 1821. He became a Chief Factor in the Hudson's Bay Company and proceeded to posts at York Factory, 1821–8, and at Moose Factory, 1831–4. Since he had been arrested by William Williams of the Hudson's Bay Company (who became Governor of the Southern Department in 1821) in connection with the dispute with Selkirk, he would hardly be *persona grata* to Garry.

[5]This letter, included in the appendix to Garry's journal, represents his official statement to Governor William Williams of negotiations he did not include in the journal itself.

renew the engagements of such Men whose Time is expired, and, even though it should be done with some sacrifice, to annul the engagements of others who may be willing to retire ...

21st July   Left F.W. & never in my life have I left a Place with less Regret.

B 2   WILLIAM McGILLIVRAY[6] TO JOHN STRACHAN[7]
[*Ontario, Department of Public Records and Archives (P.A.O),*
Strachan Papers]

Fort William,
July 26, 1821

I have been at this place since the 1st inst. settling a most important business – the carrying into effect the various Deeds and Covenants entered into on the part of the North West Company in London with the Hudson Bay Company. These arrangements are happily completed and I part with my *old troops* to meet them no more in discussion on the Indian trade. This parting I confess does not cause me much regret. I have worked hard & honestly for them, and I am satisfied that I have at least done my duty. I have been an agent or director since 1794, and Chief Superintendent since 1799. The management has not been easy for we had too many storms to weather from without and some *derangement of the household* but, thank God! the whole is done with honor and the Trade will be productive if well managed, after the country shall have been restored to order, which it will require a couple of years to effect – the fur trade is forever lost to Canada. The Treaty of Ghent destroyed the Southern Trade still the capital & exertions of a few individuals supported the Northern trade, under many disadvantages, against a chartered company who brought their goods to the Indian country at less than half the expense that ours cost us – but it would have been worse than folly, to have continued the contest further. We have made no submissions, we met and negotiated on equal terms.

B 3   REPORT OF CHIEF FACTOR JOHN HALDANE[8]
[*P.A.C., H.B. Co. Records, B-231-e, Reports on Fort William District*]

Fort William (Lake Superior)[9] 1824

The Indians about Fort William are not so numerous as they were some years ago, some having gone to Nipigon, others to Fond du Lac and a

[6]William McGillivray (1764–1825) had established the post on the Kaministikwia to replace Grand Portage as the principal depot of the North West Company. It had been named Fort William in his honour in 1807.

[7]John Strachan (1778–1867) had a number of links with the Montreal fur traders through his connection with the McGill family. His grandson, Strachan Jones, later served the Hudson's Bay Company.

[8]John Haldane (d. 1857) had been a member of the XY Company, then of the North West Company, and was named a Chief Factor of the Hudson's Bay Com-

small portion to St. Mary's [Sault Ste Marie]. The number still frequenting this establishment generally may amount to 250 men and lads. There is one principal chief to whom the others in great measure look up – the only name he goes by, even with the Indians, is "Espagnol."[10] This band are beyond the old Grand Portage, yet last year he gave us almost all his year's hunt amounting to 60 Beaver Skins besides a good many Otters and Martens. In 1822/3 there was a post appertaining to this place called "Mils Lacs" distance about 4 days in winter. It was partially relinquished by me and now made final by the Governor and Council of the Southern District.[11] The Indians belonging to that Post (12 men and 4 lads) with the exception of one, are gone to the Lines. The returns from Mil Lacs in 1823 were 5 packs of Furs principally Beaver Skins.

All this part of the country in former times produced a good many Beaver & Otters – the Indians now complain of scarcity in these Animals. There are still many Martens & Cats, but Foxes, Fishers and Bears are not numerous and the Musquash not so much so as in other parts of the country near the Lake. Formerly there were Moose & Deer – at this time not one is to be seen being literally extinct. Caribou was also at a former period, and not a great many years since, very numerous. Few now are seen – the scarcity of these Animals is greatly felt by the Indians   In Winter their sole dependance for Subsistance is on Rabbits [illegible] & Partridges of various kinds. In the Summer and Fall, the Indians are furnished with Nets & in the Fall they are supplied with a good Stock of Ammunition and notwithstanding these supplies they are often necessitated to have recourse to the establishment where we give them fish, potatoes & indian corn. Humanity and interest compel us to be kind to them, & they are generally grateful to us ...

B 4 Donald McIntosh[12] in Command at Nipigon[13]
[P.A.C., H.B.Co. Records, B-149-a, Nipigon Post Journals]

September 5, 1828.   The Indians who got their supplies for the winter yesterday are still drunk. Weather clear and calm ...

pany in 1821, in control of the whole Lake Superior District. His imminent retirement from the district was announced in the minutes of Council, August 10, 1826, and he presided over his last district Council at Michipicoten on May 21, 1827 (P.A.C., H.B.Co. Records, B-135-k).

[9]This was the common description in the Hudson's Bay records to differentiate reports from this place from those despatched from Fort Wiliam on the Ottawa.

[10]Several of the Chiefs of this period were known by French titles of obscure meaning. Besides L'Espagnol, L'Illinois was frequently mentioned.

[11]Relinquishing of posts from the control of the Lake Superior District became a regular occurrence. Those near the Height of Land – like Lac des Milles Lacs, Lac La Flèche, and New Brunswick (Missanabie) – were in turn detached from the district and added to the adjoining ones. The only post beyond the Height of Land which consistently remained within the Lake Superior District was Long Lac.

[12]Donald McIntosh (1773?–1845) had been associated with the Lake Superior

September 8.   The nets produced thirty white fish this morning. We find it the worst fish of the kind that every we tasted in the Country; it is not better than the herring of Lake Superior, nor are they much larger. The Trout is tolerable, but not to be compared with those caught in Lake Superior. Guidon was employed in cutting the barley with a scythe. Blowing moderately from the eastward.

September 16   [Copy inserted in Journal of letter sent to George Keith]
We also gave the different bands their rum separately, and sent them to drink it at some distance from the Fort in different directions. By taking this precaution they gave us no trouble nor did we hear of any quarrels among themselves. The vagabond Paul La Garde[14] was nigh rising the Indians against Mr. Benjamin McKenzie[15] and Donald.[16] Immediately upon his return here with the latter, he assured the Indians that there were still two kegs of liquor in the store. Old Le Grain, an Indian remarkable for his uprightness and attachment to the whites told Mr. Benjamin that he (La Garde) was the principal man at the time of councilling to excite the Indians to break into the store ... That wretch La Garde acquired some influence with the Indians here in consequence of Mr. MacTavish's[17] having employed him during the time he was here as an interpreter. However, I am determined not to employ him.

District and the North West Company from at least 1806. At Michipicoten in 1816 he had been arrested by Selkirk on the charge of assaulting and robbing an Indian who was carrying Selkirk's despatches. He was appointed a Chief Trader in 1821, apparently on the assumption that he was about to retire. He changed his mind, and remained at various posts in the district until 1838, when he retired to the Montreal area.

13B-149-a contains a number of post journals from Nipigon House, fairly complete from 1827 to 1829, then fragmentary from 1839 to 1844. Until 1850, when it was moved about ten miles farther south, the post was situated on Wabinosh Bay, at the northwest angle of the lake. The particular excerpts given here have been restricted to entries that seem to have been written by Donald McIntosh himself, not including those in his son's handwriting, nor any entries from the summer months when he customarily accompanied his furs to Michipicoten.

14Paul La Garde had the same name as and may have been descended from the Sieur St Pierre (a grandson of Jean Nicolet) who founded La Pointe in 1718. The La Garde referred to here received consistently poor reports in McIntosh's letters and also in John Swanston's, but his services were retained and he was apparently entrusted with some tasks involving some degree of responsibility.

15Benjamin McKenzie was the son of Roderick, Sr., at that time the Chief Trader in charge at Fort William. Benjamin was admitted as an apprentice clerk in 1825, was left in charge of the Nipigon post during the summer of 1828, and was subsequently in charge at Arrow Lake until his departure for Canada.

16The somewhat garbled reference seems to be to Donald McIntosh, Jr., who served as an assistant to his father and wrote much more literate journal entries on his behalf. No record has been found of his being under contract to the company, unlike his brother John who was a clerk in the Lake Superior District as early as 1823.

17Alexander McTavish (1784?–1832) had served the North West Company and was probably a relative of Simon McTavish, McGillivray's partner. He was clerk at Nipigon from 1824–8, when he was promoted to Chief Trader.

May 4, 1829   [Copy inserted in Journal of letter sent to George Keith]
The Indians have been murdering each other quite sober. Sebaway was killed by Kakeyekabin inland some time in February. The former's wife died of the dysentery last fall – ever since it would appear he was not in his right mind – he attempted several times the latter's life before he shot him hence it appears that it was in self defence. His loss, tho a matter of regret, will not diminish our returns much, for he was a poor hunter. The murderer is a worthless wretch who has not hunted a skin since last fall ...

April 6 [1830]   Bouchard[18] and Sabourin sawed Boards to make a coffin for old Le Grain, as the one in which his remains was put in when he died last summer[19] is a very bad one, especially as it is to remain upon a Stage where it will always be on view by all those Indians who visit the Fort ...

May 31, [1830]   Dutremble[20] and Cameron [?] with a freeman and an Indian of Fort William arrived this evening and brought me letters from the Governor and Mr. Keith informing me that I have been appointed by the Governor & Council to the charge of Fort William in place of Mr. McKenzie[21] who has been removed to the Northern Department.

B 5   GEORGE KEITH TO MCINTOSH
[P.A.C., H.B.Co. Records, B-129-b]

Michipicoten,
September 30, 1831.
Under existing circumstances, it is, I feel convinced, the wisest plan to forbear transferring the establishment of Lac La Flèche to Pigeon River. I scarcely think our opponents will anticipate us in this respect,[22] but if

---

[18]Louis Bouchard, born in Lower Canada, was a workman at the Fort William post by the mid-1820s. In 1828 he there married Charlotte Fainiant, an Indian girl, and the Bouchards thereafter appeared at both Fort William and Nipigon until they apparently settled at the latter post.

[19]Le Grain had died August 10, 1829, and Sabourin, without the help of Bouchard on that occasion, had prepared the coffin for ceremonies the following day.

[20]Antoine Dutremble (Dutremblay?), the son-in-law of Roderick McKenzie, Sr., was a workman employed at various times at both the Fort William and Nipigon posts.

[21]Roderick McKenzie (1772?–1859) was sometimes known as Roderick Senior, or Captain of the Nipigon, a region with which he had been associated from the early years of the nineteenth century. It appears that he had always served the Hudson's Bay Company, unlike several of the same name who were prominent in the operations of the North West Company before 1821. McKenzie was a Chief Trader during his command at Fort William; he was promoted to the rank of Chief Factor in 1830 and moved to Ile à la Crosse. He retired in 1843 and spent the remaining years of his life at Red River.

[22]Independent traders operating out of Fond du Lac, and the American Fur Company post at Grand Portage, were both visited on occasion by Indians upon whose furs the Fort William post depended. An occasional free trader would push

they do it will be requisite for you to station some of your people in that vicinity to oppose their views. If Ross[23] continues faithful, he will be an acquisition. The Spaniard is certainly a troublesome and expensive customer. I can scarcely believe he was so arrogant and unreasonable as to demand that supplies should be forwarded to him at Grand Marais. At any rate, I hope you did not submit to such an improper demand.

B 6 GOVERNOR SIMPSON'S OPINION OF LAKE SUPERIOR COMPANY PERSONNEL,[24] 1832
[*P.A.C., H.B.Co. Records, A-34-2, Servants' Characters*]

[Donald McIntosh] About 64[25] years of age. A very poor creature in every sense of the word, illiterate, weak-minded, and laughed at by his colleagues. Very much offended that he has not been promoted and complains loudly of the neglect he has experienced in that respect, altho' his only claim to advancement is his antiquity. Speaks Saulteaux, is qualified to cheat an Indian and can make a fishing net, which are his principal qualifications, indeed he would have made a better canoe man or fisherman than a 'partner.' 'Tis high time he should make room for a better man. He is perfectly sober and honest.

[Roderick McKenzie, Sr.] About 50 years of age – a very honest well-meaning warm-hearted correct man altho' irritable and short-tempered to such a degree that it is unpleasant to do business with him – his health and constitution broken down and worn out so that his useful days are over, and it is full time that he should retire from the service, altho' he has not held his present situation exceeding two years.[26] Indeed he never was possessed of abilities which could qualify him to fill such a situation with advantage, and he owed his late promotion entirely to the circum-

---

even closer, crossing the Pigeon River which was tacitly assumed to be the international boundary. For the Hudson's Bay Company to retaliate by placing a post right at Pigeon River and confronting the Americans seemed a dubious move, especially if the American Fur Company could be persuaded to give aid in limiting the activities of the free traders.

23Louis Ross was a half-breed and married to an Indian. He had apparently quarrelled with Chief Trader McKenzie, served the Americans for some time, then returned to work for McIntosh at Fort William. His case was typical of a good many workmen at that time, and led a number of Company officials to doubt the wisdom of employing Indians or half-breeds so near the border.

24Governor Simpson made all these private comments on Company personnel without any identifying names included. Separately, a numbered list of Chief Factors, Chief Traders, and clerks was recorded. Later experience may have modified his judgment in some cases.

25The ages given were certainly approximate. McIntosh and McKenzie were very nearly the same age, that is, just under sixty, at the time these comments were made.

26Roderick McKenzie had been in his post as Chief Factor at Isle à la Crosse for two years when this record was written.

stances of his being senior to two Gentlemen who were in nomination with him and being less objectionable in many points of view, the Company having had the choice of three very inefficient and in some respects unfit men from among whom it was necessary to fill the vacancy to which he succeeded.

[J.G. McTavish]

[He] was the most finished man of business we had in the country – well-educated, respectably connected and more of the man of the world in his conversation and address than any of his colleagues – a good-hearted man and generous to extravagance, but unnecessarily dignified and high-minded which leads to frequent difficulties with his assistants by whom he is considered a "Shylock" and upon many of whom he looks down; rather strong in his prejudices against and partialities for individuals, which frequently influences his judgment, so that his opinions on men and things must be listened to with caution; is about 54 years of age, has of late become very heavy, unwieldy, and inactive, overfond of good living and I much fear is getting into habits of conviviality and intemperance.

B 7   Thomas McMurray [27] to James Hargrave [28]
[*Glazebrook, ed.*, The Hargrave Correspondence, *pp. 93–4*]

Pic [29] 23rd May, 1832

I passed an agreeable winter at this Place and am as happy & content as a Poor old N'Wester can be, and the nature of the country admits of, not that if my Purse were well lined, I would prefer the Civilised World, but my Maxim is to endeavour to make myself content, wherever I am placed, or situated, otherwise I would be making life disagreeable. No returns this year in this Dept. Small furs failed, and Indians, for want of the Means of Subsistence owing to the disappearance of Hares, the only animal they have to depend on, suffered much from starvation, of course their exertions were damped, and they made no hunts.

[27]Thomas McMurray (1779?–1849) was born in Montreal and had been associated with the XY Company before becoming a Nor'wester. He became a Chief Trader in the Hudson's Bay Company in 1821, and, after several years at Winnipeg River and Rainy Lake, assumed command at the Pic in 1831. He was associated with that post intermittently until he went on leave in 1841. In 1843 he retired to Brighton, Canada West.

[28]James Hargrave (1798–1865) had just entered the North West Company when the union of the companies took place, and he became a clerk in the Hudson's Bay Company. By 1833 he was a Chief Trader and in 1844 a Chief Factor. In 1840 he married Letitia Mactavish, the niece of J.G. McTavish.

[29]Pic, or the Pic, was the most easterly post lying within what is now the District of Thunder Bay. The smallest of those in the district, it was situated on Heron Bay. From it the canoe route ran north to the post at Long Lac. Fairly complete journals have been preserved for the years 1828–41.

B 8   McMurray in Command at the Pic
[*P.A.C., H.B.Co. Records, B-162-a, Pic Post Journals*]

June 2 [1834] In the evening, Louis La Force and Paul La Garde arrived
from Michipicoten on their way to Lake Nipigon – they passed a large
canoe which was ashore at the White River about 4 miles from this,
manned by 8 men and a Gentleman supposed to be Henry Sayer[30] from
St. Mary's on a trading excursion along the Lake – as several of the
Indians of this Fort, Fort William, and Lake Nipigon are on the road and
who have furs in their possession, ordered McKay[31] to accompany La
Force and La Garde and, on reflection, sent an additional man, gave them
Liquor, Ammunition & Tobacco, and ordered them to make all dispatch
to secure which Furs the Indians may have. La Force will remain at Pays
Plat to watch and La Garde and an Indian will proceed on to Lake
Nipigon to advertize Mr. John Swanston. At 3 o'clock p.m. they left this
and will go on all night to get before the Opposition ...

June 3.   Sent off a couple of Indians in a French canoe to advertize
Mr. C.F. Geo. Keith of the Opposition canoe which passed yesterday.
As it is expected they intend to form an establishment at the Pays Plat
or on Lake Nipigon and should such be the case, the Gentlemen at Fort
William & Lake Nipigon are weak in men for the summer, which is my
inducement for informing Mr. C.F. Geo. Keith.

June 6.   In the evening J. Amable McKay and an Indian came back
from Pays Plat – they could not ascertain who was the trader, they were
so well manned they always kept ahead of our people – however they
had no intercourse with the few Indians who were about Pays Plat – what
few furs the Indians had were secured by our people – They appear to
be going on towards Fort William. La Force and an Indian have remained
at the entrance of Nipigon River as a watch.

June 15.   Deschamps[32] and two Indians arrived from Fort William on
their way to Michipicoten. They inform me the Opposition canoe got 15
Skins in furs which they pillaged from a Fort William Indian near the Fort
and it would appear from Indian reports that they have proceeded on to

[30]Henry Sayer was an example of the so-called "free traders" against whom
Company officials were constantly on guard. He was probably a son of the John
Sayer who had formerly served the North West Company in the Lake Superior
region, and a brother of Guillaume Sayer, the leader of the attempt of the métis to
secure free trade in 1844.

[31]The reference is to Jean-Amable McKay, a workman who appeared at various
posts in the district at different times.

[32]Jean-Baptiste Deschamps was a workman at Fort William and at other posts.
McMurray's wording suggests that Deschamps, like Bouchard, was a French Canadian from Lower Canada. Like Bouchard, he married an Indian and his descendants
continued to appear in the Nipigon records later in the century.

Fond du Lac – They give out to the Indians that they will be back and establish a trading House at the Old Grand Portage and another at the entrance to Lake Nipigon – this I consider as nonsense for was it their intent they would not go in such a hurried manner but endeavour to conciliate the Indians and remain some time to get information –

B 9   DUGALD MCTAVISH[33] TO HIS MOTHER
[*Glazebrook, ed.,* The Hargrave Correspondence, *pp. 243–5*]

Michipicoten,
26th August, 1836

My expectations of this Country are now very moderate compared with what they were at first coming out. To give you my reasons for thinking so, would probably be incompatible with my duty to the Company, and besides to enter into details about the business would be a never-ending job upon paper. I however take, I should think the wisest place, which is always to hope for the best, no odds what ups & downs I may have, for allowing any situation to be ever so bad, a man is never thought more of for making complaints. As regards John, I should be very sorry indeed to see him enter into the Service, as I already begin to think two brothers in one Concern of this kind, is exactly one too many, and of course a third still worse. I would give it as my advice, that my Father should write to Uncle [J.G. McTavish] as usual in the spring (and send his Letter to the H. Bay House) and request him to procure a situation for John in some Mercantile House in Montreal, as soon as he possibly could. Uncle I know can soon get him a place if he interests himself, which I have no doubt he will do, if only reminded a little, as Mrs. Mactavish told me before she left Moose, that he intended doing so, but I suppose he has forgotten being so busy and taken up with the Civilized world after such a long absence. About Uncle I know very little since he went down, but what I have learned is very satisfactory. His health has improved amazingly, from the change of places. He is now at one of the Company's Posts, not far from Montreal.

The past Winter was uncommonly cold. Thermometer was twice 39 below Zero, Fahrenheits scale, and from 30 to 36 below zero was perfectly common. Our House happens to be a very cold one, the consequence was that many nights I could not get sleep, although I was well wrapped in Blankets and a buffalo Robe besides, I have at times wakened in the night, and put my hand up to feel if my nose was on, for it is a fact, that there was no feeling in it, being as it were perfectly dead, and when I would put my warm hand upon it, it felt as if it was burning. You may

[33]The two nephews of J.G. McTavish joined the Hudson's Bay Company in 1833. Dugald was a clerk in the Lake Superior District in 1836–7, became a Chief Trader in 1851; William was later the Governor of Assiniboia and of Rupert's Land, 1864–70.

judge of the cold when 6 mornings out of 7 in the week I would find the water in my basin, a solid mass of Ice, at least 6 inches thick, and yet I find it adviseable to hold my tongue on the subject, especially to any of the young clerks whom I see, for I happened to tell one (the very one who had been here before in my place) the only pity he had for me, was to tell me I was an old woman, a cold-blooded animal, etc. for when he was here, he used to go to bed with his window wide open, he felt it so very sultry, only imagine sultry weather in this country in the Months of January or February, when the general average of the range of the Thermometer will be 20 below zero. Our Living here is not exactly of the best, just fancy boiled Fish three times a day, we have however tea twice a day. You seem to think that I would not find Lerwatt or Mrs Sonig so very hard now, I can assure you it is quite the reverse, for whatever I have here, I am certain that it is always the best that is going, as I see the bourgeois eating with me, whereas at the aforementioned places it would have been difficult to have found worse Provender, than we had, and what made it still worse, especially in Edinburgh, was seeing all the nice stuff in the various shops, and at the same time unable to lay hold of anything, were there only as many shops hereabouts, we would all live well in the Country.

B 10   GEORGE SIMPSON TO JOHN PELLY[34]
[*P.A.C., Series G, v. 78, pp. 491-4*]

Lachine, Oct. 31, 1836
I have the honor to acquaint you that on my arrival at Montreal from Hudson's Bay on the 5th ultimo, I noticed an article in one of the Montreal newspapers headed "Piracy on the Lakes," a copy of which is annexed, and that the following information has reached me as a result of my enquiries connected with this subject which I consider it my duty to lay before you as Governor of the Hudson's Bay Company, because I am apprehensive the party alluded to in that article are engaged in an enterprize which is like to lead to much excitement among the Indian tribes inhabiting the country situate between the banks of the Missouri and the shores of Lake Superior & Winnipeg, likewise among the numerous "half-breed" population of Red River settlement, and fraught with danger to both the British & American white population engaged in the fur trade of the Indian country and in agricultural pursuits on the frontiers of the British and United States territory contiguous to the boundary line.
The information that has reached me is to the following effect. A person named Dickson, an Englishman by birth[35] of bold & desperate character,

---

[34]John Henry Pelly (1777–1852) had become Governor of the Hudson's Bay Company in 1822, at which time Nicholas Garry succeeded him as Deputy-Governor. He became a baronet of the United Kingdom in 1840.
[35]None of these details is substantiated by Martin McLeod's account of Dickson. See Nute, ed., "The Diary of Martin McLeod."

who has for several years been resident in Mexico, made his appearance lately at Washington & New York, where he attracted considerable notice from the circumstance of his styling himself "General Dickson of the Indian liberating Army," likewise "Montezuma the Second," having the command of money, being dressed in handsome uniform remarkable in his appearance, his face being covered with huge whiskers and mustachios and seamed with sabre wounds, and of his being occupied in endeavouring to collect a strong party with the view as he said of his joining the Texans against the Mexicans. In the early part of last summer this man became acquainted with several wild thoughtless young men of good education and daring character, half breed sons of gentlemen lately and now engaged in the fur trade.[36] These young men joined Dickson's standard with about thirty others and started from Montreal for Buffalo in the month of July with all the pomp and circumstance of war, well-armed, dressed in regimentals, Dickson styling himself General, and McKenzie,[37] McLaughton,[38] McLeod,[39] and McBean,[40] half-breeds, assuming the rank, the first of Secretary of War, the second of Captain, and the other two of Lieutenants of the "Indian Liberating Army" ...

From my intimate knowledge of the Indian character, I feel such representatives from such sources might lead to much excitement among

[36]Dr Nute concludes that while the other "thoughtless young men" were in fact half-breeds, Martin McLeod was not. In 1838 he married Mary Ortley or Ouinona whose mother was a Sioux. It was their daughter, Miss Isabelle McLeod of Minneapolis, who retained the journal of the Dickson expedition and allowed it to be published in 1922.

[37]John George McKenzie (1811?–38) had been born at Long Lac, the son of "Emperor" McKenzie who continued his battle with the Hudson's Bay Company after 1821. Young McKenzie served as Dickson's Secretary of War until ill health forced him to leave the expedition at Sault Ste Marie. With his sister, Mrs Cowie, of that post, he travelled to Montreal, hoping to recover his health and rejoin the expedition in the spring. Neither hope was realized.

[38]John McLoughlin, Jr. (1812–41), the son of Chief Factor Dr John McLoughlin, had been educated in Montreal and in Paris. His attempts to secure a post in the fur trade had been denied, apparently on the grounds that the Hudson's Bay Company did not wish to employ half-breeds. After winning a Paris degree, he returned to Montreal in 1834; he was refused passage to Oregon in the Company's brigades, and, although his father agreed to finance a medical course at McGill, young McLoughlin's difficulties with his creditors landed him in jail early in 1836. Once he joined Dickson, Governor Simpson was quick to offer a three-year contract as clerk and surgeon, and, following the collapse of the "foolish enterprise," he accepted the offer and served the Company on the west coast until his murder in 1841.

[39]Martin McLeod (1813–60) was the son of Chief Trader John McLeod, who was in the far west from 1836 to 1838 as an associate of Dr McLoughlin, and retired to Canada East in 1848. Young McLeod refused Governor Simpson's offer of employment, settled in Minnesota, became a prominent St Paul businessman and member of the Councils of the Minnesota territory.

[40]Charles McBean's father, John, was another North West Company partner who had become a Chief Factor in 1821. He was in charge of the Lake Huron District at the time of his son's escapade. Young McBean returned to his father's home during the summer of 1837, but no record has been found of his being offered employment in the Hudson's Bay Company service.

the different tribes thro' whom the party would pass and expose the traders and settlers to imminent danger.

B 11 JOHN SWANSTON TO J. D. CAMERON[41]
[*P.A.C., H.B.Co., Records, B-149-a*]

Nipigon,
February 4, 1837

The establishment of the old Grand Portage by the American Fur Company, a circumstance generally known to all the Indians of the place, will cause many from this place to wish to pay them a visit next summer, particularly as it appears they have given out that they will have abundance of liquor for them. I am much afraid that our chief Michimuckwa and brothers will be one party and as they are never indebted to the Company to any extent, I am apprehensive that they will hide away some furs for this object. I shall, you may rely, do my utmost to prevent them or any others from going over to Lake Superior next summer but much fear that I shall not succeed in my wishes as they generally go out to see their brother who resorts to Fort William!

B 12 WILLIAM LOGAN'S[42] COMMENTS ON THE LAKE SUPERIOR AREA, 1846[43]
[*Logan*, Remarks on the Mining Region of Lake Superior, *pp. 3-10*]

In assuming its probable importance, I do not feel myself so much influenced by the reports that have been so diligently spread since the commencement of the present mining excitement in the United States, as by the unprejudiced account regarding the mineral riches of the southern shore furnished to the legislature of Michigan by the late Mr. Douglas Houghton[44] in 1841 ...

[41]John Dugald Cameron had entered the service of the North West Company as early as 1795, and had spent a number of years as a clerk in the Nipigon area. He became a Chief Factor in 1821, and assumed charge of the Lake Superior District, with headquarters at Michipicoten, when George Keith went on furlough. Cameron retired to Canada West in 1844 and died in 1857.

[42]William Edmond Logan (1798–1875) was born in Montreal and educated in Scotland. He became director of the Geological Survey of Canada in 1843 and continued in that post until 1870. He was knighted in 1856.

[43]These *Remarks* were written before Logan's trip to Lake Superior. They thus represent his general approach to the problem, rather than the specific discoveries and decisions included in his report to the Commissioner of Crown Lands after the completion of his expedition.

[44]Dr Douglass Houghton acted as surgeon, botanist, and geologist on Henry Schoolcraft's 1832 expedition to the Mississippi. By 1840 he had become the first state geologist of Michigan, and in that year discovered the copper ores on the south shore of Lake Superior and visited Isle Royale as well. His discoveries touched off the frantic mining rush of the 1840s; just before his death by drowning in 1845 he had also discovered iron ore in the Marquette region.

It is understood that he had visited the British shores of Lake Superior and considered their mineral character much the same as that on his own side of the water, though, I believe, he had made no published statement to such an effect ...

The minerals bearing economic value which occur on the shores of Lake Superior are the ores of copper, and though Mr. Houghton mentions that these are occasionally associated with the ores of zinc, lead, iron, manganese and silver, the copper ores appear to be those which, in my opinion, render the region worthy of mining attention ...

No surface examination can equal trial levels and shafts in the veins; it would be in the interest of the Government, as landlords and owners of the lodes,[45] to encourage to a limited extent, the working of some of them by such companies of respectable persons as might be found willing to risk their capital in mining adventures; especial care being taken in granting mining locations to secure a *bona fide* intention of working the minerals, and to avoid the encouragement of mere stock-jobbing speculation. One judicious means to this end, it appears to me, would be, that the mining locations should not exceed in magnitude the strength of the working capital of the adventurers. It would no doubt be judicious that the first adventurers should obtain their locations on the most liberal terms, but, in my humble opinion, there should be some stipulation on the part of the Government that a certain number of miners should be employed in each location. To drive one level with full vigour would require six miners who, working two at a time in *stems*, or periods of eight hours, would occupy the day.

B 13   W. NORMAN MCLEOD[46] TO JOHN MCKENZIE
[*P.A.C., MG 19 A-30, Northwest Papers*]

Pays des lièvres[47]
Saturday, June 13, 1846

I beg to acknowledge the receipt of your polite notes of the 4th and 12th instants – the latter enclosing the order in council regulating the Mineral Lands of Lake Superior of the 19th ult.[48] I avail myself of the occasion

[45]Logan was either unaware of Indian claims to the land in question, or else assumed that the Crown owned the land, and the Indians had only a claim with the Crown. In any case, the mining activity on the north shore of Lake Superior led to the agreements included in the Robinson Treaty of 1850.

[46]W. Norman McLeod was not one of the Hudson's Bay Company employees, but was on friendly terms with them. He was also clearly independent of the great Montreal mining interests which sought control of the Lake Superior area. It seems likely that he was a former fur trader, perhaps a free trader, who was briefly involved in mining explorations, then disappeared from the district.

[47]Pays des Lièvres was apparently a location between Fort William and the international boundary, perhaps in the general area where the Rabbit Mountain silver mine was to be discovered in the 1880s.

[48]During 1845 there had been 160 applications for mining locations on Lake

to thank you for the acceptable present sent to me by McKay, & especially for the polite attention evidenced in the transmission of the document referred to. This latter may prove as valuable to the man official as the former was delectable to the man natural. I think their worships might have stumbled upon a more equitable evidence of priority of discovery than mere detection and description, as it is possible that John Doe, or his especial co-mate Richard Roe, might detect a location and define its limits without surrendering their "ease in their inn" in the "goodlie city" of Montreal. However, *de auctoritatibus non est disputandum.*

I have been employed since my last communication in a further exploration of the vein at Pays des lièvres. The ore is a ferruginous sulphurit of copper; the yellow ore of Cornwall, but of a much richer quality. Its yield as compared with the same copper elsewhere is nearly twofold, but, at present, it lacks concentration to make it very productive ...

Yesterday I had a visit from Mr. Douglas[49] and his astronomers on their way to Pigeon River. Their canoe was leaking and they did not know how to find the hole. Douglas, who knew that the voyageurs applied their lips in some capacity to discover a leak, assured me that he kissed the bottom of his faithless barque with the zeal of an adoring lover, but, lucklessly, with no advantage. I sent McKay to examine it, and with a little gum, she was soon made seaworthy. The geologist & other savants attached to this expedition are on their way to copper harbor.

B 14 LOGAN'S REPORT ON THE LAKE SUPERIOR
LOCATIONS, 1846
[*Report to the Commissioner of Crown Lands, 1847*]

Leaving this [Montreal] on the 1st day of June, and joining my Assistant Mr. Murray[50] at Detroit, where he had been engaged in completing arrangements for our expedition, we proceeded to Sault Ste. Marie accompanied by Mr. McNaughtan,[51] the Provincial Land Surveyor appointed

---

Superior. The government attempted to set up some criteria for deciding among them and, when Logan had completed his survey, granted twenty-seven of the requests and provided more specific mining regulations in the order-in-council of November 2, 1846.

[49]This particular group of savants headed by Mr Douglas has not been identified. Various geological expeditions visited Lake Superior during the summer of 1846. Forrest Shepherd was acting on behalf of the group soon to become the Montreal Mining Company. J.F. Boynston worked for the Ryan-Gratiot interest soon to become part of the Quebec and Lake Superior Association. McLeod gave assistance to the Logan expedition as well, but later in the summer than June 13.

[50]Alexander Murray (1810–84) was born at Crieff, Scotland, and eventually retired there. Educated at the Royal Naval College, Portsmouth, he had served with the British navy for ten years before becoming associated with a number of Logan's ventures in British North America – the Gaspé Peninsula, Newfoundland, as well as Lake Superior. He later became director of the Newfoundland Geological Survey.

[51]John McNaughton, the surveyor with the Logan expedition, provided maps of the twenty-seven grants approved.

by the Government to survey topographically the various mining locations, the mineral veins of which it was another portion of my task to
inspect, with a view to aid in determining the direction most consistent
with the general interest, to be given to their boundary lines, in cases of
collision between the lots of neighbouring claimants. Subsequently visiting
Copper Harbour in Michigan, on the south side of the lake, for the purpose of gathering information regarding the nature of the copper lodes
which had been opened in that vicinity, we crossed over to Fort William
on the north, and entered upon the work assigned to us, commencing our
examination in the neighbourhood of the British boundary at Pigeon
River.

Mr. Murray's attention was devoted to the examination of the Kamanitiquia and Michipicoten Rivers, both of which he ascended to near the
height of land, in addition to the inspection of several sections of the coast,
his Report upon all of which I now have the honor to transmit to Your
Excellency. My own time was bestowed upon an examination of the mining locations and the coast generally; and finding it was in my power to
work in advance of the land surveying party, I was happy to avail myself
of the obliging offer of Mr. W.N. McLeod, who put at my service his canoe
and eight voyageurs to transport me round the shores of the lake, by which
I was enabled to make a more extended inspection than it would otherwise
have been possible for me to effect in the limited time one season could
afford. With the exception of Mr. Murray's excursion up the two rivers
mentioned, the examination has necessarily been confined to the coast,
and cannot be considered more than a *reconnaissance* of the district, to
be carried into farther detail at a future period as occasion may serve.

The Canadian shores of Lake Superior in general present a bold and
rocky coast, diversified in the character of its scenery in accordance with
the distribution of its different geological formations. Cliffs and eminences
rise up to heights varying from 300 to 1300 feet, close upon its margin,
and this, deeply indented in some parts with extensive bays, and in others
presenting extensive clusters of islands, is in a multitude of places carved
out into well-sheltered coves and inlets affording innumerable harbours
of a safe and commodious character, destined greatly to facilitate whatever commerce may hereafter be established on the lake, whether with
the produce of its mines or its fisheries. The timber of the district does not
seem to promise much encouragement to traffic; it is not of the size nor
the kinds most esteemed in commerce, though there is much useful wood
capable of being rendered available for mining or house-building purposes, as well as for fuel. Hardwood is scarce, red pine not often seen, and
white pine not abundant. The trees most common are spruce, balsam fir,
white birch, and poplar, with cedar in moist places. On the immediate
coast, many of the hills are nearly denuded of trees, particularly where
granite and gneiss prevail. The hills composed of trap are better clothed;
but it is in the trappean valleys and on the surfaces underlaid by sandstone, which are usually flat, that the largest growth is met with. It is chiefly
in these localities also, and at the mouths of some of the principal rivers

that is to be found whatever land may be fit for cultivation; and although of this in comparison to the great area of the district, the extent cannot be called great, nor such as even if less remotely situated would tempt settlement, sufficient would probably be found to supply many of the wants of a mining population, should the metalliferous minerals of the region be found on trial to exist in sufficient abundance to be worked with profit.

B 15   REPORT OF ALEXANDER MURRAY ON THE
KAMINISTIKWIA RIVER
[*Canada, Geological Survey*, Report of Progress, *1847*]

Woodstock, 20th April, 1847.
The Kaminitiquia falls into Thunder Bay by three different channels, nearly directly west of the Welcome Islands, the northern or main channel passing by the Hudson Bay Company's Trading Post of Fort William, which is about half a mile up from the lake. The ascending course of this channel is a little westward of south; at the distance of about a mile and three quarters, one of the other channels flows from it, and the third half a mile farther. The general course above this, turns to a few degrees southward of west, maintained for a distance which in a straight line is only five and a half miles, although the stream meanders through nearly double that distance, its deep and muddy water, with an average breadth of about 100 yards, possessing a scarcely perceptible current all the way to the lake. Above this the river becomes rapid, and the bearing against the stream is about due west for nearly ten miles, after which it bends to northwest, maintained for about three miles, and at the end of the distance the Grand Falls occur. Above these falls, which in some maps are called the Falls of Kakabica,[52] the direct course is almost due north for a distance of between eighteen and twenty miles in a straight line to Dog Lake, which is an extensive sheet of water, thickly studded with islands, occupying an area probably upwards of 200 square miles. Its shape is related to a semicircle, with the straight side or diameter running nearly north and south and facing the west. At the northern extremity a sluggish stream, known to the fur traders as Dog River, falls in. Following this, the average course would be about northwest for a distance, including its bends, of about thirty-five miles, the first twenty passing through a great swamp or marsh, with a current so slow as to be almost imperceptible; while short rapids, falling over lifts or steps of a few feet, alternating with long stretches of still water, occur in the remaining fifteen miles of the distance, until reaching the little tributary by which the Hudson Bay Company's canoes take their route to Red River. Here the river turns off nearly due north, widening out into a long narrow lake for about two to three miles, after which there follows in the same line a chain of twelve small lakes or ponds, connected by short rapid streams, comprised within the distance of ten or twelve miles. The uppermost pond appeared at its

---

[52]Kakabeka Falls. Murray's phrasing indicated how tentative many of the district names were at the time.

northern extremity to terminate in a great marsh, which was supposed to be the ultimate source of the river, and to extend far and wide along the height of land, probably joining with the great marsh of the Savannah Portage on the Red River route. From its source to its exit at Fort William, the stream, following its windings, appears to be something upwards of 120 miles long.

The last part of our ascent was performed on foot, the highest point we reached in our canoes being the lower end of the chain of small lakes, where by observations of the sun and moon, the latitude was ascertained to be 48° 56′N., while the variation of the compass taken by an azimuth of the sun was 7° 26′ E. The variation at the foot of Dog Lake by an azimuth of the sun was 7° 1′ E.

The upper part of the river between the sources and Dog Lake, for the greater part of the distance passes through a vast swamp, which is bounded on each side by low granite ridges, usually more or less covered with a stunted growth of evergreens and white birch. The timber on both banks of the river where the land is dry is generally pitch-pine, balsam-fir, spruce and white birch; where it is moist, tamarack and cedar prevail; and where the country is altogether marshy, destitute of timber, it is overgrown with willow bushes and long rank grass. In many parts large tracts have been overrun by fire, which has denuded the whole surface of its vegetation, leaving a dreary waste covered only by scorched and blackened poles. The only exception to this character is the vicinity of the chain of small lakes, leaving out the uppermost. There the valley contracts, the granite ridges come sometimes boldly to the river's edge, and the country thus diversified affords in some places interesting landscape scenery.

The country surrounding Dog Lake is of a mountainous character, thickly covered with forests, chiefly of evergreens, and among them were observed red and white pines. White and yellow birch trees are abundant, and some of them of large dimensions; it is chiefly from the neighbourhood of Dog Lake that the Hudson Bay Company are supplied at Fort William by the Indians with bark for the manufacture of their birch canoes. The bold primary rocks by which the lake is bounded, and the innumerable islands with which it is studded, afford much picturesque scenery. The water of the lake, of which the surface is probably about 500 feet above Lake Superior, or about 1,100 feet above the level of the sea, issues through a deep narrow gorge, and is precipitated over a succession of heavy falls, amounting altogether to probably upwards of 200 feet, and occasioning the Great Dog Portage, extending a mile and a half across a narrow neck of elevated land, at the foot of which our measurements on the river ceased.

Between the Great Dog Portage and the Grand Falls the river flows over a series of steps, each of them causing falls or strong rapids, with long stretches of still water in the intervals, and six of them occasioning portages, both to upward and downward voyageurs, which vary in distance from a few yards to more than a mile. The country is of a primary character all the way, and is for the most part thickly wooded with dwarfish timber, consisting chiefly of spruce, balsam-fir, white birch, and occasionally a few pine trees. The total fall in the distance is probably 200 feet.

At the Grand Falls the river is precipitated almost vertically a height of 100 feet, below which it rushes very rapidly through a deep gorge, cut through slate, to the foot of the portage, a distance of about half a mile. The difference of level from the smooth water at the summit of the falls to that at the foot of the portage was found to be 119 feet. From this point to that at which our measurements commenced, the river is for the most part rapid. It passes through a poor and unproductive country, growing chiefly the usual evergreen trees, with white birch and poplars; occasionally, however, on the high banks some moderately good pines were observed, but by no means in such quantity or general size as to be of any commercial importance. For the remainder of the distance to its mouth, the river meanders through an alluvial country without any change in the species of trees, which are, however, frequently of larger dimensions than generally seen farther up. This tract lies at the base of the high table land, which at its northern extremity is called McKay's Mountain,[53] but reaching the point where the river splits into its three exit-channels, the land becomes for the most part marshy, except at the spot on the north side, where the Hudson Bay Company's Post and the cultivated grounds belonging to it are situated. Much of the marshy ground affords excellent pasturage for cattle, and a large stock belonging to the Company was feeding on it at the time of our visit.

The waters of the Kamanitiquia are every where turbid, perhaps owing to the swampy sources from which they spring, and during the summer season they are so warm as to be scarcely potable. Many parts, however, both of the stream and its lakes, abound with fish. Some of the upper portions literally teem with the common pike, and near the mouth sturgeon and white fish are frequently found. The game of the country consists chiefly of the caribou, the bear, marten, mink, musk-rat and common hare; the first three are scarce, the last two abound. Of birds we observed several species of duck, the ruffed and spotted grouse, and the passenger pigeon. Birds of prey were likewise frequently seen, among which were numerous eagles and falcons, and several species of owls ...

B 16 LIST OF MINING LOCATIONS GRANTED[54] ON LAKE SUPERIOR, 1846
[*Printed in Logan's* Report to the Commissioner of Crown Lands, 1847]

[Pigeon River to Fort William]

1. John Stuart
2. James B. Forsyth

[53]The mountain at Fort William had no name when Garry inquired about it in 1821. McKay's Mountain seems to have been the name in common usage by the mid-1840s, and it is believed that the name came from a free trader named McKay who defied the Hudson's Bay Company in the region in the 1840s. The difficulty lies in the multitude of free traders and of Company employees named McKay.

[54]In this list there is little indication of the American influence apparent in the

3. O.D. McLean
4. W.B. Jarvis and others
5. John Prince
6. Charles Bockus and Donald Ross
7. George Desbarats

[Thunder Cape eastward]
8. Joseph Woods
9. Stewart Derbishire
10. Abner Bagg & Stanley Bagg
11. John Ewart
12. W.H. Merritt
13. S.J. Lyman
14. James Ferrier
15. S.B. Harrison
16. James Hamilton
17. Peter McGill and others
18. R.J. Turner
19. James Wilson

[Michipicoten area]
20. Charles Jones
21. Angus MacDonnell
22. Thomas Ryan
23. Arthur Rankin
24. Edward Ryan
25. John Douglas
26. Allan MacDonnell
27. W.C. Meredith

B 17   ALLAN MACDONELL'S[55] NOTES ON LAKE SUPERIOR MINING ENTERPRISES
[P.A.C., MG 24 I-8, Macdonell of Collachie Papers, Allan Macdonell Mining Papers]

The Quebec and Lake Superior Mining Company[56] is one of the first of those incorporated some years ago, and its charter confers powers and

mining companies that eventually took over the grants. Here, residents of Quebec City include the Ryan brothers, W.C. Meredith, and James Forsyth; of Montreal Peter McGill, George Desbarats (the Queen's Printer), Stewart Derbishire, and S.J. Lyman; of Toronto the Macdonell brothers, S.B. Harrison, and W.B. Jarvis; of other centres in Canada West Colonel John Prince and Arthur Rankin of Sandwich, W.H. Merritt of St Catharines, and Joseph Woods of Chatham.

[55] Allan Macdonell (1808–88) was the son of a Legislative Councillor of Upper Canada. He practised law for a time as partner of Sir Allan MacNab. He was interested over a long period of years in mining possibilities in the Lake Superior area and, along with his brother Angus, was one of the original holders of grants approved in 1846. He was later one of those most keenly interested in developing transportation routes from Lake Superior to Red River.

[56] The Quebec and Lake Superior Mining Company was incorporated July 28,

privileges upon its shareholders which are not now extended to any corporate Body, therefore it may be considered more valuable than any of those Charters granted at a more recent period. The Capital of the Company is $352,000 divided into shares – 44,000 with a limited liability upon the stockholders. The Company has also the power to increase their Capital Stock to $800,000.

The whole of the original stock of $352,000 having been taken up, under the Charter, the Company entered upon active operations but in that extravagant and reckless manner which whilst it seldom fails to ruin the fairest prospects almost always results for the advantage of those who may be in a position to profit by the experience and knowledge thus dearly purchased.

The first great error made by the Company was in seeking to possess themselves of vast tracts of mining land consisting of various choice localities along the coast of Lake Superior, these several mining locations comprising some 89,600 acres.

A large amount of the subscribed capital was necessarily expended on making explorations along the whole coast of Lake Superior and then selecting and surveying the 14 locations purchased by the company.

The payment of the purchase money consumed another large portion of the capital stock, and the consequence was that by the time the company had resolved upon which one of their mining locations to commence a mining establishment and even before the completion of the many preposterous and unnecessary expenses incidental or preliminary thereto, the remaining portion of their subscribed capital was nearly exhausted, leaving comparatively but a small amount for actual mining operations ...

Nearly one half of the stock was held between Detroit, Buffalo and this place [Toronto] and New York. The other portion was held by parties in Quebec mostly merchants in the lumber trade.

I held 3000 shares with $1 paid up this was in consideration of a mining location which I brought into the Company and is easily the most valuable on the Lake.[57]

Instalments were called in and the shares of the defaulters were sold from time to time at the office of the Company and bought in principally by the Directors. In like manner when any shares became subject to [illegible] not being able to pay they too were bought up. Thus in a short time the whole stock of the Company passed into the hands of a few parties in Quebec –

1847. Peter Patterson was its first president, and the trustees were John Bonner, Henry Lemesurier, William Petry, and Thomas W. Lloyd. Its claim to nearly 90,000 acres of land on Lake Superior was the result of taking over a number of the original grants, the Ryans, the Macdonells, James Hamilton, etc., but much of this land was forfeited to raise the purchase money on 26,000 acres. By 1864 one tract on St Ignace Island and another on Michipicoten Island were all that remained to the Company within the Thunder Bay area.

[57]Macdonell's mining location had been near Mamainse Point, on the eastern shore of Lake Superior. Like the others among the original grants, it had a frontage of two miles, and extended five miles in from the shore.

Patterson, Lemesurier, Price, Bonner, Forsyth, Rhodes etc. Subsequently most of these parties failed in the lumber trade, and funds were not forthcoming to carry on operations on Lake Superior and they were obliged to suspend & abandon all their works there. The shares of those who had become bankrupt went into the hands of assignees and were sold at auction – generally these shares were bought up by various parties, Brokers, etc. the shares at first sold for $1 1/3 a large quantity was sold at low as /9[?] per share. These were bought by some five or six Brokers.

B 18   LOUIS AGASSIZ[58] AT A LAKE SUPERIOR MINING LOCATION

[Cabot's narrative in Agassiz, Lake Superior, pp. 78–9]

July 17th [1848]   We ran into a narrow bay on the east end of St. Ignace,[59] the bottom of which approached a peak marked on Bayfield's[60] chart as thirteen hundred feet above the lake. This bay is a quiet little nook, hedged around with larches and other trees, over whose tops appeared the peak. A small clearing had been made there, it being a mining "location," and on a board fixed to one of the trees was an inscription signifying that the spot had been "taken possession of by the Montreal Mining Company, June 5, 1846."[61] They had even gone so far as to put up a log-house, yet standing in tolerable repair, and a crib for sleeping inside, and "Douglass' Hotel" written on a board for the door. This was one of the many places (there are several on this island) where works were commenced without any proper exploration of the ground, the only

---

[58]Louis Agassiz (1807–73) had left Switzerland in 1846 and two years later he became professor of geology and zoology at Harvard. The 1848 expedition to Lake Superior, the report of which was published in 1850, included a narrative by one of the members of the expedition, J. Elliot Cabot of Boston.

[59]In the locations of 1847, those belonging to S.B. Harrison and James Hamilton were situated on this large island in Nipigon Bay. The Harrison property seems to have been taken over almost immediately by the Montreal Mining Company.

[60]Henry Wolsey Bayfield (1795–1885) was appointed Admiralty Surveyor in British North America in 1817. His survey of Lake Superior took place in 1822 and 1823, and his maps were used by almost all expeditions on that lake in the next century.

[61]The Montreal Mining Company was incorporated on July 28, 1847, and at that time eighteen of the original mining grants were assigned to it. Operations were begun on St Ignace Island, Spar Island, and Prince's Bay, but all of these were abandoned within a year of two; the mining company restricted itself to its successful operation at Bruce Mines on Lake Huron and for twenty years made no attempt at developing its Lake Superior property. In 1868 silver was discovered on the Woods location which the Company had held from its incorporation and Thomas Ryan, then president, tried to secure capital in Britain to finance the Silver Islet operations. Failing in this endeavour, the Montreal Mining Company transferred its holdings to E.A. Prentice of Montreal who held, at first, a 10 per cent interest in the American syndicate that worked the mine.

indication of ore being some veins of calc-spar,[62] which by a too hasty induction was supposed to be a sure sign of copper. Small quantities of native copper were found, but not sufficient to pay for the trouble of getting it.

B 19   E.B. BORRON[63] TO HUGH ALLAN[64]
[*Montreal Mining Company*, Report, *1854*]

Bruce Mines,
Jan. 14, 1854

If the [Montreal Mining] Company could (as I doubt not they can) sell or lease on favorable terms a portion of their mineral land on Lake Superior, I think after having done so much on this Lake [Huron] for mining in Canada, they may advantageously devolve on others the honor, and to some extent the risk, of proving and opening up in the first instance the mineral resources of the North Shore.

B 20   BORRON'S ACCOUNT OF THE RUMOURED WEALTH OF THUNDER BAY
[*Ontario, Department of Crown Lands*, Report, *1870, Report of the Mining Inspector*]

The existence of silver on both the north and south shores of Lake Superior has been known for many years; on the south shore it is found associated with the native copper in many if not all of the mines, and some have produced quite a considerable quantity. Near Marquette it was found associated with lead ore or Galena. In no case, however, would it appear to have been sufficiently rich to admit of the veins being worked for the silver alone irrespective of the other metals associated with it. On the

[62]Dr John Mothersill of the Lakehead University Geology Department believes that "calc-spar" is a reference to calcide, which could have been mistaken for ore-bearing quartz by earlier exploring expeditions.

[63]Edward Barnes Borron was born in Staffordshire in 1820 and, after some time at the University of Edinburgh, joined his father and brother in mining at Leadhills, Scotland. He came to Canada in 1850 and by 1852 was manager at Bruce Mines where, in 1854, he married Marie de Laramé of Yamaska. In 1869 he became mining inspector for the Lake Superior area, a position he resigned in 1873. In the election of the following year he was chosen to represent Algoma in the Dominion Parliament. In 1879 he became Stipendiary Magistrate for Nipissing and was asked by the Ontario government to undertake various journeys to the north and west to report on the "new territory" claimed by the government.

[64]Hugh Allan (1810–82) was President of the Montreal Mining Company in 1852, the same year in which his shipping company was granted a government contract to establish a line of steamers on the St Lawrence. As founder and head of the Allan line he was knighted in 1871, just before he became implicated in the railway contract that touched off the Pacific Scandal.

north shore it had been found at Mamainse, Michipicoten Island, St. Ignace and Prince's Bay, and possibly many other places unknown to me. Many years indeed before the excitement about copper arose on this lake, a French Canadian voyageur in the service of Captain Bayfield is supposed to have discovered silver in this Thunder Bay. At a time when silver mines at all events were little thought of, this man asserted that he had found it here. So satisfied were several parties at the Bruce Mines of his sincerity that an expedition was fitted out in the year 1852 and sent up to see the vein with intention of securing and working it. Secord, as the man was called, brought the party to Thunder Bay, but once there his memory would appear to have failed him as to the exact spot, and the party returned disappointed and, for the most part fully persuaded that he had deceived them. Poor and despised, the unfortunate man committed suicide some time afterwards, the disappointment having doubtless preyed upon and affected his mind. The events of the last three or four years render it exceedingly probable that poor Secord really found silver in Thunder Bay as he asserted he had done, when Captain Bayfield was engaged in the survey of Lake Superior, and should vindicate his memory from suspicions which were in all likelihood unjust.

C 1   DR BIGSBY'S[1] IMPRESSIONS OF THE
THUNDER BAY REGION
[*Bigsby,* By Shoe and Canoe, *v. 2, pp. 218–22, 227–31*]

The Black River is now at hand. Of the islands a little to the east, and seven miles from this river, named "the Slate Islands," from their being of greenstone slate, I only know further that they are rather large and high. Captain Bayfield has visited them.

We were enabled to examine the Black River for five or six miles inland, as the fog of the morning was succeeded by a storm of wind and rain, which kept us for two days near its mouth: into which, in fact, we ran our boat. On the sudden occurrence of a storm, landing is a delicate affair in the large lakes of the interior, such as Superior, Winnipeg, &c. ...

Close to the calm basin into which we had pushed our boat, and close also to the lake, was a flourishing wood of pines. In the midst of this we pitched our tent, and set up the tripod for the *voyageurs'* fire, after having with our axes cleared a sufficient space of ground.

We were quietly at work, when one of the men informed us that the wood we were in was a mere belt, 300 yards across, and that there were extensive open plains beyond, with lofty hills in the distance. We threw away pencil and pen, and set off to explore.

The Black River, rising near Long Lake, enters Lake Superior on the west side of a small bay, with a rocky islet or two on its outskirts.

A hill of bleached granite, a mile and a half from the lake, overhanging the river, showed us the environs to advantage. From hence we see, five or six miles inland, a line of hills, bare, high, and hoary, ranging parallel with the lake shore; the space between them and it, east and west, as far as the eye can reach, being a flat of gravelly sand, bearing mosses, with a few small firs, and now and then pierced with a knoll of granite. I found a deer's antlers lying on it ...

The Written Rocks, chiefly deserving notice as a point of reference, are seven miles west of the Black River. They occur in a cluster of islets close to a large headland of glaring red colour, like all this vicinity, and which are separated from the main by a narrow, not quite a mile long, and called "The Détroit."

The drawings which have given a name to this place are made by simply

---

[1]Dr John J. Bigsby (1792–1881) was secretary to the British Boundary Commission in the 1820s, kept a diary, and made sketches during his travels. His account *By Shoe and Canoe* was not published until 1850 (London) but, although there were obvious amendments made in some sections in the light of later developments, this extract includes a number of impressions from 1823.

detaching the dark lichens from the flat red surface of the rock. At their west end there is a good representation of an Indian firing at two animals; and not far off is a cross set up by some pious traveller, in memory of a drowned comrade. Here we saw snow again.

From the west angle of a picturesque, but small bay, close to the Written Rocks, commences a line of iron-bound coast a mile long, a dangerous pass for canoes in particular winds. It ends abruptly at Cape Verd, to form the important and picturesque bay of Nipigon ...

We slept, on the 23d of June, on the edge of a beautiful basin, two miles and a half south-east of the Mammelles Hills, and next morning plunged into a charming labyrinth of porphyritic, amygdaloidal, and sandstone islands, sheltered even from a hurricane. From time to time we saw the free lake at the bottom of a long vista of pine-clad islands; and we were glad, for the sake of change, to come suddenly (nine miles from camp) into open water, opposite Thunder Mountain, seven miles from us, at Point Porphyry.

This magnificent headland is a principal feature in Lake Superior, and forms the north-west end of Black Bay. This bay, I am informed by Captain Bayfield, is forty-six miles deep, and extremely woody. It receives a large river. The mouth of the bay is partially guarded by a great assemblage of woody, and for the most part low islands.

The high hills at the bottom of Black Bay are visible from its mouth, of course much depressed below the horizon. Several islands occupy the centre of the bay.

It is not always that a boat can cross from the Mammelles to Thunder Mountain; but on the 24th of June the lake was as smooth as glass. We greatly enjoyed the gradual unfolding, as we approached, of the various parts of the great basaltic cape.

Thunder Mountain is several miles long, and of considerable breadth, except at the point, where it descends into the lake in three shelves. The west half of its summit appears to be table land; but the eastern half is hummocky. About the middle of its south side an immense crater-like cavity, with steep woody acclivities, is scooped out of the body of the mountain. The precipices are largest and finest on the north-north-west, and extend in rude colonnades over two-fifths of the whole height, terminating in naked taluses, 300 to 400 feet high, which, however, do not reach the water, but are succeeded downwards by three woody terraces, the lowest of which touches the lake.

On the side of Thunder Bay I saw no precipices.

At and about the water-level, under Thunder Mountain, I saw a good deal of fixed limestone (without fossils), the only place where it is known to exist on the north shore of this lake.

Thunder Bay, to which we have now arrived, under the shadow of its great promontory, is round, and from ten to twelve miles across. Grand Point is its western angle; its margin is swampy on the west, but its bottom is here and there bold and precipitous.

The only islands in Thunder Bay are Welcome, Hare, and Sheep

Islands, opposite the mouths of the River Kaministigua, or Dog River, where Fort William is placed.

Pursuing our journey, we made for Welcome Island, and were soon afterwards safe in the fort.

On our return from the Lake of the Woods, as we passed Sheep Island in September, we were agreeably surprised to see lines of haycocks, and four haymakers in white shirt sleeves and straw hats. This sudden coming upon one of the prettiest sights of Christendom, which we had left far away, and long ago, made us quite tender, as the Indians say.

Fort William, once the depot at which every year were assembled the wintering partners of the North-west Company, with the proceeds of their trade with the Indians, is placed on the northern of the three channels of the Kaministigua River ("River of the Isles" – Chippewa) 800 yards from the lake. It is a large picketted square of dwellings, offices, and stores, all now in comparative neglect. It is 403 miles from the Falls of St. Mary, and forty-two miles north-east of the Grand Portage, as measured on the ice by Mr. Astronomer Ferguson (Boundary Commission).

I was much pleased at Fort William. Although its palmy days were gone, when the rich furs of the Arctic circle and the Rocky Mountains were brought here by the adventurous men who alone, in those days, could conduct a distant commerce with savages, attended by a crowd of clerks, trappers, and voyageurs, still some interesting remnants of these people were at the fort during my visit.

We all took our meals together in a plainly-furnished, low-roofed hall, capable of seating a hundred persons. We were placed a good deal according to rank, the seniors and leaders at the head of the table, and the clerks and guides, &c. of respectable but humbler grade, ranged down the table in order due.

The conversation was wholly north-west and Indian.

My *vis-à-vis* was a handsome young gentleman, but pale and wasted, who told me that he had been living upon his parchment windows, and a little tripe de roche, for three or four weeks, the fish and fowl having failed at his wintry quarters.

I asked him how the Company fed their fur collectors during the idle time of summer. "We give," said he, "to each family, if in the great plains, six bullets and a quart of powder, with which to kill the buffalo. If in the lake country, they subsist upon geese and fish, and receive a net and some shot, instead of bullets, with their gunpowder."

C 2   D i a r y   o f   M a j o r   J o s e p h   D e l a f i e l d
[*Printed in McElroy and Riggs,* The Unfortified Boundary, *pp. 400–2*]

Sunday, July 6 [1823]   Fort William is a very large establishment in decay. It is contained within pickets enclosing acres and at each angle of the square has a block house, and some bastions included for artillery pieces. Two or three small pieces were mounted. The entrance also had been strengthened since Lord Selkirk's attack upon them, when he made prisoner of the principal agent, forcing the gate with fixed bayonets, before they had time to close it, sending his men down the river in two batteaux covered with oil cloths to conceal them. The gate is now secured by a portcullis & block house. Since the coalition of the Hudson's Bay and the North West Companies, this post has become very insignificant & fast going to ruin. Mr. Stewart[2] is the present agent about to be relieved by a Mr. McKenzie [Roderick, Sr.]. Both gentlemen meet me at the landing & pay me the compliment of hoisting their flag in the fort upon my arrival. Establish my camp (or rather my men do) a little above the fort where there is a plain left for such purpose & also one below. The field above was always occupied by the North Men, or people who wintered in the Indian country, and the plain below by the Pork Eaters, or people who came from Montreal in the Spring to take down packs & returned in the Summer. In former times, Mr. Stewart tells me (in 1818) he had 800 North Men encamped here, and on such occasions there was always a constant riot in the camps, there being a sort of warfare existing. Breakfast and dine with Mr. Stuart and mess, in their large hall. We were 6 or 8 at table in a hall that was large enough to dine 300, and the whole establishment look'd as if it had been run in correspondence with the hall. There is a handsome square of ground neatly levelled, &c. within the pickets, the hall on one side facing the entrance, and empty warehouses and useless offices on the other three sides.

Purchase of the company a North Canoe as it is called, to enter the interior, my Mackinac canoe being pronounced too heavy, as no two men could carry her, & the portages only admitting of such an arrangement. The men do not like the canoe now purchased but it seems that they can state no objection, except that it had been for five years in the canoe-house and no one had chosen it. There were ten or twelve new ones and as many old to choose from, but it is the custom with the Canadians always to be dissatisfied. I have faithfully tried the experiment and find that by indulging them, by giving them all things they ask for, that still some imaganary want is contrived to grumble about, and that by a strict regimen in diet and work, they are not only better satisfied, but more civil and obedient. It is rare to find a bad tempered man among the voyageurs. There are careless of all things except their money, and in all other respects very like our seamen, with the gay and singing faculties always in use.

Have my North Canoe trim'd and the men employ two squaws to stitch the bouts with watap, which they do very neatly. There are always some poor squaws about the fort for such purposes, who are compensated by a little provision.

[2]Alexander Stewart (sometimes spelled Stuart by Delafield and others) had been an apprentice clerk of the North West Company in 1796. With the union of the companies he became a Chief Factor. After two years at Fort William he moved to Island Lake, then to Chipewyan, and finally to Moose Factory, from which post he retired in 1833. He died in 1840.

Monday, July 7. At Fort William, making arrangements for the interior. The men busy preparing the gum for the canoe ... The Compy have several fields planted & I noticed barley and potatoes. Corn will scarcely ripen to eat green. Peas will sometimes ripen. They have a fine stock of oxen, horses, cows and sheep, the two former now useless for want of employ ...

Wednesday, July 9th. At day-break, Mr. Stewart of the fort comes to my Marquee to take leave, being ready to depart on his voyage to Hudson's Bay. Shortly after a salute is fired on his departure, of three guns. The first gun was the signal for the chaunt of the Canadians, and straining their pipes and their nerves to the utmost he soon passed my camp, ascending the river to take the New Road as called,[3] intending to proceed to Lake Winnipec & thence to Hudson's Bay. Mr. Stewart left with much reluctance. He married a native & has a very large family, mostly girls. His wife being in low health, and it being impossible to take her and the children along, he leaves six children and a wife behind him, most probably never to meet each other again. I heard nothing said of their manner of parting, but from appearances about his quarters, two or three days previous, I can readily imagine that the same feelings were awakened, that (when expressed with the freedom and violence that these half-breeds are apt to shew) it is as cruel to understand as to witness. Two or three of his boys accompanied him.[4] It is the diminished importance of the post that induces the change and he seeks employ of the company at some fort where he can be more useful.

C 3 RODERICK MCKENZIE[5] TO ALEXANDER
MCTAVISH
[*P.A.C., H.B.Co. Records, B-149-a, Nipigon House Journals*]

Sturgeon Lake
April 1, 1827.
I take this opportunity to write you what I ought to have done before, having forgot to mention in the winter my intention of going to Montreal.

[3]The New Road was so called to distinguish it from the old Grand Portage route – hence the Kaministikwia or Dog Lake route into the interior.

[4]The contrast with the Roderick McKenzie family which had just moved into Fort William is striking. McKenzie's wife, Angélique, was an Indian from Nipigon. The McKenzie sons, Samuel, Benjamin, and Roderick, Jr., were all employed in the fur trade; one daughter married Antoine Dutremble before her parents left Fort William, another married James Anderson, later a Chief Trader with the Hudson's Bay Company, and still another taught at the Red River Academy. Angélique certainly did not remain in the Thunder Bay area, but accompanied her husband to the west, and for many years lived at Caberleigh Cottage, Red River. She is described by M.A. MacLeod, editor of the *The Letters of Letitia Hargrave* (Toronto, 1947), as an elegant old lady, although Mrs Hargrave did not concur in that opinion.

[5]Roderick McKenzie was listed in the Company records as Clerk A to distinguish him from another half-breed of the same name and the same rank in the same district at the same time. He was sometimes entrusted with the Nipigon post in the

I now think it my duty to inform you I intend to do so. I cannot think of wintering again in such a place as this (where we are so badly off with regard to living) on the present terms. My services to the Company give me some claim to an increase in salary, having served a regular apprenticeship with hardly any, and during the last five years I wintered at *this* place   I generally made good returns. It is but reasonable when I ask an increase in salary. I only wish to be placed on a level with clerks whose length of service – and situation in the country is only equal to my own, but as I have no hopes of this, my intention is to leave the country and to go to Canada by the first opportunity the Company can furnish me a passage.

C 4   DONALD MCINTOSH TO GEORGE KEITH
[*P.A.C., H.B.Co. Records, B-162-c, Pic Journals*]

Pic

January 5, 1828

I see by Mr. McKenzie's [Roderick, Sr.] letter to me of the 18th November that he has difficulties and uneasiness. Louis Ross deserted us last fall, and is now with the Americans, working as hard against us as he can. I apprehend much that we shall have many more instances of such conduct when our men will find that they will have two trips to perform every summer to the Long Portage.[6] He also writes me that Fanyant[7] told him last Fall that he would never again go to the Long Portage upon any conditions, much less his brother, for he would not undertake to assist his son[8] going to La Fleche last autumn. What can a person do with such vagabonds – displease them in the least and they will join our opponents, treat them ever so well, they cannot be depended upon when so near an opposition. It is my own humble opinion that it is bad policy to employ Indians as voyageurs in this quarter. It may answer well enough to voyage inland or along the Bay where they can have no intercourse with Indians who resort to the Sault or the Americans; I am led to make this observation from what I have experienced of these Indians whom we have employed at the Post. For instance, there is Peau de Chat who was a good Indian and a tolerable good hunter, but I perceive that he is getting very indifferent and losing all taste for it now – he has already imbibed

summer absence of Chief Trader McTavish and, in spite of dissatisfaction, was still in the district in 1832. He is supposed to have left for Lower Canada about that time. It is not clear whether this young man or Roderick McKenzie, Clerk B, who died at Batchewana in 1830, was the son of Chief Trader Roderick and Angélique McKenzie.

[6]Usually the name Long Portage was used in connection with the route north to Moose Factory, but the context here suggests that McIntosh was referring to the route from Pic to Long Lake.

[7]The Fanyant (or Fainiant) family appear in many of the records. One of the brothers, Jacques, was still employed on Outfit 1835, although continuing to complain and threatening to leave the service.

[8]This reference seems to be to Benjamin McKenzie who was in charge of the post at La Flèche for a time.

bad ideas which is the result of his frequent intercourse with Indians from the Sault & Michipicoten. I find he is not so easy dealt with now as when I first came here; he begins to put a higher value upon his services; neither himself nor his brother have hunted a skin since the winter set in.

C 5 THE BOUCHARD-FAINIANT MARRIAGE CONTRACT
[P.A.C., H.B.Co. Records, B-231-z, Fort William Miscellaneous Items]

Contract of marriage drawn up and executed between Louis Bouchard of the parish of Maskinongé in the province of Lower Canada, party of the first part, and Charlotte Fainiant of Fort William in the province of Upper Canada with the consent of her parents, party of the second part.

The said Louis Bouchard willingly binds himself and promises faithfully in the presence of God and the church to protect, cherish, and support the said Charlotte Fainiant as his lawful wife, in sickness as in health, during the term of his natural life, and, on the first good opportunity,[9] to have their marriage solemnized according to the custom of civilized countries, and, moreover, the said Louis Bouchard, in case the said Charlotte Fainiant survives him, willingly binds himself to transfer and bequeath for the exclusive use and benefit of the said Charlotte Fainiant and any children born of this marriage all the property – in cash, furniture or other goods – of which the said Louis Bouchard dies possessed, and in case the said Louis Bouchard dies without having fulfilled faithfully the articles and settlements mentioned above – to marry the said Charlotte Fainiant – he consents and willingly binds himself to bequeath and have paid to the said Charlotte Fainiant all the credit and cash that he now has or may have in the future in the hands of the honorable Hudson's Bay Company, and out of his wages the said Louis Bouchard consents to leave a tenth part in the hands of the Company each year he remains in their service for the express purpose of making a small provision for the benefit of his family in case of his accidental death.

Drawn up and executed at Fort William, Lake Superior District, on the afternoon of October 18, 1828, and signed – except for Louis Bouchard who, having declared that he was unable to sign his name, made his ordinary mark after the document was completed.

Witnesses	His
Benj. McKenzie	Louis X Bouchard
Duncan Haggart[10]	Mark

[9]Father Pierz made two visits to Fort William in 1838–9, but by that time the Bouchards had moved to Nipigon. It would appear that the "first good opportunity" presented itself at Nipigon in 1851 or 1852.

[10]Duncan Haggart was a carpenter in the Company's employ at various posts, particularly Michipicoten. The other witness was the Hudson's Bay Company clerk, son of the officer in charge at Fort William in 1828.

C 6 REPORT OF RODERICK MCKENZIE, CHIEF TRADER
[*P.A.C., H.B.Co. Records B-231-e, Reports of Fort William District*]

Fort William,
June 1, 1829

The number of Indians that came to this establishment last autumn were forty-nine men and boys, forty-four of whom got an average debt of thirty-two skins from us which they nearly paid in small furs such as martens, minks, muskrats, cats, bears, otters, and a few beaver. In former years, one-third of the return of the post used to be beaver, and it is now nearly reduced to one-sixth ...

The population of the district is in number forty-nine men, fifty-one women and ninety-five children, by far too many for the district and the furs about it. Of the above number, there are twelve men, eleven women and twenty-one children on American territories and frequent their establishment at Grand Marais, none of whom are good hunters with the Exception of the Spaniard and his stepson and an Indian called the Balte [?] the whole of them come occasionally to Lake La Flèche and give a few skins there.

C 7 LIST OF EMPLOYEES IN LAKE SUPERIOR DISTRICT, 1829[11]
[*P.A.C., H.B.Co. Records, B-129-e, Reports from Michipicoten*]

	Wife	Children
Louis Bouchard	1	–
Pierre Camargie	1	–
Thomas Cadiont	1	4
Hyacinthe Davilleau	1	–
Baptiste Deschamps	1	4
Joseph Dubois	1	2
Antoine Dutremble	1	–
Oliver Desautel	1	–
Joseph Fontaine	1	–
George Keith, Chief Factor	1	5
Roderick McKenzie, Chief Factor	1	7
Donald McIntosh, Chief Factor	1	5
John McIntosh, Clerk	1	1
Joseph La Perdrix Blanc	1	1
Jean Baptiste La Vallee	1	2
Jean Amable McKay	1	4
John Robertson	1	4

[11]This does not appear to have been a complete list. John Swanston, for example, was a clerk at the Pic in 1829–30. Roderick McKenzie, Clerk B, was in the district

C 8 McIntosh to Keith
[P.A.C., MG 19 A-30, Northwest Papers]

Fort William,
November 4, 1834

I doubt much if Hyacinthe Davilleau will re-engage for another term with any other person but yourself. However, I shall put the question to him once. If he expresses a wish to settle with you, I shall say nothing more on the subject to him. I shall of course despatch the winter Express about the beginning of the New Year as usual via Lake Nipigon by which conveyance I shall not fail to transmit lists of supplies required by the servants from Moose Factory next summer. In compliance with your request, I have deducted the skins restored by the American Fur Company from the outstanding balance of the Indian from whom they were robbed.

There are 12 new canoes at the place at present, of these there is only one made for a light canoe. The Governor [Simpson] writes me that eight canoes will be required next spring for the brigade from Montreal and requests that three of these be of superior finish as light canoes. Collin[12] will have to make two other light canoes in the month of April.

C 9 Robert McVicar[13] to Ramsay Crooks
[P.A.C., American Fur Company Records, Miscellaneous]

Argenteuil, Lower Canada,
April 25, 1839

Having learnt that you required an experienced Indian trader to superintend some of your establishments in the interior, I made application a few days ago to your agents in Montreal. In reply they stated that they had no instructions to engage any gentlemen of my experience and qualifications but advised me to address you on the subject.

I am a retired Partner of the Honble Hudson's Bay Company. After having successfully superintended extensive departments in the Indian

---

until midsummer 1829 when he went to the Sault to consult the nearest doctor (on the American side); he was replaced, as soon as the trip could be made, by Peter McKenzie. If such omissions were possible in the list of clerks without dependents, the list of workmen is also open to question. For example, Indians like the Fainiant brothers were not classed as employees in any permanent sense.

[12]Michel Collin claimed in an affidavit sworn in 1874 that he had been born at Fort William in 1799. Like his father, Antoine, he served the North West Company and then the Hudson's Bay Company as a canoe-maker. Later, Michel Collin acted as an interpreter, and at one time was in charge of the L'Orignal post.

[13]Robert McVicar (1799?-1864) was a Chief Trader in the Hudson's Bay Company service in the Athabaska District in the 1820s. He had retired to the Montreal area in the 1830s. Twenty years later he settled in the Thunder Bay region. His son George and his daughters Victoria and Christina all had prominent roles in the early history of Fort William and Port Arthur.

country for twenty years, during which period of time it was acknowledged by the Company that I was the most active and efficient officer in
the Service. My age at present is forty years. I am still in possession of
good health ... am capable of doing every justice to your company in the
management of any of your establishments in the Indian country and
willing to enter your Service at a moment's notice provided you require
my services and that you give me reasonable encouragement. I am personally acquainted with Mr. Franchere[14] who I am satisfied would consider me an acquisition to your concern. My habits are sober and active
and the most satisfactory reference as to character and talent will be
amply furnished by the most emminent individuals in the two provinces
of Canada should you feel inclined to accept of the tender I thus make
of my services to join your Company. In that case be pleased to oblige
me with a reply immediately on receipt, stating the extent of the salary
you will allow me for a term of years not to exceed six ...

C 10   GOVERNOR SIMPSON'S CONFERENCE WITH
THE FORT WILLIAM INDIANS, 1841
[Simpson, Narrative of a Journey round the World, v. 1, pp. 34–5]

I had an interview with a band of Salteaux or Chippeways, who had
been waiting my arrival near the fort. The chamber of audience was an
empty floor in a large store, on one side of which we took our seats, while
the Indians, in all about forty men, occupied the other, Mr. Swanston, the
gentleman in charge, acting as interpreter.[15] The ceremony of shaking
hands with every person having been punctiliously performed, the Indians
squatted themselves on the boards, excepting that their chief, known as
L'Espagnol, stood forward in the centre of the room. The orator, a tall
and handsome man, somewhat advanced in years, was arrayed in a scar-
let coat with gold epaulettes, the whole being apparently spick and span
new, for the bright buttons were still enveloped in their original papers;
and whether from the want of inexpressibles, or from a Highland taste,
the tail of his shirt answered the purpose of a kilt.

Having again shaken hands with the air of a prince, L'Espagnol de-

---

[14]Gabriel Franchère (1786–1863) was born in Montreal and served both the
North West Company and the American Fur Company. By 1834 he had settled in
the United States, and for the next five years acted as American Fur Company agent
at Sault Ste Marie, Michigan. He later went into business for himself, but proved
useful to the United States government in the negotiation of the Oregon boundary
in 1846.

[15]Narrative of a Journey round the World, published in London in 1847, seems
to have been ghost-written, presumably by Adam Thom, but based on the journal
Simpson had kept during the trip. The printed and the manuscript versions of the
events of May 28, 1841, are virtually the same. Simpson's journal, however, indicated that Michel Collin also acted as interpreter, and that all strangers, with the
exception of a missionary named Cameron who happened to be in Fort William at
the time, were "carefully excluded" from the meeting. The journal does not make
clear whether the exclusion was the result of the Governor's decision or the wish of
the Indians.

livered himself very fluently to the effect, that he and his followers, after passing from the British to the Americans, had soon found reason to reflect that they had always been well treated by the Hudson's Bay Company; that, with our leave, they would now settle near the fort, so that the smoke of their homes might thenceforward rise among Canadian forests; and that, being all Catholics, they should like to have a priest among them. This speech, at its conclusion, elicited a unanimous grunt of approbation from L'Espagnol's people. In reply, I briefly reminded them that, in defiance of one promise already given, they had kept wandering from place to place; offering them, at the same time, protection, if they should decide henceforward to remain here, but declining to interfere in the matter of their religion. With the help of a present, this answer appeared to satisfy them, and the high contracting parties separated.

C 11 CAPTAIN LEFROY'S[16] LETTER TO HIS SISTER,
MRS GEORGE RICKARDS
[*P.A.C. MG 24 H-25, Lefroy Papers*]

Fort William, Lake Superior,
May 30, 1843

Fort William is the first stage of my progress, a starting point for fresh departure. We reached it on Sunday night and here I have parted with the brigade of Hudson's Bay canoes, and shall follow them tomorrow at leisure in one of my own. A journey of one or two thousand miles alone is not so agreeable as a solitary walk before breakfast, but I should have been an encumbrance had I remained with them, and there is a sense of independence, of dignity, of unity in the other mode which is almost a compensation for the 'aching void' caused by want of society. Mr. McLean,[17] the officer in charge, was a person of intelligence and information beyond what one might expect from a man who has all his life been scraping beaver skins together at remote stations. He was too very kind and accommodating to me; the rest were young men. Rather than send a son of mine to become a clerk in the H.B. Company I would see him a day labourer at home. He would there be within the influence of civilization, would have society, would suffer (probably) less from privation, and enjoy as high an average of comfort. These boys all lose that, without a compensating prospect of acquiring wealth in the long run. They lose all religious influences and restraints, frequently marry squaws and return to civilized life as old men, if they do return, with habits that

[16]Captain John Henry Lefroy (1817–90) was at this time conducting a magnetic survey of British North America. From 1844 to 1853 he was in charge of the Toronto magnetic observatory, then returned to Britain where he rose to the rank of general. He was knighted in 1877.

[17]John McLean (1797?–1890) was a fur trader and explorer who accompanied Lefroy as far as Fort William. McLean was an employee of the Hudson's Bay Company from 1821 to 1845, when he retired to Guelph, Canada West, and wrote *Notes of a Twenty-Five Years' Service in the Hudson's Bay Territory* (W.S. Wallace, ed., Champlain Society, Toronto, 1932).

make it no longer enjoyment to them ... The voyageurs are rather timid sailors, although cheerful and indefatigable. On the Sunday that we arrived here [May 28] we were 21 hours, including some hours detention, between starting in the morning and arriving for the night, the last few hours were spent in a starlight paddle across the grande Traverse as it is called, a wide bay of an ill name. It is very pretty to see a number of canoes pressing straight forwards at a rapid pace; I think the circumstance of all the paddlers facing the direction they go in, instead of turning the back to it as in rowing, gives a peculiar effect of intentness, of intelligent will, to the movement. Then they strike up old French songs, more particularly in approaching a post, many of them very pretty, almost all curious.

C 12   LEFROY TO HIS MOTHER
[P.A.C., MG 24 H-25, Lefroy Papers]

Savannah River, en route
6th June, 1843
cont'd to 1st July

... I shall begin my Journal from Fort William, where the brigade remained two days, and I three. I wrote to Fanny [Mrs Rickards] from thence, but had not time to write to anyone else in the family. Fort William was the principal depot of the Northwest Company during its rivalry with the Hudson's Bay Compy, and is one of the largest establishments in the country. The wreck, rather, of one, for as the greater part of this Company's Furs go home from Hudson's Bay they have suffered it to fall to ruin. Ranges of sheds and stores are empty, and the old mess House, sixty feet long, in which so many hardy traders used to tell of their exploits, is now a shed of canoes, half a ruin. It is situated in a swamp, on artificial ground, without any advantage of scenery, although below it on the lake, and all the way above, the scenery is beautiful. There are a dozen or two Indian wigwams about it. An old squaw in one of them washed some things for me. How they can have emerged cleaner than they entered, as they certainly did, is a mystery to me. I mention it because the difficulty in paying her lay between giving tobacco or *tea*. May not commerce triumph when squaws drink tea, and Hindoos eat ice? Acting on Sir Geo. Simpson's recommendation, I took a canoe to myself, with a crew of two Indians, videlicet Lawrent Thewhawassin and Baptiste Sateka and four French Canadians, too small a crew for the load. We were supplied with provisions, and a small tent, for my use. The provisions supplied for me were biscuit, two hams! pork, and some fresh meat, with a bag of uncommonly bad potatoes, to this was added a small keg of Port wine, which I took reluctantly solely as a "medical comfort" to be used upon occasion. At the very first portage the fellow who carried it, tapped it, and probably the whole of them drank from it, thereby losing time to say the very least, so without making any remark, I pitched the keg into the middle of the stream as soon as we were embarked again, and so had done with it ...

It is amusing to see the sort of people one finds at these smaller posts, men whose lives have been spent in the woods, who have married Indians or half-breeds, who never read because they can get no books, have but a mail once a year (this year it has been left behind by mistake) and yet by birthright or prescription are Gentlemen ... They have a curious aversion to allowing their wives to be seen. At Fort Wm. for example, although there two or three days, I could not get a glimpse of the lady, nor was I more fortunate here.[18] It seems to indicate a painful consciousness that they are not of their own rank, or an equally painful, and very false idea, that a gentleman from the settlements would ridicule their deficiencies. To be the wife of an HB officer, and most of them now are married, is no enviable lot. They must follow them to the most savage and remote stations, and take part in all the privations they encounter.

C 13   ACCOUNT OF WILLIAM McBEAN[19] WITH THE HUDSON'S BAY COMPANY
[P.A.C., H.B.Co. Records, B-231-z, Fort William Miscellaneous Items]

William McBean Dr.

To the Honble Hudson's Bay Company for the following supplies to his daughter at the Post of Fort William, Lake Superior District. *Outfit 1843.*

				£	s	d	£	s	d
1843									
Sept. 11	To	6 yards printed	cotton	3	5				
		1¾ yard blue striped	"	1	1				
1844									
May 3rd.		5 yards tartan		7	1				
		2 yards blue Shrouds		9	–				
		1 – colored thread				3			
		2 common cotton Hand k/s		1	–				
		½ Dressed Mooseskin					–	4	6
		1 Sinew					–		2

[18]Lefroy identified the gentleman in charge at Fort Frances as Isbister, but he did not make any similar statement for Fort William. At that season, moreover, the Fort William agent might well have departed for Michipicoten, leaving a clerk in charge.

[19]A William Scott McBean, probably a son of C.F. John McBean, had been a Company clerk in New Caledonia as early as 1822. By 1824, reports of his ability were far from favourable, and he found his services no longer required by 1826.

<table>
<thead>
<tr><th></th><th>£</th><th>s</th><th>d</th><th>£</th><th>s</th><th>d</th></tr>
</thead>
<tbody>
<tr><td>Paid Thomas Lamphier[20] for board and lodging of his daughter from 13 Sept. '43 a 31st May, 1844</td><td></td><td></td><td></td><td>3</td><td>–</td><td>–</td></tr>
<tr><td></td><td>1</td><td>1</td><td>11</td><td></td><td></td><td></td></tr>
<tr><td>Advance 33⅓ p/c</td><td></td><td>7</td><td>4</td><td></td><td></td><td></td></tr>
<tr><td></td><td></td><td></td><td></td><td>1</td><td>9</td><td>3</td></tr>
<tr><td></td><td></td><td></td><td>£</td><td>4</td><td>13</td><td>11</td></tr>
</tbody>
</table>

Fort William
10th May, 1844

H[ector] McKenzie

C 14 JOURNAL OF CHIEF TRADER JOHN MCKENZIE
[*Printed in Thunder Bay Historical Society,* Papers, *1915, pp. 12–13*]

[Fort William] July 17, 1845. This morning the Schooner Whitefish dropped down into the Lake there not being sufficient water on the bar to admit of her being loaded in the river. The boats were afterwards sent off with the fish and other cargo. In her were sent down to Michipicoten Mr. Begg, who had been in charge in my absence. Michel Collin, assisted by John Finlayson, preparing the wood for five additional North Canoes ...

July 30th. 7 a.m. A canoe with 2 priests and 2 nuns arrived from Montreal, having left the former place on 20th. June. They resumed their journey at 2 p.m. and by them I forwarded letters to Lac la Pluie and Red River ...

Aug. 16. Dr. Rae[21] arrived from Michipicoton in a canoe with 5 men, which place he left on the 10th inst. leaving on the following day in a new canoe with 6 men ...

Aug. 21. The Barge with our annual outfit arrived from Michipicoton everything in good order ...

Aug. 27. The Indians receive their winter supplies and take their departure.

Sept. 1. Four North canoes arrived.

He seems to have been one of the independent traders who, from time to time, did business with the Company.

[20]Thomas Lamphier was the commander of the Hudson's Bay Company's schooner, *Whitefish*. He customarily wintered in Fort William from 1838 until the early 1850s and consequently had one of the few homes in the place.

[21]Dr John Rae (1813–93) was at this time resident surgeon at Moose Factory. In the following years he undertook several trips in search of Sir John Franklin and eventually discovered his fate.

C 15   FATHER CHONÉ[22] TO A SCHOLASTIC OF THE
SOCIETY OF JESUS
[*A.S.J.C.F., Nouvelles missions, v. 1, pp. 362–3*]

Manitoulin,[23]
February 24, 1848

Imagine the situation of these isolated tribes, deprived of links with other nations, lacking the resources of information out of which intelligence can develop, confined in far too narrow a region, completely absorbed in the problems of the present life. For a long time they believed themselves to be the only inhabitants of the earth; as a result, they have not become acquainted with any ideas but their own, and to become Catholics they must enter into an atmosphere completely foreign to them. The replacing of old thoughts by new ones is necessarily a lengthy task, and to achieve it there is no other means than the teaching of the missionary who, for a long time, will be limited to the explanation of a small number of truths. There is no land set aside for these tribes; they have none of the knowledge acquired from trade with civilized people, and there has been little development of their intelligence. Thus we have the difficulty involved in learning their language but, far more important, the difficulty of translating into their original idiom ideas completely foreign to it. Failing to take this into account, the Protestant sects who had the Bible translated by some métis of the country have produced a work that is not only imperfect but false, with the grossest errors.

C 16   THE AGASSIZ EXPEDITION TO LAKE SUPERIOR
[*Cabot's narrative in Agassiz*, Lake Superior, *pp. 60–61, 74, 82*]

July 7 [1848]   Michipicotin is the principal post of the Hudson's Bay Co. in this district. From it, the other posts are supplied, and the line of communication with Hudson's Bay passes through here. It is sixteen days' journey up Michipicotin and Moose Rivers to James' Bay.

The agent's house is a little one-story cottage, uncarpeted, unpainted, and, if my memory serves me right, even unplastered, with panelling and projecting beams of pine, coloured only by age; yet it is by no means uncomfortable in its aspect. The casings of darkened wood, the heavy beams

[22]Father Pierre Choné (1808–78) was a Jesuit misisonary, born in France, active in the Manitoulin District as early as 1844. He was the senior of three men who came to establish a mission at Pigeon River in 1848, and he later supervised the building of the Fort William mission and remained in charge there for many years. His name is variously spelled in the documents, Choni, Shonny, etc.

[23]This letter was written after the preliminary expedition to the northwest which Father Choné had undertaken in the summer of 1847. It is difficult to tell how much of his description applied specifically to the Indians he saw at Pigeon River and how much applied to those with whom he had several years' experience on Manitoulin Island.

of the ceiling and cornice, the ancient unpainted settle, and the wide niche for the capacious stove, now stowed away for the summer, had all a cosy and livable look. And Mr. Swanston, although he had inhabited this wild country in the service of the H.B.C. at one or another of their posts, over twenty years, yet for anything in his manner or appearance (unless it were that he wore moccasins instead of slippers) might have left the pavement of Fenchurch Street only yesterday.

The life at these posts is a very quiet, and doubtless, monotonous one; busy during the seasons when the hunters come for their supplies, or bring in their furs; at other times, with only the fish to be seen to when the nets are drawn in the morning, some to be cleaned and salted, if there is a good haul, and perhaps put into barrels to be sent to the Sault. An arrival from some other post, a straggling party of explorers for copper, and, above all, an occasional packet of newspapers from below – these are the great events. In such a life, a man changes slowly, but gathers moss in another sense than that of the proverb.

July 15, 1848   We passed the Slate Islands, high and blue, at the distance of seven or eight miles, and ran into a cove, at the bottom of which opened what seemed to be a well-ordered lawn, with balsam firs and larches judiciously disposed at intervals. In landing, the rich green grass turned out to be bear-berry, and the soil mere sand, which the bear-berry loves, but which accounted for the scantiness of trees ...

We made a long stay here, and some of the men amused themselves with lighting a fire, which unfortunatley ran along the ridge of the beach, and, in spite of their utmost exertions, marched with a broad front into the woods. It was an exciting spectacle, the eagerness of the flames to seize upon each fresh tree, winding around it like serpents, cracking and rushing furiously through its branches to the top, until every fragment of dry bark, lichen, &c. was consumed. The fire seems too dainty to take the more solid parts, and so, for instance, the bunch of upright cones at the top of the balsams, remains distinguishable in the forest as a blackened tuft. When we left, the fire was in full progress, and was probably stayed only by the swamp behind.

Nature, however, generally provides that no land that can be of much value to man shall be subject to this fate, for the heavily-timbered (and thus fertile) land of these latitudes is mostly too wet to burn, except the solitary birches, which if you set a torch to them, go off like rockets, but do not set fire to the other trees.

July 20 [1848, Fort William]   We hear traditions of banquets, and crowds of clerks, and armies of hangers-on of all kinds. But all this has disappeared. The trade has fallen off, the gross receipts being now, they say, only about £600 per annum; and moreover the Northwest is merged in its old rival, and all these troubles at an end, so that although the court-yard is surrounded by a palisade, and there is a barbican gateway, as at the Pic, yet these fortifications are not very formidable at present; the old block-house behind is falling to pieces, and the banqueting hall has probably been burnt up for firewood, at least, we saw nothing there that looked like it. Even the little flower-garden opening out of the stone-paved courtyard was overgrown with weeds.

The general arrangement here is much the same as at the other posts, only the soil (a yellowish sandy loam) being better, and the climate less severe, the cultivated ground is more extensive, and they have a herd of some thirty cows. Sheep also are kept here, and several of the dogs were in disgrace, with heavy clogs fastened to their necks, for sheep-stealing. As the pasturage on the other side of the river is much better than about the Fort, these cows *swim across* regularly every morning and back in the evening, a distance of two or three hundred yards. I was much surprised, the morning after our arrival, when the cattle were let out of the yard, to see a cow walk down and deliberately take to the water, of her own accord, and the whole drove following her, swimming with only their noses, horns, and tails showing above the water.

C 17 SUPERINTENDENT ANDERSON AND THE INDIANS OF LAKE SUPERIOR
[Anderson Papers; copy in M.T.C.L.]

Sept. 25th [1849] ... Mrs. [John] McKenzie does not appear to be of high standing or education though in so remote a situation from Society, is, of course, a personage of no small importance and being white commands that respect which would be due to a gentleman's wife in a more respectable sphere of life. Mr. McKenzie is like all other Indian Traders of the H.B. Co. very hospitable. We lived at his table on all the good things of the season, washing the eatables down with well filled flagons of wine and brandy. He offered us beds but we preferred our tent which was pitched in the middle of his beautiful green lawn. We however accepted a spacious room in which to hold our consultations with the Indians. The scenery about Fort William is very beautiful – the placid stream in front of the dwelling unwearyingly carrying the waters from its source hundreds of miles above us through all the Great Lakes to the sea – the wild fowl paddling and winging their way from the dread shot of their enemy, man, the tormentor of all living beings even himself inclusive ... [The] aborigines luxuriating in all the filth, want and misery which an indolent and improvident parentage could for ages bestow – are objects that cannot fail to rouse the mind of those unaccustomed with such scenes to deep and profitable reflection. Then in the distance you see the mountains on all sides rising 1000 feet above your head, these are the resort of hares and winged fowls for no one else, but crafty man, can reach their summit, and were not Divine Wisdom the creator, one might be disposed to say, they were made for no purpose.

Oct. 4th – Made an early start, the wind partly ahead and partly off land – we only made 25 miles and at 8 reached Mr. La Ronde[24] in charge of the Pic Trading station or Post. Mr. La Ronde received us very kindly, took us up to his house where we had a good supper and a good night's lodging, besides gaining much information on the subject of our mission. Among other things he informs us that the Nepegon Indians almost to a man have a plurality of wives and some to the number of *seven* – the man we met yesterday had three viz., *the old woman,* her daughter by a former husband, and again a *daughter of the second wife* by another father. Mr. La Ronde further informs on this subject that parents refusing to give their daughters in marriage are almost certain of being murdered by the party applying – murders for other trifling causes are not infrequent among those Indians – surely no pains should be spared to civilize them!

Oct. 5th – Left Mr. La Ronde's at a quarter before 8 and soon after were enabled to stretch our sail to a side wind; therefore, did not stop to breakfast but proceeded passing Le Ance or La Bouteille – encamped in another nice sandy cove. In the course of this day got two fine trout from an Indian and our steersman caught two others, though his line was only out occasionally and our guide shot two fishy ducks, but all went to pot together, pork, fish, ducks, potatoes and iron cakes, and when cooked the pot generally upset on the stones to cool for hasty mastication.

Oct. 6th – Our Crew rather lazy and we did not embark until half past seven – we soon came in sight of the *Otter's Head* – which is a stone some two hundred feet above the base (a high mountain) on which it stands and at the distance appears like a huge chimney towering far above the tops of the highest surrounding trees – it may be perhaps 30 feet square but quite perpendicular until within a few feet of its summit when a projecting piece of the rock gives to the fertile imagination the appearance of an otter's head. Passing on and rounding a point we were hailed by an Indian who with his wife and family of seven children were for the time located on a rock revelling in all the luxuries of stinking fish and other like fragrances. This man has *only* one wife, but, sad to tell, our guide informs us that to possess her he killed his elder brother whose wife she was and her son now threatens to return the compliment by killing his stepfather – shortly before meeting this family, from whom we got three trout, we had passed Puc-kus-wah Sr-be and went into the most beautiful spoon shaped basin to the falls, which come tumbling down a tremendous chasm in the rocks. It hastens down with the wildest speed conceivable,

[24]Louis Laronde, who died in 1868, had been a Company servant since the early 1820s. He claimed descent from the Louis Denis de la Ronde who had been in command at Chequamegon on the south shore of Lake Superior in 1727. Although the Company found him useful it could never agree to his rising above the rank of clerk, and was reluctant to grant him pension rights. The one point on which all his superiors agreed, however, was his knowledge of the Indians.

as if to escape the threats of the over hanging precipice on either side – immense rocks have fallen into it from the height, against which, in its furious progress to the placid basin below, it dashes headlong throwing its spray all around and creating rainbows innumerable. In short, the whole scene is grand beyond description and fitted only for the pencil of artist or the pen of the poet. Continuing our route, the wind blowing very fresh from the land we were obliged to hug the shore and not wishing to avail ourselves of an early encampment we proceeded until dark when we were compelled to put in to a basin opposite to the east end of Michipicoten Island. The harbour is good but had to make our bed on boulders. Having dined heartily on fat pork fried, English rum and underdone cakes, I spent a miserable night from heart burn.

C 18   FATHER FRÉMIOT AND THE INDIANS OF
LAKE SUPERIOR[25]
[A.S.J.C.F., Nouvelles missions, v. 1, p. 381; v. 2, pp. 1, 26, 105, 168, 195, 205]

Pigeon River,
July 24, 1848.

... About noon we reached this other Jordan that waters our promised land. But there were no Jebusites to contend with, to dispute with us the peaceful possession of the country. So we set foot on this land, and what do we see? Here and there, a few unfinished houses, then, on a height of land in the centre, near the river bank, a wooden church which formerly lacked only a roof, but which now falls piece by piece; a little farther along was a house – if you would like a one-roomed cabin which lets in the light of heaven through the openings in the roof. That is the house we are to occupy. A missionary, Mr. Pirse,[26] had it built along with the church, five years ago. Then, frightened off by all the difficulties that

[25]In his series of letters to recipients usually identified only as "a Jesuit priest" or "the Superior in America" or "the Provincial in Paris," Father Frémoit touched upon a number of aspects of his work and also repeated much material for the benefit of his various correspondents. The only one of these identified in this series of letters was Father Micard, the superior of the Jesuit Seminary at St Dé in France, to whom the letter of February 2, 1851, was addressed.

[26]Father Francis Pierz and Father Frederic Baraga (who became the Bishop of the new Roman Catholic Diocese of North Michigan in 1853) were both of Slovenian birth. It was Baraga's influence that sent Pierz to Fond du Lac and then to establish a mission at Grand Portage in 1837. From this centre he attempted to serve the western Thunder Bay region as well. Political pressures seem to have been successful on two occasions in removing him from the sensitive border area, although his own preference was to work among the Ojibways rather than the Ottawas to whom he was sent on both occasions. He met Father Choné at La Pointe in 1847 and seems to have negotiated some agreement with him concerning the Grand Portage area, to which he did not return.

beset him here, he abandoned the place to go to Sault Ste Marie; he is now at Arbre Croche, a mission to the Ottawas on Lake Michigan.

Fort William,
January, 1850

Instead of a little birch-bark chapel where the wind played as it would, making mock of the blazing stove, we have had for several weeks now a fine wooden one, at least a little comfortable. Instead of a little spruce-wood cross, we have a fine iron one, supported by an imposing golden ball ...

How should we go about [the building of the chimney]? There were no bricks, not even any stones except the rocks or pebbles along the shore. We began by driving into the ground four poles the height of the projected chimney; we had to take great care to leave at the top a considerable space that would not be filled in until the chimney was finished. These four poles, bound together by cross bars six inches apart, form a kind of pyramidical ladder. Such is the frame of our chimney. To cover the skeleton we use clay mixed with sand. Over it we placed a little roller of hay which we pressed and worked with our hands until the clay was thoroughly mixed together. A second layer was then applied to first, then a third to the second. And in this way the whole chimney rose to its full height – one solid, compact mass.

Fort William
June 21, 1850.

The procession [Corpus Christi] was postponed to the following Sunday because of the bad weather. On this day, two quite simple altars of repose were set up. Ten fine spruce trees decorated the interior of the house of prayer, while others cast their shadows over the façade and rimmed the open place at the entrance as well as the paths which led to the altars. Since almost all of my congregation lacked any knowledge of what a procession was, I found no painless method of organizing even a moderately disciplined march. However, for the same reason, no matter how simple was our religious ceremony in the midst of the forest, it was a magnificent spectacle for the Indians; they all joined in admiration of it.

Sault Ste Marie
February 2, 1851

Already our glowing hopes are beginning to be realized. Last summer two families from Chippewa River in Michigan came to establish themselves here; their relatives – more than hundred in number – are coming to join them next spring. One other circumstance making a great number of Indians flock across the border is the measure adopted by the American government with the purpose of forcing beyond the Mississippi all those Chippewas who remain east of the river. This compulsory emigration is expected to take place next summer and it is to save themselves from it and the misery that will inevitably follow in its wake that the Indians of *La Pointe* and several from *Fond du Lac* wish to take refuge on English territory. But according to the clauses of the treaty which the English government has just concluded with the Chippewa of Upper Canada concerning the sale of Indian lands, the emigrants can only establish themselves on the specified reserves conceded in perpetuity to the Indians. Now the mission of the *Immaculate Conception* [at Fort William] is one of the largest, and the only one near the American border at the western end of Lake Superior. A large group is going to be driven there by the force of circumstances, and we will be able, with the grace of God, to recruit a good number to swell the decimated ranks of our little flock.[27] Recently I baptised, at the *Immaculate Conception* mission on New Year's Day, the first of these future neophytes. I opened the year 1851 with the baptism of a woman from Nipigon, a Hudson's Bay Company post six days march north of Fort William – from which hope to gather more sheep for our fold.

Fort William,
December 3, 1851

Nomadic life is the great obstacle which prevents our dealing with the majority of the Indians in any constant manner. This is especially true for the unbelievers who – for a month or two or even as little as a week or two in the entire year appear in the vicinity of the Forts – and the rest of the time live scattered thoughout the forest. This is even true to a certain extent for the Christian converts who are obliged to be away a good part of the year ... It is necessary to reach and instruct these poor people, not only family by family but individual by individual for the Indian independence of mind (or egotism) is so great that not even their nearest relations can give them advice on this matter [that is, becoming Christian] yet, on the other hand, regard for public opinion has sufficient influence that, if the head of the family is indifferent or hostile to religion, the other members of the family will not venture to take it up ...

An unbeliever from Fort William whom I believe to be nearest the truth in his statement, has made me see where I was mistaken in my idea that he had passed the age where he could keep both his wives. "Formerly," he told me, "a trader tried to make me promise to keep only one wife. I reminded him that the Pale Faces also had several wives on the sly and that I could give him more than one example." Another unbeliever from Fort William has already acquired four wives and is planning, in the spring, to add a fifth who has come from Rainy Lake. In retaliation, one of his former wives, who feels herself set aside, has left him ... Add to polygamy

[27]The letters earlier in the year described the effects of epidemic upon the Fort William Indians, and the concern among the Indians that the establishment of the mission and the tendency to settle in one place had caused the epidemic.

adultery and the whole shameful licentious paraphernalia, the common usage of magic potions to prevent conception or to destroy its effect ...

When all our Indians go to Isle Royale[28] for the fishing season you will find only a few women and perhaps one man who do not drink heavily ... One Indian sold his pipe for a dollar and rushed to spend it for brandy. Without counting what has been sold illegally on board ship, two Americans in dealing with our Indians (at Isle Royale) within the space of two or three months, have dispensed – would you believe it? – not less than two barrels of brandy, each containing 36 gallons ...

Lake Nipigon
March 19, 1852.

It is a Catholic who at the moment is in charge of the post. He is Louis Denis de Laronde, a Canadian by birth, whose father came from France. His daughters – who speak Indian far better than French or English but understand both languages – are a great help in singing the hymns. Besides the clerk, there are just six workmen here – two Scottish Protestants and four Catholics, of whom one is Canadian, one half-breed, and two Indians. Of these six men, three of the Catholics are married and they, with the clerk's family, make up the total of 27 people in the Fort. Add to their number 7 adults and 3 children, dependents of two hunters recently killed, who have taken shelter at the Fort.

Isle Royale,[29]
July 2, 1852

Some of the men about the fort [Nipigon] take care to be on the wharf to receive the bales of fur and carry them to the hall where the Indians are received. This means that the Indians do not have to climb the thirty or forty steps to the Fort with their furs. They arrive without anything more to carry than their pipes; they are usually in full regalia, having taken care to dress up before landing.

The trader or clerk shakes hands with each of them, gives each a twist of tobacco, then the products of all their hunts and all their labours are counted in their presence. Sometimes they are carrying three or four bearskins, an equal number of foxes, of wolves, beaver, muskrat, etc. This is the money with which they buy their clothing and ammunition. However, the women have remained at the water's edge, and after greeting each other affectionately, they are sent to prepare a lodging and it is only later that they will go to the Fort, if indeed they appear there at all.

[28]Father Frémiot here seems to put the blame for the conditions he describes almost equally on the nomadic character of so many of the Indians and the policy of the U.S. government, which controlled Isle Royale.

[29]Although Father Frémiot made frequent trips to Ile Royale, this particular occasion differed from the others. He had been ordered to return to Sault Ste Marie, his stay at the western end of Lake Superior over, and was awaiting transportation. Almost his entire letter dealt with the Indians of Nipigon whom he had just left.

C 19 PETER JACOBS'[30] DESCRIPTION OF THE INDIAN MISSION
[*Jacobs,* Journal, *p. 19*]

May 27, 1852. A little way up the Fort William River there is a Roman Catholic Mission which we visited, where some of the Iroquois went, made signs of the cross, and said a few prayers. The priest has gathered about 15 families of Indians; he speaks a little English and tolerably good Indian. He was busy in raising the frame of a chapel and will likely, in process of time, make a good mission of this; though now newly established, [it] is getting on wonderfully, and the Indians are living in their wigwams.

C 20 THE REV. JOHN RYERSON[31] TO THE REV. ENOCH WOOD[32]
[*Ryerson,* Hudson's Bay, *pp. 15–19, 21*]

Fort William, July 3rd, 1854.

... I baptized the infant daughter of Mr. McKenzie, the "chief trader" of Michipicoton station,[33] his lady and children not having yet gone down, he having but lately removed to that place. Mrs. McKenzie requested me to *re*-baptize another of her children, who had been baptised by a Roman Catholic priest – no other minister being accessible. But this I was compelled to decline doing, not believing *re*-baptism lawful, although the baptism had been performed by a person not duly authorized, or even by a false teacher of religion ...

[30]Peter Jacobs was an Indian convert to Methodism who became a missionary in the Lake Superior area, as early as 1838. After his ordination he returned to the Rainy River region 1844–9, and in 1852 made the tour through the Indian country that is described in his journal. In the 1857 Methodist Church *Minutes of Conference* the question was asked: "What persons who were in full connection with the Conference have now ceased to be recognized as ministers among us?" The answer was – "William Haw, Edwy M. Ryerson, Peter Jacobs."

[31]The Rev. John Ryerson (1800–78) was born in Norfolk County, Upper Canada, of Loyalist parents. Like several of his brothers, he was ordained into the Methodist ministry in which he served for over fifty years. He kept records of his missionary tour to the Hudson's Bay Company territories in 1854 which were later published.

[32]The Rev. Enoch Wood (1804–88) had been born in England but had served in British North America from the time he entered the Wesleyan Missionary Society in 1825. He was President of the Wesleyan Conference at the time Ryerson wrote him of his experiences in the north.

[33]This would seem to be a reference to the family of Chief Trader Peter McKenzie, who had first served in the Lake Superior District as a clerk in 1829. Born in Scotland, McKenzie became a Chief Trader and was in charge of the New Brunswick (Missanabie) post from 1847 to 1849, when he was transferred to Fort William. He retired from the company in 1878. He was the fourth McKenzie to have charge of the Fort William post since 1821, being preceded by Roderick, Sr., in the 1820s, Hector in the early 1840s, and John in the late 1840s.

Monday morning, the 25th, [of June] in company with Messrs. Brooking[34] and Salt,[35] in a bark canoe, I went on a hunting and fishing excursion to the mouth of the "River Du Currer"[36] a place seven miles distant from Fort William. In the morning when we started, the wind was favourable, but we had hardly got out of the river [Kaministikwia] on the lake, when the wind shifted round and came strongly against us, so that although we used our paddles and oars with all the *skill* and application we were capable of, yet we did not reach the place of our destination until after one o'clock which was two hours and a-half from the time we started. This was my first experiment in the business of hunting and fishing; and but for my fish-line breaking, and my gun missing fire, when the one should have showed itself a true conservative and the other a real progressionist, I should have caught a fish and killed a patridge – but to my great disappointment, just as I brought a large speckled trout to the top of the water, my fish-line broke and away went the trout, line, hook, and all: and after displaying some skill in hunting, as I think, I came near a partridge, which was pointed out to me by Mr. Brooking, who, by-the-bye, made as great a fuss about it as an Indian would have made in meeting with a drove of buffaloes. Well, I presented Mr. Salt's rifle in due order at the bird, which was not more than two rods from me, but the gun missed fire, and snapped the second time, when the bird walked off – not deigning to fly – with as much indifference as though I and my gun were unworthy of its notice.

The River Du Currer is about as large as the River Humber, near Toronto. Some twenty rods from the mouth there is a fall in the water of about twenty feet. The fall is not perpendicular, but nearly so, presenting to the eye a large surface of white foam, which, at a distance, has the appearance of a bank of snow. At these falls, water-power to any amount could be obtained. The land for a large distance round is very rich, and no doubt could be most profitably cultivated. At 6½ p.m. we left our fishing-ground to return home, where we arrived safely at 8 o'clock. This was my first and probably will be my last fishing and hunting-day.

Wednesday the 28th, I availed myself of the kind offer of J. Willson, Esq., Custom-House officer, at Sault Ste. Marie, who was on an exploring tour along the North Shore of Lake Superior ... to a seat in his boat, to visit the Roman Catholic Mission Establishment. This is beautifully located on the bank of the river, about a mile and a half above Fort-William depot. I called on the Rev. Mr. Shuny, the superintending priest of the

---

[34]The Rev. Robert Brooking (1813–93) was born and educated in England. He served as a missionary on the Gold Coast for seven years (1839–46), then, forced to leave West Africa for reasons of health, he came to various northern and western mission posts in British North America.

[35]The Rev. Allan Salt (1818–1911), born at Massisauga near Belleville, was early adopted by the Rev. William Case, missionary to the Indians. Ordained in 1854, Salt devoted his life to missions among his own people, principally in the Parry Sound District. The Public Archives of Canada has his notebooks for the years 1865–1906.

[36]Current River, flowing into Lake Superior just north of modern Port Arthur.

Station, who received and treated us with courteous respect. I had an half-hour's conversation with Mr. Shuny, and learned from him that it had been between three and four years since the commencement of the mission;[37] that he himself assisted by one or two men, part of the time, had built the church and parsonage; that there are now between twenty-five and thirty dwelling-houses in the village, occupied by the Indians, and that Indian families were constantly coming to the station for the purpose of building and settling in the village. The church is comfortable, and, for the place, a fine building. It is built of logs and neatly clap-boarded, it is about 30 by 40 feet in size, (with the addition of a large vestry at the back end,) and will accommodate from 200 to 300 persons. The parsonage is a neat house, 30 by 36 feet on the ground, and one story high. It is built of logs, clap-boarded, and painted white. The building of these two substantial structures, with a number of out-houses &c., was accomplished principally by Mr. S.'s own hands, and during the same time he performed his ordinary work as priest, besides assisting in the day school, visiting it twice every day, catechising and instructing the children. Mr. S. has only been eight or nine years among the Indians, yet speaks their language fluently, and preaches in it with great ease. His bed-room is also his workshop, study and sitting-room. In one corner of the room is the bed, consisting of a pillow and two buffalo skins; in another corner of the room are wide shelves, holding his carpenter and joiner tools, and in another corner is his desk, writing-apparratus, and a few books; in another part of the room a box, stool, and two chairs. I remarked to our brethren, that such laborious and self-denying zeal was worthy of a better cause than the spreading of Popery, and that it was humiliating to ourselves, contrasted with the exertion and success of some of our own missionaries, who seemed to measure out their work, both with regard to kind and extent, with as much care and exactness as a Jew would measure silk velvet. I recollect one missionary, if not more than one, who objected to teaching a day-school on the ground that it was not quite canonical, and was beneath the dignity of the ministerial office; that he was called to be a minister, and not a school-teacher. One thing is certain, that the Roman Catholic missionaries throughout these extensive regions, in zeal, in labour, self-denial, and in success in *their work*, are much, very much before us, and unless we bestir ourselves with very much more united, earnest, and *persevering* exertion than what we yet have, this whole country will be overspread and hedged in with the briars, thorns, and hedges of popery.[38]

[37]Slight errors in the reports of what Father Choné said to Ryerson may be ascribed to some difficulty in conversing in English. The account would appear to be factual, in so far as it recorded what Ryerson saw, rather than what he was told.

[38]Compare Father Frémiot's comment on the austerity of the home in which McCullough, a Presbyterian mine superintendent on Isle Royale, was living in 1849: "How can one complain about the poverty of those who devote themselves to the conquest of souls, when lovers of gold do not hesitate, in the uncertain hope of finding a base metal, to subject themselves to such privations?" (A.S.J.C.F., Nouvelles Missions, v. 1, p. 431).

At 11 o'clock [July 2] we again had divine service. Mr. Hurlburt[39] preached and led the religious exercises ... In the afternoon Mr. Salt, accompanied by Mr. Hurlburt, again visited and held a meeting with the band of pagan Indians on the other side of the river. All the Indians in the encampment attended the meeting, and, besides, there were present two or three Roman Catholics and other Indians, who had been called to the meeting by the party belonging to the camps. The brethren say that the Indians listened with great attention to their address, and manifested a still stronger desire than the last Sabbath, to be taught the *"new way"* ...

C 21   BROTHER LEISCHNER[40] AT THE FORT WILLIAM MISSION
[Woodstock Letters, *v. 37, pp. 398–9*]

He could cut a swath in anything, but another had to follow to remove the wreckage and put matters into shape. The sight of plastered or painted walls never appealed to him. He would drive a spike into anything, whereon to hang his coat and hat. He was of the pioneer, Dan Boone type of man ...

It [Fort William in 1853] was a wilderness of a place and the good Brother was in his element, clearing the ground and putting up the rough buildings of a missionary station among the Indians. Father Shoney would often ask him when engaged in such work: "Brother, did you say your beads?" and the answer always came back. "Do you think I could stay here without saying them?" The good Brother and the Indians got along splendidly together. He was invariably kind to them, so kind in fact that at times there was hardly anything left for the Fathers.

C 22   FATHER DU RANQUET[41] TO HIS SUPERIOR
[Woodstock Letters, *v. 30, pp. 182–3*]

Fort William
[n.d., likely about 1855]

Really I cannot understand our poor missions – about 2000 Indians distributed among five posts and three missionaries. Each of the latter

[39]The Rev. Thomas Hurlburt (1808–73) was a member of a family in which five brothers became Methodist ministers. He had been a missionary on Lake Superior chiefly in the Pic region from 1837 to 1842 and had occasionally held services at Fort William during those years. In 1854, when he was travelling with Ryerson, he was on his way to Norway House to assume new duties there.

[40]Brother Dominic Leischner (1814–1908) was born in Alsace and came to North America in 1848. From about 1852 to 1861 he was at Fort William as gardener, forester, cook, etc. He was later transferred to Guelph, where he delighted in battle with the local Orangemen, then to various Quebec locations. This obituary was unsigned.

[41]Father Dominique du Ranquet (1813–1900) was a member of a French noble family, one of five brothers who all became Jesuit missionaries. He came to Canada in 1842 and immediately began the study of Ojibway. In July 1852 he was sent to

ought to have 650 souls, say 400 adults at the outside for his share. What comparison with the 10,000 which each missionary has under his charge in the missions of Indian and China! And even these 400 souls it seems impossible to reach. If it be really impossible, why persist in going after them, but if it be possible to bring to this small number the help of religion, would it not be better to take the means of doing so, or else leave the field to others? Would not it be the surest means to have a missionary reside at each of the stations – Nipigon Lake, Pic, Long Lake, Michipicoten, etc.? This would make seven or eight posts to be thus occupied from s.s. Marie to F.W. A Superior of all these missions should visit them at least twice a year. This would make some 10 missionaries for 2000 souls, or one for each 200. Is it not folly to dream of such a plan?

C 23   FATHER POINT'S[42] REPORT ON THE FORT WILLIAM MISSION, SEPTEMBER 15, 1859 [A.S.J.C.F., B-1-8, Indian Missions]

The superior [Choné] has excellent qualities – a strong will, an excellent heart, courage, perfect punctuality. His rigid standards for himself and for others, impose a severe test upon his own conduct, and too severe a test upon that of others. Always, the basis of his actions is zeal for the Order. He does not know how to give way, to console, or to encourage: he strives for too much austerity and economy, and even mortification in the communal life of the mission. Firmness and a certain severity are necessary in dealing with the Indians, but he has an appearance of nervous irritation that nullifies the effect of soothing words. His is a reign of fear, not of love, especially if one judges from his general instructions. But he loves his work and he loves the Indians. When he deals with individuals, he can be patient, obliging, and charitable. In order to appreciate Father Choné, it is necessary to know him very well; to be useful to him, an assistant has to refrain from exaggerating the wrongs he suffers, and has to speak from the heart. Sharp unfeeling criticism will achieve nothing.

For his part, Father Ferrart[43] is somewhat incisive and even biting in his speech. Inevitably, both men suffer, and it is fortunate that Father Ferrart has two missions to visit, and he will not be for long at the residence.

Fort William to replace Father Frémiot and, with the exception of one year at Garden River near Sault Ste Marie, he remained in the Thunder Bay area until 1877 when he became Superior on Manitoulin Island.

[42]Father Nicholas Point (1799–1868) was born in France and came to Canada in the 1840s. He was supposed to take charge of the Fort William mission in 1855, but illness forced him to turn back at the Sault. In spite of failing health, he was counted on for particularly delicate investigations. He was the visiting Superior in 1859 when he presented his report on the western missions.

[43]Father Martin Férard (1817–91) seems to have been only briefly at the Fort William mission in the late 1850s. By the early 1870s he was Superior on Manitoulin Island, and later retired to Montreal.

C 24   RICHARD SINGLETON, THE FIRST SETTLER?
[*Thunder Bay* Sentinel, *May 26, 1883*]

With the death of Richard Singleton, the oldest pioneer of this country is removed from amongst us.[44] A young man seeking his fortune in a wild, desolate country, he came here first in the year 1849. Searching for the hidden riches which have since been and are still being unearthed, the country had a fascination for him as it has had for hundreds since then; and he toiled on and plodded in the belief that his labors would one day be rewarded. Mr. Halcrow Humphrey,[45] who is now residing in this town, tells how, in February, 1851, he found Singleton, then a hearty man in the prime of life, at Prince's Bay. In that and the previous year Dr. Rae and party were diligently searching the northern icebound regions for traces of that famous but unfortunate explorer Dr. Franklin. Humphrey, who is an Englishman, was sent by the doctor with despatches for the British Admiralty. This was in January, 1851. Leaving Fort Simpson ... he arrived with his guide in the following month on the shores of Lake Superior, and skirting Thunder Bay met the first white man during his long weary travel ...

[44]Singleton's stay in the district was much shorter than that of many Company employees. Like Laronde, Bouchard, and others, Singleton married an Indian girl. With the decline of mining on Lake Superior he moved to Bruce Mines, then returned to the Landing in 1868. Among the signers of the Indian petition to Sir John A. Macdonald in 1886 was an Alex Singleton.

[45]Halcrow Humphrey came from the Shetland Islands and was employed by the Hudson's Bay Company as a labourer as early as 1842. In 1846–7 he was employed in the Cumberland House district. After the failure of the first attempt to find traces of the Franklin expedition, he asked to be permitted to retire to Canada. He may have been asked to carry despatches on this trip; he certainly travelled through the Thunder Bay area in which he later made his home.

D. THE COMMERCIAL REVOLUTION
AND THUNDER BAY, 1855-70

D 1 WILLIAM EYRE[1] TO HENRY LABOUCHERE[2]
[P.A.C., RG 7 G-1, v. 141, pp. 311–12, 318]

Montreal,
January 12, 1857

There appears to be little doubt that the intention of the United States Government has been for some time past turned in the direction of the Red River Settlement but with what views is not clear. It is evident also that the large half breed population of which the settlement on the Red River is composed, is not easy to govern, and that the presence of the military there would aid the local authorities, and for other reasons doubtless be welcome. But whether these considerations are sufficient to overrule the objections to the Establishment of a Military Post in so remote and isolated a position, which for nine months of the year is cut off from the rest of the world it is for you to judge ...

All communication between Lake Superior and the Red River is now (according to Sir George Simpson) quite impracticable for any body of troops. A few individuals might go, but not any force. The tribe of natives who used to serve as voyageurs and have canoes, and afford assistance in passing the numerous swamps and difficulties that interpose on that route do no longer exist as traders.

If a force were sent from Canada, it would be decidedly better to send them by sea.

D 2 CASIMIR GZOWSKI'S[3] APPLICATIONS FOR TIMBER LICENCES
[P.A.O., Lands and Forests Department Papers, Applications for Timber Licences]

Kaministiquia River, Lake Superior   Rec'd March 4, 1857
Gzowski et al.[4]

Application #25

Commencing on the northerly bank of the river Kaministiquia at its mouth, thence up said River a distance of twenty miles and embracing

[1]Sir William Eyre (1805–59) was Commander-in-Chief of the forces in Canada from 1856 to 1858, and served as administrator of the united province during the absence of Governor Head in 1857.

[2]Henry Labouchere (1798–1869) made his first reported speech in the British

with a depth back of two miles & a half on said southerly [*sic*] side an area of fifty square miles.[5]

Application #26

Commencing on the southerly bank of the above River at its mouth thence up said River a distance of twenty miles and embracing with a depth back of two miles and a half on said southerly side an area of fifty square miles.[6]

D 3   JOHN SHEPHERD[7] TO LABOUCHERE
[*P.A.C., RG 10, G-1, v. 141, p. 291*]

London,
March 16, 1857

I mentioned to you that we had received letters informing us that Mr. Kennedy[8] and certain other parties had gone on from Canada to the Red River for the purpose of creating disturbance and discontent and stirring up the people of that settlement in opposition to the civil authorities ... One of the objects of Mr. Kennedy and his party is to endeavour to renew and stimulate rivalry in the fur trade, and if through their means the half breed population and the Indians should be unhappily led again to their old practices, the excessive indulgence in the use of spirits cannot fail to be the consequence and thus, the whole country may soon become involved in conflagration and bloodshed ... A spark may easily set the whole

House of Commons in 1828 on the subject of civil government in the Canadas. From 1855 to 1858 he was Secretary of State for the Colonies in the Palmerston ministry.

[3]Casimir Gzowski (1813–98) was born in Russia, son of a Polish Count. He entered the Russian army, but joined in the Polish revolt of 1830 and was exiled as a result. After eight years in the United States he came to Toronto in 1841 and was employed as an engineer with the Public Works Department of the Province of Canada. In the 1850s, after leaving the government service, he organized the firm which secured the contract for the building of the Grand Trunk from Toronto to Sarnia. His business interests extended into a number of other fields, including lumbering in the north.

[4]Other licence applications make clear that his partners in these enterprises were Walter Moberly and David Macpherson, also associated with him in his railway projects.

[5]A corrected and clarified version of this application appears in the following year – dated May 20, 1858, #103 for a tract 25 miles by 2 miles on the northern bank, #104 for a tract 20 miles by 2.5 miles on the southern bank.

[6]There is no evidence that Gzowski was aware in 1857 or in 1858 that he was applying for land previously granted to Peau de Chat and his band as a Reserve.

[7]John Shepherd was Governor of the Hudson's Bay Company for a brief period, 1856–8. E.E. Rich identifies him with the generation in power since 1821, disappearing from the scene by mid-century.

[8]Sir George Simpson, in his letter to Shepherd on March 14, identified William Kennedy and Allan McDonald as leaders in the movement to annex Company lands to Canada.

Indian population into a state of restlessness and excitement, and it would be difficult to predict the consequences of any movement of the tribes on the peaceable inhabitants of the colony at Red River, on the other trading posts of the Company, and even on the adjoining frontier of Canada ... The Hudson's Bay Company will always be prepared to cooperate cordially and promptly with the government of Canada in any measures which they may propose for the protection of British, Canadian, and Hudson's Bay Company's interests. We are convinced that notwithstanding the hostile agitation of parties in Canada against our Company, that our prosperity is not opposed to that of Canada.

D 4 HENRY Y. HIND'S[9] VIEWS ON THE POSSIBILITIES OF SETTLEMENT
[*Hind, Narrative, v. 1, pp. 14–15, 30–1*]

Early on the 1st August [1857] the expedition with baggage and stores were landed at Fort William. Mr. McIntyre,[10] the officer in charge of the Fort, received us with courtesy and hospitality, kindly placing some of his apartments at our disposal for the night. The Iroquois made themselves comfortable under the canoes we had brought with us from Collingwood, and transported by rail and steamboat to near the western extremity of Lake Superior.[11]

The present position of Lake Superior and its tributaries in relation to Montreal and the Atlantic seaboard, is wholly changed since the period when the old North-West Company ... maintained large establishments at Fort William and at Fort Charlotte, on the Pigeon River ... In these days ships can sail from European or Atlantic ports without breaking bulk, land their cargoes at Fort William, for less than one-fiftieth part of the cost involved during the period when the North-West Company became a powerful, wealthy, and influential body[12] ...

[9]Henry Youle Hind (1823–1908) was a chemist and a geologist from Trinity College, Toronto. He arrived at Fort William on July 31, 1857, on the expedition despatched by the Canadian Government to examine the country between Lake Superior and Red River.

[10]John McIntyre (1817–99) was born in Scotland. By 1841 he was an employee of the Hudson's Bay Company at Lachine and was one of those accompanying Simpson on his trip around the world. Subsequently, McIntyre was in charge of the post at New Brunswick (Missanabie) until 1855 when he was transferred to Fort William. He remained a clerk in the Company hierarchy until he became a Factor in 1872. After his retirement from the Company he became Indian Agent for the Savanne District in 1880.

[11]Professor Hind and his party travelled to Fort William on the side-wheeler, *Collingwood*, on that vessel's first trip beyond Sault Ste Marie. The Hudson's Bay Company schooner *Isobel* seems to have been the first Canadian vessel to use the new Sault Canal, in 1856.

[12]Hind included a good many statistics on the shipping already passing through the Sault Canal in its second full year in operation, and observed that this canal was the only one in the entire system that was not constructed on Canadian territory and controlled by the Canadian government.

It is worthy of remark that the flanks of McKay's Mountain support a heavy growth of hardwood timber (maple,[13] etc.) and through various sources I was informed that this heavily-timbered land stretches far to the south-west, on the side and borders of the trap range. The rock formations which comprise the country between the Kaministiquia and Pigeon Rivers indicate the presence of a fertile soil on the flank of the irregular table land; the trap with which the slates are associated giving rise upon disintegration to a soil of superior character. At the Mission, a light reddish loam constitutes the soil, having a depth of six feet, and resting upon a bluish grey clay which extends to the water's edge ...

I visited during the day the garden of the Fort; its area is about 1¾ acres. The shallots were small, but the potatoes looked well, being at the time in flower, and Mr. McIntyre thinks that varieties may be found which will ripen well near the Fort. Tomatoes do not ripen here; turnips and cabbages are very liable to be destroyed by the cut-worm or grub; currant bushes procured from the forest flourish admirably, and produce a very large berry; the red currant was just beginning to ripen. This part of the country appears to abound in currants, raspberries, strawberries, and gooseberries; they were seen growing in the woods in every direction, where direct light penetrated. A patch of oats in the garden showed a most remarkable development of stalk and leaf, and the ears were beginning to show themselves. The soil of the garden was brought from the foot of the Ka-ka-beka falls in the time of the North West Company's glory.

The average period when the Kaministiquia freezes, is from the third to the fifteenth of November, and it becomes free from ice between the twentieth and twenty-third April. The year 1857 proved an exception in many respects; the ice did not pass out of the river until the thirteenth of May, and on the first of August, the day of my visit, the waters of the river were higher than they had ever been known at that season of the year.

Indian corn will not succeed in this settlement, early and late frosts cutting it off. Frost occurs here under the influence of the cold expanse of Lake Superior, until the end of June, and begins again towards the end of August. A few miles further up the river, west of McKay's Mountain, the late and early frosts are of rare occurrence, and it was stated that Indian corn would ripen on the flanks of McKay's Mountain.

All kinds of small grain succeed well at the Mission, and the reason why they have not been more largely cultivated is owing to the want of a mill for the purpose of converting them into flour or meal. Near the lake, at Fort William for instance, oats do not always ripen; the cold air from the lake, whose surface, thirty and fifty miles from land, showed a temperature of 39°5′ at the close of the hottest month of the year, is sufficient

[13]The later, more exact report by T.W. Herrick (D 10) made it clear that any maple to be found were few. Hind's narrative had to include reports he could not always verify.

to prevent many kinds of vegetables from acquiring maturity, which succeeds admirably four or five miles up the river.

D 5   GEORGE SIMPSON'S INSTRUCTIONS TO JOHN MCINTYRE
[*P.A.C., MG 19 A-30, Northwest Papers*]

Lachine,
March 1, 1858

I note that owing to the scarcity of leather, there is a large demand for oxhide shoes to meet which a supply will be forwarded to the Sault Ste. Marie as soon as the navigation opens, to be thence shipped to Fort William by the first conveyance that may offer.

You may look out for the Northern canoes about the usual date in May. You will please have four good light canoes in readiness for immediate use, also a couple of brigade canoes. It is not improbable that besides the light canoes, there may be one or two with recruits for the service. As there is a scarcity of provisions at Lac La Pluie district, the canoes must be liberally supplied at Fort William to last them all the way to Norway House.

I trust the prospects of fur returns are favourable. The English market has been effected by the late hard times, so that the prices of all kinds of Skins have declined very much. You must bear this in mind, if you should make any cash purchases this season. We are buying martens on the Ottawa this winter @ 6/3 & 7/6 per skin – other furs in proportion.

D 6   JAMES A. DICKINSON'S[14] REPORT ON THE PIGEON RIVER ROUTE
[*Printed in Hind*, North-west Territory; Reports of Progress, *pp. 4–7*]

Red River Settlement,
8th June, 1858

Our observations more particularly commenced at Arrow Lake, as the head of this lake is the terminus of the proposed road to Point des Meurons, near Fort William, and in the case of its being made, (and it is most desirable that it should be if possible), the route between Grand Portage Bay and Arrow Lake should not be made use of. However, a short description of it may not be thought unnecessary.

Grand Portage Bay, where formerly was the chief depot of the North West Company, affords a sufficiently safe harbor for small vessels, being very shallow, however, for some distance out from the shore.

At the head of the bay commences the Grand Portage, which is eight miles thirteen chains in length; without any difficulty and with very little

14James A. Dickinson was the engineer assigned to the Gladman-Hind expedition.

expense it might be made suitable for waggons, but at present it is only a rough foot-path. As it and Grand Portage Bay are altogether within the United States territory, it is perhaps needless to propose any improvements that might be made in them. This portage is unavoidable, as Pigeon River for sixteen miles from its mouth is quite unnavigable, from the numerous falls and rapids in it.

From the end of this portage, there is one and a half miles of still water to Partridge Portage, which is four hundred and forty-five yards in length. The path is on the American side of the boundary line, as it is also at many other places along this route. In these cases paths should be sought for on British territory, and which could be obtained, as well as we could observe, without much difficulty.

Above Partridge Portage the river is deep and wide, with a moderate current for three and a half miles; but from this for one mile to the semi-décharge[15] the river is shallow and the current very strong; so much so, that canoes have to be poled up.

At this semi-décharge the path is on the British side, and is short but rough. When the water is high, no semi-décharge is required; but at the time we passed, the water here and in all the rivers and lakes was peculiarly low, the high-water mark appearing to be four feet above the present level.

The distance to the next semi-décharge is two miles, in which length there are no obstructions.

The second semi-décharge is about thirty chains long; in going down stream the portage need not be made; the path is on the American side.

Between this and Fowl Portage, a distance of three and a half miles, the river is quite navigable.

Fowl Portage is two thousand yards long, and is pretty level except at the west end, where it is very precipitous. The boundary line runs along the path, as it does also at some other portages, but the paths could be all easily made on British territory, due precautions having been taken that the boundary line be not obliterated.

We here enter on Fowl Lake, which is four and three quarter miles long; in the middle there is a narrow strait about ten chains wide and thirty chains long, part of it being rather shallow; the other parts of the lake are one mile wide on an average.

At the end of it is Moose Portage, seven hundred and twenty-one yards long; the path, which is the boundary line, could be easily improved or removed to one side.

Moose Lake is four and a half miles long, with an average width of half a mile; it is very deep, and is never frozen over till late in the season, and the ice is not broken up till long after that in the other lakes.

Great Cherry Portage is the next; it is eight hundred and forty-four

[15]Travellers to the west distinguished between a portage, where the canoe itself had to be conveyed overland, and a décharge or semi-décharge, where the canoe could proceed along the water route once part or all of its cargo was removed.

yards long, leading to a small lake quarter of a mile long, at the end of which is Mud Portage, two hundred and sixty-five yards long; and between it and the lesser Cherry Portage there is another small lake fifteen chains long.

On these three portages the boundary line, as it appears from the map, runs on the paths, although the lakes are connected by creeks. The paths are tolerably good, but better could be easily made and solely on British territory.

We then come to the beautiful Mountain Lake, which is seven and three quarter miles long and three quarters of a mile broad, deep, and navigable for boats of any size.

Watap portage, five hundred and thirty-nine yards long, lies between it and Watap Lake; the path is the boundary line.

Watap Lake is a narrow strip of water five and three quarter miles long and about twelve chains wide, sufficiently deep throughout the entire length for any kind of craft.

The Great New Portage is two thousand five hundred and seventy-nine yards long; it is rather uneven, and is crossed by some small creeks; the boundary line is on it, but judging from the nature of the ground, a good path could be made on British land.

We now arrive at Rose Lake, which is separated from Arrow Lake by a narrow neck of land, across which a portage must be made.

Arrow Lake is sixteen and a half miles long, and has an average width of one mile; but as we did not visit it, its character cannot be described.[16]

Rose Lake is three miles long, and averages three quarters of a mile across; it is deep, and well sheltered on all sides.

At the end there is a portage which is not shewn on the original map; it is only twenty yards long, and on the American side.

Mud Lake is two and a half miles long and a quarter mile wide, and from three to four feet deep, with a soft muddy bottom; the water having the peculiar property of retarding the canoe, similar to that of the Viscous Lake on the Kaministiquia route.

Between it and the next lake there is another portage which is not named or described on the original map; it is three hundred and eighty yards in length, and is the boundary line, the present path being tolerably good and level.

South Lake is the last on the east side of the Height of Land; it is two and three quarter miles across to the Height of Land Portage; the lake is about three quarters of a mile wide, and not more than four feet deep along the canoe route, the bottom consisting of very soft mud.

[16]The plan being advocated was a road from Fort William to Arrow Lake, connecting with the waterways described from this point west. However, the insistence on the feasibility of paths being constructed on the British side of the boundary along the route from Grand Portage implies the existence of a second plan – the use of the entire water route if funds for major road building enterprises were not forthcoming.

The Height of Land Portage is four hundred and sixty-eight yards long, and is one of the best on the route; a good road might be made without the slightest difficulty, there being plenty of pine and other good materials for the purpose close by.

We enter a lake now which is the head of the Winnipeg water-shed; having no name it may be considered part of Gun Flint Lake, with which it is connected by a strait two and a half miles long and varying from three to ten chains in width. The traverse across this lake is one and three quarter miles long. Near the middle of the strait there is a semi-décharge not noticed on the original map; it is but twenty yards long with about four feet fall; when the water is high the rapid could be run by canoes even when loaded.

Gun Flint Lake from the end of the narrow strait to Little Rock Portage is seven miles long, and has an average width of one mile; it is a fine open sheet of water of considerable depth. Before arriving at Little Rock Portage there is a rapid of two feet fall, down which the canoes were lowered by ropes; the rapid is caused by boulders of various sizes in the bed of the stream, but which might doubtless be removed.

Little Rock Portage is only thirty-three yards long; it is, as its name implies, over a rock, which is very steep on the west side.

From this to Mill Fall Portage is a mile; the river is about six chains wide; at the end there is a rapid with a fall of three feet, the channel being filled up very much with boulders, so much so, that the canoes were let down with great difficulty.

Mill Fall Portage of one hundred and ten yards in length, is over a very rugged rock on the American side.

The next portage is a quarter of a mile further on; it is five hundred and nine yards long, over an island; the path is very good and level except at the ends, where it is rather steep and the landings are bad, but could be easily improved, as indeed the landings at all the portages might be and without any considerable cost, as the materials for doing so can be obtained without difficulty.

This river or chain of lakelets is twelve miles long from Gun Flint Lake to Lake Seiganagah;[17] for four miles below the last mentioned portage it is full of large boulders, which make the navigation of it difficult; there are in this length six rapids, varying from five feet to one foot fall, at four of which the canoes had to be carefully let down by ropes.

From thence to the semi-décharge of one hundred yards in length and five feet fall, which is one mile from the end, the navigation is good. At the mouth of this river there is a portage which is not shewn on the original map, neither are any of the rapids between this and the last portage.

This portage is thirty yards long, over a rocky point on the American side.

[17]Saganaga is the modern spelling. The present Thunder Bay–Rainy River boundary line strikes this lake near its western end.

We now enter Lake Seiganagah, the route through which follows the boundary line or nearly so, and is nine miles in length. The greatest length of this lake is twelve miles, and the greatest width six miles. It is full of islands, from which it derives its name, affording good shelter to canoes, at the same time not impeding the navigation for large boats ...

I have refrained from offering the necessary suggestions for the improvement of this route, as I understand Mr. Dawson is to make a complete exploration and survey of it this year, and who will therefore be better able to form an opinion as to its capabilities and required improvements.

However, from even the cursory examination I was enabled to make, it appears greatly superior to the Kaministiquia route.

It is sixty-three miles shorter than the other. There are fewer portages, all much shorter with the exception of the Grand Portage, and none of them are nearly so bad as the Savanne, Prairie or Great Dog Portages. There are very much fewer rapids, and which are all more easily run. Excepting Pigeon River, it consists of a chain of lakes the whole way connected by short channels, in few of which only the current is at all strong.

I think that with a comparatively small outlay, the route could be made navigable for large row boats, and that on many parts of it, small tug-steamers could be advantageously employed.

D 7 LINDSAY RUSSELL'S[18] REPORT ON THE ROUTE
FROM THUNDER BAY TO DOG LAKE
[*Printed in Dawson,* Report on the Exploration of the Country, *p. 30*]

Indian Mission,
Fort William, January 3rd, 1859

I send a sketch shewing the Current River line, and, also, the Indian winter route which starts from Thunder Bay, about half way between the mouth of the Kaministaquia and Current River, then following the valley of the second river north of Fort William,[19] comes out on Dog Lake, about a mile and a half west of the Current River line.

A better road site can be found along the side of this little river than anywhere about the line, as the latter crosses all the hills, ravines and

[18]Lindsay Russell (1839–1912), later surveyor-general of Canada, was at this time a chairman with the Dawson exploring party. He was a cousin of the Alexander Russell, also a surveyor, who resided in Port Arthur for many years, and the two men, with initials L.A and A.L., were frequently confused.

[19]The fact that none of the rivers and brooks between the Kaministikwia and Current rivers had names in 1858 makes Russell's description somewhat difficult to follow. He did not propose to begin his route from the lake at the "second river" north of Fort William since he found both the first and second unsuitable. He thus settled for the vicinity of what was really the third stream, soon to be known as McVicar's Creek after Robert McVicar, who built a dwelling near its mouth, probably during 1859. Farther inland, however, Russell did propose to follow the valley of the second river – that is, the McIntyre.

swamps, among which the said river takes its rise, as well as those at the sources of another little river or brook between the first and Current River.

On the Indian track the country is less hilly and not so swampy. There is a mile or so of bad swamp at the outset, but it can be avoided by starting a short distance to the north, thus coming on a ridge of high land which runs down close to the shore of the lake. The next bad place is where the track first crosses the river, which here cuts its way through a range of granite hills of but inconsiderable height, but through them I think a good pass could be found as they are no worse than those on the Current River line.

There would be three or four little bridges, but they would cross mere brooks, the banks of which are low and good. In the immediate vicinity of Dog Lake there would be some rough ground, but that has to be passed through whatever be the route.

With the exception of the places that I have mentioned the country is pretty level, and the swamps few and short. The soil on the level ground and in the bottom of the swamps is a clayey sand. Under this sand is granite, and indeed, here, as in many other places, there is but little soil over the rock.

The woods are white birch, poplar, spruce, and pitch pine, on the high grounds; and spruce, larch, and cedar in the lower places.

On the sketch the red dotted line winding about the black one is where a road would have to be taken were it necessary to make it on the Current River line. Between the 2nd and 3rd mile posts is a bad swamp that would have to be passed straight through, as it runs to the river on the east side, and the other side extends even further, terminating in rocky and broken ground; it would cost more to take a road round, on either side, than it would to make it across. Near the 6th mile post is another swamp, to avoid which there is a sharp turn to the right; and the hill at the sixth post is so steep that we have to wind round its base to the left again. Between the 7th and 9th the dotted line crosses the same brook four times, but it is so small that it merely requires culverts. At the 11th post a swamp occurs, through which we pass straight, as in the one between the 2nd and 3rd, and for the similar reason, that it would cost more to get a good road round it than to make it on the line. The three brooks between the 12th and 13th mile posts are small, the width of the largest being not more than 12 feet. From the 13th to the 18th posts, the ground is good, but about half way to the 19th commence the ranges of hills which lie around Lake Pijké and Hawk Lake.[20] The best way from this is along a valley which comes out about three quarters of a mile west of the discharge of Hawk Lake.

[20]The lakes called Pijké and Hawk do not appear under those names on a modern map. Hawkeye Lake and Hawk Bay, however, perpetuate the old place names. Pijké would appear to be the lake now known locally as One Island Lake.

On the hills to the north of this valley are occasional large white pines; there are also some on the 5th mile of the line, on the shore of Current River, about 4 miles from its mouth, and on the shores of Hawk Lake.

The country to the north-east of the line is very rough. At the end next Thunder Bay, Current River, having a general course of north, winds about among steep rocky hills, which sometimes rise straight up from its edge; from the top of one of these, about 6 miles from its mouth, we could see its course for a long distance through an exceedingly rough country. It is full of rapids and falls pouring through clefts of up-heaved granite and slate. Opposite the second mile of the line it passes through slate; but higher up, through granite. About the 14th and 15th miles the ground to the N.E. of the line is more level, till near Lake Pijké, when it gets uneven again.

The banks of that lake are high, and wooded with white birch, poplar, and spruce, but the soil is of the same light sand as elsewhere on the line, and the hills are rocky, its discharge into Hawk Lake is a small and rapid stream, which falls, perhaps, nearly a hundred feet between the two lakes.

The shores of Hawk Lake are much higher than those of Lake Pijké, rising in steep rocky hills from the water's edge; the north shore of the eastern end of the lake is a wall of cliffs, about 150 feet in height, which then rises higher in wooded hills behind. Hawk Lake discharges itself into Dog Lake about a mile to the west of the line by a rapid and shallow brook, which runs from its western extremity. On it are two little lakes, and Indian Portages out of one into the other, and then into Dog Lake.

I am now going to run a line from the Mission to the thirteenth mile on the Current River line; that finished, I will locate the road from Thunder Bay to Dog Lake. I run the line first, as it will give me a much better knowledge of the country.

As I understand my instructions, I am to locate the road on the best ground I can find. I will, therefore, take it along the valley of the second little river north of the Kaministaquia, as shown in the sketch.

I would have run the line from the Mission to the 8th or 9th mile posts, were it not that I know the country through which it would pass to be bad; it would run through the swamp, on the two little rivers[21] behind the Fort, and the ground about the 9th mile at the line is very rough.

I take with me five men, the number you allowed me when I should be running lines. They are Jos. Whiteway, J. Smith, and three of the Mission Indians. I have, as yet, got only one of the Indians at 3s. 9d. per day. I may, perhaps, have to do with three men, as the people of the mission are asking exorbitant wages.

[21]These two little rivers, very close together at their mouths, are the Neebing and the McIntyre.

D 8 S.J. DAWSON'S REPORT ON THE ROUTES
BETWEEN LAKE SUPERIOR AND RED RIVER, 1859
[*Dawson,* Report on the Exploration of the Country, *pp. 27–29*]

[Feb 22, 1859]

[The Pigeon River route] leaves Lake Superior at the Grand Portage Village, and, after passing through a high and hilly region, meets the canoe route from the Kaministaquia at Nequaquon Lake, or, as it is sometimes called, *Lac la Croix*[22] ... On leaving Lake Superior the country rises very rapidly, attaining a height at Mud Lake, just above Mountain Lake, of 1053 feet in a distance, by the windings of the stream, of about 40 miles. From thence westward, it falls more gradually, Basswood Lake, which is on the opposite side of the water-shed, and distant from Mountain Lake about 80 miles, being still at an elevation of 661 feet above Lake Superior. In this high region the head-waters of four different rivers are crossed, namely, Pigeon River, Arrow River, Sageinaga River, and a branch of the Maligne. The Lakes are numerous, as they are everywhere in this district, and some of them are so small as to be barely navigable for moderate sized canoes; and in the event of a more perfect water communication becoming necessary, this being the highest land in the neighborhood, a summit in fact from which the waters run in every direction, there is no source of supply that could be made available. However, until some better sort of communication is opened, it is valuable as a route for very small and light canoes; as, although the extent of land carriage is great as compared with the Kaministaquia route, it is upon the whole shorter, and there are no rapids which could be at all embarrassing. But, though this much may be said in its favor, it is not so good as the Kaministaquia for large canoes, and ... it can never be made practicable for larger craft than canoes. The Grand Portage itself is entirely within the United States territory, and from thence westward to Rainy Lake the canoe route forms the boundary line ...

In the first instance, before traffic has assumed such dimensions as to render canals and railroads necessary, the cheapest, and indeed the only way of opening the communication that can be adopted, is to place steamers or row boats on the navigable reaches, and make good land roads where the navigation is impracticable.

This being admitted, it remains for me to describe the extent of land road that would be necessary, and the navigable reaches that might be rendered available.

To commence at Lake Superior, a land road would be required from Thunder Bay to Dog Lake, as the navigation of the Kaministauquia is utterly impracticable, except for canoes, and could only be rendered otherwise at an enormous outlay. Dog Lake is distant from Lake Superior

[22]Lac La Croix is the name now used. Dawson was familiar with both names in use in the 1850s, but Dickinson apparently encountered only one, Nequaquon.

22½ miles, and at a higher elevation by 718 feet, a difference of level which renders a canal out of the question, notwithstanding that the supply of water in the Kaministaquia would be ample. The only way of reaching it, therefore, is by land, and the surveys have progressed so far as to shew that a good line may be obtained in a distance of 28 miles.

Next follows the reach through Dog Lake and Dog River, which, allowing for bends, is equal to 35 miles; but, to render this available for large vessels, a dam would be necessary across the outlet of Dog Lake, which would have the effect of throwing back the water to Cold Water Lake, at the eastern end of the Prairie Portage.[23]

From this reach to the Savanne River there would be a land carriage of five miles, through an easy country.

From thence to the Little Falls, on the River Seine – about ten miles below Lac des Mille Lacs – the distance is about 65 miles, which might be rendered navigable, in one unbroken reach, by means of a dam at the Little Falls ...

The communication, therefore, which it is proposed to open, would afford advantages superior to any line which can be adopted in Minnesota except a line of railroad, and it is reasonable to believe that ere the United States Government can construct such a work, through an un-settled or but thinly peopled country, the trade of the Western territories will have become so much developed as to warrant the construction of railroads between the navigable reaches on the Canadian route.

When the circumstances of the country would admit of the outlay, a continuous railroad – 195 miles in length – might be made between Lake Superior and Rainy Lake, and another, of 91½ miles, between Lac Plat and Fort Garry. If this were done, and two locks constructed at Fort Frances, the Red River Settlement would be within less than two days journey of Lake Superior ... This would bring Fort Garry within five days' journey of Toronto.

D 9   GEORGE BARNSTON'S[24] INSTRUCTIONS TO
JOHN MCINTYRE
[*P.A.C., MG, 19 A–30, Northwest Papers*]

Michipicoten,
August 25, 1859

Mr. Colin Rankin[25] who will deliver this, takes his passage with his family, and will be stationed for the present with you. His able assistance

---

[23]Prairie Portage connects Coldwater Lake and the Jourdain Creek, a tributary of Dog River, with the River Savanne, by way of Lac du Milieu.

[24]George Barnston had entered the North West Company in 1820, then continued as a clerk in the Hudson's Bay Company. He became a Chief Trader in 1840 and a Chief Factor seven lears later. He was in charge of the Lake Superior District for several years, retiring in 1863.

[25]Colin Rankin, a native of Argyllshire, was then a very junior clerk. He was

will put it in your power to get through the heavy Business sometimes occurring at Fort William with ease and correctness. Now also the properly curing of fish may be fully attended to – superintendence to prevent those heavy losses and vexations that have happened of late through inexperience and unaccountable Mishaps or failures somewhere or another. I know no one can be more distressed about these matters than yourself. If fish are to be cured at all, they will have to be cured for keeping a twelvemonth, and unless persons can be employed who will give the necessary care and attention ... toward preserving the fish, it would be better not to attempt curing again. The Expenses attendant upon inspecting and removing unsound fish entail upon us loss instead of bringing profit ...

I have got a model for a new fishing Boat to be made for you, and shall endeavour to complete it for autumn 1860. It will be an addition to our other heavy work at this place, but, at present, you are too weak in people to get on with it yourself, and the trade will give full occupation to your hands.

As long as that system will pay, the furs ought to be sent for to the Indian lodges, where they are to be had always cheaper than at the Fort, and the risk of losing them altogether is less than when the Indians are left to come in of themselves to the Establishment. I would be wary also in giving debts to such as have proven themselves dishonest.

D 10 T.W. Herrick's[26] Survey of the Townships of Nee-Bing and Pai-Poonge, 1860
[Canada, Department of Crown Lands, Report, 1863, pp. 188–9]

The townships of Nee-Bing and Pai-Poonge are bounded on the south by high ranges of trap rocks, rising in perpendicular precipices some hundred feet high on their north and east sides, the most prominent point of which, – McKay's mountain – reaches an elevation of 1,000 feet. The summits of these mountains are in general covered with white and red pine, while on the sides may be seen a thick growth of birch, poplar, and spruce, and in a few spots sugar maple. At the base of these mountains we get into a comparatively level plain, forming the valley of the

---

transferred to Michipicoten in 1861, became a Chief Trader at Lindsay in 1869, a Chief Factor seven years later. He was in charge of the Lake Superior District for one of their sons, John Rankin, became M.P. for Renfrew.

[26]In 1860 the surveyor Thomas Wallis Herrick was employed to explore the north shore of Lake Superior from the Sault to Fort William to a depth of twenty-five miles from the shore, and to lay out and subdivide the townships of Nee-Bing and Pai-Poonge as well as the Town Plot of Fort William. The names of the two townships, now spelled without the hyphens, are supposed to mean Winter and Summer in Ojibway.

Kaministiqua river, and at an average elevation of 30 or 40 feet above the level of the river. The soil in this valley consists in general of a reddish, clayey loam, well adapted for cultivation, and producing a good growth of poplar, spruce, balsam, birch, with an undergrowth of hazel-nut, cherry, &c. In some places also, white and red pine of good quality, though not in any great abundance.

Between the long windings of the river, the lower part of which is exceedingly tortuous in its course, are flats of rich, dark alluvial deposit, rising 6 or 8 feet above the level of the river, and giving growth to large elm, ash, balm of gilead, &c., with an undergrowth of wild hops and flowering plants of various descriptions.

On the north as well as on the south bank of the river, rising from these flats, are banks of red clay, gravel, or sand, 50 to 80 feet in height.

The land, for a short distance from the north side of the river, is in general pretty good, and covered with poplar, spruce, birch, balsam, &c. However, proceeding further north from the river in Nee-Bing, the land in general becomes wet, and the prevailing timber is tamarack and spruce; while in Pai-Poonge, most of the country north of the river for some distance, presents a dry, sandy appearance.

Along the northern boundary of both townships the soil again improves, and continues to do so, until the range of granite and trap rocks bounding Thunder Bay on the north and ranging towards the south-west is again met with.

The country on both sides of the river is well watered by numerous creeks, affording excellent mill sites. Slate river flows with rapid current between high banks of dark argillaceous slate, lying in horizontal layers, and containing limestone in interlying masses, as well as in large rounded nodules. This slate in some places is of good quality, presenting a hard, compact appearance, while in other places it is soft, and decomposed readily – nearly pure alum being found on the surface in considerable quantity.

This formation of dark slate, intersected in places by dykes of trap, is found all through the southern portion of Pai-Poonge.

On the north side of the river are also several creeks or small rivers, very rapid in their course, and supplying easily available water power to any extent. The rocks on the north side of the river are chiefly of slaty trap, with layers of red jaspar, and intersected by veins of quartz, with traces of lead and copper ores. At the Paresseux rapids, a vein appears about 3 feet in width, chiefly of fluor spar, with particles of lead and copper ores. A small deep river flows through the north of Nee-Bing, about one chain in width, and navigable for small boat or canoe for about 4½ miles from its mouth.

Further up this river, in the north-west corner of Nee-Bing, are falls 30 to 40 feet in height. Here appears a vein running nearly east and west, 12 to 15 feet wide, chiefly of white calc spar, and containing a consider-able quantity of the ores of lead and zinc.

The only impediment to navigation of the River Kaministiqua by lake steamers consists of a bar of soft mud or sand, a couple of hundred feet wide, at the mouth of the river; over this bar in the channel there is about five feet of water. This trifling difficulty overcome, the river is navigable for good sized steamers to Point de Meuron, or about 11 miles from the mouth – there being an average width of about 5 chains, with a depth of from 8 to 10 feet.

While coasting along Thunder Bay, I had a good opportunity of examining the north shore of the Bay with reference to harbors, and found that at Lambert's Island to be the only one worth notice.

This bay, sheltered completely by Lambert Island, formed a beautiful harbor, about half a mile wide by three quarters of a mile deep – the water varying from two to six fathoms in depth. The island which protects it on the south is divided from the main land by a channel a few feet in width, and affords on its inner side a secure anchorage alongside of the island, which rises from ten to twenty feet in perpendicular basaltic columns from the water.

As far as my own experience goes, the climate at Fort William in winter is not more severe than that in the neighborhood of Montreal.

D 11   JOHN MCINTYRE TO SIMON DAWSON
[*P.A.O., Dawson Papers*]

Fort William,
February 9, 1860

Rev. P. Chonee was down here not long ago and we were speaking about the reserve at the mission and he is very much put out about the last treaty and I recommended him to get the Indians to sell their reserve at the village and he said that if the Government wanted it he had no doubt but the Indians would part with it on reasonable conditions and as the town Plot Mr. Herrick has surveyed opposite the mission is all nearly swamp it is likely that the Crown Land Dept would like to get the Reserve from the Indians: I mention this to you so as to let your brother know of it as settlers would be more likely to settle on the south side of the River as it is much better land than on the north and the only good sight for a town on this River – if the Government wishes the land they have only to write to the Revd. P. Choné about it – when he will let them know the Indians opinion and on what condition they would be willing to dispose of their Reserve.[27]

[27]Whether or not McIntyre's judgment was correct, no alteration in the limits of the Fort William Reserve was made at this time. A town was built on the site he considered unsuitable, and the Indian settlement was not moved until the building of the Grand Trunk Railway in the early twentieth century.

D 12   D.Y. LESLIE'S[28] COMPARISON BETWEEN
THE NORTH AND SOUTH SHORES OF
LAKE SUPERIOR
[*Canada, Department of Crown Lands, Report, 1860, app. 22, pp. 76–8*]

From the experience I have derived, I recommend that all that portion of the North shore of Lake Superior, similar in character to the mining regions on the South shore, be surveyed on the United States system, into Townships, six miles square, and two tiers in depth, by contract at so much per mile, with the solar compass, on true meridian, and East and West courses, or in such other manner as may be deemed best; and that no more lands be sold or patents issued, or any squatter's claim recognized, till the Township or portion claimed is surveyed, and that the $100 License system[29] be annulled. In this recommendation I believe I shall be borne out by A.P. Salter,[30] Esq., P.L.S., who has had much experience in that section of the country, intimate knowledge of its resources, and who is more capable of giving a sound opinion on this subject, than any other Canadian of my acquaintance.

My reasons for making this recommendation, knowing well that even under the American system the expense of surveying will be heavy, will be found under the various headings of my Report.

In the Spring of 1860, the time of my inspection, the white population of the North shore of Lake Superior – exclusive of the Hudson Bay Company's posts – was nine, two of this number females.

At the same time, (the census having just been taken,) the population on the American side of Lake Superior was (exclusive of the Sault District,) 19,696. The total number of Canadian Vessels, including the Hudson Bay Company's, was as follows: one Propeller, the "Rescue," and one Steamer, the "Ploughboy," occasionally running direct from the Sault to Fort William, and two Schooners in the Fur Trade.[31]

[28]D. Young Leslie reported from Collingwood, January 8, 1861, on his inspection of the previous year of all mining locations on Lakes Huron and Superior.

[29]By order-in-council of September 1853 individuals might be granted the right to prospect for minerals over a 400-acre tract of unconceded land for a period of two years upon payment of this licence fee. At the end of the period, they then had first option on the land, but the price was set at $1.50 per acre which they, and Leslie, considered too high.

[30]Andrew Pellew Salter (1815–74) was born in England. As a provincial land surveyor in the Sault Ste Marie region in 1857, he had as assistants several men important in later surveys of the Lake Superior area – Herrick and Donnelly, for example.

[31]The Hudson's Bay schooners, the *Whitefish* and the more recently acquired *Isobel*, were both in service. The *Rescue*, a twin-screw propeller, had been built in 1835 by Bidwell & Banta of Buffalo, and acquired by a Toronto group in 1858 to carry the Red River mail, making stops at the Pic, Red Rock (Nipigon), and Fort William. The *Plough Boy* began trips for a rival company in the following year, and continued to make occasional appearances on Lake Superior until its sinking in 1867.

On the American side, there were regularly running as Passenger and Freight boats, six side-wheel Steamers, ten Propellers, one small Steamer between Superior City and Bayfield, nine or ten Steamers and Steam Ferry-boats on Portage Lake, two Steam Tugs and two Steam Dredging Machines at the entrance of Portage Lake, four or five Steam Tugs between White Fish Point and Detour Channel, and upwards of one hundred first class Schooners, equal to any vessels in the world of their class, and two Revenue Cutters, carrying from twenty to thirty men each, completely armed. All of the above, with the exception of the small Steamer to Bayfield and the Revenue Cutters, depending solely and exclusively for trade on a Mineral region, said to be inferior to our's by those who ought to know.

D 13   AN EARLY LAND PURCHASE IN THE NEW TOWNSHIP OF NEE-BING
[*P.A.O., Crown Lands, Papers, Neebing Township*]

This is to certify that James Morehead purchased on the twenty-ninth day of August, 1861, Lot No. 9 in the first concession Nee-Bing north of the River Kaministiquia in the District of Algoma, containing 196 acres at the rate of twenty cents per acre and has paid ($7.84) seven dollars and eighty-four cents, being the first installment of the purchase money. Said lot is subject to settlement duty by the Crown Land Office ...

Crown Land Agency   (Signed) Robt. McVicar
Fort William,   Land Agent
29th August, 1861

Registration listed, Ottawa, 28 August, 1866

Lot No. 9 in first concession of Nee-Bing recorded in favor of John Joseph Vickers.[32]

Assigned to J.J. Vickers by James Morehead.

D 14   BARNSTON TO JOHN McKENZIE
[*P.A.C., H.B.Co.* Records, *B-135-c*]

Michipicoten
December, 26, 1861.

I am anxious you should know that an American opposition is stationed this winter at ... Bay de Quellie[?] in Nipigon Lake ... [Laronde] appears

[32]John J. Vickers was born in Ireland and emigrated to Canada as a young man. He was interested in the Thunder Bay area as early as 1859, and eventually acquired a good deal of property there. He was the proprietor of the Northwestern Express Company, and he and his wife, the daughter of J.W.D. and Susanna Moodie, were frequent visitors to Fort William.

to be apprehensive that this party of Bradshaw's will extend their exertions as far as the Albany District and it is well you should be aware of this, in case you might deem it requisite, as I imagine you will, to strengthen the Martin's Falls and Osnaburgh Posts[33] by ... keeping the Indian lodges in the direction of Nipigon Lake clear of furs, by inviting them to draw in the hunters' debts, and for surplus furs to trade any necessary articles that are wanted by the hunters during the course of the spring months, endeavouring besides to draw them out of harm's way by encouraging them to hunt for this season on the north side of the Albany River, or at as great a distance from Nipigon Lake as possible.

Bradshaw is an old experienced hunter from Fond du Lac, and is supplied with whiskey and plenty of goods. He left Fort William with his schooner and 3 half-sized canoes in the fall, intending I suppose to leave the former in Nipigon Bay to winter. He had six men, who, I dare say, were all employed in getting up the goods to Nipigon Lake until the navigation set fast; although I did not anticipate such an opposition in that quarter, yet, from hints thrown out to me, I had instructed Mr. McIntyre, should such an event take place, to send some people after the strangers to assist Mr. Laronde with goods and men to the best of his ability. He accordingly did so, and the second son of Mr. Robt. McVicar,[34] with a faithful steady Indian to assist him, is now, I believe, close to Bradshaw with a small stock of goods while Mr. Henry Laronde with a Nipigon servant, is on the other side of him, Laronde remaining at the Post.[35]

D 15   P.M. VANKOUGHNET[36] TO JOHN A. MACDONALD[37]
[P.A.C., Macdonald Papers, v. 293]

Toronto.
March 1, 1863

... And now as to C.L. Policy – a word as to the N. West. You of course

---

[33]The customary route to these posts at the extreme northeast and northwest of the modern District of Thunder Bay was naturally the Albany River. The precautions to strengthen them against possible incursions from the south indicate at least a thought of the district becoming an economic unit, as it had never been in the past.

[34]Presumably this is a reference to George McVicar, since the oldest son, John Richardson McVicar, lived in Ottawa.

[35]Louis Laronde was still in the Company service at this time, in charge of the Nipigon post. At least two of his sons were associated with the local fur trade, not always seeking to protect Company interests.

[36]Philip Michael Vankoughnet (1823–69) was the son of a Loyalist settler in Upper Canada. He had been elected in 1856 for the Rideau division as a member of the Legislative Council of the Province of Canada, and held various posts in the Macdonald-Cartier governments, serving as Commissioner of Crown Lands from 1858 to 1862.

[37]John A. Macdonald (1815–91) had few direct links with the Thunder Bay area,

know the position we always took in regard to it. 1st to avoid a ruinous or expensive contest and eventual bargain with the Hudson's Bay Co. which the British Gov't would have thrown upon us. 2nd to avoid the cost of gaining so distant a country involving as it would the armed protection of the settlers & inevitable and constant hostility with the Indians. There are I am told 20,000 Indian warriors on both sides of the Line. Already the people & authorities at Red River have petitioned the British Govt for troops setting forth the great peril they are in from the Indians. What the British Gov't could do with a few troops Canada could not effect with five times the number. The Indians have confidence in and respect for the Queen – they would have none for us. 3rd and above all we are deeply interested in Great Britain retaining a direct control in a portion of this continent. What she controls she must protect, and she cannot protect any portion without aiding the whole ... We don't want to banish Britain from the continent; we want to chain her here if we can. The time may come when strengthened by her fostering care we may call ½ of the continent ours. But even in this direction as far as one could see our gov't was not idle. 1st we had the explorations at Red River ... 2nd I laid out a Town at Fort William and two townships into farm lots to form the outpost or commencement of settlement which the visionary think should be accomplished in a day throughout the valley of the Saskatchewan. 3rd I caused (for the first time) the whole route from the Sault to Fort William along the north shore of Lake Superior to be explored with a view to its agricultural & mineral uses, & to the making eventually of a road. This work finished last summer occupied nearly 2 years. 4th I improved the roads round the Sault Ste Marie as the place likely to be of most importance in this region ... 5th In the hope of stimulating settlement throughout this region I brought the price of all the lands except immediately round the Sault to 1/ per acre. 6th I caused to be appropriated to have been spent last year $4000. on roads in and about Fort William & an agent Cumming[38] was appointed to superintend it and to take charge of the Lands with a view to promoting settlement, the post master there old McVicar whom I had appointed C.L. Agent being entirely too old for such work. This move the present Gov't stopped. Mr. Galt [?] told me he had personally urged it on them. So that while politicians have been raving about what they did not understand, we were doing during several years past all that it was possible to do towards approaching this great North West.

---

which he did not visit until 1886. His partner and long-time political associate, Alexander Campbell, however, had business associations there and seems to have served as the Prime Minister's chief source of information concerning the area for many years.

[38]Neither Cumming nor the roads appear to have materialized in Thunder Bay, whatever provision Vankoughnet made for them. McVicar served as land agent from 1861 to his death in 1864.

D 16   A. G. DALLAS[39] TO THOMAS FRASER[40]
[*P.A.C., H.B.Co. Records, A-12-43*]

Fort Garry,
November 14, 1863

The post of Fort William, under charge of Mr. John McIntyre, a clerk, though not very profitable as regards its trade in furs, is perhaps the most important on Lake Superior. It is at that place we have to watch the proceedings of the American traders who have their stations at the Old Grand Portage about forty miles distant, from whence they make excursions toward Lac La Pluie, to Nipigon, the Pays Plat, and other points on the north shore of Lake Superior. It is also the head of steamboat navigation on the Canadian side of the lake.

Near our establishment there is a Roman Catholic Indian Mission which, though small and apparently struggling amidst difficulties to maintain itself, is nevertheless the nucleus of a future settlement and already gives us trouble by affording a point of departure or base of operation for petty traders.

From Fort William several temporary outposts are established in the winter at the most vulnerable points on the frontier. Owing to the scarcity of game and fish, the interior posts are principally maintained on imported provisions, and as we always keep up an abundant supply which can be sent inland in the summer to the points where they are most likely to be required in winter, we commence operations when the hunting season arrives with a decided advantage over the petty traders, who have not the means to provide in the same way for the winter's campaign. To this cause, as well as to the experience and energy of Mr. McIntyre, is attributable the success which still attends our trade in the face of the difficulties which beset it. Fort William is to a large extent supported on fish, the fisheries at the mouth of the river Kaministaquoiah being very productive. Any surplus beyond our own wants is salted and sent to market. I understand about sixty barrels of whitefish have been forwarded to the Sault Ste. Marie for sale this season.

We formerly had a large fishery for export, but the business proved unprofitable, not from the want of good management on the spot, but from the uncertainty of the market, and great fluctuations in the demand. Another difficulty was the dishonesty of the fish inspectors and curers at Detroit and other points who, it is reported, condemned our fish on the

[39]Alexander G. Dallas (1818?–82) had been born in Rupert's Land, but his career with the Hudson's Bay Company did not begin until 1850 when he was appointed Chief Factor at Fort Victoria, Vancouver Island, where his father-in-law, James Douglas, was soon to become Governor. After the death of Sir George Simpson, Dallas was named Governor of Rupert's Land, but retained that office for only two years, retiring to Scotland in 1864.

[40]Thomas Fraser was the Corresponding Secretary of the Hudson's Bay Company from 1858 to 1867.

most frivolous pretexts, bought it for a trifle, repacked it, and sold it at a handsome profit.

There is also at Fort William a retail shop, which being the only one in that quarter, is attended with profit. It is manifestly impossible as well as inadvisable to attempt to adhere to any tariff prices at a place like Fort William, either in the fur trade or shop. I accordingly gave Mr. McIntyre full authority to vary his buying and selling rates according to circumstances and from day to day, if he found it necessary to do so. Such freedom of action could not safely be granted to every officer in the service, but it is indispensable at a place like Fort William, and hence the necessity of great care in the selection of persons to fill posts on the frontier ...

D 17   JOHN MCKENZIE TO EDWARD HOPKINS[41]
[P.A.C., H.B.Co. Records, B-134-c]

Michipicoten,
Feb. 8, 1864

McIntyre is in the "clouds" about mining – he writes me that he has had an offer of $10,000. for 200 acres of land at Fort William, & that the money is to be forthcoming in June ... Everything is couleur de rose with him. I have a location on the Current River[42] which I must see about before going south.

I cannot give you much information about the Transports of the following Summer – whilst at Toronto I saw Cooke[?] the owner of the "Rescue" who told me the only difficulty against getting a good steamer on the route was the Government not giving the mail contract for more than one year.[43] I believe however a good steamer will be on the route next year. Griffin of the Post Office Department ought to know about it ... I hope they will find a better steamer on the route than the Rescue which is the veriest tub I ever was in.

[41]Edward Hopkins, after years in the Company service at Norway House and other posts, was the Chief Factor in command at Montreal after the death of Sir George Simpson. He was much interested in the mining possibilities around Lake Superior and made a number of trips to the area. His wife, who accompanied him on some of these trips, made a number of sketches of the Thunder Bay District in the 1860s.

[42]The list of patents issued by the end of 1865 does not mention McKenzie's Current River property, but he had apparently acquired it in 1857, paid nothing over the years, then was ordered to pay $600 plus $252 accumulated interest. By 1864 this seemed worth doing.

[43]This explanation for the state of the Rescue seems to conflict with the statement in William Smith's History of the Post Office in British North America (Toronto, 1921), that the twice-weekly service from Collingwood to Fort William, begun in 1858, was discontinued after two years. In any case, the hopes of the Northwest Transportation and Land Company, which owned the Rescue, were foundering by this time. New mail contracts might secure better steamers, but they would be under different ownership.

D 18 ANDREW RUSSELL'S[44] STATEMENT OF
MINERAL LANDS ON LAKE SUPERIOR[45]
[*P.A.C., MG 24 I-8, Macdonell of Collachie, Allan Macdonell, Mining Papers*]

To whom Patented	Tract	Area in ac.	Price per ac.	Date	
Montreal Mining Company[46]	Opposite Victoria Island	6400	.40	Sept.	8/56
	Island at entrance to Black Bay	5230	.40	Sept.	13 "
	North-East shore of Thunder Bay	6400	.40	Sept.	10 "
	Fluor Island	5468	.40	Sept.	13 "
	East part of St. Ignace Island	6400	.40	"	
	North part of St. Ignace Island	6400	.40	"	
	West shore of Neepigon Strait	6400	.40	"	
	South-west shore, Neepigon Strait	6400	.40	"	
	West end St. Ignace Island	6400	.40	"	
	West end St. Ignace Island	6400	.40	"	
	East side Pigeon River	6400	.40	"	
	South part Simpson Island	6400	.40	"	
	West part Simpson Island	6400	.40	"	
	Copper Islands	7200	.40	"	
British North American Mining Company	Spar Island and tract on main shore to rear	6400	.80	Apr.	6/53
John Bonner, Jr.	Part of Michipicoten Island	6400	.80	June	17/54
George A.L. Wood	North of and adjoining the twp. of Nee-Bing[47]	400	1.00	Jan.	4/64
P.M. Vankoughnet	North of and adjoining twp of Nee-Bing	200	1.00	Jan.	26/64
Jean Langlois	North of and adjoining twp of Nee-Bing	200	1.00	Jan.	28/64

[44]Andrew Russell (1804–88) spent fifty years in the Canadian civil service. In the 1860s he was Assistant Commissioner of Crown Lands, and thus responsible for the presentation of information on the granting of mineral lands, which had been demanded by the Canadian Parliament. His statement, dated December 30, 1865, was accompanied by a similar one for Lake Huron. The total acreage granted on Lake Superior was 154,718, on Lake Huron 34,768.

[45]From this list, locations in the Batchewana and Michipicoten areas, outside the present District of Thunder Bay, have been omitted.

[46]Fourteen of the sixteen locations granted to the Montreal Mining Company lay in Thunder Bay District. All fourteen had been surveyed by John McNaughton, as had the one location of the British North American Mining Company.

[47]The surveyor for the lands described as north of and adjoining the Township of Neebing was John Francis.

To Whom Patented	Tract	Area in ac.	Price per ac.	Date
John Moore	Lot #4 on west shore of Black Bay[48]	275	1.00	Sept. 23/64
James McGregor	Lot #6 on west shore of Black Bay	391	1.00	Sept. 24/64
John J. Vickers	North of and adjoining twp. of Nee-Bing	400	1.00	Dec. 28/63
Asa D. Dickinson	Lot #8 west shore of Black Bay	400	1.00	Sept. 24/64
William B. Clarke	Lot #10 west shore of Black Bay	400	1.00	Sept. 26/64
Chas. P. Crosby	Lot #12 west shore of Black Bay	400	1.00	,,
Francis P. Montizambert	Lot #9 west shore of Black Bay	400	1.00	Oct. 3/64
Peter A. Shaw	Lot #7 west shore of Black Bay	400	1.00	,,
Frost W. Gray	Lot #5 west shore of Black Bay	400	1.00	Oct. 4/64
Donald C. Thomson	Lot #3 west shore of Black Bay	400	1.00	Oct. 20/64
Jas. F. Turnbull	Lot #18 west shore of Black Bay	400	1.00	,,
Walter Scougall	Lot #1 west shore of Black Bay	400	1.00	,,
William Shaw	Lot #19 west shore of Black Bay	400	1.00	Oct. 21/64
Rev. Andrew Balfour	Lot #20 west shore of Black Bay	400	1.00	Oct. 20/64
George Caplin	Lot #14 west shore of Black Bay	400	1.00	,,
Myron W. Stanley	Lot #13 west shore of Black Bay	400	1.00	,,
William F. Ladd	Lot #22 west shore of Black Bay	400	1.00	,,
Robert Hunter	Lot #15 Thunder Bay[49]	400	1.00	Nov. 3/64
John Mason	Lot #1 St. Ignace Island	400	1.00	Nov. 11/64
William C. Scott	Lot #2 St. Ignace Island	400	1.00	Nov. 10/64
Thos. H. Thomson	Lot #7 St. Ignace Island	400	1.00	Nov. 11/64
John C. Thomson	Lot #8 St. Ignace Island	400	1.00	,,
Chas. P. Champion	Lot #1 on west shore of Thunder Bay	400	1.00	,,
Chas. J. Johnson	Block A St. Ignace Island	400	1.00	Feb. 9/65
Rev. Geo. Duffield Jr.	Lot #2 on west shore of Black Bay	400	1.00	Mar. 3/65

[48]The considerable number of locations described as occupying the west shore of Black Bay were surveyed by J. Donnelly. He also surveyed the smaller lots on St Ignace Island, granted in the 1860s, and the one Current River location listed.

[49]Lot #15 Thunder Bay and the group of lots described as occupying the block west of Black Bay were surveyed by T.W. Herrick, who acquired one of these lots himself, along with his friends John McIntyre and the McKellar brothers. Herrick also surveyed the property which the Hudson's Bay Company acquired on the Nipigon River.

To Whom Patented	Tract	Area in ac.	Price per ac.	Date
Quebec & Lake Superior Mining Assn.[50]	#16 St. Ignace Island	6400	.80	March 17/65
Jeremiah Millbank	Lot #21 on west shore of Black Bay	400	1.00	March 28/65
Henry C. Gregg	Lot #11 on west shore of Black Bay	400	1.00	"
Wm. P. Trowbridge	Block A on Current River north shore of Thunder Bay	400	1.00	Mar. 29/65
Hudson Bay Company	Block A west side of Neepigon River	400	1.00	Apr. 18/65
Quebec & Lake Superior Mining Assn.	Block A north shore of Michipicoten Island	400	1.00	Apr. 5/65
Hugh R. Fletcher	Block B south side of Michipicoten Island	22	20	April 18/65
Jos. B.T. Grady	Lot #14 St. Ignace Island	315	1.00	Apr. 21/65
John McIntyre	Lot A in block west of Black Bay	400	1.00	Sept. 2/65
Donald McKellar	Lot B in block west of Black Bay	200	1.00	Sept. 2/65
Peter McKellar	Lot C in block west of Black Bay	400	1.00	Sept. 1/65
Thos. W. Herrick	Lot D in block west of Black Bay	400	1.00	Sept. 2/65
John S. Steele	Lot #2 in block north of twp. of Nee-Bing	400	1.00	Nov. 20/65

D 19 CHARLES DUPONT[51] TO WILLIAM SPRAGGE[52]
[*P.A.C., RG 10 C-3, Indian Affairs Letter Books, v. 574, p. 530*]

Manitowaning,
July 19, 1867

I learned that the American Traders for whose expulsion the Indians had petitioned having learnt of my coming had ten days previous to my

[50]The Quebec and Lake Superior Mining Association had lost many of its lands by the date of this list. It held on to three of its 6400-acre locations, only one of which was in Thunder Bay, and was apparently permitted to patent them at a price lower than that currently being charged, but twice the price demanded in the previous decade. Additional land which it acquired on Michipicoten Island in the 1860s was charged at the current price – $1.00 per acre.

[51]Charles Dupont was in charge of the Northern Superintendency of the Indian Affairs Department from 1863 to 1868. His experience on Manitoulin Island had led him to be most suspicious of the Jesuit missionaries, and he was almost equally suspicious of the influence of the Hudson's Bay Company.

[52]William Spragge was Deputy Superintendent of Indian Affairs 1862–73. He thus served under three Chief Superintendents (Commissioners of Crown Lands) before Confederation and three Superintendents-General after the 1867 reorganization that transferred Indian Affairs to the control of the Secretary of State.

arrival left with all their goods by schooner for the American Side of Lake Superior, and the Indians informed me they did not expect they would return. The principal object of my journey was thus accomplished ...

They as well as the Indians of Fort William, Michipicoten, and Red Rock whom I subsequently saw are very desirous of receiving their annuity money through me instead of as at present through the Hudson Bay Company and they have offered to meet and convey me by canoe from one settlement to the other without payment of any wages if I should go up for this purpose ...

Dr. Simpson[53] vaccinated large numbers at every place we stopped at, the Indians appearing to appreciate greatly the advantage. He also attended & prescribed for a great many sick.

D 20 WILLIAM PLUMMER[54] TO HECTOR LANGEVIN[55]
[*P.A.C., RG 10, C-3, Indian Affairs Letter Books, v. 575, p. 46*]

Manitowaning,
October – 1868

I have the honor of reporting to you that having been repeatedly informed that the parties on board the Steamer "Algoma"[56] and others were selling liquor to Indians at all the stopping places between Collingwood and Fort William, & especially at the latter place where the steamer stops ...

At Fort William, one Flaherty[57] has started a saloon, fearlessly sold liquor to Indians & others and I have had this Flaherty before me and fined him the full penalty for selling to Indians & also for selling without a license. I have the honor of stating however that these fines are not sufficient punishment to be inflicted on persons for bringing liquor into these remote parts where there are but few persons besides Indians ... In remote places where an officer can only make occasional visits the present law does not meet the difficulty. The enormous profit made by the sellers of liquor to Indians enables him to pay the fine.

[53]Thomas Simpson, M.D., was for a number of years employed by the Northern Superintendency. He and Dr W.S. Francis were listed among the personnel of the department in 1873.

[54]William Plummer succeeded Dupont as Northern Superintendent in 1868. He held that post until 1873.

[55]Hector Langevin (1826–1906) was Secretary of State in the first Dominion government, and as such had charge of Indian Affairs. When he became Minister of Public Works in 1869 his former post was filled by Joseph Howe.

[56]The large side-wheeler, the *Algoma*, was one of the earliest passenger boats on Lake Superior. It first arrived at Fort William in 1865, after damages during the 1864 trip caused it to stop at Michipicoten. Dupont had travelled on the *Algoma* in his 1867 visit to the Lake Superior Indians, and his comments were very similar to those Plummer made in 1868.

[57]James Flaherty arrived in the region only in 1868. He became the proprietor of the Queen's Hotel, constructed in the early 1870's, and a considerable holder of Port Arthur real estate by the 1880s.

D 21 JAMES DICKSON'S[58] FIRST SUMMER AT THE
"STATION"
[*Port Arthur,* Weekly Herald, *June 13, 1883*]

... In the spring of 1868 the enterprising firm of Marks Bros.[59] decided on opening a branch store at this place, your humble servant being selected from the staff to run the venture. In accordance with instructions I took passage on the good old lucky steamer Algoma, on her second up trip, accompanied by a fellow townsman Mr. J. Flaherty, who has since shown great energy and enterprise in erecting the Queen's Hotel, and latterly a fine mansion and first class block of stores on Cumberland Street. We were landed at what is now known as P.A. Landing, then known by the name of the Station, and consisted of one log house constructed by the Department of Public Works now appropriated as a banking institution by the Ontario Bank. The Syndicate [C.P.R.] tried hard to blow it up by blasting the way for a track along the front, but only got so far as to hoist off the verandah, they have just discovered that it was built under Conservative rule and won't be knocked over ...

As the firm had made arrangements to furnish the steamer with wood, and as she required from forty to fifty cords each trip it was necessary to construct a wharf, not only to handle wood, but to land supplies, quite a large amount being required, for the use of miners and explorers large numbers being attracted to this locality by the glowing accounts of large silver deposits one of which was then busy developed by the Thunder Bay Mining Co. Also provisions and material for a large force of men about to be employed at what has since been called the Dawson road. Seven miles of which had been completed the previous year under the superintendance of Mr. Bridgeland.

I had completed my calculations and had actually commenced dove tailing cribs intending to build a solid structure commencing at the shore and continuing out until I reached 10 feet of water so as to allow the steamer to come along the end ... Some of the employees of the H.B. Co. and others from the Kaministiquia coming along and learning what I intended doing, related a tale of an ice shove which had occurred there some 6 years past, and that an old gray-haired M.D. whose age was just the same as other gray-headed Indians, that is Ka-gau-gut-a'week which I believe means near one hundred, had told them that every seven years a "kitchee" big shove occurred in this bay, and he was certain from noticing the hair on the musk rats tail this season that the ice would be very thick the coming winter, and that the white man was foolish to try and build a

[58]James Dickson had been in the employ of the Marks family at Bruce Mines, and was entrusted with the opening of a branch store at the "Station" in 1868. He remained in the area, becoming Inspector of Fisheries for Thunder Bay in the 1880s.
[59]Thomas Marks had come to Algoma in 1849 from Limerick. With his brother Wesley he established a business at Bruce Mines, then became a permanent resident of Prince Arthur's Landing in the early 1870s. Thomas Marks became involved in a number of local businesses and in municipal politics, head of the Conservative Association, Reeve of Shuniah, then Mayor of Port Arthur.

dock that would stand ... I admit I was not as well posted then as I have been since, and the story being related by men who I considered were entirely disinterested, and being blessed with good honest looking countenances, and delivered in a style which would be very becoming in any pulpit orators. I began to think I had been landed in the spring time of an Arctic thaw. So my solid structure vanished, and a jetty substituted which I constructed in the following manner, five cribs of small size, round logs saddled at the ends, pinned together with wooden pins, half filled with brush floated into place, rocks thrown on the brush to sink cribs, put on stringers of round logs, substituted poles for planks, pinned the whole together with good tamarac pins. Sent for a small decked scow which arrived some weeks after by steamer. I then ran the business during the season of navigation with the above outfit, charged no wharfage, every man took his freight as he could catch it ...

D 22   ROBERT CRAWFORD[60] TO JAMES CLOUSTON[61]
[P.A.C., H.B.Co. Records, B-134-c]

Lake Nipigon,
Jan. 19, 1869

Do you remember my asking you for a little information regarding this place for I felt my being so long away from the Indian trade would be a great drawback ... I went to Fort Wm. found Mr. McIntyre sick with bleeding at the nose – he threw me on old Mr. Laronde who offered to give me all the information he could, he went down to the Sault by the return of the steamer in which I came up & died there. Then what with the visit of that daft man Mr. McDonald of the Silver mine (who would drain a deep mine dry if it was only filled with Eau de vie) what with the mineralogy, geology, etymology, syntax and prosidy veins, shafts, nuggets, lump mass & veins, lead indications, mica specimens, fire and earth and water I did not know where in all the world I had got to. I am thinking of sending down a few iron spoons we have here to see if the eternal chattering won't turn them into silver. Who could get any information about the paltry fur trade – not at all when I could get so much information on the formation of the crust and the bowels of the Earth & allowed to look through a little burning glass on dirty little bits of stone & told I held so many dollars value to the ton and all for nothing ...

[60]Chief Trader Robert Crawford had been in charge of various business enterprises for the Hudson's Bay Company from 1866 to 1868, travelling extensively in Canada West and the United States with Lindsay as his home base. His family ties with the Brockville area remained strong, and his relatives there possessed considerable political influence. As a Chief Trader, Crawford outranked all Company personnel in the Lake Superior District west of Michipicoten, but he soon came to regard his posting as far from a promotion. By 1873, shortly before he was transferred to Ungava, he became a Factor. He seems to have left the Company service in 1878.

[61]Chief Factor James Stewart Clouston, at the Montreal headquarters by the late 1860s, had a long association with the Company, serving at Moose Factory in the 1840s.

What a place for a Christian, why Mrs. Crawford was nearly sick long before we reached the shore (and you know she is not one to complain or be easily frightened) from the stench caused by the carcases of dead Dogs and rotten fish lying 200 yards in front of the premises ... I got ashore and found the place in ruins, not a house to put ourselves into unless we went along with the men & even then the whole & sole furniture besides the stove and goods and the walls of a ruin were 3 straight-backed chairs, a table, and a long bench on which I sat down. This is rather hard lines (I thought) coming up here blindfold, just as if I had done some great evil for which I must be punished, and therefore everyone passed me along with some excuse as if I was de trop and wishing to get rid of me as soon as possible. I was looked upon as an intruder here in the 1st, place, next I found no house to go into, & not a pot or a pan ...

Mr. McIntyre sent me late in the fall a young man of the name of Cassidy,[62] he is about as useful as a wooden eye would be, more for ornament and make believe – I can't trust or depend on him to do anything so he returns to Fort Wm. by packet tomorrow.

D 23   A. B. SCOTT[63] TO HON. STEPHEN RICHARDS[64]
[P.A.O., Crown Lands Papers, Surveyors' Accounts, 1869]

Fort William,
July 5, 1869

The weather has been unfavourable for making much progress with the survey and the black flies have been so bad that the men cannot work satisfactorily ...

Mr. Dawson has a party at work now exploring the country to change the Red River Road line. They purpose leaving the old Dog Lake trail about the seven mile post and crossing the western boundary of my township [McIntyre] about sixty chains from the southwest angle of section 12 and thence to the Mattawan River[65] – if they locate the road on that line will it be necessary to change the lots in my projected plan?

[62]Thomas Cassidy was duly reported to have returned from Nipigon on January 25, 1869. His plan was then to return to Montreal by way of Superior, Wisconsin, at the urgent request of his father, who also supplied a letter of credit to make the journey possible (P.A.C., H.B. Co. Records, B-134-c-113, McIntyre to Hopkins, Feb. 10, 1869).

[63]Andrew Brown Scott of Brampton was employed by the province to survey the Township of McIntyre in 1869. He later also conducted the survey of McGregor Township.

[64]Stephen Richards (1820–94) represented Niagara in the first Legislature of the province of Ontario. He was Commissioner of Crown Lands in the Sandfield Macdonald cabinet from 1867 to 1871, when he became Provincial Secretary. He, with a number of other members of the Legislature, had actually travelled to Thunder Bay in the summer of 1867 and had been impressed by the mining activity then under way. Shortly after this visit, a number of township surveys were authorized.

[65]The decision to alter the original plan and to build a road to the Matawin River (that is, the present Trans-Canada Highway line) was quickly seized upon by John McIntyre as a reason for building a store at Matawin (P.A.C., H.B. Co. Records, B-134-c, McIntyre to McTavish, Feb. 10, 1870).

E. THE ZONE OF TRANSIT, 1870–85

E 1 FREDERICK DENISON'S[1] ARRIVAL AT PRINCE ARTHUR'S LANDING
[M.T.C.L., Frederick C. Denison Diaries, v. 1]

25 May [1870]   turned out about 6   stopped at 7.40 near a silver mine on a small island to let off some miners.[2] Thunder cape in front of us 1300 ft high – got into "Prince Arthurs landing"[3] at 10 am   send by Col. W[4] to examine land ½ mile to left of us to see if fit for a camp. found it was – a piece about 90 yds by 50 with a nice stream of water – busy all day putting up tents and getting ashore stores.   in afternoon took a walk with Dr. Robertson R.C.R. 1½ miles down "Kaministiquia" Road – after tea Ward, St. Maur, Riddle and Dr. Young of the 60th R. and Huyshe[5] and myself took a row boat out about 3 miles and back   a lovely calm evening   the camp is on a rise, a most beautiful situation for a town.   turned in shortly after 10 PM   so cold could not sleep   had to get up and put on a pair of drawers and other things.

26 May –   got up about 6.30 am   a lovely morning   Col W started at 8 am for a ride up Govt road.   went out for a stroll in the morning.   a lot of us went for a swim in the afternoon off the buoy.   after tea at 6 Huyshe St. Maur and I went out for a ride up the Kaministiquia road going about 4 miles and then returned   turned in about 10½ PM

[1]Frederick Denison (1846–96) had already been five years in the army when an expedition was organized in 1870 to move west to Red River where Louis Riel had set up a provisional government in defiance of Canadian regulations. Denison served as an orderly officer with this expedition. He later represented West Toronto, as a Conservative, in the House of Commons.

[2]Silver Islet was on the usual steamer route at this time, and a much more flourishing community than either Fort William or the Landing.

[3]It was Colonel Wolseley who named the landing place, and, according to his own account (*A Soldier's Life*, v. 2, p. 187), on exactly the same day as Denison first quoted him. The Landing was named for Prince Arthur (later the Duke of Connaught) who had spent the previous winter in Montreal with his regiment and was still in Canada when the Red River expedition set out. Denison's description of the campsite refers to the vicinity of the present intersection of Cumberland and Arthur streets in the city of Thunder Bay.

[4]Garnet Wolseley (1833–1913) saw military service in India, the Crimea, and China, before being sent to Canada in 1861 as Assistant Quartermaster-General. A Colonel at the time he was chosen to command the Red River expedition, he later rose to the rank of Field-Marshal, and was elevated to the peerage as Viscount Wolseley.

[5]Captain G.L. Huyshe left his account of the expedition (E 6). The other officers named appear to have been sufficiently identified by Denison himself.

Friday 27th May   got up at Reveille   saw the Algoma the Brooklyn and the tug off the wharf.   they had come in during the night about 3 After Breakfast went on board the Algoma with Irvine and Huyshe commenced unloading immediately   the Chickland[6] and boats in tow sighted at 9.50 am   came to anchor at 11.45 am   Fatigue parties busy unloading vessels all day.   went with Huyshe and saw No 1 Co Ontario Batt. camped at creek ½ mile to East of us.   the Algoma left between 8 and ½ past   Went out for a short ride after tea.   Mr. Dawson lent me a splendid blanket.   a party of Mr. Dawson men and a Fatigue party from 60th working at a road from here to Volunteer Camp.   wrote to George.

28 May Saturday   Slept soundly last night thanks to Mr. D. Blanket. got up at 4 am to see 2 Co of 60th march out under command of Capt Ward   one co to be stationed at Bridge over Kaministiquia River   the other at a small Lake 7 miles beyond.   went to bed again for two hours before dinner   went out for a short stroll with Robertson   had some Pistol Practise.   bought a silk handkerchief, after dinner read etc until 5   then went out for a ride with Col. Wolseley.   after tea Huyshe came back from a fishing excursion with 5 large trout   the others of his party caught none   after dark there were 15 of us sitting round our camp fire.

29 Sunday –   turned out about 8 am   we all attended service by a Mr. Wilson an Indian missionary.   after Dinner Major Robertson and Fraser of 60 Irvine Huyshe and I were rowed over to Fort William.   we made some purchases and came back by tug.   after tea the Band played a number of very pretty pieces   this was the first time no doubt a band ever played in this part of the world   after that we sat round our camp fire – Col. W. dined with Mr. McIntyre at Fort Wm.

E 2   COLONEL WOLSELEY TO JOHN MCINTYRE
[*P.A.C., MG 29 D-10, McIntyre Papers*]

June 3, 1870

Can you assist us in getting forward some of our supplies to the Shebandowan Lake via the Kaministiquia River? If you could arrange

---

[6]Wolseley's Day Book is more explicit concerning the arrival of vessels. The *Algoma* and the *Brooklyn* arrived at 3 a.m., the *Chickland* and two schooners, the *Pandora* and the *Orion*, at 11:30 a.m. They had sailed from the Sault on May 23, after a Fenian scare. The advance party had left at the same time by the *Chicora*, the fastest ship then in service on Lake Superior. The *Frances Smith*, which had been scheduled to leave with the others, was awaited in vain on May 26 – when the *Chicora* left on its return trip. Those arriving on the 27th reported that the Captain of the *Frances Smith* had refused to enter Lake Superior without a guarantee of $65,000.

with the Indians to convey any number of half barrels of pork or biscuit from one hundred up to a thousand, it would be a great matter in forwarding the objects of this expedition. If you can do so, I should feel much obliged if you would kindly inform me of the cost of doing so.

Mr. D. Smith[7] told me I might depend upon your rendering me every assistance in your power, and your kindness to me since I arrived here Emboldens me to make this request.

It is of the most vital importance that we should receive the transport over this road to the utmost possible extent.

E 3 HUGH JOHN MACDONALD[8] TO JAMES COYNE[9]
[*University of Western Ontario Library (U.W.O.), Coyne Papers*]

Prince Arthurs Landing
Thunder Bay June 26th /70

Dear Copper

... For a time after arriving here things were very quiet fishing drinking and swearing being the only amusements, and as I don't drink I was reduced to fishing a little and swearing a great deal. About a fortnight ago a mania for boating seized the fellows, and though the heavy six oared boats to be used on this expedition are the only ones here, several good races have come off. The first of the series was between the Engineers and 60th Rifles, the course was a mile long, and the race a very close one, the Engineers winning by only a third of a boats length ...

I don't know when I will leave here and cant say that I am particularly anxious to do so, as we are very comfortable here, and the fishing and boating are first rate. I can tell you this is ahead of Law ...

I don't know when this letter will leave this as the "Chicora" was due here on Friday last and is not in sight yet.

Sincerely yours,
Doojohn

[7]Donald Smith (1820–1914), later Baron Strathcona, was in 1870 a Chief Factor in the Hudson's Bay Company. Late in 1869 he had been acting as *locum tenens* for Edward Hopkins in charge of the Montreal headquarters, and had thus been sent by the Dominion government to negotiate with the provisional government set up by Riel at Red River. He seems to have been on close terms of friendship with John McIntyre.

[8]Hugh John Macdonald (1850–1929), the son of the Canadian Prime Minister, had just graduated from the University of Toronto in 1869 and was still undecided about a legal career when he joined the Red River expedition. In 1872 he was called to the bar, and, after practising for some years in Toronto, moved to Winnipeg. He was briefly Premier of Manitoba.

[9]James Coyne (1849–1942), a college friend of Hugh John Macdonald, graduated from the University of Toronto in 1870 with very high honours, and immediately articled with a lawyer in St Thomas.

E 4 MACDONALD TO COYNE
[*U.W.O., Coyne Papers*]

Oskondaga Creek, Dawson's Road
July 15th, 1870

Things went on very quietly at Thunder Bay from the date of my last letter till Monday the 4th at three o'clock in the morning when we were all up, and ready to start on the march up the road. At about 4 o'clock the start was effected, the delay being caused by a good many of the men and some of the officers being drunk as the devil. Of course this is private and confidential as I would not like to have it circulated. However at last we got off and that day marched thirteen miles part of the time through a heavy thunder storm. The men carried everything but their knapsacks, and the officers the same with the addition of revolvers and ammunition. The Colonel marched at the head of the column all the time, the only mounted officer being the Adjutant, who had a very sore leg. On arriving at the halting ground, the men proceeded at once to rest themselves while we poor devils had to see that they had dinner and some sort of shelter before we looked after our own comforts, and I can assure you that it is no easy work to look after a lot of fellows who dont know how to do anything for themselves. This work fell particularly heavily on me as my Captain was on the sick list and the Lieut. on detachment, your humble servant being in charge of the company. Next morning we were up and off at two o'clock and marched as far as the Kamanistiquia Bridge where we halted, and camped and were just preparing to make ourselves comfortable when Col. Wolseley rode into camp and ordered our Coy and No 7 to continue the march next day. In accordance with these orders, at four next morning we began a long march of twenty five miles, over terribly muddy roads in which you would sink up to your ankles every step. The worst of it was that the soil is damned stiff red clay that sticks to one's feet like the devil. A good many men gave out on the road and came straggling into camp some time after we had arrived. As soon as we reached the place where we were to camp some men were detailed to clear the ground, which with the aid of good axes they soon did. We then pitched our tents had supper and went to bed, having first heartily cursed old Dawson. He may perhaps call this "a good road" but in any civilized country it would pass for a very respectable swamp. We are encamped about a mile from Oskondaga Creek, in a place abounding with mosquitoes black flies sand flies and other small game. None of them trouble me, thank God, but all go for the Captain. I really believe that the devil got up this expedition for the purpose of getting hold of my immortal soul, as I am already beginning to swear a little. The example set me by my Captain is not good, as I am sorry to say he does not bear the bites of the mosquitoes, doubtless made by the Lord, with the patience of a Christian, and whenever evening approaches my ears are shocked by oaths. Since our arrival here we have been busy road making not a very intellectual work, but I hope it won't last long as the first detachment of the 60th Rifles leaves tomorrow morning and we are to be the first of our Battalion to leave. Address your letters as before.

E 5 WOLSELEY TO THE MILITARY SECRETARY IN MONTREAL
[*Great Britain, Parliament,* Correspondence relative to the Recent Expedition to the Red River Settlement, *pp. 40–3*]

Camp, Ward's Landing,
3 miles from Shebandowan Lake,
16th July, 1870

I regret extremely that so much delay has occurred in starting the expedition from Shebandowan Lake, but I humbly submit that it was not in any way attributable to want of energy or arrangement on the part of the military, but has been occasioned by circumstances over which they could exercise no control whatever ...

1st The original plan of military operation was based upon the belief that the regular troops (more than one-third of the whole force), were to have left Collingwood for Thunder Bay in the first week of May, whereas they did not leave that port until the 21st, 25th and 26th of that month. This delay is attributable, in my opinion, to two causes: 1st, the slowness of the Dominion Government in making arrangements for conveying the force and its equipment across the lakes; and 2ndly, to the action taken by the United States authorities in closing the canal at Sault Ste. Marie to our shipping[10] ...

The second important cause of delay was, I consider, the want of a road between Thunder Bay and Shebandowan Lake, by means of which we could have sent forward our supplies. The original plan of military operations was based upon the belief that the road between those places would be open for traffic along its entire length before the 1st June. I write this on the 16th July, and it is now only cut out as far as this camp (about 3 miles from the lake), whilst some miles of it between the Oskondagee Creek and Young's Landing are still practically useless as a highway for constant and heavy traffic.

On the 26th May, the day after my arrival, I rode as far as it was practicable for wheeled transport, a distance only of about 28 miles; the total distance by road (as marked out) to the lake being at least 47

[10]Wolseley included a good deal of detail about the difficulties at the Sault locks. He claimed that the disputed cargoes did not contain "military equipment" but admitted that it was planned to carry such equipment on later trips had the vessels not been prevented from passing through the locks. After a delay awaiting instructions from Ottawa, he had despatched troops, horses, and supplies by steamer from Collingwood, then unloaded all ships below the locks, and, after a three-and-a-half-mile "portage," reloaded the vessels in Lake Superior.

miles. Beyond that it was a matter of difficulty to go on horseback, and could not be accomplished without danger to the horse.

On the 6th June I again rode along it, and penetrated as far as the Oskondagee Creek, a distance of about 38 miles, the last 7 or 8 miles being totally unfit for transport purposes.

The Oskondagee Creek (about 75 ft. wide) was still unbridged. From thence to the Dam Site, a distance of about 5 miles, the road was cut out through the woods for half that distance, but the stumps had not been taken out of the ground.

On the 15th June the road was again inspected by Lieutenant-Colonel McNeill,[11] who reported that between the Matawin and Oskondagee Rivers there were still about 3 miles that were almost impassable. The latter river had been bridged, and the road cut to within 1⅛ miles of the Dam Site, the remaining space being still untouched ...

I have thus given a general outline of the condition in which I found the road when I first landed, also upon the several dates when I subsequently inspected it, and its state now that it is about to cease being made use of by the force under by command.

In doing so, I have no intention of imputing to anyone's want of zeal or energy in pushing it forward. Mr. Dawson, of the Public Works Department, as well as the engineers working under his orders, have been untiring in their exertions to get the road in working order. He has had to contest with great difficulties. Fires have raged twice over considerable portions of it, consuming culverts, cribwork, retaining walls and corduroy work. Heavy rains have swamped it at other times, carrying away bridges, and rendering it impassable for days ...

The plan which I adopted for the transport of boats and stores was as follows: − To begin with boats, 28 were sent over the road as far as the Matawin Bridge upon our first arrival, and I am now bringing up a few more in that way ... Previous to our arrival here, I had been led to believe by everyone who had any previous knowledge of the country, that the only way of getting boats forward to Shebandowan Lake was by carting them over a road to that place. I was informed repeatedly that they could not be taken up the Kaministiquia river. After landing, every day's stay in the country taught me more of its geography.

Mr. McIntyre, the Hudson's Bay Company's Officer at Fort William, gave me most valuable information, and from him I learnt that it was quite feasible to send up all by boats by the river. As the general opinion of everyone connected with the Public Works Department was most decidedly against the attempt, I felt that, as a stranger to the country,

[11]John Carstairs McNeill (1821–1904) was military secretary to General James Lindsay, the officer commanding for Ontario and Quebec. He seems to have reported directly to Colonel Wolseley and to have been well regarded by both Lindsay and Wolseley. McNeill, like Denison, later took part in the Nile expedition. He had a distinguisted military career, winning the v.c. in 1864, and being knighted in 1880.

I was assuming to myself a grave responsibility in making it; but already doubting the possibility of the road being finished in sufficient time to fulfil all our requirements, I considered it worth while to risk a few men and boats in determining the point. I despatched Captain Young, 60th Rifles, with his company (two Indians for each boat as guides being furnished by Mr. McIntyre) on this service. The result was a complete success. Of all those that subsequently came up the Kaministiquia route only one has been wrecked. This boat service was of great use in drilling the men to the use of boats and their management in rapid water on portages &c., a knowledge that will be of such great importance to them hereafter. The boats were thus taken from Thunder Bay to Shebandowan Lake by water, except for the distance of five miles, where there are such a series of heavy rapids and falls that I considered it more prudent to have them carried on wagons. Had I not been able thus to have made use of river, the departure of the Expedition would have been still much further delayed ...

The troops along the line of road as far as the Matawin Bridge have been almost exclusively fed upon fresh meat and bread. Bakeries were established at Prince Arthur's Landing, the Matawin Bridge, and Ward's Landing. I have never before been with any force in the field so well fed as this one has been up to the present moment. The rations good and ample.

The absence of any spirituous liquor as part of the daily issue, is marked by the excellent health and spirits of the men, and I may add by a remarkable absence of crime.

The work performed by the men up to their arrival here has been very considerable, so much so, that many companies already begin to present a ragged appearance. This work has been especially hard upon the Militia, from the fact of their having to work in thick winter trousers when the thermometer has sometimes stood over 90° in the shade ...

Speaking generally, the personal equipment supplied to the Militia by the Canadian Government is much inferior to that furnished to the Regular Troops from our own Military Stores.

I beg to add that I have left at Prince Arthur's Landing a sufficient garrison to man the parapets and to work the guns mounted in the redoubt I had constructed there. It is of sufficient strength to hold out against any number of Fenians that could possibly be brought against it.

E 6   CAPTAIN HUYSHE'S DESCRIPTION OF THE
TRANSPORT ARRANGEMENTS TO RED RIVER
[*Huyshe,* The Red River Expedition, *pp. 28–30*]

The latter portion (600 miles) from Lake Superior presented the greatest difficulties, as the route passed through the wilderness of lakes and rivers, traversed only by the Indian in his birch-bark canoe, and never hitherto attempted by any boat of European construction. Some portion of this route had been surveyed by Mr. S.J. Dawson, of the Public Works department, who was employed in the construction of the road which was to connect the waters of Lake Superior with the innumerable lakes and rivers stretching in an almost unbroken chain to the prairies of the North-West ... He was accordingly employed by the Dominion Government in the organization of the "Boat Transport Service" and under his direction upwards of 200 boats were built in the various boat-building establishments in Canada. The boats were of two kinds, "clinkers" and "carvels." They were also of different dimensions, but as a general rule were from 25 to 30 feet long, by 6 to 7 feet wide, and were constructed to carry a weight of 4 tons, besides a crew of 14 men. Mr. Dawson also undertook the onerous task of collecting a body of trained boatmen skilled in the navigation of boats in rapid water, as it was not of course to be expected that the soldiers should understand this kind of work. He had together about 400 men, who were dignified with the name of "voyageurs" but the great majority of whom were utterly ignorant of their work, and proved afterwards to be only encumbrances in the boats. A very small percentage of them were really "voyageurs" excepting about 100 Iroquois Indians drawn from the villages of St. Regis and Caughnawaga, in the neighbourhood of Montreal, who, with scarcely an exception, were splendid fellows, and without whom it is not too much to say the troops never could have reached their destination.

E 7   LIST OF ARTICLES IN BOATS FOR THE RED
RIVER EXPEDITION [12]
[*Huyshe,* The Red River Expedition, *app. B*]

In each boat there will be the following tools and equipment: – Two felling axes, one pickaxe, one spade, one shovel, two hand axes, two Flanders kettles, two frying-pans, two sails, two boathooks, two spare oars (making eight in all) four rowlocks, one set of blocks (single and double) one boat lamp, six thimbles for setting poles, one dipper, one rubber bucket, one boat sponge, two cans of paint (black and white), five pounds of assorted boat nails, one double tin oilcan, one tin with pitch, one tarpaulin, fenders, sixty fathoms tow line, one can mosquito oil &c, & spare plank and tools necessary for repairs. There will also be the cooking utensils &c., of the boatmen, for which the coxswain of

[12]Captain Huyshe, who was on Wolseley's staff, had access to the official records in preparing his account, and was granted permission to include some of these records in the appendix to his own narrative.

each boat will be responsible. With each brigade of boats there will be a carpenter's chest of tools and a fishing net.

E 8   HUYSHE'S OBSERVATIONS ON RATIONS
[*Huyshe*, The Red River Expedition, *pp. 114–16*]

I do not hesitate to say that, had a spirit ration been issued, the results would have been very different ... I admit that, in a country where fuel is scarce, it is difficult always to get wood to make the fire necessary for tea; but this should be provided by the Commissariat, and the money and transport saved by the absence of liquor would go a long way towards supplying the fuel requisite for the tea ... There may be medical men in our army who would oppose the nonissue of spirits; it was so with the Red River Expedition; some of the medical men asserted that it was a mistake, that it would never do – but the result was a most perfect triumph for tea.

E 9   WOLSELEY'S VIEWS ON THE INDIAN ATTITUDE TOWARD HIS MISSION
[*Wolseley,* Narrative, *pp. 274–5*]

The priesthood of Canada being much opposed to this expedition had preached it down everywhere and there can be little doubt that priestly influence was brought to bear on the Christian Indians settled near Fort William to prevent them from acting as our guides ... This expedition would have been a godsend to them if they had not been tampered with, as it would have afforded them lucrative employment. They know every river, lake, and portage ... and, in previous years, when exploring and surveying parties had been at work in their country, they had done good service in a most willing and cheerful manner.

They are a simple-minded but very superstitious race, easily ruled by the Jesuit Father who has spent his life amongst them doing good.[13] Rumour was busy at the village frightening them with stories of Riel's determination to fight. These Christian Chippewas have an extraordinary dread of war – so much so that, when we reached Fort Francis the few who did accompany us so far became terror-stricken by the warlike reports that Riel's emissaries had spread among the Indians of that district, and positively refused to go any further. When a little coercion was tried by telling them that we could not afford to give them any provisions to take them back to their homes unless they kept with us, they bewailed their fate, many of them with tears, saying that they would risk anything sooner than go on where there was to be fighting.

[13]This is probably a reference to Father du Ranquet, although it would apply equally to Father Choné.

E 10   EDWARD HOPKINS TO JOHN MCINTYRE
[*P.A.C., MG, 29 D-10, McIntyre Papers*]

Montreal
August 5, 1870

This will be handed to you by the Honble A.G. Archibald,[14] the Governor of Manitobah and the Northwest, who is about to proceed to Fort Garry by the old canoe route.

I have done my best, on short notice, to get together Mr. Archibald's crew and outfit, but as he has no knowledge of canoe travelling, I must ask you to see that his arrangements are comfortably completed before starting from Fort William.[15]

I wish you would ... show Mr. Archibald how the tents should be pitched, how he is to stow away in the canoe & so forth. In fact, if you could accompany the Governor his first day's and night's march, you would set him going with comfort ...

I am inclined to recommend the old canoe route via the Dog Lake as I fancy the 40 miles jolting over Dawson's pretence of a road would seriously injure the canoe ...

E 11   JAMES H. ROWAN'S[16] REPORT ON THE PROGRESS OF RAILWAY SURVEYS
[*Sandford Fleming,* Progress Report, *1872, app. 6*]

I again sailed from Collingwood on the 10th August [1871], and reached Thunder Bay on the evening of the 14th; the *Rescue* had arrived the day previous having delivered a second supply of necessaries at the depots on the north shore of Lake Superior. By her I received the distressing intelligence of the loss of some men, by fire in the woods, belonging to party H;[17] this made me extremely anxious to visit that party and all the others along the north shore ...

[14]Adams G. Archibald (1814–92) was a Nova Scotian by birth and, after holding a number of offices in that colony, became Secretary of State in the new Dominion government in 1867. A strong advocate of Confederation, he still lacked any experience in the northwest when he became Lieutenant-Governor of the new province of Manitoba. Archibald was knighted in 1886, after his retirement from the position of Lieutenant-Governor of Nova Scotia.

[15]The tone of this letter is slightly more solicitous, but the contents are very similar to those of Hopkins to McIntyre, May 17, 1869 (P.A.C., MG 29 D-10), asking for assistance for Cyril Graham, recently retired from the Colonial Office. The instructions in the earlier letter were more specific – a half-size canoe and a crew of four men who knew the route. "Is Lambert [who had served with the Gladman-Hind expedition] too old for such a trip? He might be handy to Mr. Graham, acting as cook & servant etc."

[16]The preliminary survey groups were extremely active in the district during 1872 and 1873, before the change in government at Ottawa brought about a postponement of any plans for a transcontinental railway. Rowan, however, made it clear that he considered any such plan impracticable in the Thunder Bay area.

[17]For purposes of Commissariat and Survey, the expedition was organized in a

Leaving Thunder Bay, in the *Rescue*, on the evening of the 16th August, I reached Nepigon the following morning and proceeded along the explored line to the camp of party I, a distance of 10 miles ...

I returned to the *Rescue* the following day at noon, and proceeded down Nepigon Bay to Jack Fish River, where we arrived at 6 p.m. At this point party H had established a depot, thereby saving a portage of 14 miles along the line from Nepigon; here the effects of the fire in the woods were first seen by us, the timber and soil being completely burned up. Taking a man from the depot and two Indians I had brought with me from the Sault, I started along the line to visit the party; after proceeding about 12 miles we met Mr. Johnston and three men returning to institute a further search for the missing men.

It seems desirable that at this point I should give an account of the circumstances connected with this event, in order to shew that no blame can attach to any one in this matter, except the unfortunate men themselves: – A party of seven men, two whites and five Indians, were detailed from party H to bring forward supplies from one depot to another, (and for this purpose had cut a trail by a shorter route than that followed by the surveyed line) while the main party were proceeding with the exploration: notwithstanding their having been repeatedly urged by Mr. Johnston to push ahead and keep up with the rest of the party, they lagged behind. Their non-appearance, after some days, excited anxiety on the part of Mr. Johnston, who thought they had deserted and returned to Nepigon; he therefore proceeded there himself in search of them, but found they had not returned: then having fears for their safety, as the whole party had on several occasions, very narrow escapes from the fires, he immediately returned to the main party and sent his second in command with a number of men to search for the others. After an absence of five days they returned, having made an extensive search and found one Indian in a portion of the woods which had been burned over. He was lying on his face with his shirt, which he had taken off, between it and the ground, placed in that position to exclude the smoke from his lungs; he was not burned, but had evidently died of suffocation caused by the smoke. In a swamp near by were found six holes which had been excavated by the others, in order that by getting into them they might escape the fire, but the smoke becoming too dense had driven them away and no further trace of them could be found. The most extraordinary point in the whole sad event, being that all the supplies, together with their blankets and clothes, were found at the depot untouched by the fire.

The first party sent in search having made these discoveries, returned to Mr. Johnston, who, upon receipt of their report, had, when I met him,

---

number of lettered sections. Section G covered the district from the Little Black River to Long Lake, Section H from Long Lake to Red Rock, and Section I from Red Rock to Lac des Iles.

as already stated, started to make a final effort for finding some further traces of them.

We therefore, with the men, returned and slept for the night at one of the now deserted depots to which the supplies were being brought when the catastrophe occurred. When the whole party were first encamped at this point they had a very narrow escape, the fire having burned to within one quarter of a mile of the camp, and then leaping over burned on again beyond, leaving it intact. Leaving Mr. Johnston, the following morning, to prosecute the search (which, I subsequently learned proved useless,) I returned to the *Rescue* and proceeded down the lake to Pic, where we arrived at 8 p.m. on the 20th August.

The progress of this party had been very satisfactory, although the country passed over proved, for the most part, extremely rugged and broken, in fact entirely impracticable for Railway construction, the distance run at the time of my visit being about 30 miles.

Landing at Pic with my canoe on the morning of the 21st August, I procured some Indians at the Hudson Bay Post and proceeded up the Pic river, reaching the starting point of party G (a distance of 50 miles above the mouth of the river) late in the afternoon of the following day.

This was the point where the supplies were destroyed by fire referred to in an earlier part of this report. The manner in which it occurred was as follows: – The depot was built on a narrow terrace of the river bank, 20 feet above the water, which is succeeded by another terrace of about the same height, immediately in rear of the depot. In this building all the stores of the party were placed, with the exception of a small supply for immediate use in the camp about 10 miles distant. There was a man in charge who slept in the building; about daylight one morning he was awakened by a loud roaring noise, hastily putting on his clothes, he ran out to see the cause and found the whole of the woods on the Upper Plateau, in rear of the building, in flames. The fire was caused by some Indians who had camped there, who, on leaving at daylight, had neglected to extinguish the fire by which they had cooked their breakfast. The storekeeper had only time to roll some few barrels of flour and pork down the bank into the river and betake himself to a canoe, when the whole place was in flames.

The consequence of this was that, for some time the party was reduced to living on fish, which they caught, and some flour kindly lent to them by the H.B. officer at the Pic. As soon as possible, but not until after some time had elapsed, intelligence of the disaster was forwarded to Toronto, and the loss made good with as little delay as possible.

Starting from the Depot early on the 23rd August, with two Indians and one white man, to carry supplies and blankets, we reached the party in the forenoon of the 25th, after a most fatiguing walk of 40 miles. I found the work progressing very favourably although the party had many hardships to contend with, being sometimes reduced to very straightened circumstances as regards food, in consequence of the loss of their supplies by fire, and the great difficulty of transporting them over the rugged country they had traversed.

At the time I visited the party they were supposed to be within 6 or 8 miles of Long lake, at which point Mr. Armstrong,[18] the Engineer in charge, had directed a depot to be made. It subsequently turned out that they had 14 miles of a most difficult country to pass through, which took so long to get over that for some days before reaching the depot they had nothing to eat but a little flour and berries gathered on the hills.

The greater part of the country explored was of the most barren and rugged description, traversed by high ranges of hills of primitive rock from which every vestige of vegetation had been removed by fire, and quite impracticable for a Railway.

E 12 COMMUNITY OPTIMISM – RAILWAY CONSTRUCTION BEGINS IN THUNDER BAY
[*Toronto* Globe, *June 10, 1875*]

The energetic contractors, Messrs. Henry Sefton, Thomas Cochrane, I. Ward & Co. invited their friends at Prince Arthur's Landing to join those at Fort William in inaugurating this important undertaking, and punctually at two o'clock the steamers Jessie Oliver and Watchman, loaded with the beauty and fashion of the neighbourhood, left Prince Arthur's Landing for the scene of the operations of the day, which took place on the left bank of the Kaministiquia River, about four miles from its mouth, where were assembled upwards of five hundred ladies and gentlemen to witness the event. Among those present we observed the following, viz: – Judge Van Norman and ladies, Mr. & Mrs. John McIntyre, Mr. Thos. Marks and Miss Marks, Miss Wylie, Miss Buchanan, Mr. John and the Misses McKellar, Mr. and Mrs. D.M. Blackwood, Miss Fraser, Mr. Robert Morrison and Miss Morrison, Mr. George and Miss McVicar, Mr. & Mrs. J.C. Tulloh, Mr. and Mrs. T.A.P. Towers, Sr. and Jr., Mr. Samuel Hazlewood, chief of the "Prince Arthur" section of the Canada Pacific Railway Survey, and a large staff of surveyors, Mr. R. Maitland, Drs. McDonell, Clarke, and Cook, Messrs. L. de Carlo, J. Kerr, J. McLennan, Henry Sefton, Thomas Cochrane & Co., contractors, J. Girdlestone, Stewart B. Wallace Heath, Wm. P. Davidson, Moses Street, Noah K. Street, C.J. Brent, Manager Royal Canadian Bank, Adam Oliver, M.P., Alexander Stevenson, Jas. Flanagan, Geo. E. Oliver, Peter, Donald & Archibald McKellar, W.O. Dobie, Angus Bethune, Chief Purveyor Canada Pacific Railway Survey, and staff; Revs. Messrs. McKerracher and Dundas, Messrs. J. Preston, J. Sproule, J. Hebert, Jas. Bains, J. Parks, W.G. Dick, J. Tupper, G.

---

[18]Of several engineers named Armstrong who were briefly involved in railway surveys and railway building in the Lake Superior area, H.W.D. Armstrong, referred to in the McLennan diary (E 24), was the best known. He may have been the man referred to here.

Holland, C.C. Forneri, P.L.S., A. Tennyson, J. Furlong, G.E. Small, Hon. John Simpson, R. Carruthers, C. McIntyre, Miss McIntyre, Mr. and Mrs. Jas. Flaherty, R.B. and F.B. Horner, J. Kane, W.H. Carpenter, W. Beath, Manager Ontario Bank, J. Mengle.

Judge D.D. Van Norman,[19] on gaining the platform prepared for the speakers, spoke substantially as follows: – "It has been deemed by our wise men best to begin this tremendous undertaking right here in the heart of the continent, at the head of navigation, having for its object first to utilize the 1800 miles of splendid water navigation, and, bridging as it will the space of 400 miles more to tap the Central Provinces of our Federation, to draw closer the bonds of our commercial friendship and alliance, and also at the same time to weld into one homogeneous whole the disjointed fragments of almost alien peoples ... In my time I have seen history repeat itself on more than one occasion, and I verily believe it is about to do so again in this vicinity. Just fifty years ago as a boy I saw the great men of the day, Governor Clinton of New York and the Marquis Lafayette of France celebrate the completion of the Erie Canal at Buffalo, by mingling the waters of the Hudson River with those of Lake Erie. I also witnessed the turning of the first sod of the Illinois Central Railroad ... The village of Buffalo at that time contained a population less than Prince Arthur's Landing does today. And what at that time was called Chicago was no larger than that little aggregation of houses that goes by the name of Fort William. The breaking of bulk in the cargoes going east and west from those two has made these two cities at once, especially Chicago, the wonder and admiration of the whole world. I say I verily believe that history is about to repeat itself ... Judge Van Norman having informed Mr. Oliver, M.P.[20] that the time had now arrived for him to commence his important duty as cutter of the first sod of the great national undertaking Mr. Oliver proceeded to do so in a most workmanlike manner; a handsome spade and wheel barrow having been provided by the contractors for the purpose. The barrow being duly filled, Mr. Oliver wheeled it along the track and upset it in the most approved style, when a scramble ensued among the ladies and gentlemen as to who should possess a piece of the first cut. Great were the demands upon the supply, the requirements of those present as well as to send to friends at a distance.

[19]Delevan D. Van Norman was the first Stipendiary Magistrate of the sub-district of Thunder Bay, appointed in 1873. Like his brother-in-law, Sheriff John F. Clarke, and the Crown Land Agent, Amos Wright, he was one of that unusual group of men in their sixties who moved to a frontier village and became its most enthusiastic advocates.

[20]Adam Oliver (1823–82) was born in New Brunswick and had come to Upper Canada in 1836. By 1850 he was establishing himself as a builder and contractor in Ingersoll and in 1872, with his partners Peter Brown and Joseph Davidson, he built a saw mill at Fort William. He had been active in municipal politics in Ingersoll for a number of years, then represented South Oxford as a Liberal in the Ontario Legislature from 1867 to 1875.

E 13   THE OPENING OF THE TELEGRAPH LINE [21]
[*P.A.C., MG 29 D-10, McIntyre Papers*]

By telegraph from Prince Arthur's Landing
  June 22, 1876

To Jno. McIntyre
    H.B. Co.
    Fort William

It is the first link in the great line soon to run all the way to the Pacific. Trains will shortly follow. Prosperity for the telegraph.
    10.20 a.m.   S.J. Dawson

E 14   THE EXPENSE OF RAILWAY BUILDING
WEST FROM FORT WILLIAM
[*Canada, Senate, Debates, 1879, pp. 647, 657, May 13, 1879*]

Hon. Mr. MACPHERSON – [22] It is astonishing that the engineers should have been so much out in their calculations as they have been on the railway between Lake Superior and Red River. On the 1st section, from Lake Superior, only 32½ miles in length, there was an increase of more than 12½ per cent.[23] That is more than it ought to be in a country such as that through which the railway passes. There was no difficult work – nothing that ought to have deceived the engineers. If that had been the gross increase, I would never have asked for a committee. The next section (25) is 80 miles long.[24] The actual cost of it exceeds the estimated cost by more than one-third. That would not have occurred if the survey had been accurately made before the contract was let ...

[21]Communication between the two hamlets was all that C.P. telegraph service could offer at that time. A year later the lines were complete as far as Battleford; by 1879 the line had reached the Rockies and, it was hoped, would reach the Pacific shortly. But there was still no communication between Thunder Bay and either Toronto or Ottawa (P.A.C., MG 29 A-8, Fleming Letterbooks, June 11, 1879).

[22]Senator David Macpherson (1818–96) had been a partner of Casimir Gzowski at the time when they applied for timber grants in the Thunder Bay area. He had been a Conservative member of the Canadian Upper House since 1864, when he was elected to the Legislative Council; he was appointed to the Senate at Confederation. As the rival of Sir Hugh Allan for Canadian Pacific Railway contracts at the beginning of the 1870s, he found his party loyalty somewhat shaken, but his informed attack on the railway policies of the Mackenzie government might be taken as an indication that he had made his peace with Sir John. In 1880 he became Speaker of the Senate and a Minister without Portfolio in the Macdonald cabinet.

[23]Although Senator Macpherson did not specifically allude to it, he appears to have been referring to a part of Contract #13 awarded to Sifton & Ward, April 3, 1875. They had contracted to build the first section out of Fort William for $406,194.

[24]Contract #25, awarded to Purcell & Ryan, June 7, 1876, covered the line from Sunshine Creek to English River.

Hon. Mr. MCLELAN – [25] The people of the North-West could live without communication through their own territory, as the people of Ontario did for 30 or 40 years without communication to the sea, except through a foreign country, and the people of the North-West could have prospered as Ontario did. I say that the country has been deceived as to the cost of that communication between Manitoba and the Eastern Provinces. We were told by the late Government first, that by the construction of a few miles of road to Lake Shebandowan, and then by a slight improvement – I find the words used by the late Premier were "a slight improvement at Fort Frances" – we would have connection between Thunder Bay and Rat Portage, from which point a railway could be constructed to the Red River ...

The House can understand the character of that country when I tell them that for one quarter of the distance – for one hundred miles – the people of the country are paying $1.30 an inch for every inch of that road through it.

E 15   GEORGE STEPHEN[26] TO SIR JOHN
A. MACDONALD
[*P.A.C., MG 26 A-1, v. 267, Macdonald Papers*]

Causapscal,
August 27, 1881

Let me tell you that all the misgivings I had last year about the line north of Lake Superior, which you will remember I did not hesitate to confide in you – have disappeared, with a better knowledge of the position and of the whole country. I am now satisfied that the C.P.R. without the control of a line to the Atlantic seaboard would be a mistake. If for instance, it terminated like the Northern Pacific at Lake Superior, it could never become the property it is certain to be, having its own rail running from sea to sea. I am sure you will be glad to hear this from me, because I do not think but [for] your own tenacity on that

[25]Senator Archibald W. McLelan (1824–90) was a Nova Scotian who had been appointed to the Canadian Senate in 1869. He later resigned his seat to return to the Commons, and was serving as Lieutenant-Governor of Nova Scotia at the time of his death. A lumber merchant and ship builder who had supported Joseph Howe in his opposition to Confederation and eventual reconciliation with it, McLelan was likely to oppose large expenditures on transcontinental railways, no matter what party was responsible for them. On the other hand, his experience as a Commissioner of the Intercolonial Railway meant that he, like Macpherson, was likely to be listened to with respect in this debate.

[26]George Stephen (1829–1921), later Lord Mount Stephen, was President of the Bank of Montreal and, with his cousin Donald Smith, a member of the group which had assumed control of the St Paul and Manitoba Railway when, in 1880, he became a member of the syndicate which undertook the building of a Canadian transcontinental railway. His early inclination was to make use of American lines south of Lake Superior, linking with the St Paul and Manitoba, and bypassing Thunder Bay.

point that the line north of the Lake could ever have been built. Events have showed you were right & all the rest of us wrong.

E 16   MACDONALD TO STEPHEN
[P.A.C., MG 29 A-20, Stephen Papers]

Ottawa,
November 4, 1881
(Private)

    I note what you say about the Lake Superior shore route. I must confess a predilection for the northern Lake Nipigon route – that region, rough though it may be, will attract many settlers if the railway go that way and will have a lumber traffic going westward to supply the treeless prairies. This should not lightly be given up. The shore line will be only one-sided. It will be like the G.T.R. skirting the Lakes & controlled in a considerable degree by the water transport & the American lines on the south shore. What a Road that would have been had the policy I fought for in 1850 against Hincks been successful![27]

E 17   MACDONALD TO STEPHEN
[P.A.C., MG 29 A-20, Stephen Papers]

Ottawa,
November 16, 1881

    I am a convert to your Superior Lake shore route. It will please Ontario who are jealous of the line going far north & carrying the trade over their heads to Montreal.[28]

E 18   THE FIRST C.P.R. TRAIN ARRIVES
IN THUNDER BAY
[Port Arthur Weekly Herald, July 8, 1882]

'TIS DONE!

———

The GREAT TRANSAC-
TION'S DONE

———

[27]Sir John was obviously transposing a southern Ontario argument – and a very old and personal one at that – into a northern Ontario environment. His dreams of settlement and a vast lumber industry in the far north seem to have been less than realistic in 1881.

[28]Having conceded the argument to Stephen and his group, Macdonald perceived a political advantage in the decision he had heretofore opposed. The Hamilton Spectator and a number of other southern Ontario newspapers had been urging a route along the shoreline for some time.

The Thunder Bay
Branch Completed

The first train arrived
this morning

Only 30 Hours from
Winnipeg

Bonfire and Firing of
Guns

Great Indian War
Dance at Savanne

The Thunder Bay Branch of the Canadian Pacific Railway, connecting Winnipeg and the west with Prince Arthur's Landing, its terminus on Lake Superior, is at last completed, and the road is now in a position to admit of the passing of trains over the entire line, a distance of four hundred and thirty-six miles. If we had been told ten years ago that to-day would witness the arrival of a through train on the C.P.R. from Winnipeg, we would in all probability call the man a crank; but notwithstanding all the drawbacks and difficulties to contend with, the fact remains that the train is here.

Yesterday morning the news was received here that a through train was on its way and would arrive here late at night. The news was spread like wild-fire, and it was not long before everyone in town knew it.

About midnight a bonfire was started on the esplanade in front of the Queen's Hotel, and soon a crowd gathered around, waiting anxiously for the long expected visitor. At last, shortly before one o'clock, the sound of the whistle was heard and the headlight of the engine was seen in the distance. As the train neared the Queen's Hotel, guns were fired off, and cheer after cheer filled the air ...

PASSENGERS

Among the passengers arriving on the train were: Hon. Mackenzie Bowell, Minister of Customs, Ottawa; Hon. Adolphe P. Caron, Minister of Militia, Ottawa; A. Boultbee, Toronto; J.S. Aitkens, Winnipeg; S.O. Shorey, Montreal; Jas. Isbister, H. Sutherland, jr., Rat Portage; N.M. Fraser, England; Geo. Clarke, Niagara Falls; Geo. L. Wetmore, Tache; G.R. Kingsmill, J.M. Benyon, E. Anstruther, Winnipeg; P. O'Keefe, R. Kirkup, Rat Portage; Thos. Fraser, J.W. Blythe, Thos. Grant, Vermillion Bay; Father Baxter, P.A. Landing.

INDIAN WAR DANCE

As the train was nearing Savanne, a large crowd was noticed, and on coming nearer it was found to be about three hundred Indians, under the leadership of Chief Blackstone. They had long heard of the "iron horse" that was to come down

> From the wild of western prairies,
> From the big lakes of the northland,
> From the land of Manitoba
> Through the forests of Keewaydin,
> To the shining Big-Sea-Water,
> To the shores of Gitche Gumee.

and as the opportunity offered, while they were gathered together to receive their annuity, they concluded to have a big war-dance. All the Indians and squaws were painted up in the most approved fashion, and as the train halted a short distance from them the dance was at its height. The passengers, most of whom never saw anything of the sort before, were very much amused at the lively manner in which the Indians joined in the dance; beating their drums and tom-toms, and never noticing anything going on around them ...

E 19   STEPHEN TO MACDONALD
[P.A.C., MG 26 A-1, v. 267, Macdonald Papers]

Montreal,
August 27, 1882

We hope to have the [Nipissing to Thunder Bay] line permanently located this season except for the section between Nipigon [Red Rock] and Pic which is very heavy and any engineering mistake on it might cost us millions. We have an engineering party, our very best men, on this section between Red Rock and Pic and intend keeping them on it all winter, but no clamour will induce us to put a spade into that section till we are sure we are right in the location of the line.

E 20   WILLIAM VAN HORNE[29] TO E.B. OSLER[30]
[P.A.C., MG 28 III-20, Van Horne Letter Books, v. 1, pp. 211–12]

Montreal,
January 27, 1883

After the first of July next, when the Thunder Bay Line will be turned over to this Company, the following rates will prevail: –

[29]William Van Horne (1843–1915) was American by birth and his experience

From Winnipeg to Thunder Bay
    36¢ per 100 lbs. or 21 6/10¢ per bushel
From Portage La Prairie to Thunder Bay
    38¢ per 100 lbs. or 22 8/10¢ per bushel
From Brandon to Thunder Bay
    41¢ per 100 lbs. or 24 6/10¢ per bushel
From Broadview to Thunder Bay
    46¢ per 100 lbs. or 27 6/10¢ per bushel
From Qu'Appelle to Thunder Bay
    46½¢ per 100 lbs. or 29 1/10¢ per bushel
From Regina to Thunder Bay
    49¢ per 100 lbs. or 29 4/10¢ per bushel
From Moose Jaw to Thunder Bay
    51¢ per 100 lbs. or 30 6/10¢ per bushel

The rates from P.A. Landing to the seaboard will be about the same as those between Chicago and Duluth and the seaboard and will average not far from 15¢ per bushel.

E 21   VAN HORNE TO HENRY BEATTY [31]
[P.A.C., MG 28 III-20, Van Horne Letter Books, v. 1, pp. 694–6]

Montreal
April 20, 1883

The steam boat arrangements on the Lakes for this year are briefly as follows: –

The Collingwood Line will have boats from Collingwood four days each week to P.A. Ldg., and the T.G. & B.[32] two days each week, and I believe they have arranged between them so as to cover every day. Both will run to and from P.A. Ldg. exclusively. The Beatty Line will run

---

up to 1882 had been with American railroads. He was then appointed general manager of the Canadian Pacific Railway, and arrived in Winnipeg to begin his task of pushing the construction of that railway to completion as soon as possible. George Stephen's biographer remarks of him: "Van Horne's energy was the more boundless because he did not have to find the money which his spectacular feats required. 'Get the work done right and send the bills to Stephen' was his attitude" (Gilbert, Awakening Continent, p. 88).

[30]Edmund Boyd Osler (1849–1919) was a stockbroker who, in 1883, was the Managing Director of the Canada & Westland Company. He subsequently was elected to represent West Toronto riding in the Commons (as a Conservative, like Colonel F.C. Denison whom he succeeded) and was elected President of the Dominion Bank in 1901. He was knighted in 1912.

[31]Henry Beatty was selected to manage all the steamboat interests of the C.P.R. late in 1882. He had already had a good deal of experience in the Sarnia and Lake Superior line, known as the North West Transportation Company.

[32]The Toronto, Grey, and Bruce Railway operated a line of steamers out of Owen Sound. The Spartan and the Magnet were both owned by this company.

largely the same as last year, but giving a more frequent service on the North Shore, which will be needed owing to the large amount of work we will be carrying on there.[33]

E 22 VAN HORNE TO J.M. EGAN[34]
[P.A.C., MG 28 III-20, Van Horne Letter Books, v. 1, pp. 787–8]

Montreal,
May 3, 1883

As I wired you this morning we have arranged to take over the line from Rat Portage to P.A. Landing at once, and to complete the work remaining to be done thereon ...

The first boats of the season will probably reach P.A.L. toward the end of next week, and we must make a great effort to promptly move the freight. Our own dock at P.A.L. is not sufficient for the business, and it may be necessary to lease for a short time one of the other docks ... See what can be done in this direction. Mr. Marks has promised to deal liberally with us in this matter. I believe he is interested in two of the docks ...

It is highly important that we commence carrying passengers from P.A.L. as soon as possible, although the steam boat lines have not yet been provided with passenger rates. For a week or two coaches on the regular freight trains will probably answer the purpose.

E 23 IMMIGRANTS EN ROUTE TO THE PRAIRIES
[Thunder Bay Sentinel, Aug. 11, 1883]

In an interview today with Mr. P.A. Bogue,[35] station agent here, that gentleman referred in strong terms to the way emigrants were allowed to

---

[33]It was evident that Beatty's personal interests were closely linked with the C.P.R. at this period, although the first C.P.R. passenger boats did not make the trip to Thunder Bay until the 1884 season.

[34]J.M. Egan had moved from his former job as superintendent of the southern Minnesota division of the Chicago, Milwaukee & St Paul Railroad to become superintendent of the western division of the C.P.R. by 1882. During his years in Winnipeg, his American connections became the centre of much dispute. He was accused of dismissing Canadian employees in favour of Americans, and of having pronounced Fenian sympathies. Sir John Macdonald feared the effect of Egan's local unpopularity on the C.P.R. and the government, and questioned Stephen on the truth of the rumour that only Van Horne's friendship kept Egan in his Winnipeg situation (P.A.C., Macdonald Papers, Macdonald to Stephen, July 30, 1884). Stephen defended Egan against the charges (Stephen Papers, v. 269, Aug. 2, 1884). Subsequently, Egan left the C.P.R. and was employed by the St Paul, Minnesota, and Manitoba Railroad.

[35]P.A. Bogue was rapidly replaced as C.P.R. agent in Port Arthur. By February 1884 Van Horne was complaining about the expenses there, and the accounts submitted at the end of the previous year by one Niblock. Van Horne suggested "a general cleaning out without delay."

land without any official supervision or medical examiner. During the past few days many hundreds of emigrants for the Northwest have been put off here, and amongst them quite a number of cases of sickness were apparent. There being no officer to inspect, or doctor to attend them, these persons have been allowed to lie around until the time arrived for the train's departure. In one case, that of a woman who was confined just before the arrival of the boat, considerable difficulty was experienced in her removal. On Monday night a poor woman was taken severely ill, and were it not for the humane Bogue she would have died. Where is the Emigration Agent, and where is the contractor who has the job to put up the emigration buildings? The reputation of our port will soon be knocked into kingdom come if this sort of thing dont come to a violent and sudden end. The Government has acted promptly and generously in our interests and now it seems we are to be baulked and humbugged by officials. The lumber for the emigration building lies upon a wharf here all cut and fitted to go into place, but that is small satisfaction either to us or to the poor emigrants and their children who have been lying around the freight sheds like cattle.

E 24   DIARY OF R. MCLENNAN[36] AT PENINSULA HARBOR[37]
[M.T.C.L., Roderick McLennan Papers]

Friday, Februry 15, 1884.

In office all day making out Ests.   telegrams which I sent off Tuesday night have not been wired yet as line is down said to be broken by Whiskey Pedlars.   teams go daily on the ice now to Port Colville and most of the way to Red Rock.   temperature this morning − 24°. R.R. McDonald stayed here last night waiting on the tel. line to work in order to get some wheelbarrows and carts through from McKay's Harbor [Rossport].

Sunday, April 27, 1884

Mr. Wicksteed reports ice went of Pic River this morning and alledges further that no piles could Stand there during the passage of ice hence the bridge should be Completed over river before next Spring.

[36]Roderick McLennan (1823–1911) was born in Glengarry and worked as a surveyor in railway building in Georgia and with the Intercolonial Railway before being employed on Sir Sandford Fleming's exploratory survey in 1871. He was chief engineer of the Lake Superior division during the construction of the C.P.R., with headquarters in the Thunder Bay region. He spent much of his time at temporary locations – Peninsula Harbor in 1884 and Lochalsh in 1885 – before returning to private practice in Toronto. His eldest son, John Donald McLennan (1856–1907), was a partner of James Commee in a contracting firm which had several contracts from the C.P.R. in the area, and became involved in litigation with the railway.

[37]The modern name for Peninsula Harbor is Marathon.

Thursday, May 1, 1884

Morning clear and ice almost out of Peninsula Harbor but broken up so that the Quebec could come in with very little trouble. Mr. Armstrong came in from the east, in discussing the question of ice affecting a temporary pile bridge at Pic River Mr. Pinkerton alledged that one of his builders Mr. Meek maintained that with the Superstructure on there would be no danger from the shore as the Current was said to be not over 2 miles per hour, tho Mr. Wicksteed said it was 3 to 4, one or the other was mistaken. Mr. Armstrong who tried it today said it was only 1½ miles.

Monday, May 19 [May 11–20 at Port Arthur]

Wrote a letter to Mr. Vanhorne about spans of Pic and Black River which I handed to Mr. Ross[38] to mail lest he should wish to add a note.

Monday, May 26

This morning went in boat to Heron Bay, Messrs. Ross, Stoddart, and and Wicksteed walked over line, when I got to Pic River learned that the boom there had broken, releasing a good deal of the timber for the temporary bridge.

Saturday, June 7, 1884

This place Peninsula Harbor getting to be a fearfully rough place with vagrants and hoodlums. Got telegram from A. Piers in the Montreal office saying my letter came to him, of 19th May re bridges.

Sunday, June 8, 1884.

This morning bright & pleasant @ 6 p.m. Str. Magnet came in then Georgian, Butcher's Maid, and Quebec in the afternoon and all departed same day.　quite a fire raging s.e. of office Dinsmore out with a crowd of men turning up the sand to check it.　got telegram from Mr. Vanhorne about receiving my letter re bridges.

Wednesday, June 11, 1884.

In office all day waiting to hear from Mr. Vanhorne about spans of Pic River bridge.　this p.m. Mr. Ross Manager came on Str. "Ocean" on way to Michipicoten, also Mr. Harris of N. York and a Mr. Woods, c.e. of Detroit, from the Panama Canal who was out for his health. wrote several notices to contractors to day about their works.

[38]John Ross had been associated with Canadian railways as early as the 1850s when, during the building of the Grand Trunk, he had made Stratford his headquarters. After twenty years in railway construction in the United States he returned to Canada to assume the responsibility for the Lake Superior section. After the completion of this section in May 1885 he became President of the Rainy Lake Timber Company. In the subsequent lawsuits with various contractors Ross defended the practices of the individuals he had selected, as well as their expenses which the c.p.r. questioned.

Thursday, June 12, 1884

Expecting to hear daily from Mr. Vanhorne about bridges as time is passing rapidly. this morning Str. 'Butcher's maid' came to Pen. H. and at ten Str. Ocean on way west. weather pleasant to day. Some of the whiskey pedlars fined by Messrs Moberly and Young.

Tuesday, June 24, 1884

Siskiwit came in this morning with Mr. Van Horne and party looking for Mr. John Ross they asked me to go with them. So off we went reaching Michipicoten at midnight where we found Mr. Ross. Slept there the rest of the night.

Wednesday, June 25

Left Michipicoten at 8½ a.m. and reached Peninsula Harbor at 10 p.m. Mr. Schreiber[39] being sea sick I took him up to the house and gave him tea. when he returned to the boat, sleeping there with party. Mr. Van Horne said in speaking of the work Said it was much to be desired, yea urgently insisted that the road be built as cheaply as possible in order to keep the cost within the money loan and that the Govt officials were willing to do anything they can to help us.

Saturday, June 28

In office all day having plan of Pic River Bridge made.

Mr. Ross came in and in looking over plan said we had better make the river pier 7' wide under coping in Stead of 6' as is mostly done.

E 25 VAN HORNE TO JOHN ROSS
[*P.A.C., MG 28 III-20, Van Horne Letter Books, v. 8, pp. 201–4*]

Montreal,
October 19, 1884

More than twice as much was expended in masonry on the P.A. and Nipigon section than on all the rest of the work together and this has contributed largely to our financial difficulties ... My object in writing this is to impress upon you the *absolute necessity* of cutting every corner to save money on the work remaining to be done. We have not one dollar to spare for any work that can possibly be avoided or postponed even for a year.

The consequences of failure to complete the work inside of the Government loan would be disastrous.

The money saved on the Mountain Section is being rapidly absorbed by the Lake Superior section and we are again very near the *danger line.*

[39]Collingwood Schreiber (1831–1918) was English by birth, but had lived in Canada since the early 1850s. He was employed first on the engineering staff of the Toronto and Hamilton Railway. As early as 1856, as a member of the engineering firm of Fleming, Ridout, & Schreiber, he began his connection with Sandford Fleming whom he succeeded as Chief Engineer of the C.P.R. in 1880.

E 26   V A N   H O R N E   T O   H A R R Y   A B B O T T [40]
[P.A.C., MG 28 III-20, Van Horne Letter Books, v. 9, p. 580]

Montreal,
January 6, 1885

You have on your Engineering Staff an inspired idiot by the name of Gribble, who is writing letters here complaining of the desecration of the Sabbath Day by barbarians in your employ. These letters are very long and must have taken considerable time to write; if they were written during the week the time must have been stolen from the company's time, and if they were written on Sunday he too must have desecrated the Sabbath.

E 27   S E R G E A N T   D A O U S T [41]   O N   A C T I V E   S E R V I C E
[Daoust, Cent Vingt Jours de Service Actif, pp. 28–33]

[April 6, 1885]   Finally at six o'clock in the morning the train stopped at Heron Bay.[42] In less than five minutes, the battalion descended in order. For the first time a miserable rum ration was given to each man, and, without exaggeration, it was richly deserved. Soon afterwards we were served breakfast in the shanties of the railway construction workers ... After a very ample breakfast, the battalion again climbed on board the train and continued in the same coaches to Port Munroe,[43] which we reached about nine o'clock in the morning. Here, we left the train, and the march on foot began. Each soldier carried, besides his rifle and ammunition, all his equipment, haversack and all. After such a bad night, the twenty-five mile journey along the shore of Lake Superior made in less than ten hours was a prodigious achievement. Few men, even hardened

[40]Harry Abbott was Supervising Engineer for the Lake Superior section, and was at Bicotasing at the time this letter was sent to him. He was nominated to stand for the Ontario Legislature in the spring of 1885, but Van Horne made it clear that he could not serve two masters and he chose the C.P.R., assuming control at Port Arthur from John Ross. In the later lawsuits he also was called to testify by the C.P.R. in its attempt to collect $1,500,000. from the contractors Conmee & McLennan.

[41]Charles Roger Daoust (1865–1924) later became a journalist. In 1885 he was a sergeant serving with the 65th Regiment which moved west to suppress the North West Rebellion. His account of the four-day trip across the District of Thunder Bay in the spring of 1885 was published in the following year.

[42]The troops had been transported direct from Montreal to the unfinished Lake Superior section of the C.P.R. From Heron Bay to Red Rock they combined rail transport, walking, and transport by sleighs.

[43]Port Munroe apparently had received its name in the Nor'wester period when Dr Henry Munro and his brother William had both wintered in the Lake Superior region. It was situated only a few miles north of Peninsula Harbor, across the habour from the present town of Marathon.

veterans, would have been able to stand up to such a rigorous march so well. More astonishing still, not a man was sick! One single halt was made in the course of the march, at Little Pic, where rations, cheese and hardtack were distributed. If the sense of fatigue was great, we did have a slight compensation in the magnificent spectacle of the sun sinking over the lake ...

About eight o'clock in the evening, the whole battalion climbed aboard new railway cars, worse than the ones we had just left. These were just bare platforms, with a board on each side to serve as a hand-rail. On the floorboards, thinner boards had been laid as close as possible to each other, and these served as seats for the tired soldiers. We continued in this way for the rest of the evening, and it was one o'clock in the morning when we reached Jackfish Syndicate.[44]

The soldiers had barely got down from the train when rain began to pour down. Unfortunately, there was no shelter adequate to cover so many troops, and several companies had to wait for a good half-hour, exposed to the rigours of the climate ...

At two o'clock in the morning, after a good meal, companies 2, 3, 4, and 5 retired to the sheds of the Syndicate, while the others, 1, 7, and 8 climbed on the train again and were carried to the village of Jackfish, where a large shed had been prepared for them. A good fire was kept blazing all night in the two stoves that warmed this building, and for the first time since leaving Montreal, the volunteers slept well and comfortably ...

During the next afternoon, most volunteers took refuge inside and amused themselves with a sing-song to pass the time, for the rain never let up. A few found their way to an old tumbledown shack, attracted by the name displayed on the sign rather than by its unpretentious exterior. They sold drinks in this shanty – beer at 15 cents, and what here passes for whiskey at 25 cents a glass ...

At four o'clock the next morning the three companies which had passed the night in the village were ready for action and, since the train did not arrive, they began the march across the lake to the Syndicate. After an hour's walking, these soldiers received nothing more to eat than a slice of salt pork between two pieces of bread.

At 8 a.m. the first sleighs filled with troops began their journey, and the others were not long in following them. This new method of travelling along Lake Superior, even if we were conveyed in a vehicle, was no more pleasant than the former one. The cold was intense, and the soldiers

---

[44]The distinction made between the construction site and the village of Jackfish is an indirect reference to the extraordinary difficulty experienced by the work crews in this area. It was in the vicinity of Jackfish that the eastern and western construction crews in the district met, and the first train crossed the timber trestle at Jackfish Bay on May 16, 1885 – nearly six weeks too late to be of any use to the military expedition.

packed into the sleighs, were often obliged to get off and walk for a time, or their feet would have been frozen. About two o'clock in the afternoon, the first sleigh reached a deep bay, whose name no one knew [Collingwood Bay]. We halted for an hour and a half at this place, then climbed aboard platform cars for the journey to McKay Harbour [Rossport] where there is a hospital. Here we left our invalid, Boucher.[45]

At 7.30, the soldiers were again walking – eleven miles along Thunder Bay[46] and arrived at Red Rock at 11 p.m. Here passenger cars were waiting for the regiment, and about midnight the train left.

This day was one of the hardest for the soldiers. From four o'clock in the morning to eleven in the evening, they did not stop their journey a single moment. Fourteen miles on foot, twenty-two in sleighs, and more than a hundred in bad uncovered railway cars – in all nearly one hundred and fifty miles covered during the day.

About six o'clock in the morning, we entered Port Arthur. The soldiers were promptly awakened by the cries of the crowd which had gathered at the station. While the companies were separated into different groups to have breakfast in various hotels in the town, the officers repaired to the Brunswick Hotel[47] at the invitation of the mayor.

E 28 P E T E R N I C H O L S O N [48] T O V A N H O R N E
[*P.A.C., RG 16 A 5-7, Port Arthur Customs Records, p. 45*]

Port Arthur,
May 1st, 1885

The Canadian Pacific R. Coy on the 18th day of October, 1884, warehoused at the port 5785 tons of soft coal, and that here still remains 5468 tons of the said coal not exwarehoused as you will please observe by the enclosed statement and that according to the customs regulations all coal bonds must be cancelled and the goods exwarehoused on or before the first day of May be good enough to attend to this matter immediately.

[45]The unfortunate Boucher had apparently attempted suicide on April 5 before the really arduous part of the journey had begun.

[46]Daoust made several slips at the end of his long day's march. Nipigon he described as Michipicoten and the water along which he walked (an arm of Nipigon Bay) he confused with Thunder Bay.

[47]The Brunswick Hotel, situated at the corner of Cumberland and Lincoln streets, was one of many operating in Port Arthur in 1885. It had been newly fitted and furnished in the summer of 1884, and its proprietors, the Labby brothers, were associates of Mayor James Conmee.

[48]Peter Nicholson came to Prince Arthur's Landing with his wife and family in 1874 and was soon appointed the first Collector of Customs by the Mackenzie government, an office he held until 1895. The peremptory tone he used to the General Manager of the c.p.r. in 1885 was typical of his approach to all those who sought to circumvent any customs regulations.

E 29   VAN HORNE TO COLLINGWOOD SCHREIBER
[*P.A.C., MG 28 III-20, Van Horne Letter Books, v. 14, pp. 220–3*]

Montreal,
October 31, 1885

I have examined all of the line from Biscotasing to Nipigon with care and so far as the track and bridges are concerned I am very sure that $25,000 – will be sufficient to bring the road up to the requirements of the Company's contract with the Government at all points; and nearly all of it will be far beyond the requirements of contract ...

More than half the depots are under roof and will be completed during the coming week, and the material is provided for the remainder, and a few weeks more will see them all in use.

The Engine house at Chapleau is well advanced and the turntable is in; and those at White River and Schreiber[49] are started, all the material is on the ground and they will be ready for use in two or three weeks.

The water tanks at all points are completed except one at Schreiber which is now going up.

I hope you will touch as lightly as possible in your report on the approaches of the Big Pic bridge. These have been very much improved since you saw them and made entirely safe. We have decided however to put in say 450 feet of iron trestle at the East end of this bridge and 200 at the west end early next year, not because the present trestle is not entirely safe, but because of the danger to the main bridge from the possible burning of the approaches.

E 30   JOHN ROSS AND THE CONSTRUCTION OF THE
SUPERIOR SECTION
[*Port Arthur* Weekly Herald, *October 31, 1885, reprinted from the*
Stratford *Beacon*]

Between Nipigon and the Pic there are five tunnels; and not less than ten rivers had to be diverted from their natural courses and carried through rock tunnels excavated underneath the road bed. One of these rivers measures in width one hundred and fifty feet. There are along the coast eleven miles where in the living rock a shelf has been formed for the road bed of the railway, averaging twenty feet in width; in some places considerably wider. The rivers crossed by the line are spanned by iron bridges; the abutment – indeed the stonework throughout – being the best kind of masonry. There is some trestle work which has mostly now been filled in. As a further evidence of the quality of the work, it may be remarked

[49]The small community called Isbester's Landing had grown up in the early 1880s as a C.P.R. construction camp. In 1885 it was renamed in honour of the Chief Engineer of the railway and became, like Chapleau and White River, a divisional point for the new transcontinental line.

that no grade exceeds fifty-two feet to the mile, and the curvature is generally good, only two curves exceeding six degrees.

The social life of the community governed by this great captain of industry possessed features of interest. Mr. Ross is himself a staunch teetotaller in principle and the vast interests committed to his charge, alike impelled him to a vigorous prosecution of the whiskey peddlers who were bold and unscrupulous, and who gave him great trouble. To keep the liquor evil in check several jails were built and a big force of constables and detectives employed, the rough justice necessary to be visited on such a community, so situated, being in the hands of fifteen magistrates. We fear that no provision was made for the spiritual wants of the men other than by the whiskey ring, when they got a chance, there being no churches or chaplains; but the physically sick were cared for by several medical men who, as the phrase goes in more pretentious circles, "walked the hospitals," five in number, where provision was made for from four hundred to five hundred patients. These were for the most part typhoid fever patients, the infection, curiously enough, being caught in the cuttings, possibly from the foul air escaping from the crevices in the rocks.

There were few accidents to call the hospitals into requisition, and such was the care exercised in the dynamite factories that no casualty whatever arose in the manufacture of tons upon tons of explosives. There was, however, one serious result from culpable ignorance and temerity – four men having brought dynamite into one of the houses and placed it on the stove to thaw! The experience was a severe one – but to these poor fellows it carried no benefit. The survivors were more cautious. After the works were completed care was taken to demolish the dynamite factories, so as to render them innocuous.

E 30   VAN HORNE TO H.E. HOBART[50]
[P.A.C., MG 28 III-20, Van Horne Letter Books, v. 14, pp. 899–901]

Montreal,
January 8, 1886

The amount of the frauds attempted upon the C.P.R. by some of its contractors and engineers, while large, has been greatly exaggerated in the newspaper reports. They were almost entirely limited to the section of the work in a remote district north and east of Lake Superior and until the completion of the railway quite inaccessible during the winter months. The principal frauds seem to have commenced in September of last year[51]

[50]H.E. Hobart was editor of the magazine *The Railway Age*, published in Chicago. As rumours surrounded the launching of court proceedings against some engineers and contractors by the C.P.R. late in 1885, Van Horne felt it was necessary to write his version of the proceedings.

[51]Van Horne seems to have forgotten he was writing in the first week of a new year. The reference, of course, is to September 1884.

The work of construction was then within a few months of its close and winter was near. All of the work was planned to be completed before the opening of spring, and advantage was taken of this favorable and apparently last opportunity to make a "haul." Before midwinter the extraordinary quantities returned for the contractors on monthly estimates as compared with the total work to be done and with the force supposed to be engaged attracted the attention of the officers of the Company and full payment of the estimates was withheld until the matter could be investigated. On the completion of the work and as soon as the snow had sufficiently disappeared to admit of remeasurements, these were made to a sufficient extent to indicate extensive frauds and the most thorough reexamination of the work was then decided upon. It turned out that the amounts withheld from the contractors were not sufficient by several hundred thousand dollars to cover the discrepancies and suits were instituted to recover the differences. Cross suits were brought by the contractors and the whole matter is now before the Canadian courts.[52] In the legal skirmishes so far the Company has come out ahead in every case and the officers of Company are confident of recovering every dollar overpaid.

E 32   VAN HORNE TO LADY MACDONALD
[*P.A.C., MG 26 A-1, Macdonald Papers, v. 288*]

Montreal,
July 7, 1886

I am delighted to learn that Sir John has determined to start this week for a trip over the Canadian Pacific ... If you should conclude to adopt this suggestion, the car [the Jamaica] will be left at Chapleau on Sunday evening at eight o'clock. The car would be taken by special engine Monday morning at 7.30 to Jackfish Bay, reaching there in the evening, and leaving there the next morning at eight by the regular train, reaching Ignace Tuesday evening at 9.00, leaving there by a special train the following morning at eight o'clock. Winnipeg would be reached about six o'clock Wednesday evening. Any one of these special runs might be omitted for the return trip ... I think sleeping accommodations can be found for the two secretaries you mention at Chapleau, Jackfish Bay and Ignace, although it may not be quite equal to that of the Windsor Hotel.

[52]"We have won first blood in the contractors' costs, the court having refused them a jury trial and having decided the certificates of Ross and his engineers of no value against error and fraud" (P.A.C., MG 28 III-20, Van Horne Letter Books v. 14, p. 293, Van Horne to Stephen, Nov. 23, 1885). The cases thus initiated dragged on for most of a decade. The case of Conmee & McLennan, of particular local interest since Conmee was Mayor of Port Arthur and later M.P.P. for Algoma West, went to the Supreme Court in 1891. The particular contract under dispute in this case lay outside the Thunder Bay District to the east of Lake Superior.

F. THE ECONOMIC DEVELOPMENT OF ONTARIO'S FRONTIER, 1870–92

The Mines

F 1 A.H. SIBLEY'S[1] DEFENCE OF THE ONTARIO MINERAL LANDS' COMPANY[2]
[P.A.C., MG 28 III-19, Algoma Silver Mining Company Papers]

On the 28th July, 1847, by chapter 67 of 10 and 11 Victoria, a company called the "Montreal Mining Company" was incorporated, with power to acquire mineral lands on the north shores of Lake Superior and Lake Huron and to explore, develop, sell, lease, and otherwise dispose of them ...

[In 1868] assays were made by Professor Chapman, Dawson and others which indicated the existence of silver ore on some of these lands and especially Silver Islet.

The Honourable Thomas Ryan,[3] then the President of the Company, endeavoured to procure the assistance of English capitalists in London,

[1]Alexander Hamilton Sibley, president of the Silver Islet Mining Company, was a son of Judge Solomon Sibley of Detroit and a brother of Brigadier General H.H. Sibley, the first governor of Minnesota, who had commanded the American campaign against the Sioux in 1863 and had given up with reluctance the idea of exterminating all Minnesota Sioux who had fled to Hudson's Bay territory. Several of the Sibley brothers had worked for the American Fur Company in the 1830s and 1840s, and the records of that company indicate a connection between the Sibley and Trowbridge families long before the Silver Islet project. A.H. Sibley had been a '49er and by 1870 had built up wide interests in mining and banking. Although Detroit was his permanent home, he spent most of the summers in the early 1870s at his twenty-one-room mansion on the shoreline facing Silver Islet. Sibley died in 1878, but the interest of his family in the Silver Islet property continued for a number of years.

[2]Sibley and his associates obtained a charter from the Ontario government as the Ontario Mineral Lands' Company, but their title to the most valuable part of the land was challenged by a Colonel Albert Seymour of Toronto, and the government came close to recognizing this counter claim. Sibley only heard of the threat to his company in December 1871, and he immediately began his defence of his claims, a defence that had proved successful early in 1872 when the Seymour petition was refused.

[3]Thomas Ryan (1804–89) had come to Lower Canada from Ireland as a child, and by the 1840s his extensive business interests included the Quebec and Lake Superior Mining Association. By the 1860s he had withdrawn from most of his business activities, although still retaining the presidency of the Montreal Mining Company, and was involved in politics. A Liberal-Conservative, he was a member of the Legislative Assembly from 1863 to 1867. He was appointed to the Senate at Confederation.

but reported on the 9th March, 1870, as appears from the Minute Book of the Company "that although he gave some time and attention to the matter in London, he found little disposition to embark capital on distant mining enterprises." At the same meeting, it was also reported that Messrs. McDougall and Davidson, who had made a conditional offer for a portion of these lands, including Silver Islet, "after a lapse of four months found themselves unable to accomplish the formation of a company in England."

Then, on the 16th February, 1870, an offer was made to me and W.B. Frue, Esq.,[4] by an agent of the Company for the sale of part of these lands, which fell through.

Subsequently, negotiations were carried on between the Montreal Directors and certain parties in Montreal who again endeavoured to place the property in England, where they partially succeeded in negotiating a sale, but, not being able to provide all the money needed, the English parties telegraphed to me, in August, 1870, in New York, offering one-half of the property on the terms of a bond which would expire on the 1st of September. I accepted this offer, went to Montreal, and on the day when the money was to be paid over the English parties represented by a solicitor sent from London declined the purchase, withdrew, and left me to find all the capital or abandon the purchase.

On the 1st September, 1870, having succeeded in getting some other persons to join with me,[5] I became the purchaser of these lands for myself and them, for $225,000.00, which has been paid in full. Captain Frue, at once, on a telegram sent from me in Montreal, chartered a steamer and left Houghton, in the State of Michigan, with about thirty men, mining tools, supplies, etc., for Silver Islet, and took a large scow and heavy raft of timber, to commence the construction of a breakwater for Silver Islet, which the Montreal Company had failed in mining.

From that time and until the 10th May, 1871, Captain Frue engaged in constructing works to protect the mining on Silver Islet at enormous cost. A breakwater was at first constructed which enabled us to begin the work of mining in about thirty days. In November a heavy gale carried away a part of this structure but it was repaired and mining began again which, however, was several times interrupted owing to the difficulty of getting a structure which, in size and weight, would be sufficient

[4]William Benjamin Frue had been born in County Down, but had spent most of his life in the United States. He was appointed general superintendent by the Silver Islet Mining Company in 1871, at a salary of $5000, plus an addional $25,000 bonus if the mine should produce within one year sufficient net profits to pay the total purchase price. Frue won his bonus, and the great success of the mine occurred during his few years as superintendent. During these years he was a permanent resident of the area with many interests in mining. He left Silver Islet in 1874 and died in the late 1870s.

[5]Sibley's associates were, besides Frue, E.B. Ward of Detroit; Edward Learned of Pittsfield, Massachusetts; Charles Trowbridge, Peleg Hart, William H. Zabriskie, and George S. Coe of New York; and Edward A. Prentice of Montreal, who had taken part in the unsuccessful attempt to secure English capital.

to withstand the heavy seas which sometimes prevail there. On the 8th March, 1871, a heavy sea bearing a large body of ice, carried away nearly half the crib-work and filled the mine with water and ice and the works were not restored until the 10th. During the summer of 1871, large additions were made to the crib work (the more exposed part being 75 feet wide), and it was loaded with 50,000 tons of rock, carried from the main shore.

On the island and breakwater there are now erected a large boarding house, blacksmith's shop, engine house, assorting house, shaft house and an engine is at work on it, and mining operations have been carried on uninterrupted since 10th May last.

Our expenditure in and about Silver Islet within a year has been about $200,000.00 exclusive of the purchase money ...

The number of men employed on and about Silver Islet is 170 summer and 130 winter, apart from the force employed in smelting and otherwise.

In addition to the expenditure and works on Silver Islet, improvements have been made by us on the mainland, opposite the Islet, and last summer we began to mine there also.

There being no lighthouse on the coast, we have kept, at our expense, during the season of navigation on Silver Islet, a large light at a height of forty feet, and the range lights on the mine were continually alight from dark to daylight, for the benefit of steam and sailing craft plying along the coast and the lake.

We have also kept in constant use three steam tugs, two large scows and fifteen smaller boats.

We have, on more than one occasion, relieved a government steamer with surveying parties on board, at great inconvenience to ourselves, with coal without which she could not have left our harbour and ours is really the only "harbour of refuge" in the Thunder Bay district as the masters of the Chicora, Manitoba, Cumberland, Algoma and other vessels can testify.

We have had our large steam tug employed, during the summer, in carrying men and supplies at different points in our lands where explorations are being made, with a view to development and bona fide mining operations, and Government surveyors with supplies, as well as Indians, have been transported by us whenever they needed it, from point to point on the lake shore, which are not visited by other steam craft (and without our having, in any instance, accepted remuneration in any shape.)

We also offered to the late government, and are willing to give to any government,[6] any land in our territory that they require for public works, free of charge.

We have given a great deal of encouragement to the Indians. We

[6]Sandfield Macdonald's coalition government had been defeated in the House at the end of 1871 and R.W. Scott had become Commissioner of Crown Lands in the new Blake government. Other records suggest that the Silver Islet Mining Company was more closely linked with politics than Sibley stated.

employ them in large numbers and give them the same pay as we give to others.

Almost the whole force employed by us are Canadians. On the Woods' Location,[7] within a year, we have established a colony of about 300 souls, almost all Canadians.

We understand that it has been objected that all the money realized is carried away to the United States. This is not the case. We have paid about $240,000.00 to Canadians for their rights and besides the money earned by the large number of Canadians to whom we give employment, we are obliged to spend money in Canada in very considerable quantities.

During the last year we paid for supplies in Toronto about $40,000.00 and in Collingwood $15,000.00 besides paying freight and other incidentals. We have paid the Government for timber and have been taxed large sums. We are obliged to keep up an organization in Ontario which involves the expenditure of money. We have, by our success, caused large additions to be made in one year to the revenue of the Crown Lands' Department than had been made from the same source for many years before, I believe; and what is better still for the country, we have been the direct and immediate cause of directing capital into the Lake Superior region, which had almost become a sealed country.

Owing directly and exclusively to our successful venture, several mines are to be opened this spring for bona fide operations, with large capital – one of them, the Jarvis Island,[8] with a capital of 100,000 pounds sterling, raised in England and by Mr. Mandelbaum[9] ...

When I made the purchase from the Montreal Company in September, 1870, the whole country about Thunder Bay was in a state of torpor.

The companies there, the Thunder Bay Mining Company of Montreal, after expending $50,000.00 and the "Shuniah" about $25,000.00, discharged their workmen and virtually abandoned their mines. The latter company, encouraged by our success and by Mr. Mandelbaum's exertions, has resumed its work of mining with very flattering prospects of success ...

If Ontario, itself, has not the means to develop the mineral resources of this region, they must either remain unproductive or they must be developed by foreign capital.

[7]The Woods Location of 1846 was an oblong grant five miles east of Thunder Cape. Its 6400 acres were made up of a strip of land along the coast, as well as offshore islands. Continued description of the property by its old name was a convenient way of avoiding a detailed statement of construction on Silver Islet itself and on the shore opposite.

[8]W.B. Jarvis, like Joseph Woods, had been one of the original holders of mining locations on Lake Superior. This property, situated between Fort William and the American border, also included a section of the mainland and an island in front. Sibley and his associates had acquired it in the negotiations of 1870, but sold it in the following year to an English company.

[9]Simon Mandelbaum of Chicago was associated with the Silbley group in a number of ventures in the Lake Superior area. He was one of the purchasers of the Enterprise Mine on Black Bay, which John McIntyre, T.W. Herrick, J.J. Vickers, and Peter McKellar originally owned.

F 2   S. J. D A W S O N   T O   A L E X A N D E R   C A M P B E L L [10]
[P.A.O., Alexander Campbell Papers]

Lac des Milles Lacs,
September 12, 1871

A discovery has been made not far from Shebandowan Lake which, if it is anything like what it is reported to be, is destined to have a very important effect on this part of the country.

Gold and Silver have been found "in place" a little beyond the Height of Land at a distance of some three miles beyond the western extremity of Shebandowan Lake and the rock which contains it has been traced over a considerable area. I have myself seen some of the specimens containing both gold and silver and assays have been made shewing as much as twelve hundred Dollars to the ton. The discoveries were first made by men who had been employed on the Public Works and they are now being followed up by parties who are at the present moment laying off the ground.

Three provincial land surveyors are at work in the interests of some Americans possessed of large capital, who, it is said, have combined with the agent of the Hudson's Bay Company to lay off extensive tracts. The land is in the North-West Territories, that is, if Ontario is to be bounded by the water-shed ... Of course nothing can be more gratifying than to know that such a discovery has been made in Canadian territory and so near the Red River route. The Thunder Bay road, apart from its being a link in the route to Red River, will become a travelled highway to a gold region – but, in view of all the circumstances, it will become a question, on the one hand, to what extent individuals should be allowed to absorb the titles to the land and, on the other, how they may be best restrained in this regard and development at the same time promoted.

F 3   W I L L I A M   B .   F R U E   T O
C H A R L E S   A .   T R O W B R I D G E [11]
[P.A.C., MG 28 III-19, Algoma Silver Mining Company Papers]

Silver Islet,
October 26th, 1871

This week, so far, has been very unfavorable for our operations; a light s.e. wind has been blowing and a heavy sea has been setting in, so as to make it very unsafe to land at the Islet since Monday last.

[10]Alexander Campbell (1822–92) had been for a number of years the law partner of Sir John Macdonald. He had been Commissioner of Crown Lands before Confederation, but, in 1867, he was appointed to the Senate and served as Postmaster-General until the creation of the new Department of the Interior in 1873.

[11]Charles A. Trowbridge of New York was the secretary of the Silver Islet Mining Company when it was established in 1870. He was one of the original

Yesterday several of the miners were tossed about like nut shells, they being at work upon the centre line of crib-work. The sea rolled up and picked five of them up at ease, throwing them up on top of the lumber pile, which is 14 feet above the level of the lake and forty feet from the front line of crib-work; so you can picture to yourself the gigantic size of the waves and the immense volume of water which passes over the crib-work at a height of 10 feet above the level of the lake ...

The new boarding house [as of] noon today was standing two stories high, built out of 7 inch flattened timber, thoroughly belted together, with nearly all of the windows in place and the roof half boarded; what the condition is now heaven only knows! Still, the foundation of the house is well protected by a line of crib-work, which has already been extended over two hundred feet.

I write you, however, more especially in regard to gold, as I have positive information that the patents for the three locations purchased will be issued forthwith, and, further, that the patents for the other 6,000 acres will be all right and issued in a week or two.

F 4   FRUE TO TROWBRIDGE
[P.A.C., MG 28 III-19, Algoma Silver Mining Company Papers]

Silver Islet,
February 19th, 1872

... Something ought to be done by the managers of the company by way of advertising through the columns of the newspapers for men. I believe that if $200. or $300. were put to use in this way the money would be spent profitably. Such notices should be put in the papers at once, and be kept in until the opening of navigation as I do not approve of sending around to drum up men having to pay their fare to the mine. I look upon it as so much money thrown away. The men thus brought into the country are worthless both to themselves and to their employer. They get their ideas up and labor under the delusion that you cannot get along without them. I believe that by advertising in one of the Galena papers in Illinois that a good class of miners such as Americans and Germans might be obtained. I have lost quite a number of the miners brought up here by Captain Trethewey.[12] In fact I settled with them to get rid of them as I did not look upon their labor as profitable. The Captain has often expressed himself that he never was [so] deceived in such a party of men.

---

partners in that Company, whose wealth depended on railway construction and mining in the United States. Adverse economic conditions there after 1873 had an important effect on the history of the Company.

[12]Both Richard and John Trethewey served as mine captains at Silver Islet, and both were linked with the importation of miners from their native Cornwall. The brothers and their families moved to Prince Arthur's Landing in the early 1880s and were associated with other silver mining ventures, notably those of Oliver Daunais.

I have no doubt that they were good men but paying their fare spoiled them.

F 5   The Thunder Bay Mail in 1872
[P.A.O., Crown Lands Papers, Surveyors' Accounts]

Receipt   Thunder Bay,
$\quad$ $10   xx   March 20th, 1872
$\qquad\dfrac{}{100}$

Received from the Department of Crown Lands by the hands of E.B.

Borron, Mining Inspector, the sum of Ten Dollars ($10.$\dfrac{00}{100}$) towards

the expenses incurred by me bringing the mail from Duluth
$\qquad\qquad\qquad\qquad\qquad$ (Signed)   D. McKellar[13]

[Notation on reverse side]
This payment was made in the form of subscription to defray the expense of bringing the Canadian Mails from Duluth where they had been left for several weeks in consequence of the refusal of the United States Contractor to carry the Canada Mail from Duluth to Pigeon River.[14] Knowing that I might expect official letters and that an indefinite delay or detention on the way might not be desirable, I contributed the above sum of ten dollars towards the expense of getting the overdue Mails reporting the matter to Washington and Ottawa so as to ensure regularity in future.

F 6   Frue to Sibley
[P.A.C., MG 28 III-19, Algoma Silver Mining Company Papers]

$\qquad\qquad\qquad\qquad\qquad\qquad$ Silver Islet,
$\qquad\qquad\qquad\qquad\qquad\qquad$ April 4th, 1872.
... The work on the gold mine was unexpectedly stopped two days after I left the diggings owing to the Indian Chief Blackstone[15] putting

[13]Donald McKellar, in partnership at this time with his brothers John and Peter, was an experienced bush traveller. Finding weather conditions worse than he had expected, however, he with five local Indians took thirty days to cover the 400-mile distance. This business transaction throws some light on the extraordinary position of a mining inspector in Thunder Bay at that time, although Borron in his notation made it clear that he got in touch with the appropriate authorities and that he could not demand recompense from the Ontario government which employed him.

[14]The mail crisis was precipitated by the rapid growth of Silver Islet in the previous year. American carriers had been willing to transport a few letters and papers with their deliveries to Pigeon River, but could not handle the volume of mail in the winter of 1871–2, which accordingly piled up at Duluth. Even after provision had been made to deliver this mail to the boundary, Silver Islet's difficulties were not over, as the Canadian government had not made provision for the new situation either (Frue to John Cousins, March 1, 1872).

[15]Blackstone was Chief of Indians living in the Shebandowan area. He had halted

in an appearance and ordering the men to discontinue their work. Had it occurred a month earlier I would have undoubtedly sent back another party of men well armed so that they would have been able to have protection against any raids Mr. Blackstone saw fit [illegible] all for the best as the Government will undoubtedly perfect the treaty early in the summer which by the way you want to say to Mr. Crooks, Scott, and others that Blackstone protests in the strongest possible way against Mr. Simpson's[16] return. He says that he will not treat with him but will treat with any other man the Government will send up. There is something connected with Blackstone's sister-in-law and Mr. Simpson that the former is exasperated about.

F 7   FRUE TO ADAM CROOKS[17]
[*P.A.C., MG 28 III-19, Algoma Silver Mining Company Papers*]

Silver Islet,
April 4th, 1872

I enclose to you herewith a copy of a letter I have written to Mr. Scott, Commissioner of Crown Lands which will give you some idea of the uncertainty of mining or even the title to such property.

If you can do anything to reinstate me in my right you will place me under many obligations. I believe that if you could manage to have a committee appointed to investigate the disbursement of money supposed to be expended upon the Red River Road sufficient evidence might be obtained around Prince Arthur's Landing and Fort William to establish the fact that a considerable amount of the public funds was expended for the survey and explorations of land for private interests.[18]

This you will please consider strictly private.

---

activity on the Jackfish Lake Mine on the grounds that the Dominion government had not yet concluded any agreement with the Indians living beyond the Height of Land. He was later one of the Indian spokesman at the negotiations for the North-West Angle Treaty of 1873.

[16]Wemyss McKenzie Simpson, a cousin of Sir George's, had served the Hudson's Bay Company for about twenty-five years, and had some acquaintance with the Sault Ste Marie area. In 1867 he had been elected to represent Algoma in the Dominion Parliament. In 1871 he had become Indian Commissioner.

[17]Adam Crooks (1827–85) was the Attorney-General of Ontario at this time. He became Provincial-Treasurer later in the same year. There are a number of letters in the Silver Islet papers that indicate the personal friendship of Captain Frue and this particular cabinet member.

[18]The animus against Simon Dawson is quite clear in this letter. Frue certainly believed that it was Dawson who had attempted to check the activities of the Jackfish Lake Mine. It is interesting that the suggested investigation does not seem to have taken place, and that Dawson was the next representative of the district in the Ontario Legislature, sitting as an Independent but supporting the Mowat government.

F 8 FRUE TO JOHN MCINTYRE
[*P.A.C., MG 28 III-19, Algoma Silver Mining Company Papers*]

Silver Islet,
April 4th, 1872

In thinking over the matter of trust deeds,[19] I believe it would be to the advantage of all interested to have the deeds made out in the name of Alexander Hamilton Sibley (A.H. Sibley) of the City of New York.

All that is necessary to be inserted in the deed is as follows: viz. In trust for McIntyre, McKellar, White, Herrick, W.B. Frue and associates. From this you will notice that A.H. Sibley stands entirely as a disinterested party holding the property in trust for us and no advantage can be taken of any of the parties interested. It is not necessary to explain the exact interest of anyone in a deed of trust.

Go ahead now and have it made out at once. It would be of immense interest to me if the property could be transferred two or three times, considering the present state of affairs. Every transfer makes the original doubly strong, and I am of the opinion that should Mr. Mathers agree with me in the above, it would be well for you and others to deed directly to me and I would make the transfer to A.H. Sibley.

I speak of this because in the States when the title stands in the name of the first party, the Attorney General for great cause or reason can set aside such title but when the original party has conveyed it to others the Attorney General can not annul the title. I merely mention this [so] as to post you and then you can do as you think best.

F 9 FRUE TO SIMON MANDELBAUM
[*P.A.C., MG 28 III-19, Algoma Silver Mining Company Papers*]

Silver Islet,
June 10th, 1872

Mr. Sibley arrived here on Tuesday, the fourth instant and told me that you wished a few men sent without delay to location G at the head of Black Bay to commence work and forward to you in Boston a few barrels from the large lode there as soon as possible.

As no road or trail has been cut out, I sent word to Mr. John McKellar to find out from him whether three or four Indians could be hired at Fort William to pack the ore from the mine to the shore and received an assurance that he would be here so as to proceed with them in person yesterday morning, but he has not yet made his appearance. I intended to send with him from here about five additional men with directions to cut out and bush a road so that a yoke of cattle could get through.

---

[19]Frue had every reason to reflect on this particular date on the subject of trust deeds for various pieces of property in which he and the associates named in the letter were interested. The property referred to here may have been the very Jackfish Lake Mine where Blackstone had intervened.

Then I proposed to send you a single piece of ore weighing about a ton. If he does not make his appearance tomorrow I shall send Duncan Laurie with some men to commence work and I do not anticipate any difficulty about sending you three or four tons within the present week similar to a small specimen which I forwarded to you by this boat. As requested in your letter I also enclosed you my report on the property which I visited and thoroughly examined the latter part of August 1871 in company with Messrs. Burbank and Beaupré from St. Paul, Minnesota.

These gentlemen were fully satisfied with the property and priced me in its purchase but the sale fell through in consequence of a defect in the title as a Mr. Turner of Illinois claimed one quarter of it.

F 10 FRUE TO OLIVER BURKE OF DETROIT
[P.A.C., MG 28 III-19, Algoma Silver Mining Company Papers]

Silver Islet,
July 22nd, 1872

You will please ship by the first boat 10 gallons of your best old Bourbon whiskey, 5 gallons of your best Holland Gin, to the care of Smith & Harris, Houghton, Michigan.

You will also purchase from some glassware establishment (I think the one within a stone's throw of your place would be the best) two dozen goblets, two dozen champagne glasses, two dozen claret glasses and two dozen wine glasses. This glassware must be selected with the letter "F" ground upon it. When in Detroit last I visited the house and saw that they had a complete stock of such glasses. Please ship the glassware to same address as the whiskey and forward invoice to my address in Hougthon.

F 11 FRUE TO TROWBRIDGE
[P.A.C., MG 28 III-19, Algoma Silver Mining Company Papers]

Silver Islet,
July 30th, 1873

The Norwegians arrived here, unfortunately, for since their arrival we have had constant trouble and vexation. After being here a very short time, long enough however to arrange for drafts to be sent to their respective wives, they decided on clearing out. I took occasion to remark casually that drafts might be rendered worthless by means of the telegraph provided I was not satisfied and the men then concluded, unfortunately for me as it turned out, that they would remain and work. I can best explain what sort of miners they are by stating the manner in which they could make themselves most profitable, viz: by doing away with the expense of a hoisting engine. If the mines were dry, no machinery would then be necessary, for the men by taking knapsacks with them in the morning would be able to take up on their backs at night the ground they had broken during the day. Our old hands, the regular miners, began to raise objections to the foreigners, and at length many of them refused to work in the company of men who would fire off their blasts without giving the regular warning to others. There were but two courses to pursue, either to let the old hands go or to discharge the Norwegians. However much I might have preferred the latter expedient, its employment was rendered impossible by reason of our contract with these new men. I was in a position where nothing could be done, and with sorrow I saw many of my old tried miners going, leaving with me a lot of men I feel grieved at keeping from the bosoms of their families.

Our last assortment of Cornishmen turned out as troublesome as the Norwegians. Ten of them stole off the day after their arrival, the remainder all struck work after some of them had passed one day underground. As [to] the reasons offered, they are as many and as opposed to compromise as the quills on a porcupine. The longest and strongest quills appeared the poor board, foul air in the mine and the payment of passage money to this place. There is a wonderful difference in the sensitive organizations of Cornish miners. Among this lot there were three well marked classes, each of which could put up with two of the above evils but was totally incapable of bearing up under the third. The passage money was the last straw to one party; the board completely upset the delicate internal arrangements of another; while the remainder exhibited signs of having been suffocated by the foul air. Besides these great evils, there were several minor objections these men had to suffer, such as the fatness of the fresh beef, sourness of bread, light air, coal damp, loss of appetite, uncivility from the boarding bosses, and so on.

I saw I could not keep all of them very long and in order to make a separation of the good men from the grumblers, I offered to pay the passage money of those who would stop and work. About half the number were satisfied with this, the remainder said they would not work underground at the Islet but would at any other point. As I could not with convenience move Silver Islet to the top of Thunder Cape, I told these men to take their baggage and go on shore.

F 12   FRUE TO JAMES FITZGERALD [20]
[P.A.C., MG 28 III-19, Algoma Silver Mining Company Papers]

Silver Islet,
February 19, 1874

I am most comforted by the intelligence conveyed in your letter concerning the coming election. You can safely count on 65 to 70 votes from Silver Islet straight for Scott.[21]

[20]James Fitzgerald was the first lawyer to practice in Prince Arthur's Landing and, in the election campaign of 1874, served as secretary of the committee working for the election of the Conservative candidate.

[21]William James Scott, Jr., of Batchewana, contested the Algoma federal seat in 1874 and emerged with 258 votes to the winner's 436.

I have had the pleasure of meeting Messrs. Dobie and Strobie[22] and have no doubt they will return to Thunder Bay and fully endorse my reputation as a plain spoken man.

I firmly believe they are using their influence in behalf of Borron for the purpose of securing Simpson's election.[23]

In haste –

F 13 SICKNESS AND ACCIDENTS BENEFITS, 1880
[*Lakehead University Library (L.U.L.), Silver Islet Papers, Constitution and By-Laws of Silver Islet Employees Benefit Society*]

CONSTITUTION

Art. 1 – Name of Society
The Society shall be called the Silver Islet Employees Benefit Society.

Art. 2 – Object of Society
The object of this Society is to assist any of its members who may be sick from natural causes, or who may receive any injury while at their daily labor, or while going to or from such labor, to the place of their abode; and also to see that all of its members who may die from natural causes, or are accidentally killed during the hours of employment are decently buried. The remainder of their dues from this Society shall be refunded to their nearest relative as provided in the By-Laws.

Art. 3 – Qualifications for Membership
All, and only those persons in the employ of the Silver Islet Consolidated Mining and Lands Company at Silver Islet or its vicinity, and under the jurisdiction of the Company's Medical Officer, not actually suffering from disease contracted, or injury sustained, previous to entering the Company's employ, and not exceeding 50 years of age, shall be eligible for membership.

Art. 4 – Exceptions to Claims for Benefits
No Members shall be entitled to any Benefit for sickness or accident

[22]The reference here is to Prince Arthur's Landing citizens supporting the opposite party. W.C. Dobie, born in England in 1842, came to Canada in 1849. He arrived in Prince Arthur's Landing in June 1872, after more than ten years at Bruce Mines, and opened a grocery store. He was later appointed a police magistrate. No record of a citizen named Strobie has been found. Either this is an error in the transcription of the letters, or Frue intended to ridicule his political opponents thus.

[23]E.B. Borron was the Reformer candidate, and the eventual victor in the election. In his previous position as Mining Inspector, he had many dealings with Captain Frue, but Frue was careful, even in such a hasty communication, to present his opposition on other grounds. W.M. Simpson, the former M.P. from Algoma, was suspected by Frue of various plots and schemes, although this letter does not make clear the precise nature of the current one.

brought on by fighting, except in self-defence, wrestling, intoxication, debauchery or other misconduct.

BY-LAWS

Art. 3 – Subscriptions

Each member shall pay a monthly subscription of 50 cents if his wages exceed $25 a month. Each member whose wages do not exceed $25 a month shall pay a monthly subscription of 25 cents, but shall be entitled only to half benefits.

Art. 5 – Benefits in Case of Sickness

Any member paying a monthly subscription of 50 cents, being disabled through sickness of a specified disease from attending his daily labor, usual business or other occupation or work of any kind at home or elsewhere, shall receive a weekly benefit of $5 and fractional parts thereof after the expiration of two weeks' sickness, but shall not be entitled to anything for the first two weeks – such benefits to continue for any period up to three months – after that time only as the Society may determine by a majority in meeting assembled. Any member receiving benefits, found or known to do anything contrary to the rule laid down in this By-Law shall be at once expelled from the Society ...

Art. 7 – Benefits for Accident

Any member paying a monthly subscription of 50 cents, who may receive an injury ... severe enough to disable him from working, shall, while so disabled, receive a weekly benefit of $5 and fractional parts thereof from the date of accident; such benefits to continue for any period up to four months, after that time only as the Society may determine by majority in meeting assembled ...

Art. 10 – Injury through Carelessness

If any member misses a hole he may uncharge it with a scraper, picker and swabstick, or gun; but if he is injured by using any other instrument in uncharging, or, in any other case where a member may receive injury or death through his own wilful carelessness, or, by self-destruction, such member, relative or person designated by will shall have no compensation from the Society ...

Concluding By-Law – Disposal of Funds in Event of the Works Closing Down.[24]

It is hereby enacted: That should the Company at any time reduce

[24]Insertion of this clause as late as 1880 was highly necessary. There had been predictions for several years that the mine would close operations, and there had been one interval in 1877 during which all workers had been discharged.

their working force so as to reduce the membership of this Society to the number of 20, those members when they think it likely that the Works are about to close or change hands may by a two-thirds majority of their number in meeting assembled, draw from the Company's office all the funds on deposit in the said office to the credit of the Society, and also dispose of the effects of the Society, and the money so obtained with the amount drawn from the Company's office, shall be equally divided one with the other.

F 14   ARCHIBALD BLUE'S[25] ACCOUNT OF THE END OF OPERATIONS AT SILVER ISLET
[*Ontario, Bureau of Mines,* Report, *1896, pp. 156–7*]

The year 1883 closed with a deficit of $45,682. The receipts were mostly derived from bonds, assessments and call loans, and the straits to which the Company was reduced is shown by the sale of such articles as a tug boat, old crushers, ore-bags and laboratory fixtures. The sale of fine silver fell to 1,874.15 oz., which netted $2,010.41, and the value of ore on hand was estimated at $7,500.

The list of directors for 1884 comprised the following – two of whom had been on the board of trustees when the Company was organized in 1870, Messrs. Learned and Trowbridge, and only one other besides these, Mr. Coe, was an original shareholder:

Edward Learned	Pittsfield, Mass.
William A. Booth	New York.
William A. Langley	New York.
George S. Coe	New York.
C.A. Trowbridge	New York.
B.E. Strong	New York.
John J. Marvin	New York.
George C. Moon	New York.
Myron P. Bush	Buffalo, N.Y.
John S. Newberry	Detroit, Mich.
T.C. Weeks	Boston, Mass.

Their report refers to a proposal to secure financial relief by the sale of Mamainse location on the east shore of lake Superior to English parties, with whom negotiations were proceeding. Further explorations

[25]In producing his official report for the Ontario Bureau of Mines in 1896, Archibald Blue seems to have had access to documents that have not survived. Even then, he found it necessary to interview some of those who had been associated with Silver Islet in its heyday, so much change having taken place in a decade.

downward at Silver Islet, they said, had been discontinued and operations were being confined to the upper part of the mine.

The report of the superintendent, Mr. Trethewey, showed that the main shaft had been sunk to the fifteenth or 1160-foot level, drifting upon that level north and south and sinking two winzes upon it, and back-stoping at encouraging points in some of the upper levels. The explosion of a boiler in January caused the stoppage of pumps and machinery for twenty days, during which the water rose in the shaft 330 feet, and the shaft was not pumped out until 15th March. Drifting was immediately commenced on the lowest level, and was carried south 227 feet and north 81 feet. "The vein though well defined," Mr. Trethewey stated in his report, "and carrying quantities of minerals, has not produced the expected amount of silver. A deposit of silver was opened into during the summer, near the end of the north drift, but proved to be small in extent. At this point and in this run of ground a winze is being sunk toward the 1260-foot level, hoping that in its course other bunches may be found. A winze has also been commenced toward the 1260-foot level near the end of the south drift, in the same run of ground in which silver has been found above. In the levels where back-stoping has been carried on, the vein, although of a very encouraging nature, yielding minerals which are always found accompanying silver, has not produced silver in paying quantity; still it will be remembered that heretofore we have worked for long periods in ground such as described, and finally been rewarded by encountering rich deposits, and there is no reason why we should not expect similar results again. Ere long," he went on to say, "we shall find ourselves placed in a serious dilemma owing to the non-arrival of our winter supply of coal last fall – a vessel with a cargo of nearly 1,000 tons having failed to reach here, being laid up while en route. The present supply of coal is sufficient to run with until about March 1st, after which we shall find it extremely difficult to carry on the work."

This was written under date of January 20, 1884, and what was feared came to pass a little earlier than was expected. The cause is best told in the words of trustees John J. Marvin and Henry S. Sibley in an official letter printed under date of July 10, 1890:

"When work ceased at Silver Islet in February, 1884 (owing to the non-arrival of coal, unfortunately shipped in charge of an intemperate captain in the fall of 1883), the appearance of the vein in that mine was in every respect encouraging."

The incline shaft had reached a depth of 1,160 feet, or to the fifteenth level, and the winze from that level north of the shaft was sunk to a further depth of 90 feet, being a total depth of 1,250 feet upon the vein.

All the property of the Company has since been sold under fore-closure of mortgage and has been vested in the two trustees above named with a view of prospecting it as to mineral, timber, quarry, farming, water power, harbor, fisheries and other values, in order to facilitate its sale in locations or in lots.

F 15 PETER NICHOLSON TO THE ASSISTANT
       COMMISSIONER OF CUSTOMS
[*P.A.C., RG A 5–7, Port Arthur Customs Records, v. 2, p. 82*]

Port Arthur,
September 2, 1885

I also enclose one of a no. of communications from Mr. James M. Cross,[26] preventive officer at Silver Islet. You will no doubt still recollect of my speaking to you last spring when I was in Ottawa in reference to Mr. Cross — there is no necessity of employing him at Silver Islet as this office received neither customs duty nor vessel report from Silver Islet since May, 1884, as the place is out of the way for vessels to call there and there are no business of any kind on the Islet since it was abandoned. Therefore I will most respectfully suggest that whatever salary is due Mr. Cross (justly) be paid to him and that his services be discontinued.

F 16 A.L. RUSSELL'S REPORT ON MINING
       DEVELOPMENT
[*Ontario, Department of Crown Lands, Report, 1885, app. 20, pp. 30–1*]

Port Arthur, Ontario
December 30th, 1885

I beg to submit the following brief description of the various mines in operation in the Rabbit Mountain Mining Region, a portion of which is incorporated in the Township of O'Connor, which I had the honour of surveying, last summer under instructions from your Department.

All of these mines are situated from twenty-five to twenty-eight miles from Port Arthur, or about twelve miles from Murillo Station, on the line of the Canadian Pacific Railway.

The new Colonization Road,[27] built by direction of your Department, affords constant and convenient access to the majority of these mines at all seasons.

In alphabetical order, the mines are as follows: –

First. – Beaver Mine. – 97 т.

This mine at present employs some forty-three miners and is operated by wealthy American capitalists, who are so satisfied with the large

26It was upon the narrative of James Cross that Archibald Blue relied for a number of details in his "The Story of Silver Islet." The Cross family continued its interests in navigating, engineering, and mining – cf. the twentieth century link between Julian Cross and the Steep Rock Iron Mines.

27The Rabbit Mountain and Whitefish Lake Road provided access to the new mines, only a year after the first mineral discoveries in the region. The construction of this road marked the first large-scale operation in the district for nearly a decade. It was also in marked contrast to the history of the road to Silver Islet, which was just nearing completion when the mines closed down.

amount of splendid silver ore in sight, that they have contracted for the erection of an extensive mill for the treatment of ore on the spot, thereby saving the almost ruinous expense of teaming the same to Port Arthur and shipping from thence to New York.

This is undoubtedly a most valuable and promising mine, with a good strong vein, which has been developed, both horizontally and vertically, by tunnels and shafts to such an extent as to insure a steady industry. The new road passes within less than one mile of this mine.

Second. – Rabbit Mountain Mine.

The Rabbit Mountain Mining Company are operating on Mining Locations 39 T and 40 T. A great deal of work has been done here, about thirty-five men being constantly employed.

This was the first discovery in the region and has yielded a large quantity of rich ore, which heretofore has been shipped to New York at enormous expense.

Some of the nuggets of silver found near the surface were several pounds in weight, rivalling the ore obtained from the famous Silver Islet. There is a large quantity of low grade ore in the various dumps, and the Company have stipulated to erect a stamp mill before the snow disappears.

A very comfortable and commodious hotel and store, besides numerous other buildings, make this place quite a village. It has also a Post Office, which is supplied with a weekly mail.

This mine can be reached by either the Colonization Road and a branch road of four miles, or *via* the ferry over the Kaministiqua River and the nine miles of road which the original miners made at great personal expense.

Third. – Rabbit Mountain, Junior.

Mining Section 57 T, or Rabbit Mountain, Junior, as it is called, is immediately adjacent to the west of the Rabbit Mountain mine. Silver has been taken from the veins, and the owners are sinking a shaft with the view of intercepting the main Rabbit Mountain lode, which, they affirm, dips under this property.

Fourth. – Twin City Mine. – 96 T.

Considerable work has been done at this mine and many very rich specimens were obtained, as well as a large quantity of low grade ore extracted.

Five miners are at work on this property, the rock from which will probably be treated at the mill to be erected near the Beaver Mine. The new road passes through this property.

Fifth. – Silver Creek. – 140 T.

Little work has been done on this property as yet, although very rich specimens of silver have been obtained from the surface. About five men are now employed at this promising mine, which will also have the advantage of the mill to be erected in the vicinity on Silver Creek. The new road passes through this property likewise.

F 17 RUSSELL TO GEORGE B. KIRKPATRICK[28]
[P.A.O., Crown Lands Papers, Surveyors' Accounts]

Port Arthur
1 June '86

Now as regards the account.[29] I feel that we have overrun the $1000. by a little over $200. The two surveyors, McDougall and myself is the chief cause of this also the very out of the way locality and consequent cost of transport, uncertainty of time, etc. The remoteness of the region also caused a great loss of time going and coming which of course could not be avoided as no men could be depended on out there.

I don't know whether your dept like the Dominion allows full amount for the camp equipage and have it placed with agent here or as is frequently done pay half cost only and make surveyor keep the outfit. A survey in spring when water is over the ice is very hard on outfit and snowshoes and sleds. The greater part of the snowshoes are not worth even mending and a good many pair were used up and thrown away. The sleds are not worth storing away and the tents, stoves, etc. are badly wrecked by constant and rapid travel. I think it would be fair to the Department to assume cost of snowshoes as agreed upon and charge me with half the cost of the camp outfit of which some of it will be useful in the survey of Conmee.

F 18 THOMAS KEEFER[30] ON MINING IN THUNDER BAY
[P.A.C., MG 29 B-10, Keefer Papers]

... During these discoveries [1866–70] silver was also found within the present town limits of Port Arthur at the Singleton Mine and in its very streets for a tea chest full of very rich ore containing native silver was

[28]George B. Kirkpatrick was the Chief Clerk of Surveys in the Department of Crown Lands throughout the 1880s. S.J. Dawson, in a speech early in 1889, commended the work of Kirkpatrick in that department.

[29]After the flurry of township surveying that marked the early 1870s, no new townships in Thunder Bay were surveyed between 1875 and 1885. The mining excitement then resulted in Russell's survey of O'Connor Township, and T.O. Bolger's surveys of Gillies and Lybster. Russell had just completed the Whitefish Lake survey at the time of this letter, and was proceeding to the new area immediately to the west of Oliver Township and north of O'Connor.

[30]Thomas Alexander Keefer arrived in Prince Arthur's Landing in the spring of 1883 and set up a law practice in partnership with E.R. Cameron. From the first, however, it was mining rather than the law that absorbed his attention. He

taken from a very small vein or seam a few inches wide that crossed the street in front of Thomas Marks & Co.'s store.

The Gold excitement commenced with the discovery in the winter of 1870 and 1871 by two Indians named J. Baptist and M. Puchot in the employ of the Hudson's Bay Company of a gold and silver bearing vein in which free gold was afterwards discovered by Peter McKellar[31] in the year 1871. This discovery was named the Jackfish Lake Mine.

The discovery of this Mine created much excitement as it was the first free gold discovery on the North Shore of Lake Superior.

At that time the Indians occupying that portion of the country had not been settled with and no treaty existed between them and the Dominion Government.

The territory was also in dispute between the Dominion and Ontario Governments and patents to the lands therein could not be had from either Government.

To add to these difficulties, a fierce contest arose between rival claimants of this find, an attempt having been made by some influential wihte men of means to 'jump' the claim of the original discoverers. By an arrangement between the Dominion and Ontario Governments the latter were allowed to issue patents of the land in that part of the Country and patents began to issue in 1871 the first being that of the Jackfish Lake Mine.

In 1872 a party directed by Peter McKellar and employed by Captain William B. Frue (then of Silver Islet) who had become interested in this discovery began operations in this gold region. But they were stopped by Chief Blackstone and his band of Chippewa Indians until a treaty was made with them. However a treaty was made with them by the Dominion Government [Treaty 3, North-West Angle Treaty, 1873] soon after, and a conventional boundary established between the two Governments which was shortly afterwards annuled and now by a recent decision of the Privy Council of England the true boundaries between the Province

---

already knew the area well, having visited it at various times in the previous decade, while his brother, Francis H. Keefer, was a resident. Later the two brothers were to enter a law partnership, but in 1883 the *Herald* described Frank Keefer as a metallurgist, occupying offices in the same building as his brother. Both brothers had precise knowledge of the mining boom of the 1880s, in which they participated. Thomas Keefer was the better known promoter at that period, but derived little profit from his enterprises and died comparatively young. Francis H. Keefer became a prominent barrister and represented the area in both the Ontario and Dominion Parliaments as a Conservative.

[31]Peter McKellar was born in 1838 in Middlesex County, Upper Canada, the second son of Captain Duncan McKellar. The family moved to northern Michigan in the early 1850s and it was there that young McKellar began his training and experience in surveying, mining, engineering, and geology. From 1863 on, he had successfully built up his mining interests in Thunder Bay. He was later to contribute to the journals of several of the societies of which he was a member: the London Geological Society, the American Geological Society, and the Association for the Advancement of Science.

of Ontario and Manitoba have at least been defined and this troublesome boundary question for ever settled ...

Some of the mines were first pointed out by Indians. The Rabbit Mountain Mine location was told by Louis Bokachanini ("Weesaw") to Oliver Daunais[32] a French trapper who had married an Indian woman.

It is a fact of common knowledge in this and other mining districts of the north west that the Indians as a rule have a superstitious objection to making known the locations of Mines and while some of the most valuable ores in the district, except Silver Islet, were pointed out by half-civilized Indians, yet, at first, none of them could be induced to tell where they were situated or to take white men near them.

Weesaw would not go within twenty miles of the Rabbit Mountain mine to point it out though he gave such a perfect description of it as enabled his white trapper friend to find it readily.

This trait of the Indians is ascribed to his idea that these deposits are of a sacred character the making known of which will cause him trouble and an early death.

The Indians are now known in different places to possess richer specimens of Gold than any hitherto obtained by white men in this district ...

For want of good roads railway facilities and sufficient capital the owners of the other discoveries are unable to develop them and the exorbitant prices asked by some of their owners for these undeveloped, or in some instances only partially developed locations retard the progress of the Country.

Some practical lessons were taught these high priced owners of prospects during the year 1885, and a much more sensible way of bringing Capitalists into a new Country has been shown in the policy pursued by the owners of the Beaver Mine.[33]

They agree with a capitalist who agrees to furnish a stipulated amount of money required to work the property and to build a mill to give him an undivided one half interest in the Mine and as somewhat similar conditions were attached to the sale of the Rabbit Mountain Junior and

[32]Oliver Daunais was born in St Ours, Lower Canada, in 1836, and had worked in the United States, Red River, and the United States again before he came to Silver Islet in the 1870s. He then branched out for himself in trading and prospecting, ranging from Lake Nipigon to the Minnesota boundary. He married Hélène L'Avocat, the daughter of the Chief at Lake Nipigon. His mining successes brought his existence to the attention of his first wife, living in Minnesota, and he was charged with bigamy but acquitted. His fame as the Silver King was limited in time, since by 1890 the mining boom was over and the fabulous era of Oliver Daunais virtually ended with it. He died in 1916.

[33]The Beaver Mine had a history of six years, about two of which had passed at the time Keefer was writing. Locations were staked on that property early in 1884 by Oliver Daunais, and grants issued to T.A. Keefer, Daniel McPhee, and Oliver Daunais. Soon thereafter, the American financier R.G. Peters acquired a one-quarter interest (presumably part of Daunais' share) and then bought out T.A. Keefer.

Silver Creek Mines the success of these has so modified the ideas of the owners of other prospects in the district that at present time reasonable working arrangements which would lead to the development and probably sale of their prospects could be made with their owners.

The Farms and Forests

F 19   HUGH WILSON[34] TO HON. R.W. SCOTT[35]
[P.A.O., Crown Lands Papers, Surveyors' Letters]

Mount Forest,
December, 1872

I have the honor to transmit my final report of the survey of the township of Blake in compliance with instructions issued from your department in February A.D. 1872.

I started from Toronto on the 10th of February last for Thunder Bay, Lake Superior, via Duluth and walked from Duluth to Prince Arthur's Landing distant by the coast about 250 miles.

The coast from Duluth to Pigeon River has very little protection and is open with floating Ice during the greater part of the winter. From Pigeon River to Fort William the coast is protected by numerous islands outside and the lake is generally frozen over for several miles out. After a delay of 4 days at Silver Islet I proceeded to procure camp Equipage, Supplies and men for the survey which had all to be procured there as I could not bring anything with me but my Surveying Instruments. After considerable time and at great expense, I succeeded in getting up a camp outfit and on the 10th of March commenced to move in my supplies to the south east angle of the township of Neebing and thence to Loch Lomond. First by having them sent about 6 miles up the Kaministiquia River with sleighs and from that point by packing them in places and by Tobogans in others, making my first depot near the shore of Lochlomond ... I would here beg to state that by commencing the Survey at that season of the year, there were but few men in the country that had any experience in work of the kind and that consequently I laboured under great inconvenience and heavy expenses in prosecuting the work till I got a party of good new men up from Garden River and Sault Ste. Marie about the 1st day of June. And owing to the demand for good

[34]Hugh Wilson of Mount Forest had already been employed by the provincial government on the surveys of McTavish Township in 1870 and the townsite of Prince Arthur's Landing in 1871. After completing the survey of the Township of Blake he proceeded to the new townships of Pic and Sibley in 1874.

[35]The name of Richard William Scott (1825–1913) is identified with two important pieces of legislation – the Separate School Act of 1863 and the Canada Temperance Act of 1878. In the interval between these labours he was Commissioner of Crown Lands for Ontario, 1871–3.

woodsmen for exploring, mining, and surveying parties at Prince Arthur's Landing, wages to men ranged at from $45.00 to $50.00 per month. My average rate of wages paid to men throughout the survey was $45.00 per month exclusive of Board and all Travelling expenses and no deductions for lost time ...

Carp River is the outlet of Lochlomond and is a meandering stream with a succession of Chutes and Rapids and has a fall of about 200 feet and affords excellent mill sites[36] both at or near the mouth on Lake Superior and at various points up the stream to the level of Loch Lomond, reached at about ½ mile from the Loch. A road could be easily constructed along the valley of the River from Lake Superior to Lochlomond and from the extreme west end of the Loch a valley extends through the country running nearly due west into the valley of the Slate River, thus giving easy access into the interior of the Township. I recommended in my previous report during the progress of the Survey that a small reserve be made at the mouth of the Carp River for a Government Town plot – That being the only point that access can be had to the interior of the Township excepting by Neebing and Pai Poonge, north of the McKay Range of Mountains[37] into the valley of the Slate River.[38]

F 20   C.F. AYLSWORTH[39] TO SCOTT
[P.A.O., Colonization Roads Papers]

Toronto,
25th Oct. 1873

In obedience to Departmental Instructions, I have examined the Pigeon River road, and beg to lay before you, the following report thereon.

[36]The firm of Oliver, Davidson & Co. was building a saw mill on Island No. 1 (also known as McKellar Island) at the mouth of the Kaministikwia River but had discovered during the summer of 1872 that it could not take advantage of its licence to cut saw logs on the Indian Reserve unless those logs were sent down the Carp River (now known as the Lomond River).

[37]Whereas Nicholas Garry could find no name for any of the mountains in the range, Wilson ascribed the name of one mountain to the entire range, now known as the Nor'westers.

[38]Plans for providing access to the most promising land in the area were advanced by both Wilson and Adam Oliver, M.P.P., who apparently selected the name for Blake Township. Their suggestions were not followed and the Slate River region was not settled for another decade. The project of a town at the mouth of the Carp River and a road from it was never carried through.

[39]C.F. Aylsworth was an Inspector of Colonization Roads sent to Thunder Bay in 1873 to check on the roads then being built – the Black Bay Road, the Fort William Road, and the Pigeon River Road here described. Procedure seems to have altered somewhat once T.R. Secord was appointed to oversee Thunder Bay roads and took up residence in Prince Arthur's Landing.

I found upon examination and measurement that Mr. Carrell[40] the contractor has cut out and removed the timber from Twenty-four miles and seventy one chains and eighty links of road. This work has been done in three different sections.

The first section commencing at the east side of Fort William Town Plot and running westerly along the North side of the Kaministiquia river; crossing it at point Demeuron, on lot twenty, in the first concession of the Township of Neebing; and at the distance of six miles and forty-six chains and fifty-five links, and extending south-westerly beyond the river four miles and seventeen chains, making in all, in this section, ten miles sixty three chains and fifty five links. This section is well cut out and cleared and a small amount of levelling has been done but not sufficient.

The culvert have not been made satisfactory, not being constructed in the style required in the specifications nor made out of the most durable timber procurable in a reasonable distance. A considerable amount of crosswaying is also required.

The second section commencing at Pigeon Bay, and at the distance of about one mile north of Pigeon river, and extending northeasterly along the road line, one mile and twenty-six chains; this section is only cut out and the timber removed; the road bed has not been levelled, nor culverts and crossways made where required.

The third section commencing at Pine River and extending northerly along the road line twelve miles sixty two chains and twenty-five links. This section has been cut out and the timber removed, a few culverts and some crossways have been made, but not sufficient in number, nor in accordance with the specifications; the timber used being deficient in size and quality, while more suitable timber was available in a reasonable distance.

No levelling has been done on this section and the stumps where the road bed has been cleared are not cut sufficiently close to the ground.

I pointed out the above mentioned defects to Mr. Carrell the contractor, who was present during the measurement and examination of the road.

I would advise that the sum of one thousand dollars per mile be retained from the contract price of this road until it is completed satisfactorily.[41]

[40]John Carroll, a road builder from Harrowsmith with several years' experience as a railway sub-contractor, had been given the contract for the Pigeon River Road in 1873. In the fall of the same year he secured the contract for the bridge across the Kaministikwia.

[41]Aylsworth made similar recommendations concerning the work of Sutherland & Co. on the Black Bay Road at the same time. The Crown Lands *Report* for 1873 shows that $6,600 was spent on the Pigeon River Road in that year, plus an additional $200 for work begun in 1872 on a preliminary mail track to Pigeon River. This *Report* indicates the expenditure of $53,126.80 in the province's Eastern Division, $59,641.32 in the Western Division, and $24,037.43 in the Northern Division, of which Thunder Bay's total was $20,655.65. Such an apportionment of funds was never repeated.

F 21   WILLIAM GAMMOND'S APPLICATION FOR A
HOMESTEAD[42]
[P.A.O., Crown Lands, Papers, Township of Oliver]

I *William Gammond* of the *Kaministiquia District of Hudson Bay* in the ————————[43] make oath and say, that I have not been located for any land under the "Free Grants and Homestead Act of 1868," or under any Regulations passed by Order in Council under said Act, that I am the *male* head of a family having *two* children under eighteen years of age, consisting of *one* son and *one* daughter residing with me, and that I desire to be located under the said Act and the Regulations of the 27th May, 1869, made thereunder, for lot number *nine S, part* in the *sixth* concession and lot number ———————— in the *sixth* concession of the township of *Oliver* containing *200 acres*, and that I believe that the said land is suited for settlement and cultivation and is not valuable chiefly for its mines, minerals and pure timber, and that such location is desired for my benefit, and for the purpose of actual settlement and cultivation of such lands, and not either directly or indirectly for the use or benefit of any other person or persons whatsoever, nor for the purpose of obtaining, possessing, or disposing of any of the pine trees growing or being on the said land or any benefit or advantage therefrom, or any gold, silver, copper, lead, iron, or other mines or minerals, or any quarry or bed of stone, marble or gypsum thereon.

[Signed] William Gammond

Sworn before me at *Prince Arthur's Landing*
this *Seventh* day of *June* A.D. 1875
[Signed] Amos Wright[44]
  Crown Land Agent

I *Cosford C. Forneri*[45] of the *village* on *Prince Arthur's Landing* in the *District of Thunder Bay* make oath and say, that I am well acquainted

[42]As soon as the new township was opened for settlement under the Homestead Act, the first applicants were all from the immediate district, and not until September 20, 1875, was an application made in southern Ontario – in this case, Nicholas Hogg of Grey County. Gammond's application is the earliest one recorded.

[43]Both Gammond and the Crown Land Agent seem to have had some difficulty in understanding what was to be filled in the blank spaces on the form. The description of Gammond's previous address hardly conforms to any expected pattern. Throughout the document, a number of words were crossed out as inapplicable. The number of acres was also inserted incorrectly.

[44]Amos Wright (1809–86) acted as both Crown Land Agent and Indian Agent from April 1875 until 1883. His dismissal from the Indian agency resulted in some difficulty for S.J. Dawson, M.P., since a number of local Conservatives wished him to remain in office in spite of his advanced age.

[45]Cosford Chalmers Forneri was a provincial land surveyor who, in the previous year, had surveyed the Dawson Road lots. One supporting signature was apparently considered sufficient in this case, whereas in other cases two were required. The form used differed considerably and, with the passage of time, a shorter and simpler form was used by most applicants.

with *William Gammon* of *the Kaministiquia* mentioned in the above affidavit, and that he is the head of a family, and has *two* children, consisting of *one* son and *one* daughter under eighteen years of age residing with him.

[Signed] C.C. Forneri

Sworn before me at *Prince Arthur's Landing*
this *seventh* day of *June* A.D. 1875
[Signed] Amos Wright
    Crown Land Agent

F 22   TEMPORARY ARRANGEMENTS FOR THE GRANTING OF TIMBER LICENCES
[*Ontario,* Sessional Papers, *1885, no 20*]

The Commissioner of Crown Lands has the honour to report:

That several applications have been made to his Department for authority to cut timber on the Public Domain in the Thunder Bay District, Lake Superior, to be used in the construction of the Canada Pacific Railway, the locality for which applications have been made being in the vicinity of the railway line westwards from Prince Arthur's Landing to Lac-des-Milles-Lacs, and others will probably be made for ground between Lac-des-Milles-Lacs and the provisional westerly boundary line of the Province.

No licenses to cut timber have hitherto been granted west of Sault Ste. Marie, nor any explorations made as to the character of the country for timber.[46] From Batchewaning River west of the Sault to Thunder Bay, Lake Superior, maps indicate occasional pine clumps at a considerable distance back from the shores of the lake, the timber on the territory appearing, from the same source of information, to be spruce, birch, maple, and other hard woods.

In the vicinity of Thunder Bay and for some distance westward, pine of poor quality generally scrubby and stunted, is found sparsely scattered throughout the district, which may be suitable for rough work in connection with the C.P.R., and will no doubt be cut by contractors on the road and appropriated to their use, should provision not be made by which it may be cut under authority.

In order to meet the case, the Commissioner herewith submits for approval a temporary "arrangement" by which license or permission to

[46]This statement seems remarkable in the light of the fact that Oliver, Davidson & Co. was cutting timber in the Fort Wiliam area from 1872 on, and an order-in-council of June 29, 1872, authorized the sale of timber on lands on the north shore of Lake Superior. The record of applications to the Crown Lands Department, however, does show that, after a brief flurry of applications in 1872, virtually no applications were received during the rest of the 1870s. The publication of this statement in the *Crown Lands Report* of 1885, moreover, indicates how few licences had been granted even a decade later. The first sale of timber berths in the Thunder Bay District did not take place until 1892.

cut timber may be granted in the locality referred to to parties desiring the same, under which trespassing on the Public Domain may be to a large extent prevented and revenue collected on timber cut.

October 3, 1876   Hon. T.B. Pardee[47]
                                                          Commissioner of Crown Lands

F 23   WALPOLE ROLAND'S[48] REPORT ON THE
       SLATE RIVER LANDS, 1887
       [*Roland*, Algoma West, *pp. 80–3*]

Meeting Mr. Roland on his return from an extended examination of the above district, a *Sentinel* representative gleaned the following interesting information touching the settlement of that favoured tract –

"It is now about ten months ago since I made a particular topographical examination and valuation of a considerable tract of patented mineral, timber and agricultural lands along the valley of the Slate River, belonging to Toronto people, as well as a general report upon the great natural advantages of that district generally as a field for agriculturalists, a brief report of which appeared in the *Sentinel* of July last.

At that date I placed an estimate upon the value of lands in this particular section that caused quite a ripple of excitement among practical men both within and without our own community, not only as a field for agriculture, but also as a sheep and cattle ranche. Foremost among the few practical men who tested the accuracy of those highly favorable reports upon its great capabilities may be mentioned Mr. D.F. Burk,[49] who examined the country in South Paipoonge for himself and immediately afterwards secured the lease of a large area of this extensive park-like grazing range, whereon he placed a large stock of young cattle with splendid results, notwithstanding the fact of its being an exceptionally dry

[47]Hon. T.B. Pardee was Commissioner of Crown Lands from 1873 to 1889, when he was succeeded by A.S. Hardy. Pardee, like Adam Crooks, Adam Oliver, and Edward Blake, had a Thunder Bay Township named in his honour.

[48]Alexander Walpole Roland was a civil engineer linked with the district from the early 1870s on. Born in England sometime in the reign of George IV, by his own account, he made his first appearance in the Prince Arthur's Landing press in December 1875. A decade later, he was frequently being interviewed about the new mining activities, and a number of these interviews were included in his book on the areas, *Algoma West*, published in 1887. In 1912 he published another work called *Under Five Flags* which dealt mainly with his experiences as an eighty-three-year-old man lost in the bush and his delight in the premature obituaries composed on that occasion.

[49]Daniel F. Burk (1840–1917) came to Prince Arthur's Landing in the early 1870s as manager of the Ontario Bank. He later became involved in many land and railway ventures, acting as President of the Port Arthur, Duluth and Western Railway in the early 1890s, for example. He was twice a Liberal candidate in federal elections, losing to S.J. Dawson by only eleven votes in 1887, and to George H. Macdonnell by a wider margin in 1891.

summer. Up to this date, or for a period of twenty-six years, (date of survey 1859–60) comparatively little was known of this rich and practically inexhaustable soil as a field for settlement. True applications were made as long ago as 1878 for free grant sections in this direction by well known old residents of Port Arthur, and the traveller throughout the township of Blake to-day, who happens to run against a certain southeast quarter post in the 7th concession, may read the following legend: – 'This lot claimed by Charles Augustus Everitt'; while upon another may be observed: 'Claim of Mr. Geo. Hill Kennedy, 5th March,' and upon the north-east quarter of lot 10 in the 8th concession, 160 acres, 'Geo. F. Duggan, July, '78.' What becomes of claims like the above? If ever placed upon record I presume they have long ago been cancelled, but whether the rich lands in the concessions 6, 7 and 8 are yet open for homesteading we shall probably never know definitely until some practical man like Mr. Burk goes out there, and after demonstrating what the soil is, makes application for a tract for a "model farm."

"Yes, I will explain: At the time Mr. B. examined the lands in the valley of the Slate, there was not one solitary settler or applicant for a free grant, where to-day there are upwards of twenty-three entries and many actual settlers there, while some six or seven others are out there at the present moment, making arrangements for putting in some crop and otherwise fulfilling their homestead duties.

"Many of these are old countrymen, Scotch and English, while others are practical Canadians who have lived and hunted in vain throughout the storm swept prairies of far west Dakota and Minnesota for such a place as this favored portion of Algoma alone can offer. Four at least of the old countrymen have very emphatically expressed their opinions regarding their claims in the 3rd, 4th and 5th concessions, (lots 12, 13, 14, 15 and 16) in the following characteristic manner: – First the hardy Scot observed that 'Right here in one line are my own and my two brothers' lots, or 300 acres altogether; you valued the private lands out here, I believe, at one pound ($5) an acre last year?' 'Yes.' 'Well, I have seen our free grants now – there they are, Nos. 14, 15 and 16 in the 4th concession, and, believe me, I think they are good value at $1,000 each. Ech, mon! I only wish we had the auld mon here; how he would appreciate the scene. Here are real grand mountain ranges surrounding our well watered table land – there is nothing like it between here and John O'Groat's.' 'Not even in Midlothian?' I suggest. 'Ah, weel, the Lothians are fine certainly, but ye ken there are nae free grants there.' " This was Mr. Alexander McDonald, of Point de Meuron farm, who, with his two brothers, George and Angus, appear to be more than pleased with their homesteads.

Another settler, Mr. Newton, (central counties, England) secured some time ago a homestead and pre-emption upon lots 12 and 13 in the 4th concession, immediately east of Alexander McDonald and adjoining the lands of ex-Governor Morris, of Manitoba, Mr. Newton has lived for some time on farms in the vicinity of Brandon and Oak Lake in Manitoba, and marvels much that nothing has ever been done by our citizens to divert a portion of the practical class of old country emigrants or capitalists into this district. Mr. Newton estimates his two sections or lots worth a thousand dollars each. Immediately south of Newton on the 5th concession are the lots of John and Angus McClure, father and son. Mr. McClure, senior, is a practical Scotchman, who fully appreciates the value of his really fine lots, and who with his energetic and resolute-looking son Angus, intend to begin seeding "right away."

"How is this desirable tract of good land reached?"

"At present you have your choice of two or more routes, including the old ferry road, along the north bank of the picturesque Kaministiquia River to the Rabbit Mountain crossing, thence south over a comparatively open and rather sandy ridge in concessions A and I; or you can take the Pigeon River road through the Point de Meuron farm and crossing by the new and substantial Government bridge across the Kam, follow the Pigeon River road for about 1,320 feet to a point where a new road is being constructed in a general westerly course throughout the second concession of Paipoonge. Beyond or even up to the crossing of Slate River little effective work has so far been carried out, and at the present time is hardly available for horse or foot ...

"Is all the lands in that quarter (Slate River) taken up?" "Almost. Certainly all the open or burnt tract. A few sections of partly wooded land remains unsettled, settlers as a rule preferring the cleared ground, timber and thick underbrush being regarded by many homesteaders as a most unfavorable aspect of affairs. I have, however, seen some good land in the burnt portion of Blake, and quite a number of intending settlers are here in Port Arthur to-day for the purpose of consulting the Government Agent for Crown Lands, Mr. Margach,[50] with regard to this township. The settlers with whom I conversed respecting this section of country, express great satisfaction with the Local Government and its officers here, for their uniform courtesy and strict impartiality in the manner of dealing with applications from all classes. Returning by way of the ferry, I noticed a nice frame dwelling house on lot 13 in the 1st concession south of the Kaministiquia. This building belongs to a young homesteader, Mr. Hunt, whose long experience in the North-west convinced him that he had at length found what he had so long pined for – a good homestead possessing the great natural advantages of fuel and water combined with the charms of a most delightful climate and scenery. Near to Hunt's claim is a large area of improved land upon which a log house has been erected by Mr. D.F. Burk, the pioneer of the Slate River country.

[50]William Margach was appointed Crown Timber Agent on November 15, 1882, and was a resident of Port Arthur and a member of the town council. In the spring of 1889 he was transferred to Rat Portage and Hugh Mumro succeeded him in Thunder Bay. Unlike Amos Wright, Margach did not have the title of Crown Land Agent, although he fulfilled some of Wright's former duties.

F 24   THE PORT ARTHUR, DULUTH & WESTERN RAILWAY[51]

[Thunder Bay Sentinel, September 30, 1887]

The Port Arthur, Duluth & Western Railway was originally incorporated by the Ontario Government as the Thunder Bay Colonization Railway. At the last session of the provincial legislature the name was changed to that which it now bears. The route is from Port Arthur southwesterly through the townships of McIntyre and Oliver, crossing the Canadian Pacific about two miles east of Murillo, thence to the Kaministiquia, crossing that near the junction of the Whitefish, following the valley of that stream, and by way of the Beaver, Rabbit, Porcupine and Silver Mountain mines to the north of Whitefish lake, thence north of the Arrow lake chain to the international boundary at Gunflint lake on the Pigeon River system of water stretches.

The present position of the line, which it is intended to build from Port Arthur to the boundary is about eighty-six miles in length. At the last and previous sessions of the dominion parliament it was subsidized to the extent of $3,200 per mile or in all $275,000. The work for the first forty miles has been let to the firm of Grant & Ross, who are also to complete it ready for traffic by July 15 next, and they are also to build the remainder as soon as this section is well under way ... The enterprise was organized in Port Arthur and the credit for its present success is due to the promoters who have been indefatigable in their efforts in the past two years, and now have the pleasure of having their efforts crowned with success and an additional stimulus given to the advancement of their already thriving town. The board is composed of Thomas Marks, president; D.F. Burk, vice-president; Mayor Macdonell, Dr. Smellie, George T. Marks, Michael Dwyer, W.G. Smith, and Allan R. Macdonell, directors.[52]

F 25   ALEXANDER NIVEN'S REPORT ON TIMBER AREAS

[Ontario, Department of Crown Lands, Report, 1890, app. 34, p. 52]

The country along the whole line[53] has been burned at various times from seventy years down to seven years ago – large portions of it about

[51]The P.A.D. & W. was intended to serve the mining communities in Thunder Bay and also to link Port Arthur with the iron deposits of northern Minnesota. The Canadian section of the line was complete by 1891, but the Duluth section was never built, and the collapse of the silver boom seriously handicapped the enterprise. It remained as a local carrier, however, until the end of the 1890s.

[52]Thomas Marks and D.F. Burk had both been directors of the Thunder Bay Colonization Railway, but on that occasion their associates had been Toronto and New York businessmen. Although the first sod had been turned on November 25, 1884, construction had not begun. After the reorganization of 1887 under a new name, all the directors were Port Arthur business and professional men.

[53]Niven was at that time engaged in a survey of the line dividing the districts of Thunder Bay and Rainy River. The Crown Lands *Reports* did not publish the plan to which he referred with his description.

eighteen or twenty months ago. The portion tinted pink on the plan shows the outlines of the brule of comparatively recent date upon which white birch, poplar, cherry, spruce, pitch pine etc. are now growing varying in diameter from two to five inches and on large portions of which is still standing the dead timber killed by the fire.

Considerable green timber of about six to twelve or fifteen inches in diameter is to be found in the country – spruce, tamarac, pitch pine etc.

Considerable tie timber of tamarac and pitch pine is met with in many places along the line notably north of the C.P.R. along the English River.

A few groves of white pine were met with, but there is none of any consequence north of the Seine River.

F 26   EXPERIENCES OF SETTLERS IN THUNDER BAY
[*Ontario, Department of Crown Lands*, Northern Districts of Ontario,[54]
p. 74]

Xavier Laplante's Experience.

I am 55 years of age. I went from St. Martin, near Montreal, in the Province of Quebec, to Pembroke, and from Pembroke to Port Arthur six years ago. I bought 160 acres of land on the Oliver Road, seven miles from Port Arthur, for which I agreed to pay $720 in annual payments. At that time I had $50 and a team of horses. I have three boys. I have met all my payments as they came due. I have now on the farm a good house, 22 × 26, with a 16 × 22 kitchen; a horse stable 22 × 26; cow stable 28 × 30; barn 30 × 50, root house, chicken house and pig house. I have since purchased 320 acres adjoining, and 160 acres in the Township of Oliver, on which there is a house and stable. I have now a farm for myself and one for each of the boys. I have 68 acres cleared, six horses, fourteen milch cows, eight other cattle, twelve pigs, chickens and all the necessary farming utensils. With two teams and one hired man I am making $12 per day. My property, real and personal, is worth $6,750. I have $200 in the bank ready for my next payment, and I owe $800. This country is good enough for me.

Settler's Testimony.

W. Piper. – I have a good dairy farm; a comfortable farm house; a big barn 40 × 80, with a full sized basement full of cattle. Any man who is willing to work can do well at farming in this district. I have grown 1,100 bushels of oats on ten acres.

[54]This pamphlet was published by the Crown Lands Department in 1899 but the experiences described here generally relate to the early 1890s. The purpose of the pamphlet was obviously to induce settlers to move to the northern areas, but this, the fifth edition, was the only one to include Thunder Bay in its appeal. Algoma and Nipissing received fairly full treatment in all editions, while the Rainy River District was receiving a good deal of attention by 1899.

Isaac Ryde. – I came to this district a poor man; I have a good farm in Oliver Township, with good out buildings and as good a house as any farmer needs. I make a comfortable living and I owe no man a cent.

Wm. Reese. – I have a good farm which I have cleared up myself. I am willing to furnish the milk of twenty cows to the first dairy that will start within a reasonable distance from my farm.

Jno. McKay Hunt. – I have a farm in Paipoonge; have 70 acres cleared; my crops are good. I have good health; make a good living; lay up something every year in the way of improvements, implements and clearing and find plenty of work in connection with the farm the whole year round.

Craig Greer. – I came here with a team of horses; I have 120 acres cleared up on the homestead. I sometimes grow two or three thousand bushels of potatoes. We can grow almost anything. My boys are all getting farms for themselves.

Roly Martin. – I generally get the first prize for wheat. I grow from 25 to 40 bushels of it to the acre. I have now about 100 acres cleared up. This is the greatest country for roots I have ever seen.

G. ON THE FRINGES OF SETTLEMENT, 1870-92

G 1 WILLIAM K. BROUGHTON[1] TO ALEXANDER HARVEY[2]
[L.U.L., Hudson's Bay Company Letters]

Martin's Falls,
March 16th, 1870

The usual packet from Albany reached us yesterday afternoon & will I trust start for your quarters [at Osnaburgh House] tomorrow morning.

I would now beg to acknowledge the receipt of your favor of the 3rd Jany under cover to Mr. Wm. MacKay by which I was sorry to learn that some of our Indians had gone to A/O [Albany and/or Osnaburgh?] although at the same time it must be acknowledged that you acted properly in supplying them rather than run the risk of their leaving the District, however I hope that you will give Cr. for any Furs they may give in after paying the advance they recieved from you. "Moss" has been here with a few skins & has been supplied with a few necessaries, so that he can have now no excuse for leaving this post, & should he again visit you I hope he will meet with a similar reception to what you gave him last fall.

The Tobacco 150 lbs. which you requested, is herewith forwarded & I trust will reach you safely, it has been well put up so that I do not think it can come by any harm.

Our Potatoe Crop having failed last season, I have been instructed by Mr. C.F. A. Macdonald [at Albany] to apply to you to bring down 4 or 5 kegs of seed for us when you come down with your returns, this it is to be hoped you will be able to supply as I am sorry to say the greater portion of the few we had for next year's seed have unfortunately got frozen ...

The Result of this Year's Trade will I fear be anything but good, as I hear from all quarters dreadful accounts of starvation among the Indians, & although I do not hear many complaints of the sort here, all complain of the great scarcity of marten & wishing you a pleasant spring etc.

[1]William K. Broughton remained at Martin's Falls at least until 1876, sometimes taking charge of the Albany post, as he did in 1871 during the absence of Chief Trader Alexander Macdonald. All these posts were under the supervision of Chief Factor James Anderson of Moose Factory, a son-in-law of Roderick McKenzie, Sr.

[2]Alexander Harvey was the Hudson's Bay Company post master in charge at Osnaburgh from 1868 to at least 1876, except for the year 1871–2 when he appears to have been on leave. His pay was the equivalent of a clerk's, but it seems doubtful whether he was given that rank.

G 2   ROBERT BELL'S FIRST SURVEY NORTH
OF THE HEIGHT OF LAND[3]
[*Canada, Geological Survey*, Report of Progress, *1870–1, p. 350*]

Sands.

The shores of Long Lake are mostly rocky, but banks of light colored fine clayey sand are met with in some parts, and are conspicuous at the narrow place, which takes its name Ka-wa-ba-tongwa, or the White Sand Banks, from this circumstance. Here, on the east side, this sand rises to a height of upwards of 100 feet over the lake.

North-west of Long Lake House, the country is overspread with a sandy and gravelly deposit, which appears to be too light to form a good soil, except in some places. Owing to its level character, much of the surface is swampy; but as nearly as can be judged by our explorations, only a comparatively small portion of the whole area is rocky. These sandy deposits, as already mentioned, are underlaid by a lightcolored clay, which occasionally comes to the surface, and in cross sections, shews lines of stratification. The Hudson Bay Company's farm at Long

Clays.

Lake House, is situated on this clay formation, and a specimen taken here at a depth of about two feet, was found by Dr. Hunt to contain over twenty per cent. of carbonate of lime; while one from another part of the deposit, in the valley of the Making-ground River at the Summit Portage, proves to contain little or no lime. Mr. Walter Beatty, P.L.S., informed me that the surface is of a similar character all along his line from Humboldt's Bay on Lake Nipigon, to Long Lake, and also along the canoe-route from Poplar Lodge to Long Lake House.

Soil.

It has been already mentioned that a brownish gravelly loam is exposed in the banks of the English River, and that at a distance back from the stream, much of the surface is swampy, especially in the lower portions explored.

In a general way, it may be said that the whole country examined, north of the hilly region around Lake Superior and east of Lake Nipigon, is comparatively level, with a sandy soil, generally dry, but in places interrupted by shallow swamps and low rocky ridges. The soil appears to be for the most part naturally poor, and, over a considerable proportion of this area, it has been rendered worse by the burning-out of the vegetable mould by repeated fires.

[3]Robert Bell conducted the first of many exploring expeditions to the Thunder Bay area in the late 1860s. This particular survey was influenced, as were the missions of E.B. Borron for the Ontario government in later years, by the desire of both Dominion and provincial authorities to know more about the land which the Hudson's Bay Company claimed until 1869, the year of this particular survey.

The old timber consists in order of abundance, of spruce, balsam-fir, tamarack, white birch, aspen, white cedar, Banksian pine or "cypress," and balsam-poplar; but after the fires the new growth consists principally of white birch and aspen. The tamarack, Banksian pine, and white cedar will prove of value for sleepers and ties, culverts, telegraph-poles, &c., in the construction of the proposed Canadian Pacific Railway; while the country along any route through this region will always afford abundance of wood for fuel.

The climate appears to be no worse than that of parts of the Province of Quebec, which are already inhabited. In going from Lake Superior to the valley of the Albany, no difference was observed in the character of the vegetation; which may be accounted for by the greater elevation of the southern part, together with the cooling influence which Lake Superior exerts upon it.

G 3   FATHER DU RANQUET TO FATHER BAPST[4]
[Woodstock Letters, v. 1, pp. 25–6]

Thunder Bay Station,
Sept. 24, 1871

Since I last wrote you from Grand Portage in June, I have been away nearly all the time travelling or on sick calls. A type of measles, called by our doctor "malignant measles," has swept off fifteen of our poor people in less than a month, and threatens to make still further ravages. Truly a terrible scourge for our poor mission! We have had the consolation of seeing the greater part of the victims prepare themselves for death as true Christians. Others have been called away so suddenly that I have hardly had time to give them extreme unction. Very few whites have been attacked; but it would seem as if no Indian or half-breed were to be permitted to escape. Fr. Choné, here at the mission where the greater number of deaths has occurred, is extremely fatigued. Fifty Indians have died of the same disease at Rainy Lake. I have had no news from Lake Nissigon [sic], or the stations north of Lake Superior since my visit to them. I am very anxious about them; this terrible plague seems to ferret out the poor Indians in every corner; whereas the whites, as I was saying, have almost all escaped. I wish I were able to go and examine for myself the state of things at all points of the mission, but I would not venture to leave Fr. Choné here alone in his already exhausted condition.

If the sickness lasts another fortnight, our Autumn fishing will be lost, and those whom the disease will have spared, will fall victims to the famine. The foremost officials in charge of the public works have already

[4]Father John Bapst became Superior of the New York and Canada Mission in 1869, and held that office until 1873. The division of the Canadian Jesuit missions from New York did not come until late in the 1870s.

given some relief to our unfortunate people, and hold out hopes of still further assistance. I have not yet attempted to make a collection, but the compassion for our poor Indians which their great distress excited, should move people to be generous towards them.

The Daughters of the Immaculate Heart of Mary have nearly all their children sick.[5] They also devoted themselves, as far as in their power, to the assistance of the other sufferers.

The visit to our Christians at Michipicoten, Pic, etc., without offering any very remarkable results, has yielded its ordinary share of consolation. At Red Rock, at the mouth of the Nissigon river, seven men, five of whom were Christians, in the employ of the engineers of the Pacific Railroad, were overtaken by the fire which had broken out everywhere through the woods, and were suffocated by the smoke. This accident and the sickness have left many orphans on our hands. The sisters have taken charge of the little girls.

G 4 WILLIAM PLUMMER TO JOSEPH HOWE
[P.A.C., RG 10 C-3, Indian Affairs Letter Books, v. 576, pp. 38–9]

March 3, 1872

Enclosed is a letter of John McIntyre accompanying an account from Dr. Clark[6] of P.A. Landing, Lake Superior, for medical attendance to the Indians residing near Fort William, the same having been addressed to Mr. W. Simpson, Esq. [Indian Commissioner] and forwarded by him to me. Mr. Simpson in writing to me says "I have answered Mr. McIntyre's letter and told him that the Indians of Algoma are under your superintendence and therefore the account has been sent to you, but that as I was personally able to state that the facts mentioned in his letter were true, I would recommend your trying to get Dr. Clarke's a/c paid and his appointment made as surgeon to the Indians of Fort William.

Enclosure		Indian Department to Dr. Clarke						Dr.
1871								
Sept.	14	For professional services and medicine for 33						
		Indians at Mission for measles						$24.75
	16	For professional services. Medicine for 42 Indians						$31.50
	20	”	”	”	”	” 46	”	34.50
	22	”	”	”	”	” 47	”	35.25
	27	”	”	”	”	” 40	”	30.00
Oct.	9	”	”	”	”	” 6	”	6.00
	12	”	”	”	”	” 4	”	5.00
								$167.00

[5]Four members of this order arrived at the Fort William mission in 1870. Miss Josephine Martin, their superior, was listed in the Indian Affairs Department records as a teacher to the Indians during the next few years. The orphanage and Indian school which the Daughters of Mary conducted became the responsibility of the Sisters of St Joseph after 1885.

[6]Dr John F. Clarke (1827–87) was born in England, and had practised medicine

G 5 NIPIGON'S BID FOR LEADERSHIP
[*Roland*, Algoma West, *pp. 3–4*]

Lake Nipigon, situated between the parallels of the 49th and 51st degrees of latitude and the 88th and 89th degrees of longitude, measures nearly 70 miles in length by about 39 miles in width, and in consequence of its numerous and deeply indented bays, has a coast line of nearly 600 miles. This magnificent sheet of clear, deep water, with its innumerable islands, great and small, was, until the commencement of exploratory surveys in connection with the Canadian Pacific railway, comparatively unknown to the outer world. During the years 1872 and 1873 extensive explorations were being carried out upon all sides of this inland sea by the Government engineers, under the direction of Mr. W. Murdoch, then chief engineer of the Lake Superior divisions of the Canadian Pacific railways. It was one of these parties, accompanied by Chief Murdoch, that in the winter of 1871 and 1872, made a bee line from Fort Garry to Nipigon House, a distance of about 410 miles, making a topographical survey of this hitherto unbroken wilderness, on their journey.

At this period in the undeveloped scheme of our great national trans-continental railway, the Government had seriously entertained the idea of making Red Rock, near the mouth of the Nipigon River, the Lake Superior terminus of the road. This scheme had many warm advocates among the engineers, who were of course thoroughly conversant with the great natural advantages of the harbor. A change of Government, however, occurred about this period, when the advocates of the amphibious route came into power, and of course abandoned the north shore for all time, as they supposed. Anyhow, another selection was made.

About this time many important improvements were made in the appearance of the Red Rock post by the officer in charge, Mr. Robert Crawford, now of Indian Head. Docks, houses, stores and commodious officers' quarters were rapidly constructed, and in an amazingly short time the once desolate and weird looking shanties were transformed into an orderly and prosperous station. All this was done in anticipation of the promised terminus. The terminus, however, did not come. The great company of merchant adventurers were disappointed and disgusted with the expenditure, and then and there resolved that as soon as they could discover a post belonging to their ancient corporation where wood or building material did not exist, to that place they should send the offending agent, though said place be the north pole itself. The opportunity soon occurred. A vacancy was made in far away Ungava, and to that place, the nearest

---

for many years in Norfolk County. He represented North Norfolk in the Ontario House in the 1870s and was appointed the first Sheriff of Thunder Bay in 1879, a post he held until his death. His interest in the district antedated the appointment, since two of his sons operated a drug store in Prince Arthur's Landing from the early 1870s, and their father was a fairly frequent visitor to the district while he was still an M.P.P. He never became "surgeon to the Indians."

post to the north pole, Mr. Crawford was exiled. "Lumber," writes Mr. Crawford, "is entirely out of the question here. I used to think $55 and $60 a thousand dear at Red Rock, but here everything is constructed of ice," and unfortunately for Mr. Crawford, ice palaces had not then become fashionable.

G 6 THE PETITION OF THE MUNICIPALITY OF SHUNIAH,[7] 1874
[The Question of the Terminus of the Branch of the Pacific Railway North Shore of Lake Superior, *Ottawa, 1874*]

The petition of the Municipality of Shuniah in behalf of the inhabitants of the District of Thunder Bay

HUMBLY SHEWETH

That your petitioners have lately been informed that Nepigon Bay is looked upon with favor as the terminus of the Canada Pacific Railway on Lake Superior.

That an attempt has been made to place evidence before Your Honourable House by a few parties who have taken up large tracts of land in and about Nepigon for speculative purposes, tending to prove that Nepigon Bay is the most favorable point on Lake Superior for the terminus of the said Railway ...

That Nepigon Bay cannot in any one point claim the advantage either as a terminus for a railway or as a harbour for vessels, owing to the dangers of navigation in consequence of the numerous islands, reefs and shoals in and about the said bay, the early formation of ice and the late date of its breaking up in Spring, and the prevalence of fogs in the latter, which is hereby verified by the affidavits attached, viz: Deschamps, a resident for twenty years in Nepigon Bay,[8] Clarke a resident for ten years;[9] Lambert, sailing master of the Hudson Bay schooner for twenty years;[10] also the statements of Fathers Chone and Duranque Roman Catholic missionaries in this district for over a period of twenty years, which are also further substantiated by affidavits of surveyors, explorers, and other old residents of this district.

[7]The new municipality of Shuniah had been created by Ontario statute in 1873 (36 Vict., c.50). It included both Prince Arthur's Landing and Fort William, as well as the recently surveyed townships near them.

[8]Peter Deschamps was undoubtedly associated with Nipigon over a long period. However, the close association of the Deschamps family with American traders and their continuing battle with the Hudson's Bay Company, Robert Crawford in particular, might be significant here.

[9]Among the attached affidavits there was none sworn to by a man named Clarke, nor by anyone claiming ten years' residence, except John McKellar.

[10]Michel Lambert had the longest acquaintance with the district, with the exception of old Michel Collin. Lambert had come from Sault Ste Marie in 1839 when the *Whitefish* was first put in service on Lake Superior. He had made Nipigon his headquarters for one year, and Fort William for the next thirty-four years.

That the country through which the railway would pass from Nepigon, is neither agricultural nor rich in minerals, but rocky and mountainous, and in view of a railway from that point, there is no road to the interior for the purpose of conveying the plant and provisions necessary in carrying out such an important work.

Whereas Thunder Bay can, in every particular, claim to be the most advantageous point for the terminus of the Canadian Pacific Railway on Lake Superior, having a Bay sufficiently landlocked, forming one of the best natural harbours on the Continent, and which is free from all obstructions to navigation, such as shoals, rocks, and sunken reefs, so that sailing vessels and steamers can approach in safety, both day and night, any of the settlements on the said Bay, that the Harbour is free from ice six weeks later and from two to three weeks earlier than Nepigon, as from the evidence of the Hudson Bay journal embracing a period of nineteen years, and other affidavits attached, Thunder Bay opens on an average on the sixth of May, and closes on the thirtieth December.

That the proposed line of Railway from Thunder Bay would pass through the agricultural valleys of the Kaministiquia, Matawan, Sunshine and Raining rivers, and also through the Gold fields of the Shebandowan and height of Land, in fact, through the whole mineral region of the North-West, so that it would be a great assistance in the direct development of that Country. Miners in the interior would have an outlet for their products as well as the means of supplying themselves with the necessaries needed in opening and working them to advantage.

That along the proposed Railway route from Thunder Bay, the established road and water communication of the Dawson Route would greatly add to the cheap construction of the Railway, as the line would run parallel with it, and by its aid could be commenced in several sections simultaneously, provisions, plant, etc. deposited at them; thus overcoming the great difficulties of building a railway through an unsettled country, and of necessity shortening the time of construction. That Thunder Bay is open longer than any harbour on the South shore which connects with the Railway System of the United States, thereby insuring the longer period of communication during the season with that system which could be obtained by steamer or vessel, and therefore could be maintained long after Nepigon and the Sault Ste. Marie had closed. That there is already at Thunder Bay the nucleus of a large city; the inhabitants now numbering upwards of four thousand ...

[Signed]   PETER J. BROWN[11]   [Signed]   JOHN MCKELLAR[12]
    Reeve   Deputy Reeve

By Order of the Council   [Signed]   ROBERT MAITLAND[13]
               Clerk

[11]Peter J. Brown of Ingersoll was a partner in Oliver, Davidson & Co. He was elected Reeve by his fellow members of the first Shuniah Council, and became noted chiefly for the number of times he was absent from meetings. Having done

G 7 MEMORANDUM PREPARED FOR MEETING OF
CHIEF COMMISSIONERS, HUDSON'S BAY COMPANY,
MONTREAL, FEBRUARY 11, 1875
[P.A.C., MG 29 D-10, McIntyre Papers]

Fort William Employees	John McIntyre, Factor
	Alex. R. Arnot, Clerk
	Fred. Kirkpatrick ″
	James Warnock ″
Nipigon	Henry Laronde, Clerk
Red Rock	Neil Whyte ″
	Alfred P. Vennor ″
Flying Posts	Nicholas Bouchard, Postmaster
	Charles F. Laronde ″
Pic	David McLaren, Clerk
Long Lake	John Finlayson, Post Master
Michipicoten	Peter W. Bell, Factor
	Gilbert Spence, Post Master

G 8 DESCRIPTION OF TRAVELS BY E.R.–
A MEMBER OF THE SOCIETY OF JESUS[14]
[Woodstock Letters, v. 5, pp. 60–2]

F[ort] W[illiam]
Oct. 24, 1875.

At one hundred and eighty miles from Sault Ste. Marie we sight Silver
Islet, where the mines are worked by an American company. They are

with non-residents, the Council chose Thomas Marks as Reeve for the next nine
years.

[12]John McKellar, the eldest of the brothers, had been born in Middlesex County,
Upper Canada, in the 1830s, and had reached Thunder Bay prospecting for
minerals in the early 1860s, after about ten years in the copper-mining region of
northern Michigan. He represented Neebing in the first Council of the municipality
of Shuniah, and later was the first Mayor of the town of Fort William (1892–8).

[13]Robert Maitland moved to Prince Arthur's Landing at the beginning of the
1870s as an employee of the land office. He served as Clerk of the municipality
and Clerk of the division court for some time, and was Deputy-Sheriff for three
years. Extremely successful in his business enterprises, he retired early in the 1880s.

[14]This priest remains anonymous in the Woodstock Letters and no reference
has been found to one with these initials associated for any length of time with the
Fort William mission. The only information given about him in the Letters is that
he had served for a time in the West Indies and was thus qualified to comment
upon a variety of climates. The description of his travels was published in English,
but there are a number of indications that E.R. was French-speaking, and that his
remarks were translated for the benefit of American readers.

picking out silver five hundred feet beneath the lake's bed, the miners, however, living above ground. None but the Americans could succeed here. A Canadian company had tried it and given it up as a hopeless job. Captain T[rethewey], who superintends these works, allows Fr. Baxter[15] to come first in the religious services of Silver Islet, though he himself is a Protestant. The reason he gives is that the priest needs no breakfast before his service. He also defrayed most of the expenses for the chapel, and made a present of a bell to our church at the Landing. Besides this mission, Fr. Baxter visits Ile Royale and La Pointe a Miron[16] ...

Out of a population of six hundred [at the Landing] two or three hundred are Catholics. Father Vary goes there every Sunday to say Mass[17] ... Those poor people have Mass, and sermon in French and English – there are no Indians there – once a week on Sunday and nothing else except catechism for the children.

Our mission is seven miles from Thunder Bay up the river Kaminis-tiquia. For sick calls from the Bay, the messenger has to paddle all the way, often in the dark; true, there is a carriage road, but not on our bank of the river, though one can generally find some means of crossing. Often enough, too, Father Baxter is to be found at the Bay during the week, but not always, as he has other missions to attend to ...

What shall I say of the country? Would it be too much to call it a wolfish country, owing to its climate and a land of adventurers – Indians, half-breeds, whites toiling in the gold, silver, and copper mines? Among the whites are all nationalities – English-speaking, Germans, French-Canadians, etc.

Well, I have come to the conclusion that it is very hard to say which climates are the best, the least demoralizing, hot or cold? A problem I will not undertake to solve. In these icy regions, the devil getting no assistance from atmospheric heat makes great use of internal fires kindled by

[15]Father Richard Baxter (1821–1904) was one of the legendary figures of Thunder Bay history. Born in England of Irish parentage, he was educated in Tyrone, Toronto, Montreal, and Fordham. In 1872 he came to the village of Prince Arthur's Landing, and his missionary duties took him not only to Silver Islet but later to the workmen along the C.P.R. line. He was credited with the building of many of the Roman Catholic churches in the area, at White River and Schreiber, as well as in the Landing and Fort William.

[16]Point de Meuron on the Kaministikwia River had been the site of a fort when Lord Selkirk challenged the Nor'westers at Fort William. By the 1870s it was the centre of a tiny settlement.

[17]It was with Father Baxter that the congregation in the Landing had the closest ties. One of his early letters (*Woodstock Letters*, v. 34, p. 167) reported: "I said Mass in several buildings and sheds, and in Mr. Dawson's house, alongside Flaherty's hotel ... I had hard work in erecting St. Andrew's Church. Mr. Dawson's Glengarry men gave me a hundred dollars. That start produced the Scotch titular for the church, which was burnt down and rebuilt immediately." For several years advertisements in the Landing newspaper listed St Andrew's as "served from the Mission" since Father Baxter's activities took him elsewhere on Sundays and often through the week as well. Father Vary seems to have been at the Fort William mission only briefly.

whiskey. The consequences are self-evident. Happily, the scourge has not succeeded in gaining a foothold on the Indian Reserve, thanks to the zeal of our Fathers ...

The school is not yet opened;[18] it will be at All Hallows; at present, an eclipse of children. I don't know where they are. You must know that English is very useful here; it is the ordinary language of the whites around us. I trust I shall not forget it.

G 9 FATHER HÉBERT[19] TO A JESUIT FATHER
[Woodstock Letters, *v. 7, pp. 95, 99*]

Fort William,
November 22, 1877

... Horses, as you are aware, are not known hereabouts. Dogs have to take their place. Accordingly, when we were about to start [from Nipigon], and the sleds and harness with their many strings of little bells were brought out, all the dogs of the fort began to bark at once, showing, some told me, their desire to take part in the journey. But the happy privileged ones were to be but eleven, six to draw the sledge of the Rev. Fr.[20] & five for mine. This preference gave rise to jealousy and a general battle followed. Those sharing in the fight barked and howled and our men shouted until their throats were sore to bring back quiet ...

[Postscript]   December 31, 1877

The goodness of God enabled me to catch two white fish at Grand Portage, one was a Methodist and the other a Presbyterian. I instructed and baptized them a few days before my return.

G 10 REV. E.F. WILSON'S[21] ACCOUNT OF A
LAKE SUPERIOR MISSIONARY TOUR
[Algoma Missionary News, *v. 1, pp. 118–20, September 1, 1878*]

July 22   Our party consisted of the Bishop,[22] Mr. McMorine,[23] myself and 4 of our Indian boys. Mrs. Wilson and our two little boys remained

[18]The Daughters of Mary were running a school for Indian and some white children. By this time also, Fort William's first public school had opened with Miss Groom, an Irish woman, in charge.

[19]Father Joseph Hébert (1835–93) had been born in Three Rivers and for a time practised law there before he entered the Society of Jesus. In 1876 he left the Collège Ste Marie in Montreal, where he had been professor of theology, to enter the mission field. He spent the rest of his life at Fort William and was buried at the mission in 1893.

[20]It was Father du Ranquet who mapped out the arduous missionary journeys of 1877. The new missionary and the veteran travelled together as far as Nipigon, then Father Hébert proceeded to Red Rock, while Father du Ranquet went east to Pic and Michipicoten.

[21]The Rev. E.F. Wilson of Sault Ste Marie was the editor of the *Algoma Mis-*

behind at the lodgings [in Prince Arthur's Landing] and three Indian boys in their tent. We reached the Town Plot about 4.30 a.m. and the train was to leave about a quarter of an hour later. It was a novel sight, an engine and five or six gravel trucks piled and being piled with trading goods of every description for barter with the Indians; and the owners of the goods, and other travellers sitting on the top; while beneath, on the floor of each truck was a goodly supply of "Mr. Mackenzie's steel rails." I took a sketch of the scene just as we were starting. No conductor, no tickets, nothing to pay, the only conditions being that you should hang on and look out for yourself. In this manner we had to travel seventy miles over a terribly rough unballasted road, reminding one rather of a tug towing some barges on a somewhat stormy sea, than of a railway train, for our engine pitched and tossed and rolled like a propeller, our trucks following in her wake. At seven a.m. we were switched off on to a side-line, and had to wait an hour for a gravel train to pass. This suited us very well, the boys made a fire and got the kettle boiling, and we all had breakfast on the bank. It was a wild journey through the dense forest; occasionally a glimpse of the Kaministiqua River, which, for twenty miles, or so kept alongside us, occasionally a log shanty where men employed on the line found board and lodging, the soil generally rocky and sprinkled with huge boulders, the bush on either side charred and blackened by fire, in some places all in a blaze, and huge columns of suffocating smoke curling upward to the sky, once or twice the heat of the fire on either side of us was excessive, and once the railway ties themselves were burning, and had to be replaced before we could proceed. About 1 p.m. we passed through the tunnel, cut through a rocky ridge and not more than 500 yds. in length. At length after a long journey (of hours if not distance) we reached Savanne at about three p.m. Savanne consists of a river going one way and the railway track going the other way, three log houses and a barn or two; this was the end of our journey, thought not the terminus, which is at present a moveable institution some ten or twelve miles further on upon the route to Winnipeg. One of the first persons we encountered on alighting from "the cars" was the redoubtable chief "Black-stone" who, dressed up in paint and feathers, had given the Bishop

---

sionary News and Shingwauk Journal which began its monthly publications in 1877. He was also superintendent of the Shingwauk Home for Indian Boys.

[22]Frederick Dawson Fauquier was the first Bishop of Algoma from 1873 to his sudden death in 1881. Two of his journals, for the years 1878 and 1880, have recently come to light at Sault Ste Marie. Anglican missions in the Thunder Bay area appeared much later than Roman Catholic and Methodist, partly because the Diocese of Rupert's Land did not include Thunder Bay nor was that area considered as part of the responsibility of the Bishop of London as were other areas of Hudson's Bay territory not included in any Canadian diocese (see Thomas C. Boon, *The Anglican Church from the Bay to the Rockies*).

[23]The Rev. John Ker McMorine had recently left Almonte to assume his duties at St John's Church in Prince Arthur's Landing, succeeding the first Anglican clergyman in the area, the Rev. C.B. Dundas. Mr McMorine later became Archdeacon of Ontario.

a piece of his mind last year on the subject of Paganism *versus* Christianity and is said to have dyed his hands in the Minnesota Massacre. He was accompanied by one of his councillors, and both were, on this occasion, in European dress. We were also much gratified in meeting Mr. McLeod Maingy of the C.P.R., who takes great interest in the Indians, and with whose estimable wife I had had some correspondence besides receiving material help for our institution [the Shingwauk Boys' Home].

Mr. Wright[24] was expecting a tug to arrive to convey him and the traders, and ourselves as a portion of his party down the Savanne River and through the Lake of the Thousand Lakes to our destination, the "Height of Land" where the Indians were to gather for their annual payments. The tug, however, was not on hand, so we had to camp until morning. Several Indians were about awaiting Mr. Wright's arrival, and there was a wigwam full of them close to our tent; they were all pagans, and their appearance very different to those of our neighbourhood; the men had their hair plaited in two large plaits, the tails of which were joined halfway down the back, generally they had no hats and their costume consisted of a shirt, a beaded belt around the waist, trousers and moccassins. They were evidently dressed in their best for the grand occasion. Nearly all wore silver earrings, some of them consisting of a string of five-cent pieces, and others had necklaces of bear's claws and other strange fancies; their pipes were carved out of soap-stone polished smooth, many of them were armed with ornamental tomahawks, and they had long knives concealed in bead work sheaths.

G 11   FATHER HÉBERT TO FATHER PERRON[25]
[Woodstock Letters, *v. 9, p. 25*]

Long Lake,
May 27, 1879

I was very kindly received by Mr. Bell,[26] the great man of the Hudson's Bay Company. He is a Protestant, but intends becoming a Catholic as soon as he is disentangled from the affairs of the Company. God grant it. There are a great many Methodists in this place. They were baptized, I

[24]Amos Wright of Prince Arthur's Landing was both Crown Land Agent and Indian Agent at this time; he had offered to take the missionaries and the Indian boys with him on his expedition west.

[25]Father Jean Jacques Cuillier Perron had served the New York and Canada Mission since 1860, and was Superior of that mission in the early 1870s, although not at the time this letter was written.

[26]Peter Warren Bell was the son and grandson of Nor'westers. By the 1870s he was a Chief Factor and the acknowledged "great man" of the Lake Superior fur trade. The Hudson's Bay records indicate that he was transferred to Esquimaux Bay in 1879, but there are references to him at Michipicoten as late as 1882. In 1893 he was granted two years' leave by the Company, prior to his retirement. No evidence has been found to indicate that he ever became a Roman Catholic, as Hébert believed he intended.

was told, by Fr. Kohler[27] and some by Fr. Hanipaux,[28] but after their departure, the enemy came in the garb of a Protestant minister, and sowed cockle among the good grain. Many of these poor wanderers have since returned. We have a very neat little chapel at Michipicoten, the only one that is finished between Prince Arthur's Landing and Sault Ste. Marie. It was built by Father Du Ranquet. He was liberally assisted by Mr. Bell in finishing it.

G 12   HÉBERT TO PERRON
[Woodstock Letters, *v. 9, p. 131*]

Fort William,
February 24, 1880

Mr. Bell, the bourgeois of the fort, divided the sum of about $400 given by the government of Ontario among the Methodists and Catholics. The Methodists resolved to buy provisions with their portion of the money and the Catholics put theirs together for the purpose of building a school-house. To renounce Methodism was, therefore, to deprive oneself of pork and flour which, I assure you, is a great sacrifice for a poor hungry savage. I am glad the Methodists expended their money for food instead of expending it as our people have done; for if they had a school, it might do much harm to the rising generation.

G 13   LAWRENCE VANKOUGHNET[29] TO
SIR JOHN A. MACDONALD
[*P.A.C., RG 10, Indian Affairs Letter Books, v. 1081, p. 369*]

July 5, 1882

One cannot but be impressed with the opinion that undue pressure was brought to bear upon Chief Binessie[30] to induce him to sell his land, also that considering the rates at which lands were being sold locally in the same locality Binessie might probably have obtained a higher sum for the land than was paid him by Mr. Wright. There can be little question that Mr. Wright's conduct in this matter has to say the least materially

[27]Father Auguste Kohler (1821–71) belonged to the original group of Jesuit missionaries in the Lake Superior area, travelling to Fort William in 1855, for example, in the party with John McIntyre and his family en route to a new position. Much of his work was in the Michipicoten area. He was drowned near Sault Ste Marie in 1871.

[28]Father Joseph Urban Hanipaux (1805–72) was also one of the original group of Jesuits who came from France in the 1840s. He seems to have made only one expedition to the Lake Superior area.

[29]Lawrence Vankoughnet was the son of Hon. P.M. Vankoughnet. He became Deputy Superintendent-General of Indian Affairs in 1874, a post he held until 1893.

[30]Pinessi or Penassie were the usual versions of this name current locally.

impaired his usefulness as Agent to the Indians of whom Binessie is the Head Chief, and considering this fact as well as Mr. Wright's advanced age, namely 73 years, the undersigned is of opinion that it would be advisable that he should be placed on the retired list, and he sees no reason why Mr. McIntyre ... should not also have charge of the Indian Bands on Lake Superior[31] ... Mr. Wright's present salary is $600. per annum. Mr. McIntyre receives $730. per annum. The population in Mr. Wright's agency number 1782, that of Mr. McIntyre 874. Mr. Wright's duties consist principally of paying the Indians their annuities as the most of the Indians under him are of nomadic character and only appear at the places of payment on the days appointed. Mr. McIntyre's Indians are making an attempt to settle down upon the Reserves ...

With regard to the question as to whether Mr. Wright can be legally compelled to restore Chief Binessie's land to him, the undersigned takes it that this is a matter for the courts of law to determine ... and he is of opinion that Chief Binessie should be informed to this effect.

VANKOUGHNET TO MACDONALD
[*P.A.C., RG 10, Indian Affairs Letter Books, v. 1082, p. 190*]

December 13, 1882

The document referred to, namely the Surrender,[32] is utterly spurious and invalid, if no stronger terms may be used to characterize it, for it is clear from the evidence that the surrender of the timber on their Reserve was never made by the Indians and that the document was not signed by all the men whose names are upon it, that Mangading whose name appears first on the surrender swears positively that he never signed or touched a pen; that Crow could not possibly have signed as he was away on the Red River Expedition ... Upon looking at the Reverend Father Choney's petition of January 15, 1874 ... it is found that ... Mr. Plummer, when he came to Fort William for the purpose of submitting to the Indians the question of surrendering the timber, finding the majority of them absent came to him [Father Choné] and that only two Indians were present on that occasion ...

[31]John McIntyre had been appointed in 1880 as Indian Agent for the Savanne District, immediately to the west of the area then administered by Amos Wright. The suggestion that the two areas be combined under McIntyre's control reached the stage of a recommendation to the Council, which Vankoughnet withdrew on the advice of S.J. Dawson. Dawson had expressed doubts over the McIntyre appointment in 1880, but too late to effect any change. This time his intervention was decisive (P.A.C., RG 10, v. 1081, p. 565, Vankoughnet to Sir John A. Macdonald, Sept. 27, 1882).

[32]The reference is to the July 8, 1871, document in which the Chiefs of the Fort William Band were supposed to have surrendered timber rights on the Reserve. Superintendent William Plummer had been in Fort William at that time to conclude the agreement. At least from 1881 on, the Fort William Indians had been claiming that the document was "spurious and invalid."

Mengandine is described in the evidence of Mr. John McIntyre ... as having been the Head Chief of the Band at that time, and William Crow as Second Chief ... All the signatures apparently are in the handwriting of Mr. Plummer ... Mr. McIntyre in his evidence states that when any important event ... was to be considered by the Indians, it was usual for a Council to be called and every man over the age of 21 years had a right to vote on the question. Mr. McIntyre alleges that he remembers nothing about the aforesaid surrender stated to have been made by the Indians of their timber; he however remembers Mr. Plummer being at Fort William at that time but nothing further.[33]

G 15 MAGISTRATE BORRON'S JOURNAL EN ROUTE
FROM NIPIGON TO LONG LAKE[34]
[*Borron*, Report of the Stipendiary Magistrate, *1884, pp. 7–11*]

June 13th [1883] – At this Post [Nipigon] I expected to be able to obtain reliable information in regard to the route to Long Lake, and to secure the services of a competent guide. I hoped too, to have been able to exchange my canoe for another, or others more suitable for the route I proposed following. I was sorry to find that the route to Long Lake, although practicable for small canoes, would, at least, present great difficulties to our passage over it in a large four fathom canoe, and that the trip would, at best, be slow and laborious. Mr. [Henry] DeLaronde informed me that there were no canoes such as I wanted at the Post, and that it was even doubtful if another man could be got.

June 14th. – The Hudson's Bay Company's establishment here is not as large as I expected to see. The site is rather pretty, and very well sheltered by an island, so much so that, on approaching it from the open lake, it cannot be seen by the voyager until he is close to it. A catholic mission has been established a mile or so to the eastward of the Post, which is conspicuous at a distance of four miles.

I was not very favourably impressed with either the climate or the soil. In fact, with the exception of a few hours, it rained almost the whole time we remained at the Post. The soil fit for cultivation, so far as it fell under my observation, is only found in patches here and there, between exposures of rock ...

June 15th. – Today we had one of the severest thunder storms I ever

[33]Plummer's memory was scarcely more reliable. He denied he had used bribery, declared he might have distributed crackers and tobacco on the occasion, since that was his usual custom. Father Choné, he did remember, had acted as interpreter and signed as witness of the validity of the signatures which Plummer might have written down himself when the Indians were unable to write. Father Choné had died in 1878.

[34]E.B. Borron had retired from federal politics and had been appointed Stipendiary Magistrate for the District of Nipissing. His special commission was to explore the "disputed territory."

remember to have experienced in this country. It lasted five or six hours, the rain descending in such torrents that our camping ground was flooded, and we were literally "drowned out" of our tents. But for the kindness of Mr. DeLaronde, who provided us with shelter and dry blankets we should have been obliged to pass a very uncomfortable night.

June 16th. – A fine morning at last, but most of our things being wet, I concluded to delay our departure until the afternoon, in order that they could be at least partially dried.

Mr. DeLaronde had engaged a man to accompany me to Long Lake. Unable to obtain half-sized canoes, two of which would have answered me better, there was nothing for it but to make the trip in our large canoe, which, if once at Long Lake, would thereafter be more suitable in some respects than smaller ones. In order to lighten our load and lessen the labour of portaging, which I was led to expect would be severe, I parted with almost all superfluous articles of luxury that Mr. DeLaronde was willing to take off my hands.

At 2 p.m. we got under way, and pursuing an east south-east course for about 12 miles, camped on an island near a point, at which my guides said a long traverse would be necessary. We had barely got our tents pitched when rain, accompanied with thunder, lightning and wind again came on – but very moderate as compared with yesterday. Even this storm, however, would have been far from pleasant if it had overtaken us when making any of the traverses referred to.

June 17th. – This being Sunday we remained encamped.

June 18th. – Started at 6 a.m. and took a south-easterly course across the lake for the mouth of the Mamaominikon [Namewaminikan] or Sturgeon river. This we reached about four o'clock in the afternoon. The distance is about 20 miles – and made up of long traverses, from island to island. In crossing to the north and east of Gros-Cap, we were able to form some faint idea of the size of this lake. Fogs are seemingly frequent, and "the mirage" is also seen elevating and distorting objects at a distance. The temperature of the air during the day varied from 49° to 59°, and of the water from 40° to 49°. Ice was seen on the islands in one or two places – an evidence of the coldness and backwardness of the season. The islands we passed were mostly composed of trap-rock; and though less elevated, reminded me of those seen in the neighbourhood of Thunder Bay, on Lake Superior. Vegetation was very backward; and the timber, where exposed to the sweep of the wind, was stunted and poor. Although I have been disappointed with that portion of the country bordering on Lake Nipigon, now for the first time seen, I have no doubt, however, that on the west side, and up the rivers which empty into the lake, more or less land fit for cultivation will be found.

The Sturgeon river is about two chains in width, with a moderately strong current. The water is much darker than that of the lake itself. Near the mouth, sandstone, slate and conglomerate rocks were met with "in place."

We ascended the river about three miles, and camped a little below the first rapid and portage.

The soil on the banks is a sandy loam reposing on clay, and from the appearance of the timber, I should take it to be a tolerably good soil. The timber consists of aspen spruce, tamarac and birch, with some rough bark or banksian pine.

June 19th. – It commenced raining yesterday afternoon, and has continued to do so with little or no intermission all night. It had not abated this morning, and knowing the state the portages would be in, and how drenched everything would get, I waited until mid-day to see if it would not clear up. Disappointed in this, and impatient at the delay, we started at 2 p.m. The first portage, which was close at hand, turned out to be quite short, not more than 100 yards in length. The fall here is about ten feet. In two miles more we came to the second portage, about two hundred yards in length, with an estimated fall in the rapids of fifty feet. Both these portages are on the south side. In another two or three miles we arrived at the third portage, where we camped for the night.

June 20th. – The temperature of the air fell to $32°$ or freezing point. This (3rd) portage is a mile and a quarter in length, and the fall in the rapids probably not less than forty feet. But little rock is visible on the portage, but that seen was trap. Owing to the length of the portage, and difficulty experienced in getting the canoe across, it was two o'clock in the afternoon before we were ready to start again. In three or four miles more we came to the fourth portage, 200 yards long with a fall of about ten feet in the rapid. A short distance above this, a demi-charge was necessary, and at the end of another mile, or say about two miles from the fourth portage, we arrived at the fifth portage, and there camped. The timber met with on this stretch was mostly spruce, banksian pine, tamarac and cedar. On the low, flat river bottom, between the third and fifth portages, there is a considerable quantity of tamarac and cedar. At the upper end of the third portage I measured aspen, poplar and balsam trees that were 42 inches in circumference, spruce 70 inches, and white birch 40 inches. The rock at fourth portage and demi-charge consists of greenish grey slates with veins of quartz. At the west end of the fifth portage we found a tree blazed, and marked "C.P.R., September 17th, 1881."

In ascending the river our course thus far has been, on the whole, pretty steadily eastward. The average width of the river has been about two chains.

Black flies were out in force to-day. It is the first time they have been troublesome this season ...

June 23rd. – At this camping place, I measured aspen that were four feet in circumference, white birch five feet and tamarac four feet. The soil is light and sandy, but is covered by a good thickness of vegetable or leaf mould, and even at this elevation (and we must be now almost on the water-shed) I have no doubt excellent crops of potatoes could be grown on land of this description.

Joseph, a native, and one of my guides, encouraged by the other voyageurs, favoured us with a specimen of his vocal powers in the language and style of his race. Each verse of the song began with "Yea yea, yauchee, O yea," and was continued and ended by a quick succession of nasal sounds and grunts that I am utterly unable to describe. He accompanied himself by drumming on the canoe, which, after being unloaded, had as usual been hauled out and turned bottom up. This song, or others set to the same air, is known to and sung by the Indian medicine men and conjurors, not only of the Ojibbewas but other tribes, and has, I suspect, its origin in some form of religious incantation. The drum and these original songs are rapidly disappearing, but may still be occasionally heard in the solitudes of the wilderness, and generally in the dead of the night on the Height of Land.

June 24th. – This being Sunday, and my crew in need of rest, we remained encamped, although morally, I think, we would have been quite justified in going on, as there is no little probability of our running out of provisions before we can reach Long Lake and replenish our stock.

June 25. – Rising at 4 a.m., we got once more under way about 5 o'clock.

This lake cannot be less than ten miles, I think, in length; and appears at its greatest to be about four miles in width. The number of islands, however, prevents anything like a comprehensive view being obtained of it. The longer axis bears as usual about N.N.E. and S.S.W. Pursuing a direction between N.E. and E.N.E., diagonally across the lake, we came in about an hour to where the fifteenth portage takes off on the east side of the lake. This is, I believe, the Height of Land Portage on this route.[35] It is about a quarter of a mile in length, and passes over a ridge 40 feet or so in height of drift gravel and sand. It terminates at a small lake about half a mile wide. No rock was met with in place on our route through the large lake on which we were last camped, but numerous pieces of fossiliferous limestone were seen at the bottom and on the gravelly beaches.

The small lake north of the water-shed is, I think, a little higher than the larger one to the south, but not more than eight or ten feet. Crossing this small lake we came to its outlet, a small stream only a few yards in length, and running into another little lake. The water is very clear and many pieces of limestone could be seen in the gravelly bottom. A partial unloading or demi-charge was required here. Crossing this second small lake in an easterly direction we came in a mile to the commencement of the next or sixteenth portage. This is level and swampy, and in 250 yards brought us to a pond about one-third of a mile wide. This crossed, we landed and found ourselves still in a swamp. Here commenced our seventeenth portage, one of the longest and worst, not only on this route but any other I have yet passed over. It is about three miles in length, and

[35]This uncertainty about the Height of Land is added evidence to support the description given by Dr Bell to the Select Committee on Boundaries (A 22). Borron made it clear that all his measurements particularly of altitude were very approximate.

for the most part over muskegs so wet and soft that the men with loads
on their backs frequently sunk down almost to their knees. At the end of
the first mile the portage is interrupted by a small pond which it was
necessary to cross in the canoe, but the whole is reckoned as one portage.
After making three stages, or about two miles, we camped for the night,
my men being very much tired.

June 26. – Calling all hands soon after four o'clock, a hurried cup of
tea and a bit of biscuit were taken, and once more they set to work on the
portage. The chief difficulty was the canoe, which was much too large and
heavy for the route. The black flies and mosquitoes, kept back by the cold
spring, now seemed determined to make up for lost time, and harrassed
us almost beyond endurance. About 9 a.m. everything had been got over,
and we embarked on a small lake. We had not gone, however, more than
half a mile when we came to another, the eighteenth portage. This was
only, however, seventy-five yards in length. It terminated in a stream
fifteen to twenty yards wide, the water of which flowed towards the east.

G 16 FROM OUR OWN CORRESPONDENT
[*Port Arthur*, Weekly Herald, *January 10, 1884*]
McKay's Harbor[36] Items

December 31st, 1883

Work is going on very busily on both sides of us, but not right here.
The proposed line to replace the old right-of-way, which was found to be
impracticable, owing to the late slide, has not yet been fully decided upon.

The weather has been very changeable. As yet we have very little snow.
scarcely enough for sleighing, and such roads! I had heard of the rough-
ness of "tote-roads" but never imagined them as bad as what I see. Just
to the west is a hill, which a horse can hardly climb to say nothing of
drawing up a load. We have to draw up the sleighs by ropes from the top,
and occasionally we have to attach a rope to the horse and draw him up
in a like manner. Of course all these difficulties will shortly be overcome
by cuts and fills.

Accidents are continually happening at the different works; and our
doctor, Mr. Beck,[37] who has a beat of about twenty-two miles, is kept
continually on the road. I tell you he works faithfully and is the right man
in the right place. We have also had Drs. Black and Courtney ... One is
now at Jackfish and the other away below, at some other point.

Most of our vegetables are a total loss, owing to the slide occurring so
late in the season, leaving us no time to prepare for the severity of Jack
Frost. Some of the contractors, however, were more fortunate, but those

[36]The present name for McKay's Harbour is Rossport. It derived its earlier name
from Charles McKay who came to the area as early as 1874 from Sault Ste Marie.
It was renamed in 1885 after the C.P.R. contractor.

[37]Dr G.S. Beck was a member of the original staff of the hospital opened at
Prince Arthur's Landing in the spring of 1883; in 1891 and 1892 he served as
Medical Health Officer for Port Arthur.

having vegetables cannot be induced to part with them under any circumstance ... Flour and fresh meat are all right, and everything else that cannot be hurt by frost, so we need not fear famine.

G 17   VANKOUGHNET TO MADAME FARIJANA[38]
(PRIVATE)
[P.A.C., RG 10, Indian Affairs Letter Books, v. 1085, p. 667]

Ottawa,
April 12, 1884

I am in receipt of your private letter of the 4th instant relative to the trouble you are having with Father Hébert. I am writing you officially in reply to your official letter to the Minister to the effect that you have the remedy in your own hands against all trespassers upon your limit. I am sorry that you are being given so much trouble and sympathize with you. I think, however, that a spoonful of oil is of more effect than a gallon of vinegar in such cases, and that you could probably, with that suavity of which you are such a rich possessor, induce the Reverend Father to cease troubling you. There is no doubt that he has great influence with the Indians, and it would be in your interest, in order to avoid trouble with them, to pacify him.

G 18   VANKOUGHNET TO MACDONALD
[P.A.C., RG 10, Indian Affairs Letter Books, v. 1085, p. 706]

April 22, 1884

With reference to Sir Hector Langevin's letter of the 14th and the Hon. Dr. Costigan's[39] of the 16th instant – both returned herewith – relative to Father Hebert's timber transactions on the Fort William Reserve, I beg to inform you that Madam Farijana's allegation, through Archie Stewart,[40] is that Father Hebert was cutting timber and selling it. She wanted the Department to interfere. I informed Mr. Stewart that the licensee had the remedy in her own hands, as her license covers the timber of certain

---

[38]Colonel Farijana had taken over the timber licence for an area of about 20 square miles on the Fort William Indian Reserve from G.W. Monk, then assigned half of the licence to Vallières de St Real. Farijana died in 1882, and his partner in the following year. The two widows secured a renewal of the lease but entered into an agreement with George Thomas Marks to share the profits and superintend operations locally. By the end of 1883 Madame Farijana was concerned that Marks might manage to have the new licence issued in his name and cut them out of the limit altogether. In the following year a new problem arose over Father Hébert's authorization of the cutting of wood within the limits for which Madame Farijana held a licence.

[39]John Costigan (1835–1916) had been born in Lower Canada, but moved to New Brunswick as a young man and represented a New Brunswick constituency in the House of Commons continuously from 1867 to 1905. He was Minister of Inland Revenue in the Macdonald cabinet in 1882–92.

[40]Archibald Stewart, an Ottawa barrister, was Madame Farijana's lawyer throughout the various problems connected with her Fort William timber licence.

dimensions and it was for her to take any proceedings to protect herself from trespass that might be necessary.

With regard to timber required for buildings within the Mission, I do not believe that Madam Farijana would interfere with Father Hebert's taking such; it would be bad policy on her part to do so. But Stewart assures me that Father Hebert has cut and sold quite a large quantity of timber from off the Reserve.

I think the best way will be to allow them to fight the thing out between themselves. We have got our money for the timber and that is all we need care for, and Madam Farijana has her own remedy at law in view of the license issued to her.

G 19 The Jackfish "Demi-Monde"
[*Port Arthur* Weekly Herald, *November 27, 1885*]

Jackfish Bay, one of the stations east of here, on the c.p.r., is one of the many that has still continued to live (as the frontier saying goes) along the immense line, since the greater part of the construction has stopped. Quite a thriving trade is done among section men and others employed in the vicinity. The staple article of consumption, however, is whiskey, and quite a little gambling takes place. Several members of the demi-monde also hold forth there. With such attractions as these, it had the effect of embracing among its denizens one Edward McMartin, a notorious individual who has often been hunted by the officers of the law, both at Port Arthur and at other places. He was arrested once in connection with a robbery and for assaulting one Agnes Steele, some time ago. It appears that on the morning of the 16th of November he had a quarrel with a man named Herritt, a boarder of Mr. James McKay, who keeps a boarding house at Jackfish Bay, which led to a fight ending in the beast McMartin biting off the nose of Herritt. This had the effect of causing McKay to order the man from his premises. One word bringing on another, a fight ensued in which McKay decidedly had the best of it, when suddenly having got the whole of McKay's index finger between his teeth, he with a most ferocious snarl severed it from the hand, near the second joint. They were finally separated and the injured man was attended to as well as possible without medical aid, there being no physician near. But subsequently the wound became fearfully inflamed and McKay suffered most excruciating pain, which finally led to dilerium. At this juncture, an effort was made to capture the perpetrator of the outrage, but as two days had elapsed, and anticipating trouble, he skipped westward. Constable McIntyre was put on the offender's track, but on his arrival at Port Arthur he found his man had left for the east on one of the boats.[41]

[41]McMartin was later shot and killed while resisting arrest in Cartier, January 12, 1886.

G 20   A.L. R U S S E L L ' S   S U R V E Y S   O F   I N D I A N
R E S E R V A T I O N S   A T   N I P I G O N ,   1 8 8 7
[*Roland*, Algoma West, *pp. 149–51*]

The route to the scene of Mr. Russell's surveys of Indian reservations was along the (for the most part) frozen rapids and chutes of the Nipigon River, and from the Little Flat Rock rapids across the magnificent inland sea known as Nipigon Lake. This immense water stretch possesses a deeply indented coast line of nearly 600 miles. Voyaging along this route in summer was of course familiar to the entire party,[42] but the experience of travelling on snow-shoes over the frozen chain of lake-like expansions composing the swift flowing Nipigon River, was to some of us quite a novel one.

This river measures some 33 miles from its source at Victoria Falls to its inlet into Nipigon Bay, Lake Superior. No less than fifteen falls of more or less magnitude occur in its impetuous course. Many of these falls are of unrivalled grandeur, and even in their present partially frozen-over state, present new charms and impressions from every point of view.

The topography of this country is perhaps more diversified with islands, lakes and streams, with rocky mountain ranges and fertile belts interlarded therein, than any other portion of Ontario.

To the south and westward of the big lake with the euphonious Franco-Indian name of Nipigon, much fertile land and good timber abounds, and the country in the neighbourhood of the English church mission, where the Indians cultivate a great variety of root and other crop, is no exception.

This mission was established some ten years ago by the late Bishop of Algoma (Fauquier), who endeared himself to the small but devoted band now permanently settled in McIntyre Bay on the south side of Lake Nipigon. Here some five or six frame and log houses, including a good school, have been erected under the superintendence of Rev. Mr. Rennison,[43] a graduate of Trinity College, Dublin.

This well chosen site has not yet been secured to the Indians. I am, however, informed upon good authority that both the Dominion and Ontario Governments are about taking steps to construct a good wagon road from Red Rock on the Canadian Pacific railway to this mission. This is rather a better route for the road promised to the Nipigon people by Mr. Conmee,[44] M.P.P., during the closing days of last session, and for

[42]Among the group making these surveys in the last weeks of February and the first weeks of March 1887 was Walpole Roland, C.E., who wrote the account first for the local press, then included it in his book.

[43]The Rev. Robert Renison had come to Canada from Ireland in 1883 and had almost at once taken charge of the Nipigon mission. His son, the future Archbishop of Moosonee and Metropolitan of Ontario, was educated at Trinity College School, Port Hope, while his father was in the north.

[44]James Conmee (1848–1913) was born in Grey County and, after service with the 8th N.Y. cavalry in the American Civil War, became involved in a number of railway construction projects in the United States and Canada before arriving in

which the sum of $1,000 has been voted in this year's estimates. Mineral lands have been applied for in this vicinity. "Possibly," observed the intelligent chief of the band, "the Government think we have moved away. And as white men have already applied for mineral lands right at our doors, we should like to see this question of ownership settled in a friendly way, as we don't want to keep out miners or settlers."

During our trip we experienced some unusually severe weather, notwithstanding which work was vigorously carried on every day. Over 11,000 acres of land were instrumentally surveyed, and repeated observations were taken upon clear nights throughout the progress of the work.

In addition to the above survey, consisting of some twenty miles of line cutting and traversing, Mr. Russell also made a track survey across Lake Nipigon by pacing and prismatic compass bearings, thereby fixing the position of many islands and essential points in this lake of magnificent distances. This latter proved a most fortunate undertaking, as on the return trip, and during a piercingly cold north-east wind and blinding snow storm of sleet, our Nipigon Indians, who might reasonably be supposed to know the route thoroughly, became hopelessly lost, and it was only owing to the fact of Mr. Russell's observations on the up trip and his early detection of their aimless and irregular course that saved us being placed in a very unenviable position to say the least.

Indians like others are often slow to admit their errors, but in this case they frankly admitted that "Indian was positively lost" ...

The fur trade near the lake is said to be fairly good this season, but owing to a decided paucity of supplies at the Hudson Bay Company's interior post of Nipigon House, the Indians complain that they would be compelled to seek other sources of supplies. Our party were, however, fortunate in obtaining just sufficient food for time actually employed. This, under the peculiar circumstances of the case, may be looked upon as a very great concession on the part of the Hudson Bay Company. Mr. Russell proves to have been an old acquaintance of the agent at this post (Nipigon House) and this doubtless accounts for his successful negotiations respecting the commissariat department.

In addition to the above reserves on the Big Lake, another reserve was last season surveyed by Mr. A.L. Russell, for the band of Chippeways belonging to Red Rock and Lake Helen. This reserve is on the west bank of the Nipigon River near its inlet to Lake Helen, where the Chief Pierre

---

the Thunder Bay District in the 1870s. With his partner, J.D. McLennan, he received the C.P.R. sub-contract for the sixty-four miles of track from Missanabie to White River. He was later associated with the building of various sections of the Canadian Northern Railway, the Port Arthur, Duluth and Western, and the Algoma Central, while the lumber trade also absorbed much of his interest. After a brief career in municipal politics as Councillor and then Mayor of Port Arthur, he represented the newly created provincial riding of West Algoma from 1885 until 1904, when he resigned to enter federal politics. He was returned for the constituency of Thunder Bay and Rainy River in the Liberal victories of 1904 and 1908.

Deschamps and other civilized Indians have made comfortable homes and well cultivated gardens. Here also reside the most experienced and trusty voyageurs and guides to the numerous fishing places of note. Among the best known of the guides I may mention Pierre Bonnetcarie, Jose Bouchard, John Watt, Alexe La Ronde and Dennis Deschamps.

G 21   NEWTON FLANAGAN'S[45] REPORTS ON FISHING PERMITS
[*Ontario, Department of Crown Lands, Reports, 1887, app. 13, p. 21; 1889, app. 11, p. 21*]

One hundred and two persons made applications for and received special permits to fish; of this number, seventy-three were issued to residents of the United States, two to gentlemen from England, and twenty-seven to inhabitants of our own province. The sum of $375. was collected for permits ...

Fishing for pleasure with fly and hook and line have been the only methods practiced here during the past season. No netting or other illegal means of procuring fish have been resorted to. In this connection I have no complaints to make, nor has any infringement of the fishery laws been brought to my notice.

The River Nepigon was throughout the season in very fair condition for fly fishing, the water being low and remarkably clear. Any quantity of fish was in the stream, still complaints were made that the trout would not rise readily to the fly. Many fine catches, however, were made and large fish taken.

Not so many anglers visited the Nepigon the past season as during the previous year, owing in great measure to the exorbitant charges made during 1888 by the Indians and halfbreeds who act as guides and boatmen. This great objection was, however, much mitigated during the past season by having men brought in from other localities.

G 22   VANKOUGHNET TO JOHN MCINTYRE
[*P.A.C., RG 10, Indian Affairs Letter Books, v. 1091, p. 372*]

Ottawa,
July 18, 1887

Mr. Dawson, M.P. handed me your letter to him of the 27th ultimo requesting him to see me regarding the travelling expenses deducted from your account to and from Savanne. In reply, I have first to remind you that it is looked upon as an act of insubordination for an Indian Agent or

[45]Newton Flanagan spent half a century as a Hudson's Bay Company employee before retiring in 1890 to St Paul. His first report from Red Rock concerning the Nipigon fisheries was made in 1887, by which time he was overseer for the Department of Fisheries, responsible for Lake Nipigon, the Nipigon River, and adjacent waters. In 1890 he was succeeded by William McKirdy. The salary in both cases was $50 per year.

other official of the Department to communicate on such a matter as the above with any other than the officers of the Department.

Secondly, if you will refer to your instructions when you were appointed to the position which you at present hold, you will see that you were then informed that you were to reside at Savanne, and that was the condition on which your appointment was given you as stated in the Order by His Excellency the Governor General in Council appointing you. You will therefore observe that there should be no necessity, if you followed the instructions of the Department by residing in Savanne for the Department to pay your expenses to and from Fort William and the same cannot be paid.

As to your postal matters not being so conveniently obtained if you were to take up your residence at Savanne, I beg to state that you would be in no worse – not in as bad a position as many of our Agents located upon Indian Reserves who have not Post Offices in their neighbourhood but who nevertheless manage to have their postal matter transmitted to them. The same remark applies to your cashing cheques and drawing salaries, etc.

An Agent should certainly reside within the District for which he acts as Agent, and not outside it, as Fort William is. As far as that goes, we might very properly dispense with your services entirely as Indian Agent if you are to continue to reside at Fort William and delegate the duties to Mr. Donnelly[46] who resides in Port Arthur, which is within a few miles of Fort William.

G 23   PETITION OF FORT WILLIAM INDIANS TO SIR JOHN A. MACDONALD, 1887
[Document in the possession of Dr P.M. Ballantyne, Thunder Bay]

We again write you concerning Chief Thomas Bouche.[47] The Indian Act provides that any Indian Chief may be deposed by the Governor for dishonesty intemperance, immorality or incompetency. Chief Bouche has deserved to be deprived of his chieftainship for each of the causes above mentioned.

[46]James P. Donnelly was appointed Indian Agent "for that part of Ontario lying between the 48th and 52nd degrees of latitude and the 84th and 95th degrees of longitude" in January 1883 and retained the office well into the 1890s. His appointment had come about on the recommendation of S.J. Dawson, who described him thus: "(He) is a Roman Catholic and will be acceptable to Bishop Jamot who insists so strongly that as the Indians are R.C. their agent should be one too. Mr. Donnelly is a very respectable man with a large and exemplary family and he speaks and writes both French and English" (P.A.C., Macdonald Papers, v. 289, Dawson to Vankoughnet, Jan. 10, 1883).

[47]Thomas Boucher was elected Chief on March 18, 1886. His election was opposed from the beginning by Father Hébert, and supported by J.P. Donnelly. Protests over irregularities in elections were not new, since the 1883 election of John Pierre as Chief had also produced a complaint in that case that Amos Wright, the Indian Agent, had used his influence.

First, for dishonesty. He is openly and publicly known as a liar – no person of sense believes a word that he says. Here is an instance of his dishonesty – We have a large book where we keep a minute of the Resolutions and By-Laws of the Band Minute Book. In the Spring of 1886 three white men who had married squaws were allowed to live on the Reserve, but under certain conditions which were registered in the Minute Book. Later on, that is last winter, Thomas Bouche, not liking any longer those conditions, secretly tore up two leaves from the Minute Book.

Secondly, Intemperance – Last Summer while in Liquor he had a quarrel with one of the Missionaries domestics. Again, last Summer he sent a Frenchman named Blais to fetch liquor, when it had been brought, he, Thomas Bouche, his sister Ann, his niece Elizabeth Kebeis, sang and Blais drank together. That took place on the Reserve in the bush. Lately on Dominion Day, he drank again – he continually does so. Nevertheless the Indians are told never to drink.

Thirdly, for Immorality. Last Summer on Dominion Day, being on board the Kakabeka with three Indian girls, he attempted to take extraordinary liberties with them, and moreover he encouraged some whitemen to do the same. Again, last Summer, he has been seen very often in the evening, and at night, paying visits to a woman who was living alone in her house. In the Fall of 1885, at the fishing place he gave great scandal with an Indian girl. Last winter a great many Indians of this Reserve spoke against him, saying that he had unlawful intercourse with a married woman. This last Spring an Indian of this Reserve, Gwinguish, saw him, Thomas Bouche, taking unlawful liberties with the woman just mentioned, which scandalized him though an infidel yet. Towards the same time, or a little before, a half-breed who is a near relation of Thomas Bouche, gave warning to the woman above mentioned, that Thomas Bouche had, or was endeavoring to have, unlawful intercourse with his wife. Finally, Lately, on Dominion Day, the same, the same Thomas Bouche, behaved shamefully with that woman. In the after-noon they went behind the big pile of lumber of James Conmee at Port Arthur. An Indian woman of the Reserve having seen that, told the woman, now I see that those who last winter said that you and Thomas Bouche were misbehaving together, said the truth. When the night had already set in, it being already nine o'clock if not later, Thomas Bouche and the same woman were seen together at the outskirts of the town of Port Arthur. Several persons have seen them. The woman returned home only the next day, being yet half drunk ...

Fourthly – Incompetency. When he gathers the Indians together, if he be contradicted, he becomes furious and insults those who oppose him, using the most awful language. Last Spring, towards election time[48] he insulted three Indians most shamefully, though he had received no provocation whatever. He speaks without any reason, against the Missionary, and is most impolite towards him. He spoke most impolitely of yourself

[48]This reference is to the Dominion election of March 3, 1887, not to the election of Boucher the year before.

last Summer when you visited us.[49] He wished to go to Ottawa, and you remember, he asked you to pay his travelling expenses. Your answer was that you had no power to do that. He then said in presence of many men – See how the old man son of a bitch is lying. Last Spring an Indian of this reserve, remarked to him that some of the trees which were cut by Indians, employed by Madam Farijana, were too small. Thomas Bouche insulted him telling him, you had better to take care of your wife, whenever you go away, she cheats you openly so that many persons know it.

He is most unworthy to be chief. And now this is our resolution – We reject said Thomas Bouche as chief. We will not have as chief, an immoral man an insulter, a man of bad conduct. We chose as chief, John B. Pinessi.

It is not astonishing to see him behaving as he does now, for until his election as chief, his conduct was very bad, he having been repeatedly sent to jail at Port Arthur.

The Indian Agent, last Spring gave us oat seed. Thomas Bouche secretly appropriated them himself, thirteen bushels of them

Solely without any provocation he struck Andrew Bannon, second chief and was fined at Port Arthur for that offense.

He struck brutally last Winter, a young boy, who is now in the Hospital at Port Arthur, on that account.

(sgd.)[50] –

Andrew Bannon[51]	Joseph Penassie
John Pierre[51]	Thomas Penassie
John Pinessie[51]	Stephen Joseph
William Crow	Alexr. Chab
Louis Kebewinsee[51]	Moses Louis
Michael StGermain[51]	Alexie Debakonang[51]
Baptiste Collin	Joseph Sebastian Nenaigahaish
Simon Webabikenze	Michael Madjisanany
Simon Penassie	Gwinquishineanan
Simon Collin	Alex X Singleton
Simon Louis	Joseph Debaconang
Peter Salamon	Michael X Collin
Frank Salamon	Joseph Nenrkas
Frank Majeweskkan	James McErtts
John Manitou	Squimawaguick
Frank Bellon	Peter Jourdain

[49]Sir John A. Macdonald had visited the Fort William Indian Reserve on August 26, 1886, and, in addressing the Indians, impressed upon them that their duty lay in obeying the missionary. This advice might partially explain Boucher's comments concerning the Prime Minister.

[50]Beside the signatures on the document is the following notation: "This is the original Petition drawn up at my house and that sent to the Department taken or copied from it are the same. (Signed) John Pinessi" No copy of this petition has been discovered in the Macdonald Papers or in the Indian Affairs documents. It appears to have been written in the summer of 1887.

[51]Each of these men had served as head or second chiefs during the 1880s. Elections were held every three years.

G 24 FATHER JONES' INQUIRY[52] INTO DIFFICULTIES ON THE FORT WILLIAM RESERVE
[A.S.J.C.F., D-8, Memoir of Father Jones]

From a careful perusal of the above enumerated papers,[53] it would seem that the trouble began as far back as June 1885. On the 25 of that month the Indian Agent Mr. Donnelly convened an assembly with the view of electing councillors. The election resulted in the choice of objectionable persons. The respectable portion of the Indians had the matter laid before His Lordship, the late Bishop Jamot[54] and this through their missionary priest, the Rev. F. Hebert. The department in turn took the matter in hand and, in an official communication to Mr. J.P. Donnelly, the agent, annulled the election.

This, according to F. Hebert, was very distasteful to the agent, who on many occasions reproached him with his having been intermediary.

On the 26 November of the same year, the Indians petitioned against the illegal election of Pierriche Deschamps as Chief [at Red Rock]. This also took place within the limits of Mr. Donnelly's agency.

In the spring of 1886 a reserve was established at Red Rock with the assurance on the part of the agent to the missionary that the Red Rock mission would not suffer thereby. But from that moment, according to the Father, the agent and Pierriche Deschamps, the latter more especially, have not ceased to work injury to that mission.

On the 18th March, 1886, Thomas Boucher was elected Chief, the same whom at the present date the missionary and a number of Indians would have removed as totally unfit for the position, and whom the Agent and the remaining portion support.

Later on, that same spring, the Agent, Mr. J.P. Donnelly (according to the Father's statement) in the Father's room and in the presence of the Indian, Jean Pierre, Mr. Donnelly declared that M. Farijana was to receive 5 cts. a foot for the timber the Indians would use in constructing or repairing bridges. Thereupon the Indians reported this to the Department, and Mr. Donnelly, the agent, was officially informed that M. Farijana could claim nothing. The agent on his side denied having made the statement which gave occasion to the official communication.

It was in the summer of '86, on the 26 August that Sir John A. Mac-

[52]Father Jones was asked by the Superior of the Society of Jesus in Canada, Father Hamel, to visit Fort William and investigate the difficulties between Father Hébert and the local Indian Agent. He cited documents dated up to October 1888 and likely prepared the report very soon after that date.

[53]Father Jones cited eighteen documents, many of which were referred to in his report but none of which were included with it. He also relied to a great extent on interviews with the contending parties.

[54]The Lake Superior District lay within the Diocese of Peterborough. Bishop Jamot, who died in 1886, had communicated a number of the protests from the Indians to the Indian Affairs Department. When an Indian Agent was being appointed in 1882 he had recommended J.J. O'Connor, but Dawson had urged the government to appoint Donnelly who, in his opinion, was "far superior to O'Connor." Dawson's advice prevailed over that of the Bishop.

donald visited the mission, and in addressing the Indians he took occasion to impress upon them that their duty lay in obeying the missionary.

In the course of the following spring, 1887, the missionary states that the agent informed him that Fehagash [?] the chief of the Pays Plat had lodged certain complaints against him, Mr. Donnelly, and that Alexis Memashkawash and some others had behaved badly, and that consequently hereafter there would be no chief of the Pays-Plat; that furthermore he would take from the Indians residing there what the Department had allowed them, viz: implements, oxen, etc. The Father subsequently met Charlie McKay,[55] who, as he states, told him that the Indians of the Pays Plat had had word of Mr. Donnelly's threats, but they were in no wise disposed to leave their place. The Father thereupon wrote to Mr. Donnelly and pointed out to him that the Indian Act granted them the right of having a chief etc. He transmitted in return a written answer to the Father denying ever having said what was related in the Father's letter; who asserts however that Mr. Donnelly from that time had on every given occasion reproached him with intermeddling with the affairs of the Pays Plat.

The general elections were to take place on the 9 March of that year, 1887, and the election franchise had been extended to the Indians.[56]

The Father received the following telegram by the C.P.R. dated 28 Feb. 1887. "By telegram from Ottawa to Rev. Father Hébert, Fort William 'Please give my friend Dawson a helping hand in this election' "[57] ...

Although I have not yet completed the report I was to make out at your request, and which on account of numerous side issues involved threatens to be a lengthy paper, I think with the knowledge I now possess of the documents and facts I can conscientiously form a judgment of the case. Two general questions seem to cover the whole ground.

1. Has the Government any reasonable ground of complaint against the Father?

2. Has he as a religious & a Jesuit forfeited by his conduct his claim on the protection of his Superiors?

– I –

The complaints of the Government, those at least put forward, are no others than those of the Indian Agent himself, though circumstances point to another grievance not openly avowed.

As for Mr. Donnelly's heads of complaints, they are in my humble

[55]Charles McKay, after whom the settlement later called Rossport was first named, lived with the area Indians for several years, and later became a lighthouse keeper.

[56]By the Act to Amend and Consolidate Laws Respecting Indians (43 Vict., c. 28) certain Indians were to be enfranchised, provided they held land on a Reserve and had the consent of the Band to which they belonged. The 1887 election appears to have been the first in which Fort William Indians voted.

[57]According to the list of documents cited by Father Jones, this telegram was signed by Hector Langevin. He also lists a telegram from Van Horne to the agent at Port Arthur, containing a similar message.

opinion reduced to their proper proportions by F. Hebert's reply, which I find covers every point of importance. So much so that even were I not acquainted with the father's trustworthiness and sound judgment, I should unhesitatingly say that he and not the agent is the aggrieved party.

I said that there seems to be a complaint which is not avowed, and to which I would ascribe the government's dissatisfaction. I mean the Father's refusal to canvass for the government candidate at the general elections, which took place on the 3 March, 1887, and what certainly must have been very distasteful to the Department of Indian Affairs at Ottawa, he advised the Indians, when his advice was privately solicited, to vote for the opposition candidate.

My reason for coming to this conclusion is that up to that date, though there had been more than one issue in which Mr. Donnelly had taken his stand against the missionary, F. Hebert's representations had been favourably received by the Department. In proof of which the annulling of the election of councillors of the 25th of June, 1885 may be instanced. Nor was any exception taken to the petition against the illegal election of Pierriche Deschamps at Red Rock on the 26 Nov. of the same year. There were various other points of disagreement between the missionary and the agent in that and the following year, and nevertheless on the occasion of the visit of Sir John A. Macdonald on the 26 Aug. 1886, the latter had nothing but words of praise for F. Hebert, and he even took occasion to impress upon the Indians that it was their duty to obey their missionary priest.

As soon however as the elections were over a change took place in the manner of treating certain representations and at Ottawa F. H. was forthwith set down as a firebrand and the cause of all the trouble. The agent in his injudicious zeal accused the father of taking an active part in the elections, unaware that the Father had been solicited directly and indirectly by telegrams from members of the Government and their partisans to throw in all his influence and vote in favour of the administration candidate.

It is needless therefore to add that as the Father has effectually vindicated his own conduct in his dealings with the agent, that the Government by soliciting him to use has influence with the Indians in its behalf has forfeited all right to complain of the missionary's independence in advising the Indians to vote otherwise.

And should further complaints be forwarded from Ottawa for your Reverence's consideration, I should advise a copy of the Father's reply to his accuser and his countercharges be forthwith sent to heads of the Department for their edification.

— II —

I come now to the second question — Has Father Hebert as a religious and a Jesuit forfeited by his conduct his claim on the protection of his superiors against the Government? If for me the question takes this shape, it is because I think that is really the import of the present investigation. To my mind, the good name of a man who has surrendered it to the keeping of a kind mother, the Society, must be held by her beyond all else as sacred, and no consideration of worldly loss or worldly advantage should be entertained for one moment as being able to outbalance it in price or value.

But I make haste to say that in this present case I think the Society has little to lose and everything to gain in the above named order of temporalities by showing a little firmness in favour of one of her persecuted children. For, before God, I heartily endorse your Reverence's sentiment in writing to the Father last July, "Ils veulent que vous ayiez tort car ils veulent vous persecuter."

To withdraw the Father is in my estimation little else than to sacrifice him. That is to say to sacrifice one who has toiled a score of years for God's glory among a band of degraded savages, who has by untold and unremitting labour mastered a language in which it takes a life time to become proficient, one who has served the Society faithfully, and though in his present disposition he offers himself a willing victim of obedience, one who should have the undivided support of the Society to maintain him in his position.

I am, as I said, led to think that in face of a firm stand on our part, the government will not dare to curtail its yearly subsidy to the missions, as the measure, as soon as known by the public, would eventually turn to its own disadvantage by estranging many of its present supporters, and would be quickly rescinded. A show of weakness on the part of the Society by withdrawing the Father would make the position of his successor untenable. He would either have to become the obedient subordinate of the agent, and thus lose all powers for good over the minds of the Indians, or make but a feeble opposition to any demoralizing measure the agent might devise, fearful that, like his predecessor, he might not meet with the support of his Superiors. It would also be most detrimental to the good of the mission to replace the Father before some other missionary, destined to replace him, should have acquired a knowledge of the language ...

The government itself must have foreseen that by extending the franchise to the Indians it was sowing the seeds of discord for ever among them. It is not for me to discuss the expediency of a measure which made mere wards of the government, placed under the tutelage of an agent, voters at the elections, but even the least perspicacious must see that such a situation is incompatible with the independence required to record a vote freely. In the present case, it is not easy to prove that the agent, who depends for his position on the good will of the government, induced certain Indians to vote for his patrons. But the fact is there, that the minority faction whose cause he has all along espoused, voted for the government candidate. To say the least the measure is calculated to lead to interminable abuses. Now in the case of an unscrupulous agent with sufficient cunning to conceal the undue influence he is exerting, who but the missionary is left to advise the unsophisticated savage? It is not a case of a missionary's showing favour to the officials of an unlimited monarchy where Indians are placed under a paternal government, to which the conditions of the bands, previous to the extended franchise, bore some analogy, but it is a case under a constitutional government. In such case, every man has the undeniable right of consulting with whomever he chooses, and as long as no undue influence is used no government can reasonably find fault with the missionary priest who makes use of his reciprocal right of imparting advice.

Nor can I see how a missionary can be advised by his Superiors otherwise than in general terms to use great circumspection in the use of that right, to refrain from giving unnecessary offence, and to abstain from intermeddling in elections when the good of the country at large or of the mission is not in any way interested. But once admitting the right of the Indians to vote he cannot reasonably be deterred from prudently and according to his conscience assuming the part of the natural adviser of the Indians. And an enlightened government, especially if it has placed the Indians in this false position of voters and of wards, should rather rejoice to see the all-powerful influence of an over-zealous agent tempered by watchfulness of the missionary.

H. THE RIVALRY OF THE PORT AND THE FORT, 1870-92

H 1 HUGH WILSON TO THOMAS DEVINE[1]
[P.A.O. Crown Lands Papers, Surveyors' Accounts, 1871]

Prince Arthur's Landing,
30th Sept. 1871

I beg to forward to you a trace of the working plan of the survey of Prince Arthur's Landing shewing the subdivisions as far as the Survey is completed.

I was obliged to deviate considerably from the projected plans in order to suit the streets to the nature of the ground and at the same time clash with buildings as little as possible.[2]

So far nearly every lot is claimed and it will be necessary for me to subdivide another tier of Park lots to supply the demand in that locality.[3] I purpose completing the survey on south side of Arthur Street before proceeding with the north side so as to give time to decide on the propriety of setting appart a Dominion and Ontario reserve.[4] If it is the intention of the Government, I would recommend that it be done at once for as soon as I commence to lay it out Every lot will be squatted on at once.

H 2 PETITION OF THE INHABITANTS OF PRINCE ARTHUR'S LANDING
[Canada, Sessional Papers, 1877, no 57]

The petition of the inhabitants of Prince Arthur's Landing, Thunder Bay, February 26th, 1875, humbly sheweth:

That the inhabitants of Prince Arthur's Landing having learned with surprise and regret that it is the intention of the Government to make the

[1]Thomas Devine was the Surveyor-in-Chief for the Ontario Crown Lands Department in 1871.

[2]That the 1871 survey was the official one and that those occupying property at the Landing before that date could claim only squatters' rights is borne out by Wilson's reports, by various claims of individuals to land held in the 1860s, and by contemporary accounts like that of Walpole Roland (*Algoma West*, p. 20). The belief that the history of the Landing dates from an 1857 survey and the subsequent sale of lots appears to rest on precarious foundations.

[3]This is a reference to Wilson's decision, in view of the nature of the terrain and the direction taken by the Dawson Road, to provide for a park (the present Waverley Park) in the centre of the townsite. His decision made it necessary to extend lots farther south of Park Street than had been originally intended.

[4]The main east-west thoroughfare was Arthur Street, the beginning of the Dawson Road. In this initial planning stage it was obvious that Prince Arthur's Landing was being regarded as the site for government buildings. The government reserves were accordingly laid out.

Town Plot of Fort William, on the Kaministiquia River, the terminus of the Fort Garry branch of the Canadian Pacific Railway, beg leave to bring before you our claims to a continuation of the railway to this point.

Prince Arthur's Landing is a flourishing town of twelve hundred inhabitants, composed chiefly of active and enterprising men, who have been the means of opening up this isolated section, enduring the usual disadvantages and hardships of pioneers, and deserving therefore of recognition at the hands of the Government, a large amount of capital, over $300,000, has been expended in actual building improvements, and consequently the value of the land greatly enhanced; whereas the town plot of Fort William is almost uninhabited, and is owned almost entirely by speculators, so we pray that Prince Arthur's Landing, being the older and already established settlement, may not be ignored, but receive the advantages of the railway starting from it.

There is already at the Landing, besides an open roadstead for any number of vessels, a good substantial dock, which, with a comparatively small additional expenditure, would be amply sufficient for all the requirements of trade for several years to come. There are only two or three days during the season when vessels would have any difficulty in discharging or shipping, with the accommodation the dock possesses at present, but a breakwater of six hundred feet or less would obviate this, and as only four miles of perfectly level country intervene between Fort William and this point, the cost of continuing the railway would be very small.

It is an undisputed fact that the Kaministiquia River is closed by ice several weeks earlier than the Bay, the average time of the River freezing up, being the first week in November; this is a disqualification affecting the River for being made the final terminus of the railway on Lake Superior, the importance of which cannot be over-estimated, as the fall of the year is the period during which the heaviest shipments are made; therefore, if the railway terminate at Fort William, all late freight would have to go by Duluth, thus losing a large amount of money for Canada, besides building up American lines in opposition to ours; in the same way shippers in the West would ship *via* Duluth, rather than run the risk having their freight left over for an entire season at Fort William ...

(Signed) PETER NICHOLSON
And over 100 others

H 3   THE EARLIEST NEWSPAPER IN
PRINCE ARTHUR'S LANDING[5]
[*L.U.L., The "Thunderbolt," April 15, 1875*]
A.D. 1900

At our feet lay the valley of the Kaministiquia, where its muddy little stream trickled down as of yore. I noticed that at its mouth "outwork"

[5]During the winter of 1874–5, residents of Fort William produced a few hand-

was built out on each side for about half a mile, but no shipping was to be seen. I looked for the *city* of Eden, but found only a miserable village ... "Look farther ahead (a mist was just then rising) and you will behold the city of Prince Arthur's" – I could not believe my eyes, for it was far ahead of my utmost expectations. On the north side of McVicar's creek stood the Union Station for the Canadian Pacific & Duluth & Thunder Bay Rail Roads, about a mile from the shore stretched a mammoth breakwater two miles in length, named after its great builder "The Uncle Oliver Breakwater" – a range of docks (which put me in mind of Liverpool more than any I had ever seen) stretched from "Buffalo Creek" to Current River, lined with a perfect forest of masts. Row after row of princely villas dotted the hills on all sides. A second St. Paul's Cathedral stood in the midst of Waverly Park, in the dome of which was an immense clock just on the stroke of seven – at that moment a score of bells from the factories and mills at Current River with St. Paul's Bell rang the hour. I awoke with a start and found the Government bell ringing getting up time ...

The Future of Prince Arthur's Landing

There is at least a gleam of hope that Prince Arthur's Landing is destined to be ranked amongst the great cities of this continent. The contract for the Telegraph communication between Thunder Bay and Fort Garry has already been given, as also that for a branch for the Canadian Pacific Railway between the same points. It is confidently hoped that the latter will be completed within three years; this will be the beginning of the opening up of the great Nor-West Territories which will unite our Bay and Lake Superior with the Pacific, when we may look forward to this Port as the outlet of importations of the produce of China in the shape of silks, teas, etc., and British Columbia and Manitoba of gold, silver, and cereals. The shipment of "pig-tails from China," "Jugglers from Japan," and Grasshoppers from the Nor-West Territories, will break bulk at Fort William Townplot, those from China to meet many old friends, those from Japan to instruct the unlearned of that Plot in the art of that science which they are well adapted for, and those from the Nor-West Territories (viz) grasshoppers to feed on the mosquitos and black flies, the former of which get in the logs and bark and many of them will neigh around. It is well that the latter can find abundance of the insects above named as their prospects of procuring vegetation in that Locality would be rather poor ...

---

written issues of a newspaper called the "Perambulator," no copies of which seem to be extant. Prince Arthur's Landing retaliated with the "Thunderbolt." The tone of both publications was decidedly partisan, but at this stage in the rivalry probably intended to be humorous. The "Thunderbolt" was edited by G.F. Holland and George Thomas Marks. The three extracts are from the opening editorial, from a letter to the editor signed c.o.d., and from the news items.

That Ice-House

The "Perambulator" compliments Mr. Wm. Blackwood[6] on erecting an ice-house at Ft. William *Town*; it is truly said that some things have small beginnings, and we believe it when one of the first buildings erected in a *would-be* town is an ice-house. We think when Mr. Blackwood has lived six months, in that mosquito-blown, fever-stricken and inhospitable region, he will require an ice-house to preserve his remains.

H 4   THE PLOTTERS OF FORT WILLIAM
[*Thunder Bay* Sentinel, *July 12, 1877*]

Names of Persons Who Sold Property for the C.P.
Terminus

Recapitulation

Jos. Davidson	$10,930.
Caroline Davidson	600.
Jos. Davidson & Hellen E. Leys	3,250.
Helen E. Leys	2,025.
Mary J. Brown (wife of P.J. Brown)	735.
Thos. Wells (partner of P.J. Brown)	1,000.
Neebing Hotel (O.D. & Co.)	5,029.36
John McLaren	4,000.
Sam. Hazlewood (Engineer of C.P.R.)	1,575.
M. & N.K. Street[7]	3,000.
Mary J. Street	1,300.
Moses Street	900.

Recapitulation $34,731.[8]
Total as published   51,700.18

Land bought from the Government in Town Plot $8.00 up per acre, and outside (18 lots alluded to) only 20 cts. an acre, and purchased back *by* the Government at $475. per acre! ! !

[6]The Blackwood family seems to have been far more closely associated with the Landing than with Fort William. Robert Blackwood had been a signer of the 1875 petition (H 2) and D.M. Blackwood became Port Arthur's first Postmaster.

[7]Moses Street and his younger brother, Noah K. Street, had established a general store at Prince Arthur's Landing in 1871 and later opened a Fort William branch as well, hence they could not be considered absentees. After the death of the senior partner, N.K. Street continued to operate both stores under the name of Street Brothers.

[8]This Recapitulation is remarkable for its omissions. The recipients of small amounts were understandably omitted (although the fact that Thomas Marks of Prince Arthur's Landing received $80 had later to be defended by the *Sentinel*) but several names of men receiving as much or more than those included were left off the list – J.J. Vickers, for example, received $1200 and John McIntyre $2025. It was evident that the immediate targets in the summer of 1877 were the partners in Oliver, Davidson & Co. and the Street family. McIntyre would qualify later.

H 5 AN INTERVIEW WITH "GOVERNOR MCINTYRE"[9]
[*Thunder Bay* Sentinel, *October 18, 1877*]

Mr. McIntyre would have it that "the Kaministiquia channel is 400 feet at its mouth, 500 feet at the division of the two islands and 400 feet at the Government Dock." It has never been pretended here by the most ardent friends of the River that the *channel* was over 50 feet wide (while many of the most intelligent people of the District deny that width). Even the *Manitoba* upon her last rest at the Bar was not claimed to be over 100 feet off her course – that bright, calm morning.[10] We are perfectly willing to let the Government survey disprove the wild distances given by Mr. McIntyre.

It would almost seem unnecessary to discuss the extravagant use of language in which the late "Governor of Fort William"[11] indulged as we presume the subject will be before the Senate, if not the Lower House, also, when testimony will be taken under oath, and "bottom facts" reached. However, we will ask attention to a few of the figures given by Mr. McIntyre; it is true he refuses to admit there is any comparison between Prince Arthur's Harbor and that of the River, and goes on to compare the Kaministiquia with the St. Lawrence and the Clyde Rivers! Comparisons are said to be odious ...

Mr. McIntyre might have described how the ice coming down the river effected his property at Point de Muron, and also how the banks of the river are disappearing, leaving trees and stumps many feet now from the shore, and how near the Mission the banks are caving in, and filling up near the Mouth of the Mission River,[12] and elsewhere, but that would not answer his purpose; he had to go the whole length even to the whopper of saying there was not too much paid for the "Neebing Hotel,"[13] and when disclaiming that politics had anything to do with his opinion, he

[9]John McIntyre had recently paid a visit to Ottawa and had there been interviewed concerning the location of the railway, then under investigation by the Senate. It was his comments reported in the Ottawa press that aroused the *Sentinel*.

[10]Captains of the various vessels coming into Thunder Bay were under constant pressure to support one or other community in its claims. Captain J.B. Symes of the *Manitoba* was supposed to favour the Fort William interest (See McKerracher Diary, Sept. 6, 1874: "Steamer 'Manitoba' came in this evening. The Captain was in a fearful passion and swore fearfully at someone who taunted him with going up to Fort William before coming to the Landing"). It was thus a source of special delight in the Landing when this particular vessel ran aground in the Kaministikwia River.

[11]The Hudson's Bay post at Fort William was being closed at this time, but the use of the term "Governor of Fort William" was satirical to an extent that the editor of the *Sentinel* could hardly have realized. McIntyre only became a Factor, and hence acquired the title Governor, in 1873 when the future of any Hudson's Bay Company operation at Fort William was very much in doubt. Throughout his long years with the Company up to that time, McIntyre was a clerk.

[12]The most southerly of the three mouths of the Kaministikwia.

[13]Fierce local controversy raged over the purchase of this hotel, owned by Oliver, Davidson & Co., and its transformation into offices for the railway company.

carefully forgot to say anything about his property up the River having a good deal to do in "warping his judgment." It is a great pity that Mr. McIntyre was not cross-questioned just a little to see what effect a life-time trading with Indians had upon his answers to certain questions.

H 6 The Prince Arthur's Landing and Kaministiquia Railway [14]
[Prince Arthur's Landing and the Terminus of the Canadian Pacific Railway, *pp. 1–2*]

The people of Prince Arthur's Landing having built a short railroad as a line of communication between their harbour and the terminus of the Canadian Pacific Railway, nearly five miles inland on the Kaministaquia, and having been debarred from the privilege of forming a connection with the Pacific line at the latter place, for reasons which, if any exist, have never been explained to them, are naturally desirous of having a clear and unbiassed statement of the circumstances connected with the deplorable position in which they find themselves placed by, as they believe, an arbitrary exercise of power, laid before the public.

Among the grounds on which they claim consideration are the following:

(1.) That from the time when it was first contemplated to open communication with the territories of the North-west, up to the fall of 1874, every Engineer who had been employed by the Government in exploring the country, reported that the harbour, now known as Prince Arthur's Landing, was the best starting point, and that this led to the formation of their settlement.

(2.) That the Government had formed a depôt and built a wharf at the Landing, confirming them in the opinion that it would ultimately be the terminus of a railroad.

(3.) That the Government of Ontario laid out a town site on the ground which they occupied, and compelled them to pay a high price for their holdings.

(4.) That they have built up a town of respectable proportions, with churches and other public edifices.

(5.) That the population of their town now numbers nearly two thousand.

(6.) That, on finding that the terminus of the Pacific Railway had been fixed at a point some distance inland on the Kaministaquia, they made a line of railroad, at great expense to themselves, so as to form a connection

---

[14]This pamphlet, published in 1878, represented an attempt to win support in the rest of the country for the linking of the railway built by the municipality of Shuniah (with Thomas Marks as Reeve) with the Canadian Pacific line. It also provided an opportunity to submit evidence that the decision to begin that line several miles up the Kaministikwia River was an unfortunate one.

with it, well knowing that, without this connection with the leading highway, their settlement must languish and decay.

(7.) That in laying out this line they were guided by the advice of experienced engineers, and that all disinterested persons familiar with work
of the kind are unanimous in the opinion that their line is located in the
proper place.

(8.) That they were first trifled with and eventually denied the privilege of connecting their line with the Pacific Railway, at the instigation
of parties interested in crushing their settlement and building up a town
on the Kaministaquia.

(9.) That through the sinister influence of these parties they have
been subjected to the most cruel persecution, involved in litigation, and
grossly misrepresented to and placed in a false light before the Government and the country; and

(10.) Lastly, they claim and can prove that Prince Arthur's Landing
is the natural and proper place for the terminus of the Canadian Pacific
Railway; that the reports as to the harbour being exposed are untrue, that
it can easily be made to accommodate any number of vessels; and that
within the past eight years there have been 1,575 arrivals of large vessels
at the port,[15] without so much as a single wreck or even accident of the
most trifling nature occurring; that their statements and complaints are
well founded, can, they assert, be made abundantly clear, and a number
of documents are annexed, from which it will be seen that they – the
people of Prince Arthur – have at least had reason on their side and that,
under very trying circumstances, they have acted with becoming and com-
mendable energy in the endeavour to extricate themselves and their
settlement from a very embarrassing position, and it may be added have
shown much moderation and forbearance in urging their claims.

Apart from any consideration as to the superiority of Prince Arthur's
Landing as a harbour, it will readily be admitted that, as a matter of simple
justice, the people of that place should not be denied such privileges as
are accorded to communities elsewhere throughout the Dominion, and
it has yet to be shown that the inhabitants of any district, on making a
branch line of railway, have been debarred from connecting it with a
leading line. On the contrary, branch lines are always considered an
advantage to a main line, and that an exception should be made in the
case of the Prince Arthur's line must be due to exceptional causes. Such
is, at least, the natural inference and what these causes are or have been
is a fair subject of inquiry.

The people claim that they were led to form their settlement by the
reports of Government Engineers who, for a long period, had coincided
in the opinion that the harbour now known as Prince Arthur's Landing,
was the proper starting-point for a line of communication with the north-
west, and although this, in the event of a better place having been found,

[15]The statistics had been supplied by Peter Nicholson, one of the most ardent
advocates of the claims of Prince Arthur's Landing.

might not, of itself, be an admissable argument, in favour of adopting their harbour, it should at least entitle them to friendly consideration in their endeavours to establish communication with that better place. This is about all that they now claim, but at the same time they deny that a better place has been found and assert that the government and the country have been deceived by interested land speculators, through whose influence the terminus of our great national high-way, instead of being at a harbour on Lake Superior, has been fixed at a point nearly five miles inland, on a narrow winding stream which is not adapted for an extended traffic and which freezes up so early in the fall as to cause the loss of a very considerable part of the season during which navigation is open on the great lakes.

H 7 PETER NICHOLSON TO THE COMMISSIONER OF CUSTOMS
[P.A.C., RG 16 A 5–7, Port Arthur Customs Records, v. 1, p. 182]

Prince Arthur's Landing,
July 25, 1879

I have the honor to acknowledge fyle no. 2844 of the 17th instant relative to the seizure of the Tug M.I. Mills, Mrs. Catherine Cousins,[16] owner, and beg to say that the complaint of the said Mrs. Cousins is incorrect.

Mrs. Cousins states that the said Tug Mills has been allowed an unlicensed engineer to run her during a number of years by the collector and inspector of steamboats. Inspector Risley can testify to the uncorrectness of said charge.

Mrs. Cousins states that on this particular occasion no doubt refering to the date of the seizure of her boat that the Tug M.I. Mills was run by a licensed Engineer with American papers but the said engineer told me distinctly that he never had a license! Mrs. Cousins also states of the false security she was lulled into by the collector and both the customs officers at this Port deny having any conversation of any nature with Mrs. Cousins relative to the Tug or the Tug's Engineer either this season or last season ...

When I received instructions from Mr. Inspector Risley to seize and detain Tug Mills for contravention of the steamboat act, I at once did so, but the captain of the said Tug got the start on me and got down to the bottom of Thunder Bay with said tug for a couple of days. However

[16]This was the first public statement of the Nicholson-Cousins conflict which was fought on a number of battlefronts in the following years. John Cousins, in charge of the Fort William Customs at the time when his wife so enraged Nicholson, was suspended from his position in December 1879. The Dominion government, acting on Nicholson's complaints about alleged infractions of the regulations at the much smaller port of entry, dismissed Cousins early in the following year. Later, however, he became a magistrate in Port Arthur, sometimes handing down decisions which involved the Collector of Customs and his employees.

as I was on the lookout for her as soon as she returned I followed her up the Kaministiquia River and had her tied up to Mr. Ingall's[17] dock where she is now resting and lastly if Mrs. Cousins was ignorant of the laws regulating steamboats and their engineers, her husband Mr. John Cousins, landing master of H.M.'s Customs Outport of Fort William ought to have instructed her differently.

H 8   THE CONTROVERSIAL NEEBING HOTEL
[*Fleming*, Report *to the Minister of Public Works in reference to the Canadian Pacific Railway, 1879, p. 131*]

Contract No. 38
For converting the Neebing Hotel of Fort William into offices for the engineering staff, Prince Arthur District, including all labour and materials, according to plans and specification.

Name of contractor .... Edmond Ingalls
Date of contract .... July 26th, 1878
Date for completion .... 26th September, 1878
Estimated amount of contract $3,261.00

This contract has now been completed:

Amount paid .... $3,456.85[18]

H 9   GEORGE STEPHEN TO JOHN MCINTYRE
(PRIVATE AND CONFIDENTIAL)
[*P.A.C., MG 29 D-10, McIntyre Papers*]

Winnipeg,
August 14, 1882
Referring to Mr. John McKellar's offer of 100 feet right of way through his property, which you handed me at Thunder Bay, it is all very well as far as it goes, but it is necessary to have a larger frontage on the water both in his case, in McVicker's and any other property through which the line will pass if Fort William is adopted as the Lake terminus. We should have 600 feet depth on the River. The land is not wanted for speculative purposes but to enable the Railway Company to offer facilities for the building of Docks, Elevators, and Warehouses to accommodate the public ...

[17]Edmond Ingalls was the contractor in charge of remodelling the Neebing Hotel to serve as railway company offices.
[18]Although the local outcry was about the purchase price of the hotel and the question of its suitability as a location for offices, the railway company was publishing all even marginally relevant documents.

It is desirable that the negotiations should be kept entirely private for the present, as the Company must look elsewhere if land suitable for our purposes cannot be obtained in Fort William. We have to provide for our own future as well as present requirements and before committing ourselves to a definite policy we must have a clear understanding with the present proprietors. I shall therefore be much obliged if Mr. Carpenter[19] and you will see what is the best that can be done to secure the 600 feet frontage all along from the Railway reserve to the Hudson's Bay Company property – and then *telegraph* the result of your negotiations to Mr. W.G. VanHorne, our General Manager, at Winnipeg.

I suppose you will experience some difficulty with the McVickers who desire to influence us in another direction, but you can point out to them that if we go to Fort William, their property both there and at the Landing will be greatly increased in value and if they drive us away they will permanently lose their opportunity.

H 10   WILLIAM VAN HORNE TO C.P.R. BOARD OF DIRECTORS
[P.A.C., MG 28 III-20, Van Horne Letter Books, v. 1, pp. 414–23]

Montreal,
March 2, 1883

As I understand it to be the present intention of the Government to turn over the line from Prince Arthur's Landing to Rat Portage to this Company on the first day of July next, as it is exceedingly important both to the Company and to the people in the Northwest that the necessary facilities should be provided at Thunder Bay for the handling of coal, lumber, grain and other freights by the time the line is to be opened, I beg to urge in the strongest terms the importance of taking immediate steps toward providing the necessary dock room, machinery for handling coal and elevators for handling grain.

There will undoubtedly be a large surplus of grain for shipment from the Northwest from the coming season's crop and elevator facilities must be provided at TB by the middle of August.

A cheap and abundant supply of coal is of vital importance both to the Railway Company and to the people along its line. The supply from Iowa and Illinois is limited as is the means of transportation from that quarter.

The coal is also of a very inferior quality and before another winter ample provision must be made for a full supply from the Lake Erie ports.

The supply of lumber from St. Paul and Minneapolis is also inadequate and large quantities must be brought in from the Georgian Bay District.[20]

[19]W.H. Carpenter was the proprietor of the second saw mill in Fort William, which opened after Oliver, Davidson & Co. closed their business in the late 1870s. Carpenter was later Sheriff in Fort William.
[20]Van Horne's advice to the Company (of which he became a Vice-President in

There are already facilities at Prince Arthur's Landing sufficient perhaps for the ordinary merchandise shipments, but not for coal, lumber, grain or other coarse freights.

I have looked over the ground repeatedly and carefully and am of opinion that the natural advantages of the Kaministiquia River should be utilized for the coarse freights, whether or not the general merchandize and passenger business may be done at Prince Arthur's Landing.

In order to make the Harbour of Prince Arthur's Landing secure a long breakwater and a substantial pier to resist the shoving of ice will have to be constructed. This I think should and undoubtedly will have to be done under any circumstances.

I am informed that vessels drawing sixteen feet of water can pass through the new locks at Sault Ste. Marie. Vessels of this draft can now reach the docks at PAL but cannot reach the K[aministikwia] River on account of the bar across its principal mouth.

I am informed that a channel twenty-two feet in width was dredged across this bar some years ago, but it soon filled up again.

In a recent interview with the Chief Engineer of the Department of Public Works, I was informed that the reports upon this work indicated that this filling up was caused by the deposit of silt from the River.

I am confident from repeated examinations of the River that this is a misapprehension and that the narrow channel referred to was filled from the sides by the action of the waves, which in the case of northeast winds run heavily along the shore.

The water in the River in my opinion carries little or no silt and I think this is conclusively proved by the fact that the River within the bar maintains a uniform depth of from 16 to 23 feet notwithstanding the fact that during the prevalence of east winds the current in the River is checked to such an extent that silt would be deposited were any present.

There are two outlets to the K. River in addition to the principal mouth and the dispersion of the current caused by these prevents the natural scouring of the bar at the mouth.

I believe that jetties of reasonable length and cost at either side of the principal mouth of the K together with the closing of the other two outlets referred to will be all that is necessary to maintain a sufficient depth of water across the bar when it is once dredged out.

There is not sufficient available ground at PAL for the business of the immediate future. The lumber business will require several hundred acres for assorting and piling. Storage room for coal to the extent of at least 100,000 tons must be provided, which will require greater dock room than can well be provided at PAL.

The K River within the bar is now equal to the Chicago River after

the following year) makes very clear on what basis, at this period, Canadian products might be preferred over American. The attitude of the c.p.r. toward Macdonald's National Policy might be expected to become much more respectful, once the line was completed.

forty years of improvement and in my opinion the business of the Northwest will at once require the combined facilities afforded by the harbour of PAL and the K River, and it seems of the greatest possible importance that the Government be urged in the strongest possible terms to take the necessary steps toward the improvement of both harbours, that is, to the construction of a breakwater and pier at PAL, to the closing of the minor mouths of the K, to dredging the bar of the principal mouth, and to confining the current between jetties, or in such other manner as may be deemed sufficient and expedient.[21]

H 11   THE C.P.R. CONTRACT WITH THE MCVICARS
[Port Arthur City Files]

This indenture made in triplicate the ninth day of August A.D. 1883 between the Canadian Pacific Railway Company, of the first Part

Christina McVicar,[22] formerly of the Town Plot of Fort William in the District of Thunder Bay but now of Prince Arthur's Landing in the said District, spinster, of the Second Part

Victoria McVicar of the same place spinster of the Third Part and

George A. McVicar of the same place Esquire of the Fourth Part

Whereas the lands and water lot firstly and secondly hereinafter described have by conveyance bearing even date herewith been conveyed by the said Christina McVicar to the Canadian Pacific Railway Company their successors and assigns

And whereas considerations for said conveyances are that the Canadian Pacific Railway Company shall locate their Railway Stations for Prince Arthur's Landing now called Port Arthur with the General Passenger and Freight Depots for Prince Arthur's Landing aforesaid on the lands firstly hereinafter described at a place on the said lands on the north east side of McVicar's Creek in the township of McIntyre, the westerly end of said General Passenger Station or Depot to be not less than one thousand and eighty feet east of the centre of said McVicar's Creek and the

---

[21]Here in considerable detail Van Horne expressed his own view of the effective development of two sets of harbour facilities at the Lakehead ports. His contentions, disputed on many counts particularly by Port Arthur interests, form the basis of many of the disputes of the next decade.

[22]The daughters of Robert McVicar, who had died in 1864, claimed the property on which he had built a house near the mouth of the creek named after him. Before any settlement of their claim was possible, Christina had been appointed postmistress, provided she established her office near the Hudson's Bay post in Fort William. Fifty acres of land, at $1.00 per acre, were then granted to Mrs Robert McVicar. The daughters eventually secured 600 acres in the vicinity of Prince Arthur's Landing for twenty cents an acre. Their brother George had been a partner with Duncan McKellar in the Shuniah Mine, near Current River, and was also the holder of considerable real estate by 1883. The family thus had financial interests in both communities, and felt itself in a position to dictate policy to the C.P.R. Christina remained postmistress in Fort William until her death in 1895, when she was succeeded by her sister, Victoria.

General Freight Station or Depot to be at a place on the said lands further east than the said General Passenger Station[23] ... That the said Company will locate and erect on the lands of said Company adjacent to the south east corner of the lands of said parties of the second third and fourth parts thirdly hereinafter described the General Passenger Station of said Company for Fort William when the main line shall have been extended through said lands.

H 12   VAN HORNE TO J.H. EGAN
[P.A.C., MG 28 III-20, Van Horne Letter Books, v. 4, pp. 138–41]

Montreal,
January 3, 1884

There is now a strong possibility that the Government will commence work on the dredging at the mouth of the Kaministiquia River immediately on the opening of Navigation and, if a narrow channel is cut to begin with, it will only take a few weeks to enable any ordinary lake vessel to get into the river. That being the case, we should avoid, if possible, any further outlay on docks at Port Arthur.

Walsh[24] is anxious to lease us the Bell, Lewis and Yates dock, and says it can be made available for handling a large amount of coal by putting in a sunken track alongside, which can be done at a comparatively small Expense ...

Provide a sufficient quantity of piles for any probable dock work and also for the foundations of an elevator of say 600,000 bushels capacity, which we will probably build on the river during the coming season ... Keep dark about the river plans for the present – we will move very soon in the matter of property there and it is important that our plans should not be known until we have secured what we want.

H 13   VAN HORNE TO EGAN
[P.A.C., MG 28 III-20, Van Horne Letter Books, v. 4, pp. 322–6]

Montreal,
January 15, 1884

There is a road allowance all along the River front from the Government reserve to the mouth which we must secure. The Hon. R.W. Scott,

---

[23]There was general agreement on the part of all but the McVicar's that this location was most inconvenient.

[24]Major James M. Walsh had been born in Prescott, Canada West, in 1843. He had served with the Red River Expeditionary Force in 1870, and in 1873 had become an inspector for the newly formed Royal Northwest Mounted Police. In 1883 he resigned to devote his time to the establishment of the Dominion Coal, Coke & Transportation Company. Subsequently he returned to the mounted police and was Commissioner of the Yukon District in 1897.

who acted for us at PA, had an understanding with the FW people about this, and he has prepared the necessary papers to secure the title from the municipality. It will require, I think, one month's advertisements. I do not think we can get the road allowance in front of the McKellar property as Grahams[25] is occupying a portion of it and different individuals own the lots fronting on the River. The McKellars have agreed to give us right of way across their land and they told me last year that they would give all property they yet own within 600 feet of the River, but I do not think that is much, and you had better try to get a slice in addition – as much as possible – but locate the line and secure the right of way at all events. You will probably have to expropriate through McIntyre's lot and you may have to expropriate some lots in the angle where the projected line runs off from the Government reserve.[26]

Some understanding should be reached about the removal of the cemetery, but that need not delay matters as we can corner the graveyard by running tracks around it[27] ...

Major Walsh is very anxious to have us do something on the River and, as he is intimate with the McKellars, I think you can use him to great advantage. His anxiety to help the Company may not be entirely disinterested, but knowing that you can use him just as well.

H 14   VAN HORNE TO MAJOR J.M. WALSH
[P.A.C., MG 28 III-20, Van Horne Letter Books, v. 4, pp. 319–21]

Montreal,
January 15, 1884

I did not misinterpret your anxiety to help us in the Fort William matter and I am very much obliged to you for your kind offer ... What we may do there will depend upon the Fort William people themselves, mainly; but the whole matter must be decided within the next two weeks as if we can do nothing on the River, we must go on with extensive docks in PA. We have already expended so much money at PA that it is a matter of some indifference to us whether we make all our arrangements there or take advantage of the River. We have to erect a very large elevator in time for the next crop and must commence work on it within a few weeks, and

[25]George A. Graham and Thomas Horne were steamboat agents and lumber dealers; their mill was situated on the left bank of the Kaministikwia in Fort William. Van Horne here merely abbreviated the firm name of Graham & Horne.

[26]It was clear that Van Horne wished to use expropriation procedures for the smallest possible amount of land, but that, when he did resort to such procedures, the property of presumed friends of the Company would not be exempted.

[27]Van Horne's suggestions were followed. The old cemetery near the Hudson's Bay fort remained, "cornered" by the railway tracks, for some years. In 1884, new property was obtained in Neebing Township for a cemetery, but the old one was not closed until 1902, when a number of bodies buried there in the days of the fur trade were moved to the new cemetery.

where that goes our principal business will go permanently. If the McKellars and others will deal with us liberally, we will put the Elevator on the Hudson Bay property near the old fort, but we cannot commence operations there without being assured of ample room for all our business in the future.

H 15   VAN HORNE TO JOHN McKELLAR
[*P.A.C., MG 28 III-20, Van Horne Letter Books, v. 4, pp. 729–32*]

Montreal
February 10, 1884

If we can get the necessary property on the north side of the River between the old town plot and the Hudson Bay Dock, we will commence operations there at once and construct a large elevator and coal and other docks, and if this is done the present line between the town plot and PA will be changed so as to run the way of the old Fort. It is not yet known what the Government will do toward dredging a channel across the Bar at the mouth of the River; but it is certain that the Government will do nothing in the River itself, and as a large expense will have to be borne by the Company in order to make the river available and to supplement the Government work at its mouth, they feel that they would not be justified in undertaking the work without ample provision for their future requirements in the way of land on the north bank of the River ...

A freight and passenger station is also contemplated on the River and will be provided if your people will meet the requirements of the Company as before stated.[28]

H 16   VAN HORNE TO SIR HECTOR LANGEVIN
[*P.A.C., MG 28 III-20, Van Horne Letter Books, v. 7, pp. 830–1*]

Montreal,
October 1, 1884

The large elevator will be completed about the first of January[29] and with the temporary warehouses now provided on the River, I think I am

---

[28]It was quite evident in this correspondence that Van Horne did not intend to allow the McKellars to dictate the location of the Fort William station. In his letter to Egan of May 3, 1884 (P.A.C., Van Horne Letterbooks, v. 5, p. 900), he wrote: "It would not be to our interest to put the depot on the McKellar property at Fort William. We own one half the HB property and want to make it as valuable as possible. The depot should go somewhere east of the old burying ground, as should the first elevator and the coal docks."

[29]Van Horne's report to the Minister of Public Works contains one of the first references to the building of Lakehead elevators. The so-called King's Elevator had been built in 1883, was of wooden construction, with a capacity of 350,000 bushels. The large elevator here referred to – later called Elevator A – was also of wooden construction, built to hold 1,039,880 bushels of grain (John E. Young, *Grain Elevator Construction and Shipping in the Lakehead Harbour since 1883*).

safe in estimating that there will be in store at that point and ready for shipment by the opening of navigation 1,500,000 bushels of grain.

H 17   VAN HORNE TO LANGEVIN
[P.A.C., MG 28 III-20, Van Horne Letter Books, v, 11, pp. 631–2]

Montreal,
May 27, 1885

I have received with dismay your note of yesterday saying that nothing can be done at present about dredging the bars in the Kaministiquia between its mouth and the elevator and coal docks.

In the belief that the work could be done, we have constructed there one of the largest grain elevators in the world and have in it now a great quantity of wheat awaiting shipment. We have also provided expensive machinery for the quick and economical handling of coal. As the matter stands, neither the elevator nor the coal docks are accessible and it will cost, at least, four times as much to handle the coal at Port Arthur as at these new docks, and the extra expense the people of the North West must, of course, pay.

H 18   VAN HORNE TO LANGEVIN
[P.A.C., MG 28 III-20, Van Horne Letter Books, v. 15, pp. 563–5]

Montreal,
March 5, 1886

I notice a disposition on the part of some people interested in PA to urge political reasons for making no improvements at the Kaministiquia. Looking at the people of the two places from a political standpoint, I do not think, so far as I can judge, there is much to choose between them.

The coal and lumber and grain business cannot be done at PA except at greatly increased cost and this will affect the interests of the whole country west of Lake Superior.

PA has advantages in the way of the general merchandise business and will undoubtedly hold all business of the higher class. The Kaministiquia, however, has advantages for coarse freight business unequalled in the whole range of the Great Lakes and it seems to me that it would be an enormous mistake to ignore these advantages.

Surely PA cannot complain if three times as much Government money is expended there as on the Kaministiquia and it will take much more than that to make it a good harbour, and no amount of money will provide the necessary facilities there for handling coarse freights, which require a large amount of room.

H 19 W.H. LANGWORTHY[30] TO WILLIAM WHYTE[31]
[Port Arthur Council Minutes, v. 2, pp. 397–9]

Corporation Offices,
Port Arthur, February 21, 1887

I am instructed by the Council to inform you that with reference to the amount of Taxes levied against the various properties of your Company in the first two years namely,

Amount for taxes for 1885	$2189.67
Amount for taxes for 1886	$2954.95
	$5144.62

it is prepared to take all steps which may be legally requisite and necessary for the granting of a bonus to your Company for the sum of $2572.31 which is equal to a rebate of fifty per cent on the amount of the said Taxes.

Respecting future assessments on your Company's property the Council are willing to undertake to submit to the Ratepayers of the Town a By-Law exempting from taxation all existing improvements – not including lands together with any hereafter to be made by your Company so long as the said improvements are in actual use by your Company.

The Council would strongly urge upon your notice the pressing necessity for our "up town" station being built at or near the foot of Arthur Street. Whilst not expressing any opinion on the question of the present station remaining the Company's headquarters, I am instructed to point out the great annoyance and loss caused to the citizens of the Town as well as to passengers travelling to and fro by your Company's boats during the season of navigation through having to enter the cars at the present station. Such a building might also be used as a telegraph office and thus avoid the danger which now exists of any person who is a telegraphist tapping a message although standing outside the present building.

The Council would further bring to your notice the danger which exists from fire to your present station-house arising from the bush on the land surrounding the said station and would respectfully suggest that for this reason as well as for the greater improvement of the appearance of the approach thereto the said land should be properly grubbed and cleared.

I am further instructed to inform you that in the summer time a very serious nuisance arises from the accumulation of stagnant water on the

[30]William Howard Langworthy was appointed Clerk and Treasurer for the new town of Port Arthur at the first meeting of the Council, May 12, 1884, and held that office for a number of years. His son, W.F. Langworthy, was later a prominent lawyer in Port Arthur and, briefly, a member of Parliament.

[31]William Whyte (1843–1914) was born in Scotland. His career with Canadian railways had begun with the Grand Trunk in 1863. In 1884 he became Superintendent of the Ontario division of the C.P.R. and two years later moved to Winnipeg to replace J.M. Egan. At the time of his retirement from the Company in 1911 he was knighted.

low land (previously forming the lake shore) lying to the west of the track and abutting on the east side of North Water Street and would recommend that the said low ground be drained by one or more culverts running under the track and if possible filled in which would allow of the Company's track now standing on North Water Street being moved further east and off the street allowance as also to request that as early as may be convenient to your Company's interests the line of rails laid by the Construction Company and now crossing the said North Water Street be taken up as the street is rendered impassable for vehicles and practically useless in consequence of this obstruction.

With regard to the application of this Council to the Ontario Government for a portion of the Government Reserve, I am instructed to inform you that the Council originally applied for a portion of the Reserve "B" lying West of Court Street but were informed by the Honourable the Commissioner of Crown Lands that such application could not be entertained but that a portion of the Reserve "A" lying between Cumberland and St. Paul Streets might be acquired. You will therefore perceive that on the part of the Council there is no manifestation of a spirit of opposition to the claims of your Company. The Council however would respectfully suggest that as the Honourable the Commissioner of Crown Lands has sold portions of such Reserve and as the balance west of Cumberland Street is practically useless for the purposes of your Company, it is advisable that the Council should procure the legal right to the said lands for Municipal and Governmental buildings.

The Council learns with great satisfaction of the contemplated improvements and extensions to your Company's dock at the foot of Arthur Street and will be glad to find the work proceeded with as early as can be arranged for.

H 20   VAN HORNE TO WHYTE
[Port Arthur City Files]

Montreal,
February 28, 1887

As regards an uptown passenger station, I must say that I do not see how we can establish one without violating our agreement with the McVicars. The principal citizens of Port Arthur will remember the circumstances under which the McVicar property was acquired. It was necessary for the Company to procure a considerable amount of land for its immediate and future needs if any large business was to be done at Port Arthur and if the land could not be had there, we had no alternative but to do the business at Fort William. The Town was not in a position to offer the Company the necessary land and the negotiations for the land, which we have since acquired from the McVicars, were carried on with the full knowledge of the principal citizens and officials of the town, who wisely thought it would be better to submit to a little inconvenience in the matter of the location of the passenger station than to lose the important business that we proposed to do there. We could only get the McVicar property on the condition that the station would be located where it now is, and before closing the agreement I talked it over with the Port Arthur people and heard no objection from any of them, although they all expressed a preference for the station further south if it could be brought about. The Company would much prefer to have the passenger station at or near the foot of Arthur Street if that could be arranged, but I do not see how that is possible.

As to the danger that is claimed to exist from fire in the vicinity of our present Station arising in the bush surrounding, I would say that if there is such danger you should take steps to obviate it. It would be better to slash the trees and burn them while the snow remains on the ground. It does not seem to me that the expense of grubbing is necessary.

As to the water space between our main track and North Water Street, I will say that it has been the intention of the Company all along to fill this whenever our operations in that vicinity require any earth to be moved. Our embankment along the water front is composed mainly of rock through which the water freely circulates and I don't see how the water can properly be termed stagnant. I have seen it frequently during the summer and the water always seems to be clear and fresh. If it does not amount to a nuisance we do not of course wish to spend any money on it unnecessarily.

As to the tracks on North Water Street, I must say that I think they ought to be moved in the spring ...

As to the Government Reserve, I would be willing to recommend to our directors the release in favour of the City of the Company's rights to that portion west of Cumberland Street if the city would cooperate with us in securing the patent from the Ontario Government to the portion lying east of Cumberland Street.

H 21   THE PORT ARTHUR COUNCIL AND A POLICY OF
APPEASEMENT
[Port Arthur Countil Minutes, v. 2, p. 421, March 17, 1887]

Present: George MacDonnell,[32] Esq. Mayor
           Councillors Brown,[33] Smith[34] Cordingly[35] O'Connor,[36]
           Dickson, MacKay[37]
Moved by Councillor O'Connor, seconded by Councillor Brown
"That this Council believes it to be in the best interests of Port Arthur that the Canadian Pacific Railway Co. should obtain an absolute title to that part of Reserve "A" lying east of Cumberland Street providing the

[32]George Hugh Macdonnell was born in Toronto in 1851. He became a Port Arthur contractor and served as Mayor 1886–8. In the years 1891–6 he represented

C.P.R. Co. withdrew their claim and assist the Town in obtaining a title to that part of the Reserve lying west of Cumberland Street and that a copy of this resolution to be forwarded to the C.P.R. Co. and the Honble the Commissioner of Crown Lands."

The Yeas and Nays being called for the motion were recorded as follows: –

Yeas – the Mayor, Councillors Brown, Cordingly, O'Connor and Mackay

Nays – Councillors Dickson and Smith

Moved by Councillor Cordingly seconded by Councillor Smith

"That the Council acknowledge the receipt of Mr. Whyte's letters and also that from Mr. Van Horne but as they are not sufficiently satisfactory the Council are desirous of a reply to the matter of a reduction of taxation and the intentions of the Company in respect of future improvements."

On the motion being put to the vote, the Mayor declared the same lost.

H 22   THE COUNCIL OF 1889 AND
RAILWAY BONUSES
[Port Arthur Council Minutes, v. 3, pp. 300, 392]

Report of the Finance Committee, March 25, 1889

That the Clerk be instructed to inform Mr. Whyte that this Council regrets its inability to procure any amendment of the Bill[38] and informing

the District of Algoma in the House of Commons as a Conservative. He later left Thunder Bay, it is believed for the District of Assiniboia.

[33]George Wesley Brown was elected to the Council in 1886 and, with the exception of the year 1888, continued to sit on the Council for a number of years. He had moved to Prince Arthur's Landing from Collingwood in the mid-1870s.

[34]W. George Smith sat on the Port Arthur Council in 1887 and 1888. He was a partner in Smith & Mitchell, butchers who held the C.P.R. contract.

[35]William Cordingly, like Smith, was new to the Council in 1887. This seems to have been the only year in which he served as Councillor.

[36]J.J. O'Connor was a Councillor 1886–8 and a controversial figure in the battles in the Council during 1888. The power struggle which went on during that year between the "appeasers" who had sat on the previous Council and the new Mayor, T.A. Gorham, ended in a temporary victory for Gorham and the way clear for the 1889 confrontation with the C.P.R. O'Connor's previous efforts to become Indian Agent in succession to Amos Wright in 1883 had been frustrated by S.J. Dawson. Later, O'Connor became a magistrate in Port Arthur.

[37]John T. MacKay was Chairman of the Finance Committee in 1887. He had been a member of the first Town Council in 1884, then, after an interval, had returned to municipal politics. He also was at the centre of the controversy with the new Mayor in 1888, and was not returned to the 1889 Council.

[38]A motion of December 16, 1888, moved by Gorham and seconded by Rutton, had instructed the town Solicitor to take the necessary steps to secure a provincial act empowering Port Arthur to pass by-laws exempting C.P.R. improvements from taxation. On January 21, 1889, with Gorham as the new Mayor, the Council voted to dispense with the services of a permanent Solicitor. Attempts to have Bill 38 (An Act Respecting the Town of Port Arthur) amended came to nothing.

him that it is advised that the Canadian Pacific Railway Company's personal property is now and always has been exempt by the Assessment Act (Section 34) from assessment and that it is prepared to submit to the rate-payers a By-Law to remit fifty percent of the taxes levied on the property of the c.p.r. Co. for the years 1885 and 1886, to remit the taxes levied on the said Company's property for the years 1887 and 1888, and to grant exemption from taxation on such property as the Company now owns or may hereafter acquire within the town of Port Arthur for the period of ten years commencing January 1, 1889, or as long as the said Company continues to transship its passengers and packet freight between Rail and Boat as heretofore at Port Arthur.

Meeting of May 13, 1889
Moved by Councillor Shera,[39] seconded by Councillor Brown:
That a $25,000 bonus be granted for the p.a.d. & w. & Ontario & Rainy River Rlwy.[40] if their terminal buildings, workshops etc. are within 3/4 m. of Arthur Street & if they build & equip 50 miles of railway.[41]

H 23   AN EARLY ATTEMPT AT AMALGAMATION
[*Thunder Bay* Sentinel, *August 3, 1889*]

Undoubtedly a topic which has been discussed to a considerable extent during the past week has been the union question of Port Arthur and McKellar ward[42] ... There is the important consideration contained in Mr. Van Horne's statement to the Council committee, that in the event of the proposed union taking place, the c.p.r. Company would undertake to build up the property between Port Arthur and the elevators, or, in other words, to fill it up as a portion of the town. To both places, this is certainly a very important proposition, and worthy of the fullest consideration. Looking at this question of union either from a McKellar ward or a Port Arthur standpoint, it appears as the most sensible and natural thing to do. The matter should be easily decided by the ratepayers of both places.

[39]Caleb H. Shera, a drygoods merchant, was first elected to the Council in 1888, and re-elected for 1889. His tenure thus coincided exactly with that of Thomas Gorham, whom he seems to have supported throughout the battle with the c.p.r.
[40]The Ontario and Rainy River Railway was eventually constructed some years later by McKenzie and Mann who, at that time, bought the p.a.d. & w. Port Arthur's second railway link to Winnipeg did not materialize for another decade, and its link with Duluth never materialized.
[41]This particular motion, like Shera's earlier one at the May 9 meeting, was lost, but it was agreed on June 5 to submit the matter to the voters at the next municipal election. Conmee and Middleton asked for an additional bonus for the p.a.d. & w. in October 1889.
[42]That is, the section of East Fort William lying closest to the town of Port Arthur. Amalgamation at this time was not intended to include West Fort William.

H 24   W . S .   B E A V E R [43]   T O   W H Y T E
[*Port Arthur City Files – Taxation*]

Port Arthur,
November 19, 1889

In the course of my duties as Tax Collector I served upon the Company's Representative here the Tax Bill relating to this Town on October 11th; it was subsequently found out that interest had not been added to the amounts of arrears, so on the 20th October I delivered at the Asst. Superintendent's Office an amended statement of amounts due, which together with local improvement taxes totals something like $15,000.

I have called upon the Asst. Superintendent three times but so far without finding him in his office. His clerks however inform me that the two statements of a/c were sent to Mr. Aitkins[44] at Winnipeg. I have written to this gentleman but up to date have received nothing definite from him ...

Now as I have to get my Books closed up and matters in shape for making my returns I must ask that you inform me by the end of this week – say 23rd instant – when I may look for the amount due, so that I may know what to expect. Enclosed find stamped envelope for reply.

H 25   K E E F E R ,   T H A C K E R   &   G O D F R E Y , [45]   B A R R I S T E R S ,
T O   B E A V E R
[*Port Arthur City Files*]

Port Arthur,
November 27, 1889

Replying to your letter of yesterday's date asking what, if any, property of the Canadian Pac. Ry. Co. would be exempt from seizure under a warrant of distress for municipal taxes, we are of opinion that none of the articles you mention are exempt from such seizure.

In the case of freight on boats, or loaded cars, we would suggest that you do not make any seizure upon the freight either upon the boats or cars upon which you may think it advisable to seize. This would obviate any trouble or difficulty with the consignees of the same, which considering that the property of the Company would be ample, would render such unnecessary for the purpose of realizing the arrears of taxes.[46]

---

[43]William Sydney Beaver was assessor and tax collector for the town of Port Arthur. He also acted as bailiff in the seizure of C.P.R. property.

[44]James Albert Manning Aitkins (1851–1929) was western solicitor for the C.P.R. from 1881 to 1911. In 1916, he became Lieutenant-Governor of Manitoba, a post his father had held in the 1880s.

[45]Francis H. Keefer, formerly in partnership with his brother, T.A. Keefer, was by this time senior partner in a new firm.

[46]Both this legal advice and later letters of protest from William Whyte make it clear that the town did not impound a silk train, as local legend would have it.

H 26   The Failure of Mayor Gorham's[47] Efforts
[*Thunder Bay* Sentinel, *November 29, 1889*]

A majority of the members of the present Council, including the Mayor, have signified their intention of not presenting themselves as candidates for another year[48] ... There is now no denying the fact that an effort will be made to elect for next year's "railway" council, men who will be at the beck and call of the railway companies who have in hand the schemes for pushing lines of road to the west and southwest.

H 27   An Exchange of Telegrams, November 30, 1889
[*Port Arthur City Files*]

Understand from Keefer that Town of Port Arthur intends seizing Company's property today for Taxes.[49] If the Town takes such action they do it in violation of an agreement made with the Co. by a previous council.

Wm. Whyte

Can't interfere with tax collector.

T.A. Gorham

H 28   The Seizure of a C.P.R. Train[50]
[*Port Arthur, Weekly Herald, December 14, 1889*]

The engine and cars were offered for sale on Thursday [December 12] but as it was known that Mr. Whyte intended making the town an offer no one bid on them and the sale was adjourned. Later on Mr. White tendered $12,800 to the mayor and the collector, each of whom refused

---

Reminiscences of the seizure of C.P.R. property continued to be published as long as pioneer residents lived, and many errors inevitably crept into these accounts (*Port Arthur News-Chronicle*, June 23, 1934, interview with Colonel S.W. Ray, in 1889 an accountant with the Ontario Bank).

[47]Thomas A. Gorham was a young lawyer who, with his partner, Gilbert Ware, followed the Keefer example in combining law practice and prospecting, and two townships surveyed in 1891 were named for the partners. Gorham's career in municipal politics was a short one: Councillor in 1888, Mayor in 1889.

[48]When the new Council met on January 20, 1890, with Mayor Aaron Squier in the chair, Johnston, Bawlf, Brown, and Fraser were the only old members present. Of the 1889 members, J.T. Ruttan was to reappear as Mayor in 1891, but Gorham himself and his supporters Shera and McTeigue withdrew from the battle.

[49]Whyte, like the *Sentinel*, expected the climax to occur on November 30. The train was not actually seized until December 9. Rumours that the town intended to seize the last boat of the season apparently caused the C.P.R. to leave Port Arthur off the itinerary. The boat sailed direct from Fort William to Sault Ste Marie.

[50]Local newspapers gave surprisingly little coverage to the seizure of C.P.R. property, confining their reports to one edition only, and refraining from editorial comment, although sometimes publishing accounts of the incident from other newspapers in Winnipeg. Both the actual seizure of the property and the Council's acceptance of the C.P.R. offer occurred between weekly editions.

it. The mayor informed Mr. Whyte that he would call a meeting of the Council, which he did. At the meeting a letter was presented from Mr. Whyte tendering $11,807.11 the full amount of five years' taxes, without interest. It seems that in making up the $12,800 the C.P.R. people had made a mistake of $1,000. Mr. Whyte also offers to leave the matter of the interest and compound interest to any proper tribunal.[51] The council discussed the matter and came to the conclusion to take it, provided the C.P.R. paid the bailiff's costs; meanwhile Mr. Whyte took away his engine and cars. Yesterday, the Council waited on Mr. Whyte and found that he was firm, that he thought he had done more than fair. The Council met again and accepted his offer.

H 29   THE ARCH-PLOTTER, DONALD SMITH
[*Thunder Bay* Sentinel, *May 15, 1891*]

The Athabasca has landed her through freight at Fort William.[52] To do this it has taken a great deal longer time and many more men than would have been required at Port Arthur, but when the C.P.R. undertakes to do anything a little cost never stands in the way.

The removal of the C.P.R. boats and ticket office to Fort William East means a great deal to Port Arthur and it may, perhaps, be well to inquire the causes which led to this action on the part of the railway company.

The immediate cause was the seizure of the Company's property for the taxes. It was a very shortsighted policy on the part of Mr. Gorham the then mayor to force an issue with the C.P.R. It is well known to many persons that Mr. Van Horne, and Mr. Whyte, were both consistently in favor of continuing the arrangements which subsisted up to the end of last season, and it is known to some persons, the writer included, that very strong pressure was being brought to bear to effect the removal of the boat business to Fort William.

The force of the last paragraph can be gauged when one reflects that Sir Donald Smith is heavily interested in both the Hudson Bay and Canadian Pacific Railway Companies. The former Company had given the land needed for the Canadian Pacific Railway service and half its lots as an inducement, and Sir Donald Smith was not very likely to spare his efforts to have the remaining lots increased in value.

It appears to us, therefore, that it was only a question of time as to when the change now made would be brought about. The change has come and it appears to us that the only reflection at all reassuring is that offered by the fact that the C.P.R. has done about all it can in the way of removals.

[51]A year and a half later Port Arthur was still trying to collect $3703.31 from the C.P.R. in unpaid interest on the bills paid in the 1889 settlement, and in interest on interest (J.A.M. Aitkins to W.S. Beaver, July 23, 1891).

[52]The arrival of the *Athabaska* in May 1891 had been the cause of jubilation in Fort William, since it marked the transfer of C.P.R. business from Port Arthur. Fort William thus became the port of embarkation for all C.P.R. steamers.

H 30 PORT ARTHUR AND THE C.P.R.
[*Thunder Bay* Sentinel, *June 5, 1891*]

In talking with the old citizens of Port Arthur about the C.P.R. question reference is frequently made to the time when Mr. McIntyre was president of the road and when he had great designs for Port Arthur. At that time construction was well under way and the owners of the docks were literally coining money from their properties. Therefore when the C.P.R. tried to get private owners to sell out the Company found that the owners were valuing their properties at a price in ratio to their income producing powers. It is alleged that the C.P.R. was scared off by the large amount demanded for wharves, docks, and water frontage. So again it is said the C.P.R. made an earnest effort to buy out the McVicar estate in Port Arthur, but the Misses McVicar are reported to have valued their property at a higher rate than the C.P.R. would pay, and thus the company is alleged to have been scared off a second time.

Now it may be that the Misses McVicar and the other property owners wanted too much money for their property, but it may also be that the C.P.R. would not give a fair price. It must always be remembered that the C.P.R. could at any time have expropriated any property they desired for terminal facilities, but that it could not expropriate any for town lots.

Is it possible that in either of these reported negotiations the C.P.R. was trying to get a bigger offer elsewhere? It is quite certain that they got more given to them at Fort William than they could possibly have got at Port Arthur, and we trust it is not very uncharitable to harbor the thought that the C.P.R. intended to do from the first what they have now done.[53]

H 31 THE CITY OF THUNDER BAY
[*Thunder Bay* Sentinel, *September 18, 1891*]

There are a few men in Fort William who believe in the sincerity of the C.P.R., but not many. There are a few people in that place, and another few in the outside world who believe that the C.P.R. can down Port Arthur and uplift Fort William but they do not know the circumstances of the places.

Port Arthur's manifest destiny is to be the city of Thunder Bay, and it is equally the manifest destiny of Fort William to be a bustling railway suburb of Port Arthur.

Our Fort William friends will get angry over the above words we know but the truth must be told.

[53]By this time the *Sentinel* emphasized that Port Arthur was still the capital of the district and that the coincidence of Fort William and C.P.R. interests had affected the economic, but not the legal, position. The heading of the article was "A Stiff Upper Lip."

H 32 FORT WILLIAM'S PROTEST AGAINST AMALGAMATION
[*Fort William* Journal, *March 16, 1892*]

Port Arthur a few years ago claimed a population of 6000; the Dominion census of last year showed a population of less than 2700; it probably contains today somewhere between 2000 and 2500 actual residents. One would naturally suppose that an area large enough for a population of 6000 would suffice for one of 2500, especially when the tendency is in the direction of a still further decrease. Such, however, is not the view taken by our Port Arthur neighbors; as the population decreases, as the value of real estate grows less, their ideas in greater proportion expand, and they seek, by ways that are dark and tricks that are vain, to at least extend their limits if they cannot add to their numbers. Land grabbing has become a mania with them, and, on the one hand they seek to purchase territory from Shuniah, on the other they are endeavoring to steal from the present Municipality of Neebing and the proposed incorporated town of Fort William large tracts of land to which they have not the shadow of a right, not an iota of a claim. Between the territory which they seek to filch and the remainder of Fort William there is no natural boundary, and the line to which they would fain extend the limits of Port Arthur is crooked as a ram's horn; but what matters that to them? The territory is here – valuable today, its value rapidly increasing – and Port Arthur is eager to realize from it the revenue accruing from taxes ...

Some arguments of our Port Arthur neighbors contain a strange blending of the amusing and the absurd. They assert that they were treated with great harshness and injustice by the Canadian Pacific Railway Company, and that injury has been inflicted on their town by making Fort William the lake terminus of the road. Then they claim that they should be reimbursed for this injury. By the C.P.R.? No, but by Fort William.

H 33 A NEW TOWN ADOPTS A SYMBOL
[*Fort William Council Minutes, July 26, 1892*]

Moved by Councillor R.J. Armstrong,[54] seconded by Couns. Hammond[55] "That the Corporate seal of this Town be as a design a Locomotive surrounded by the Words Corporation of the Town of Fort William and that the Clerk[56] be instructed to order one at once." Carried.

[54] R.J. Armstrong, a locomotive engineer, was elected to represent Ward 2 in the first Council of the town of Fort William. John Armstrong represented Ward 4 in the same Council.

[55] James Hammond was a general contractor from West Fort William, elected to represent Ward 4 in the first Council.

[56] Edward S. Rutledge had been appointed clerk *pro tem* at the first meeting of Council, July 18, 1892.

I. A SENSE OF COMMUNITY

I 1 A VIEW FROM THE EAST – A TORONTONIAN IN THUNDER BAY[1]
[*J.C. Hamilton,* The Prairie Provinces, *pp. 5–6*]

At the east end of the village [Prince Arthur's Landing] is a little river – McVicar's Creek – round which are piles of lumber and log and clapboard houses. Close to the creek is the bark conical wigwam of an Indian. Along the shore boys pick up agates. The village site, with its scattered white houses, gradually rises. We pass up Arthur street, leaving the reservation for a park of some ten acres on our left, and the commodious grounds, residence and offices of Mr. D.D. Van Norman, Stipendiary Magistrate and Registrar, on the right, the land rising gradually, so that after a half-mile walk we are on high ground, with a fine view of the harbour, village and surroundings. This street we have been on turns to the left, and, in the course of a few rods further, runs into the well-known road, the Dawson route to Manitoba.

Prince Arthur's Landing received its name from Colonel Sir Garnet Wolseley, in honour of His Royal Highness, then in Canada. It was at this, then insignificant hamlet, that the Expeditionary force, on its way to Red River, disembarked on the 25th May, 1870.

The inhabitants of the Landing are such as an adventurous wild life, the outskirts of civilization, and the speculation in minerals and lands bring together, to which, in the season, are added tourists from far and near; from Nova Scotia – from many other parts of the Dominion. But here passes a black-robed man – a priest from the Mission up the river. This half-score of rough fellows are navvies from the railway line. Three young gentlemen, undergraduates of Yale, with their guns and fishing tackle, were here. They had seen the falls of the Kaministiquia, and fished there and elsewhere in the region, and were about to start for prairie chicken shooting on the plains of Minnesota. The number of saloons and drinking places in the village was astonishing. All seemed only too well patronized. Strong rough fellows from the woods often pass, with coarse brown dress and unshaved faces. One stout man of more than middle age, whose hair hung in curls, in which grey and black were equally mingled, was pointed out. He was a graduate of Cambridge, but, years ago, gave himself up to a roving life and dissipated ways. He discovered several mines, made large sums by selling his rights, which were soon spent in sprees on the South Shore. His countenance still retains many traces of

---

[1]James Cleland Hamilton (1836–1907) was a native of Belfast. He had been called to the Bar in Canada West in 1861. This description of his trip "from Lake Ontario to Lake Winnipeg" was published in 1876.

intelligence, and we saw him last as a deck passenger on the way to Duluth, addressed with some attention and civility by those who knew him. When not actively engaged he lives a hermit life. How the inhabitants of the Landing spent their time was a matter of amusement. At the hotels and like places of resort, and not at offices or shops, we must seek them. One talks of Silver Islet, another of Shuniah, the Cornish, 3A, the Bruce mines, Thunder Bay, or Shebandowan, and each pulls from his pocket a specimen of the ore or quartz supposed to contain silver, as "blende" or "native," or in sulphates and other forms. Various as the specimens may be, and to the unskilled, scarcely differing in structure and appearance, yet our friends here will at once name the mine whence they come.

I 2   Amos Bowerman[2] to the Chief
Superintendent of Schools[3]
[*P.A.O., Education Office, Incoming General Correspondence*]

Prince Arthur's Landing,
District of Thunder Bay,
5th Sep. 1873

I have the honor to inform you that an election of School Trustees was held on the 1st inst. for the first time in this place for the school section No. 1 in the new municipality of Shuniah at which myself and two other gentlemen were elected.[4]

As the Act passed last session by the Ontario Legislature incorporating the Municipality of Shuniah only vested in the Council the powers of Township Councils you will observe that we have no County Inspector to apply to nor as far as I can see any immediate prospect of any such Inspector.

Therefore I take the liberty of applying directly to the Department of Public Instruction for the School Manual and such explanations and regulations together with Daily Register for Public Schools as are necessary for our guidance in the discharge of our duties as Trustees of a rural school.

The Clerk of the Municipality, Mr. Robert Maitland, acted as Chairman at the School Meeting and probably has ere this notified you officially of our return.

[2]Amos Bowerman, with his wife and family, had moved to Prince Arthur's Landing at the beginning of the 1870s, and the name Bowerman was to appear frequently in a number of connections in the next decade – the Methodist Church, the Masonic Lodge, the schools, homesteading in Oliver Township, etc.

[3]Bowerman and Maitland were writing to Egerton Ryerson, who still held this post in 1873. All answers to correspondence from Thunder Bay came from J.G. Hodgins, who was shortly to succeed Ryerson.

[4]Maitland's letter, also dated September 5, listed the other trustees for Section 1 as Delevan D. Van Norman and Thomas Woodside; Section 3 (Silver Islet) had chosen Richard Trethewey, John Livingston, and Lachlan Morrison; Section 2 (Fort William) had not yet chosen its trustees.

Our communications with Toronto after the first of November are both uncertain and tedious and if our wants above stated are not complied with on or before that time, we can only receive them through the United States via Duluth sometime in the middle of the winter. For that reason, may I ask of you the favor of an early and prompt reply to these our pressing wants.

As we can receive no aid this present year from the Legislative School Grants, can you aid us in any way from the Poor School Fund granted by the Ontario Legislature?

P.S. Our address is Thunder Bay P.O., Ontario.[5]

I 3 P. NICHOL[6] TO THE REV. DONALD McKERRACHER[7]
[*Unitd Church Archives, Victoria University (U.C.A.), McKerracher Diaries and Correspondence*]

Thunder Bay,
June 11, 1874

The town [Prince Arthur's Landing] will never be in a worse financial state than it is this very time, but will have a more gradual & solid growth I think than if the railway had come here this year or been begun at least. Mines not much worked but confidence that they will pay when worked fully is still strong. They have a small sum at the Fort for a schoolhouse-church & really they need some kind of church in more ways than one.

I 4 DIARY OF THE REV. D. McKERRACHER, 1873–5
[*U.C.A., McKerracher Diaries and Correspondence*]

May 16 [1873]   Made arrangement with Halstead[8] to preach on Sunday morning in his meeting place in the basement of his church.

---

[5]Thunder Bay was the correct name of the post office, but very few residents remembered to include the correct superscription on their letters.

[6]Peter Nichol, not to be confused with Collector of Customs Peter Nicholson, was the Knox College student who served as summer supply at Thunder Bay during the spring and summer of 1874.

[7]The Rev. Donald McKerracher (1840–81) was born in Perthshire, came to Canada as a child, and shared Glengarry schooldays with the Rev. C.W. Gordon (Ralph Connor). He had done some building as well as some school teaching before studying for the ministry, and all his acquired skills were to be useful to him in the north. As a student, he spent the summer of 1873 in Thunder Bay, then, after his ordination, served as Presbyterian minister, 1874–80. He moved to Wallaceburg, Ontario, where he died in the following year.

[8]The Rev. William Halstead (1833–1905) was born in England but, like McKerracher, had lived in Canada from childhood. He had been ordained in the Methodist Church in 1862 and, ten years later, had volunteered for a western post. He was in Prince Arthur's Landing from 1872 to 1876, when he left for Portage La Prairie.

May 17   First trip to the Fort ... saw Mr. Oliver[9] & made acquaintance of some others. Tug costs 25 cts. each way.

May 18   Congregation of about 50 for P.A.L. services, about 20 at the Fort. Went thence to Mr. J. McKellar's – kind and intelligent people. He took me across the river to his father's – with whom I had some conversation – rather tending to worldliness. (Must guard against such influences specially on Sabbath evenings)   Spent the day chiefly at Mr. McKellar's, and in the evening went to Mrs. McVicar's, but returned for the night to McKellar's ...

July 14   Called on early by Mr. Arnot with a note from Mr. McIntyre requesting me to go to the Fort to the funeral of an old lady who had been at one time in the H B Co. employ ...

August 1   Wrote to the Crown Lands Department for patent for church lot here ...

Sept. 16   Roused in the morning by Mr. Dickson in fits from excessive drinking. Thought that he was dead several times ... Went to the Fort ... to John McLaren's where we had tea. His wife would not talk any English; it is a pity that he has thus thrown himself away.

August 7 [1874]   Baptized Mr. Dobie's child – my first official act here since my return. The occasion lacked solemnity and the evening was not spent in a becoming manner.

August 8   "Chicora" with the Gov. Gen. and party on board.

August 9   Preached in the morning in the Methodist church, P.A. Landing from St. John VI-68 and in the evening in Mr. Oliver's office at the River to his men. The presence of the Gov. Gen. and his party at the Fort interfered with our regular services there.[10]

August 10   Had a meeting of the managing committee in the evening at Mr. Dobie's. Messrs. Maitland, Grant, Dobie & McDonald appointed to solicit subscriptions for building a church. Gov. Gen. & party gone up the Dawson Road to Lake Shebandowan, to return by the Kakabeka Falls tomorrow ...

August 24   In the morning went to see the lumber for sale at the dock. Found them unloading, and Mr. Nicholson assured me if we needed the lumber for a church, we should have it at cost, which is $13. for 1000 feet of wharfage ...

---

[9]This was Adam Oliver, at whose home in Ingersoll McKerracher had visited on April 8, when he was en route to Chicago, a few days after he had decided to go to Thunder Bay for the summer.

[10]The progress across the country of the Marquess and Marchioness of Dufferin occasioned considerable excitement in 1874, but McKerracher was not unduly impressed.

Sept. 25   Three tenders for the work –

Cummings & Humphrey	$650.
Stonehouse	$500.
Woodside	$450.

There were no tenders for the material, and evident dissatisfaction among some of the builders.

October 10   Set contract for church to Mr. Jos. Ross for $420.

October 13   Seeing the difficulties in the way of obtaining the material for the church, I drew out a plan for a Lecture Room, which I find commends itself to most of our people. Called on Mr. Halstead about the heating of the church, and was told that they considered it would cost $100.00 of which we would be expected to pay half.

October 15   Saw Mr. Oliver this morning and found that he must get 2/3 cash down, and the other 1/3 next summer, a proposal which we are unable to meet. Gave Mr. Oliver a Bill of the lumber required for the smaller building ...

October 21   Reached Duluth about 11 o'clock and found Miss Matheson waiting for me ... owing to Mr. Heberton's absence, we decided to come to Silver Islet and be married by Rev. Mr. Caswell ...

November 29   Organized a Sabbath School at Ft. Wm.
Superintendent – Mr. Peter McKellar
Teachers   Mrs. Neil White, Miss C. McVicar, Miss M. McIntyre,
            Miss C. McKellar

December 23   Christmas tree in aid of the Presbyterian church, P.A.L. in the dining room of the Queen's Hotel. Solely under the management of Mrs. D.M. Blackwood. The attendance was good, good order was kept.

The ending, which was a dance, caused some unpleasantness to Mrs. McK. and myself. We both took a decided stand which we do not yet regret.

December 27   Opening of our new Lecture Room for divine worship ...

March 9 [1875]   Funeral of Capt. Duncan McKellar. Have learned since that I must be more careful of what I say on such occasions ...

June 9   Mr. Neil White who mysteriously disappeared on Saturday was found in the Bay, in 18 inches of water. Another instance of the doings of liquor ...

July 2   Baptized Mr. D.C. McKinnon's child, *Simon James* for Mr. Dawson

Sept. 17   Rev. Mr. Halstead this evening baptized Robert Murray[11]

[11]Robert Murray was McKerracher's infant son, baptized by the Methodist clergyman. The staunch Presbyterian baptized on July 2 by McKerracher was named for the village's leading Roman Catholic layman. The McKinnons, however, had refused to have their older children baptized by a Methodist, and called on the services of the Rev. Mr Black of Kildonan on his trip east.

November 8   Had duplicate deeds drawn up for Lot No. 5 on Elizabeth Street, said lot being the gift of Mr. W.W. Russell

I 5 DIARY OF PETER MCKELLAR, 1874–5
[Original in the possession of Mrs Gordon McLaren, Paipoonge]

Nov. 6 [1874]   Ran into Nipigon Bay and sent some freight ashore in small boats. Arrived at Silver Islet about 5 p.m. very dark. Arrived at P.A. Landing at 11 O'clock. The sea was running over the dock. Capt. Anderson, Capt. Symes and I got a team from Summers and drove over to the Fort, & got home about 2 a.m. Don and I had a sit-up.

Nov. 7   Katie and I drove over to the Landing with the team. The *Quebec* left before we got there, but the *Frances Smith* was there until 4 p.m. Mr. Moberly and wife, Mr. S.J. Dawson, A. McKenzie and a number of the C.P.'s [?] left on her. We brought all our freight home by the *Watchman* except a barrel of apples which John brought home on Monday ...

Nov. 10   I wrote a letter to C.B. Black, Secretary of the T.B. Mine[12] to transfer one third of our stock for working capital. I wrote a letter to Dr. G.B. Hall about Archie.[13] I settled with John McLaurin and W. Pritchard about the sale of the gold and silver lode down the lake.[14] I paid them their full amount, to each a check on the bank for $497.50 in the morning and in the evening $124.75

Nov. 11 (Wed.)   Donald and I went to the Landing, called at the Fort & McIntyre and I signed the trust deed & the agreement of the Silver Lake property & Donald witnessed it & he made an affidavit before Duggan for which I paid $2.00. The second river frozen. The *Quebec* did not arrive from Houghton ... We mailed all the letters and papers at the P.A.L. & I enclosed a few lines to Eckart. The plasterers got through papering etc. the House and we paid in full $7.00

Nov. 12   I went to the Landing, saw Mrs. Blackwood at Cameron's. She said she would take an interest in gold as offered yesterday ... I saw Marks.

---

[12]The Thunder Bay Mine had been discovered by the McKellar brothers in 1866 and a company formed to develop it in the following year, with Edward M. Hopkins of the Hudson's Bay Company as the first president. The forest fires of 1873 had destroyed some of the buildings on the site, but there was still hope of realizing money from the investment.

[13]Archibald, the youngest of the McKellar brothers, died in 1886. There were frequent references to his poor health in the diary. Several of the other references – Donald, John, Katie, Susie, etc. – were to other members of the family.

[14]The reference is to the discovery of silver near the Little Pic River by Donald McKellar, Warrington Pritchard, and John McLaurin. Peter McKellar had spent the month of October 1874 in Toronto, seeking financial support for the development of this new mine.

He offered to give us everything we would want all right along, and give us the balance we would want to raise the notes in the Bank, so I told him I would see. 1st river frozen.

Nov. 13, 1874 (Fri.) John and I went to the Landing and agreed to Marks' terms. I bought from him on a/c 29 yards carpet @ $1.25 a yard, 12 picture nails – $.50, 2 brooms, 70 ft. of braid. 2 schooners came into the river. No snow yet. Cold clear weather. The Kam River for the most part coated over with ice but we cross with the small boats. The Watchman brought a raft of timber down the river and over to the Landing. We hauled two of our small boats ashore tonight.

Nov. 14 I am writing a report of the McKellar gold lode to Mr. Courtenay.[15] What little ice there was nearly all went out of the River. Paid $28.75 taxes. We hung the pictures in the parlor and put down the new carpet.

Nov. 15 Mr. McKerracher held service as usual. There were 32 in church.

Nov. 16 Crossing at the Mission, not strong enough here. I finished the gold report. John and Susie went to the Landing. School commenced in the New house – Miss Brown[16] teacher, 15 scholars were present.

Nov. 17 9 inches of snow fell last night, there was only a couple of inches before. The ice is full of holes – cannot cross here ...

Nov. 30 St. Andrew's Day – had a surprise party at Mr. McIntyre's house – gay time. The Marks and [illegible] were there from the Landing ...

Dec. 6 Drs. McDonald and Clarke paid us a visit. First meeting of the Sunday School scholars ...

Dec. 11 The Marks family were spending the evening, also George and Christy McVicar, Violet and Mary McIntyre.

March 7, 1875 Father departed this life peaceably at one o'clock and thirty minutes a.m.

March 12 I wrote to Himes & Banes [?] offering them for the $1000 received last winter $5000 of stock in the Jackfish Lake Mine, $4000 in

[15]At other places in the diary, Courtney is the spelling used. The October 27, 1874, entry (in Toronto) recorded that William Cayley, J.B. Robinson, M.P. for Algoma, and Courtney each put up $1000 and promised a further $2500 in the spring, to be used toward the development of McKellar property on which gold had been discovered the previous summer.

[16]The lady's name was Miss Groom. In the following winter she and Peter McKellar were joint editors of Fort William's first (handwritten) newspaper, the "Perambulator." Miss Groom, an Irish woman, was the teacher in the first public school in Fort William. Earlier private schools for children of Hudson's Bay Company employees had been carried on intermittently since 1870, and the school of the Daughters of Mary since 1870.

the Highland Mine and $4000 in the Neebish Mine. In case they refuse, we pay the rate of 20% interest.[17]

April 4   Miss McIntyre, Violet, Katie & myself taught.

Number of scholars	17
Collection	1.42
I gave Warnock for Roderick McL. for putting on fire	.50

April 11   Miss McIntyre and I were present and about 12 scholars. Collection 70 cents.

April 18   12 scholars, Mrs. Whyte, Katie & I. Agreed to give a soiree on Friday next. I dismissed the Sabbath School for the two following Sabbaths. Collection 50 cents ...

May 23   About 15 children in Sabbath School I was the only teacher. The first boat, the *Quebec*, arrived at P.A., the *Asia* right after on the 19th. They had to cut their way through the ice from Passage I. 9½ feet on the Bar, measured. *Asia* ran into the river. *Normand* arrived on the 20th. *Chicora* arrived at the mouth of the river at 11 a.m. on the 23rd and sent the passengers ashore in small boats, could not get to the Landing with the ice. The *Manitoba* arrived in the evening and got through the ice. The *Chicora* followed and got to P.A.L. The *Manitoba* came into the River on the morning of the 24th.

May 30   8 Sabbath School scholars and none of the teachers but myself. Miss McIntyre resigned. No church held.

June 1 (1875)   Hired Antoine David and four Indians for Little Pic at $20. per month.

June 3   Turning of the first sod of the Canadian P.R. took place on the Kaministiquia River on the 1st of June, 1875. Mr. Van Norman was chairman. Mr. Oliver turned the sod. Woods, M.P. Borron, Oliver, and Van Norman spoke ...

June 13 (Sunday)   Tug *Watchman* with our party ran from Welcome Islands to east end of Nipigon Bay.

June 14   Arrived at Little Pic Bay about 10 a.m. I paid tug for trip by check $80.00. Landed stuff, took dinner after loading tug with wood, then all took packs and reached the mine about 3¼ of the clock. I set 3 miners to open number 1 shaft, 2 Indians to cut trail, and others to clear ground and set up tent ...

---

[17]There was no reference to this particular business arrangement in the diary of the preceding year. The three mines alluded to, on adjoining properties, were later formed into the Shebandowan Mining Company in which both Peter McKellar and J.J. Vickers were associated, but real development had to wait for the completion of the C.P.R.

Friday, Aug. 13   Rained all night. Drove Indians out of their camp and covered the floor of the mine. I gave Michael's wife an order on the Pic for $15.00 Rained at intervals all day. The miners of No. 1 shaft are blasting on the vein in the hill.

Aug. 14   Miners finished in No. 2 pit – sank 4 or 5 feet – good show of ore, looks rich in silver like that of No. 1 shaft.

Aug. 15   Rained heavy last night and a considerable today. Waters nearly as high as ever, about 24 feet in shaft.

Aug. 16   I sent 3 Indians to bail No. 1 shaft, and 3 Indians to blast at the shaft opening west of No. 1 shaft. The Indians forked out all the 50 tons of water, or about 24 feet of depth in the shaft ...

Aug. 19   Tug arrived last night – Mr. Robinson, Mrs. McNabb, Katie, Effie, Donald, Pritchard and McLaren ... Hired Antoine brothers at $1.00 per day. I pay all the Indians $1.00 while packing, commencing today ...

Aug. 27   I left Fort William with 22 barrels of L.P. silver for Toronto on the propeller *Asia*. Passage to Windsor $12. We reached Bruce Mines about dark on Saturday (28th) ...

Novels Read[18]

Feb.   *Nicholas Nickleby*

June   *Like a Snowball* – a story of 7 links in a chain by *Gentleman's Magazine*
       Bessy on the Moor by J. Latimer
       Grant's Grave
       Queen of the Pixies
       Wrecked in North Seas
       Barren Honour by Guy Livingstone
           [List of major characters follows]

July   *Cometh Up as a Flower*
           [List of major characters follows]

June   *Midnight Queen*
           [List of major characters follows, also note: Setting: Plague of London, 1665]

July   *John Halifax, Gentleman*

August *Put Yourself in His Place* by Charles Reade
           [List of major characters follows]

[18]Diary entries were fragmentary from November 1874 on, and during April and May Sunday entries covered the important events of the week. This list, written on the last leaves of the 1875 diary, consists chiefly of books read at the Little Pic mining location.

16 REPORT ON POOR SCHOOL APPLICATION,
JANUARY 1875
[P.A.O, Education Office, Incoming General Correspondence]

The undersigned Trustees desire to report to you the following facts –

1. This school is known as Section No. 1 in the H.B.Reserve & Neebing.

2. The estimated population of school age (5 to 16 years) in the section is 35.

3. There have been 28 pupils in the Roll of the School during the last 1½ months

4. There has been an average attendance of these pupils of 5½ during that time.

5. They employ a A 1 class Teacher at a salary of $400.00 per annum.

6. The assessed value of taxable property in the section is $47,575.00.

7. The assessment levied by the Trustees this year, was at the rate of 1¼ in the Dollar.

8. The assessment raised for Federal purposes during the past twelve months was $30.00.

9. The whole apportionment made to the school by the Inspector during the past twelve months was nothing.

10. The total receipts of the school from all sources during the last twelve months were $80.00.

11. The School Accounts of the Section were audited on the 12th Jany 1875.

12. The School has received aid from the Poor School Fund during the last _____ years Nothing.

13. Our reasons for applying for aid from the Poor School Fund for this year are as follows:
There being only 5 resident freeholders & 7 householders in our school section, the burden of Taxation is too heavy to be bourne by residents & freeholders. Most of the lands assessed are absentees.

(signed) JOHN MCKELLAR
J. WARNOCK[19]
JOHN MCLAURIN[20]

[19]James Warnock was a clerk at the Hudson's Bay Company post at Fort William during the 1870s. As Secretary-Treasurer of Section 3 Shuniah (later renamed Section 1 Neebing) he had been attempting to persuade the government to contribute money from the Poor School Fund during 1874. Prince Arthur's Landing had extracted $58 from the fund in that year, but no evidence has been discovered concerning the effectiveness of the Fort William plea.

[20]John McLaurin, the associate of the McKellars in a number of business enterprises, was the commander of the tug *Watchman*.

17 LIST OF ADHERENTS AT FORT WILLIAM [21]
[*U.S.A., McKerracher Diaries and Correspondence*]

1. Jno. McIntyre (wife & fam.)
2. Morrison (wife & fam.)
3. Mr. & Mrs. Finch
4. Mr. & Mrs. Mauzer
5. Rowan, Capt. tug
6. McLean, Capt. tug
7. McKenzie, Laborer   left
8. Mrs. McVicar – two sons & two daughters
9. D.E. McDonald
10. Capt. McKellar & wife & four daughters
11. Jno. McKellar – single
12. D. McKellar   single
13. P. McKellar   "
14. A. McKellar   Single
15. Pritchard   wife & fam.
16. Jno. McLaren   wife & fam.

18 A NEW SCHOOL OPENING
[*Thunder Bay* Sentinel, *December 7, 1876*]

In our issue of 23rd ult, we announced the completion of our new School House, and stated its size to be 46 × 31 feet, two stories high, with a neat porch in front, and outside covered stairs in the rear, reaching to the upper appartment – a cupola upon the front part of the roof. Carpenter work by Messrs. Neil Shaw & Co., and painting by Mr. J.B. Tall. all work done satisfactorily.

Tuesday evening was set apart for the Grand Opening of this important feature in our local history ... The people began to fill the Upper Department [the lower floor was occupied by Primary Department] and pretty soon the desks, seats and benches were occupied: Miss Nichol having taken her place on the platform as Organist, Mr. Wright, teacher, moved that Mr. W.C. Dobie, Chairman School Trustees, preside for the evening, and see to the carrying out of the programme. Carried unanimously. Mr. Dobie said he saw the Chairman's Address was the first thing in order, and proceeded to make some timely remarks, expressing great pleasure at the present state of affairs.

1st – Singing "The Lord's Prayer" by the Pupils.
2nd – Chairman's Address, in which Mr. Dobie exhibited his usual happy vein.
3rd – Reciting "Meddlesome Mattie" by Miss Kate Casey.

[21]This note in the McKerracher Papers has no date, but it appears to have been written about the end of 1874, certainly before the death of Captain Duncan McKellar, March 1875.

4th – "Happy School Children" by the Pupils, accompanied with music by Miss Nichol.

5th – Address by Rev. W. Hicks, in which the Rev'd gentleman was brief, not wishing to prevent the evident enjoyment the pupils were giving to the audience.

6th – Recitation, "Timothy Brown" by Master Rob't Emmons.

7th – Reading "The Irish School Master" by Mr. R. E. Mitchell, causing some amusement.

8th – "Be kind to the loved ones at home" with music.

9th – Address by Rev. D. McKeracher, the Rev'd Speaker making the principal address of the evening.

10th – Recitation, "Canada" by Miss Polly Warren. We give upon our first page this patriotic piece which was creditably rendered and met with applause.

11th – Recitation, "The Clever old man" by little Miss Tulloch, in good style, causing mirth and approval.

12th – "The Seasons," Misses Mary Humphrey, E. Bowerman, F. Wood, and M. Nichol, with music.

13th – Address by Mr. Hagan of the *Sentinel*, past, present, and future prospects of the town alluded to.

14th – "Pull for the Shore" by pupils. Music.

15th – Address, by the Reeve, Thomas Marks, Esq., who gave interesting particulars of the action of the Council in promoting the prosperity of the town, and aiding the School Trustees in the good work of securing the present fine school building, at an expense of $2,100 – paying $1,200 and leaving $900 to be settled hereafter.

16th – Prologue, "The Miser Punished" Masters A. Wiley, H. Bowerman, and W. Humphrey, sustaining their respective parts well.

Votes of thanks were unanimously passed to the Chairman, Ladies of the Committee, Speakers, the Organist and Teacher, and the evening's entertainment then closed by singing "God save the Queen."

I 9   MCKERRACHER'S BATTLE AGAINST THE SALE OF LIQUOR
[*U.C.A., McKerracher Diaries and Correspondence*]

On board the *Frances Smith*[22]
November 8, 1876

I had a long talk with Judge Van Norman today. I find first that the charge against W.J. Clarke was dismissed – his Bro. the Dr. assuming the responsibility.[23]

[22]The *Frances Smith* was a sidewheeler owned by the Collingwood Transit Company and making weekly trips to Thunder Bay in the 1870s. The unsigned letter written on board and the following one from William Kennedy were from officials of the Ontario Temperance Lodge in whose activities McKerracher was deeply involved.

[23]W.J. Clarke, like the other druggists of the time, sold a variety of medicinal

Second, I learned that Mr. Marks had paid a visit to Mr. Mowat in Toronto and was there shown a letter with my signature to it. I presume it is the same one I sent to our grand worthy Sec'y – at any rate Marks is pretty well exorcised over it and so is Judge Van Norman.

I have no doubt Marks has represented things to suit himself and counteracted any good the letter might have done. Now I must checkmate him if possible & to do this I must see Mr. Mowat & when I do see him I must have something to show the confidence of the Temperance people of P.A. Landing.

Owen Sound,
February 24, 1877

In Thunder Bay the Inspector is E.P. Langrel,[24] Esq., the Commrs are the old ones reappointed – in this matter Mr. Dawson has played false – he led me to believe that D.D. Van Norman would be one of the Commrs & John McKellar the other ...

I am sorry to hear of the disasterous fire that you had in P.A. Landing[25] – much cause as I have to dislike hotels & hotel keepers I would rather know that they had been turned into respectable houses than that they should be destroyed. I also learn by the Thunder Bay Sentinel [January 25, 1877] that Mr. Lobb *died from the effects of a cold that settled in his lungs.* When will newspapers learn to tell the truth?

I 10   PETER NICHOLSON TO GEORGE P. DICKSON[26]
[*P.A.C., RG 16 A 5-7, Port Arthur Customs Records, v. 1, p. 73*]

Prince Arthur's Landing,
Algoma District,
February 2, 1877

I beg leave to enclose you herewith a requisition from Mr. Henry Weiland[27] of this village for license for malting and brewing for his one-

---

products, and the Temperance Lodge had him arrested. It was Clarke's father, not brother, who was the influential Dr J.F. Clarke.

[24]E.P. Langrell was the principal of the two-room school at Prince Arthur's Landing. His appointment as Inspector of Licences was apparently not so great an affront to the Temperance Lodge as were those of the Commissioners. All these appointments were made by the Lieutenant-Governor-in-Council.

[25]Many of the buildings constructed in the Landing in the early 1870s were destroyed by fire. The *Sentinel*, while giving much attention to the activities of the volunteer fire brigade, seldom recorded the early fires. Neither the hotel fire of 1877 nor the destruction of St Andrew's Church in 1881 seems to have warranted newspaper coverage. Later, the fire that destroyed St John's Church and parsonage, and the Cumberland Street fire of 1887 which destroyed several hotels and business offices, received headline treatment.

[26]George P. Dickson was Inspector of Inland Revenue for the District of Algoma, with headquarters at that time in Sault Ste Marie.

[27]Henry Wieland had moved to the Landing after many years in Beaver Bay, Minnesota. He may have been the first to apply for a licence, but he was not the

horse brewery rather a new enterprise on his part – he have this day with his requisition deposited $50. at this off. on a/c and for said license and if more money is required, he will pay it.

This Brewing is something new to me therefore you will be pleased to send me instructions in full and as plain as possible and I will comply with same to the letter.

I judge a rule is required for the measurement of the utensils used such as mash & fomenting tubs – they cant do much until navigation opens as they have only about 100 Bushels of Barley. I am told Mr. McIntyre the Hudson Bay agent have some if they will [give] him his price.

I 11   DIOCESAN NEWS FROM PRINCE ARTHUR'S
LANDING
[Algoma Missionary News, *March 1, 1878, v. 1, p. 76*]

The ladies of St. John's Church,[28] here, held a very successful bazaar on Wednesday, the 19th December. On the one side of the room was a table abundantly provided with the good things of this life; and on the other was a great variety of articles, useful and ornamental, which willing and unwearied hands had furnished. Nearly every item was disposed of, and $172.90 were realized after all expenses had been paid. This amount is to be applied to the diminution of the debt on the parsonage. The church was very tastefully decorated for Christmas. Six beautiful illuminated texts presented by L. De Carle,[29] Esq., were in themselves a valuable help to the adornment of the edifice. The white cloth which covered the holy table was wreathed with green, and in the centre was the sacred mono-gram, I.H.S. also covered with green. The prayer-desk and pulpit were hung with white, and here as well as in texts of Scripture, and festoons which encircled the whole building, the fir tree was employed to beautify the place of God's sanctuary. The offerings amounted to $32.87, and several generous gifts from members of the congregation were sent to the parsonage on Christmas Eve. A very handsome altar-cloth is the kind gift of Mr. De Carle, and on it the monogram I.H.S. has been beautifully embroidered in gold-colored silk by Mrs. Frank Moberly. Velvet hang-ings for the pulpit and prayer-desk have also been presented by Mrs.

---

first to establish a brewery. Conrad Gehl, who had emigrated with his two brothers from Bavaria, was already in business in 1876 and on March 31, 1877, his brewery and all contents were seized for failure to obtain a licence from the Department of Internal Revenue. The dispute ended with Gehl paying the $50 licence fee and establishing a successful business.

[28]St John's parish was originally in the Diocese of Toronto when the first church was built in 1872. In the following year it became part of the newly created Diocese of Algoma. The parsonage had been completed in 1875.

[29]L. De Carle lived in the Landing for a few years in the mid-1870s, at the time when railway surveys were being made. Besides his contributions to the Anglican Church, he was noted locally for his artistic skill in producing programmes for such social events as the Bachelors' and Benedicts' Ball.

Moberly[30] and Mrs. Clarke,[31] and will replace the Christmas decorations as soon as these are removed. Some other requisites for the chancel have been promised by another lady member of the congregation, and when these are supplied, the furniture of the church will be almost complete.

I 12   THE CHURCH OF ENGLAND IN THUNDER BAY
[Algoma Missionary News, *April 1, 1878, v. 1, p. 80*]

The following contained in a private letter from the Rev. J.K. Mc-Morine recently appointed to P.A.L. will, we think, be read with interest: "I think that numerically we are the weakest body here. I think the R.C. is strongest; then Presbyterian, then Methodist. On the other hand, it is asserted even by outsiders that ours is the largest Protestant *congregation*, I am anxious only to hold my own, and to feel that the Church's strength depends upon character rather than upon numbers. However we have thirty-five avowed Church families at or near the Landing, twelve at the Town Plot and Fort William, two at the Shuniah River[32] and a few more up the line whom I have not been able to visit yet. There are also a number of young men who attend service very regularly, and thirty are professed communicants, although only about fifteen have communicated since I came here.

"Mr. De Carle has kindly taken charge of the Sunday School at the Landing (about thirty scholars) and is well fitted for it, having been superintendent of the Brockville s.s. for years. So I have my afternoons to myself, and have taken up a regular service at the Town Plot, seven miles away. I go every Sunday afternoon at 3 o'clock; we worship in 'an upper room' and so are apostolic in this respect. It is above a building which Mr. Marks has erected for a store, but is at present unoccupied. I sometimes walk, but generally drive, and the offerings pay for the horse. The congregation is small, twenty-five thirty and so on, but we will have more in summer and I am determined to keep it up as there are a few earnest Irish and American Church people there, and almost every individual attends.[33] We began on the second Sunday in February."

[30]Georgina Moberly (née McIntyre) had come to Fort William as a child in 1855, and died in 1880. The McIntyre family divided its support between the Presbyterian Church to which the "Governor" belonged and the Anglican Church of his wife. Frank Moberly was a civil engineer who had come to the Landing in connection with the railway surveys of the early 1870s. A decade later, when he was police magistrate at Michipicoten during the construction of the C.P.R., he had married his deceased wife's sister.

[31]This was likely Mrs A.A. Clarke, wife of one of the partners in the early Landing drug store. The Clarke family were Congregationalist, but, lacking any church of their own in Thunder Bay, supported both the Anglican and the Methodist churches.

[32]Mr McMorine had only been in the Landing a few months at the time this letter was written, and his geographical references were vague. The railway line then extended about fifty miles west from the Town Plot, but he gave little hint as to the location of the river he called the Shuniah.

[33]The *Sentinel* of October 15, 1880, suggested a different national origin for some

I 13   S.J. DAWSON TO COLONEL CHARLES CLARKE [34]
[*P.A.O., Clarke Papers*]

Queen's Hotel, Toronto,
May 7, 1878

A report has become current in my constituency to the effect that I opposed the Orange Bills, and if uncontradicted it might lead to the loss of some votes.

You may perhaps remember that I did not vote at all on these Bills and if so you would greatly oblige me by writing me a letter which I could show stating the fact.[35]

I would not of course publish the letter, but only show it to some of the leading Orangemen who would at once contradict the report. The effect would be all the better from the fact that you were looking after the votes on the ministerial side when the Bill first came up.

I have made up my mind to run for the Dominion and we are to have a convention soon when a candidate will be selected for the local. We will have no difficulty in putting in a supporter of Mr. Mowat's government.

I 14   DR T.S.T. SMELLIE [36] TO THE REV. MR HAMILTON [37]
[*U.C.A., McKerracher Diaries and Correspondence*]

Fergus,
7th December, 1878

Circumstances have arisen which render it probable that I shall not find Fergus a resting place for the sole of my feet after the coming session of

---

Anglicans when it commented upon the marriage "at the residence of Mrs. MacLean, Town Plot, on Thursday the 14th last, by Rev. J. Ker McMorine, William Jackson, Esquire to Mrs. Grace Macgregor MacLeod MacKenzie."

[34]Colonel Charles Clarke (1826–1909) had been a resident of Elora since 1843. From 1871 to 1894 he represented Wellington Centre, and became Speaker of the Assembly, 1880–5.

[35]An Orange Lodge was established in Thunder Bay by this time and by the 1880s had about fifty members. Orangeism can hardly have been as intense an issue in Algoma as it was in Wellington Centre, but Dawson, as a Roman Catholic, had to look to his record of abstentions if he was to win the Dominion seat he was then resolved to seek.

[36]Dr Thomas Smellie (1849–1925) was born in Fergus, Canada West, and set up a medical practice in Prince Arthur's Landing in 1879. In 1882 he was appointed Superintendent of the Medical Department of the C.P.R. for the district stretching two hundred miles to the east, and in March 1887 became Medical Health Officer for Port Arthur. He wrote voluminous reports until 1890 when, convinced that the town had no future, he left for Manitoba. A year later he returned and established a practice in Fort William as well. He subsequently represented Fort William riding at Queen's Park, 1905–11, as a Conservative.

[37]The Rev. Mr Hamilton is not identified in the letters except as a friend and classmate of Smellie, a visitor to Thunder Bay in the mid-1870s, and a clergyman at Winterbourne in 1878.

Parliament is over ... Politics and whiskey are the main reasons for wishing to leave Fergus. The first is interfering sadly with the practice, and the second shocks and drives away many who would cling to Dr. Orton[38] in spite of the disadvantages consequent upon being patients of a political doctor. The terms of our partnership prevent me from beginning by myself, and there are now so many doctors in the place that I would not consider such an idea a very good one. If I cannot better myself, I suppose, I must remain and make the best of it but I am persuaded that there are many places in the province where a medical man is needed. I have no objections to roughing it and would rather go to the back country & grow up with the place than languish in a large town or city waiting for practice which may never come.

More than one person to whom I have spoken in confidence has spoken favourably of Fort William or P.A.'s Landing and considering the rapid growth of the North-West, the position of these places as the eastern terminus, for many years to come, of the C.P. R.R. while communications will probably be made with Manitoba in two years or so, I think that these places will soon grow and be but little behind some of our small Ontario towns. One at least of those who have spoken of this place is a residenter and a business man. And at the present stage of Canadian history I do not think that my politics would stand in my way though to be sure I have always abstained from doing more than entering into fireside discussion on that subject.

I know that you spent some time at Fort William a year or two ago and I would be very much obliged by hearing from you and learning what you think of the proposal. I am a little afraid of receiving coloured statements from those to whom I have spoken on the subject, and would like you just to speak candidly & from your own experience. I have made one mistake already in choosing a location & I wish to avoid a second. I am obliged to remain in Fergus till after the next Session of Parliament is over, but then I hope to be able to leave here. But I must come to some understanding with Orton before he leaves for Ottawa, and I would like to have some plan pretty well arranged before expressing any dissatisfaction with the present position of affairs ...

I have not hinted to Orton as yet that I am dissatisfied though only a man thoroughly soaked in liquor could fail to see that my present position is intolerable. I am anxious however to do my best for him during his absence, and any rumour floating about that I was soon to leave would operate against me, as people who might otherwise patronize me would prefer employing a doctor whom they could count upon as employing permanently.

[38]Dr George C. Orton, Smellie's partner in Fergus, represented Wellington in the House of Commons as a Conservative at this time. After Smellie's departure, Orton moved west also, and Sir John A. Macdonald made this comment about Orton in his letter to George Stephen, January 19, 1888 (P.A.C., MG 29 A-20): "He is a very able medico and will be of great use politically at Winnipeg. He takes a horn now and then but that won't hurt him."

I 15   SMELLIE TO MCKERRACHER
[*U.C.A., McKerracher Diaries and Correspondence*]

Fergus,
12th December, 1878

I have just received a note from my friend and fellow-student, Rev'd
Mr. Hamilton of Winterbourne, informing me that he has forwarded my
note to him to you along with an explanatory note from himself ...

You will judge from the foregoing whether I will suit the place; now
will the place suit me? Do you think that there is an opening at P.A.'s
Landing for me, without turning out anyone already there, or is there a
prospect that the influx of population in the spring will be sufficient to
support another doctor? It may not be amiss to state that I am prepared
to marry as soon as there is a decent prospect of securing a living. A fear
that my present partner may break faith with me & thereby necessitate
a postponement of my contemplated marriage is an important factor in
my present intention to leave Fergus. Please let me know all you can
regarding the social and moral standing of the medical men you already
have, and be good enough not to hold out any inducement to come to
P.A.'s Landing unless you feel that there is really an opening.

I 16   DEPARTMENT OF EDUCATION MEMORANDUM TO
THE MUNICIPALITY OF SHUNIAH
[*Thunder Bay* Sentinel, *July 30, 1880*]

By Section 10 of the School Act, of 1879, the 33rd section of the Public
Schools Act was amended, and its terms so clear that there need be no
difficulty excepting as to the state of facts to which the terms of the Act
are to be made applicable. The Municipality of Shuniah is a Municipality of more than one Township, and without county organization. Its
Municipal Council has therefore discretion to manage school matters in
these two ways, either by forming school sections, or by establishing a
School Board. The board to be legally constituted, should comprise two
members for each Ward, when not divided into Wards, for each Township. It is clear that the Municipality of Shuniah has been divided into
Wards ... Neebing, Blake, Pardee, Crooks, McKellar, Paipoonge, Mc-
Intyre, McGregor, Island, and Prince Arthur's Landing (two) being in
all 11 wards. So soon as the Act of 1879 came into effect, on the 11th
March, 1879, all its provisions would apply, whatever might have been
the constitution of the Board previously, and the By-law of December,
1878, which formed 5 wards, would necessarily become of none effect,
at least at the end of the year, if it was not illegal at the time it was passed.

EDUCATION DEPARTMENT
    19th July, 1880   Signed

ADAM CROOKS
Minister of Education

I 17 EDITORIAL COMMENT ON THE ACTION OF
THE DEPARTMENT OF EDUCATION
[*Thunder Bay* Sentinel, *August 20, 1880*]

What a farce, burlesque, pantomime, extravaganza, anything, everything ridiculous and absurd is the present educational muddle relating to
Shuniah; twenty-two able bodied men called upon twice a week to superintend two males and one female who are teaching our schools. Not only
the Shuniah act now to wory the brains of those who would attempt to
understand it, but the school law also has assumed such shape, and
under the perfectly ludicrous ruling of the present Minister of Education
has become so terribly bungled that the Hon. Adam Crooks virtually
admitted by his conspicuous inactivity of decision in our case, his inability to unravel the tangled threads he has woven around us. Surely it
is time that the responsible portfolio was assumed by some one capable
of performing the duties more to the satisfaction of the entire educational
interests of the Province than at present, for almost every section of
country is suffering from one or another of the unjust inflictions, rulings,
or indecisions of the present Minister of Education.

I 18 THE BOOM OF 1882-3 AT THUNDER BAY
[Prince Arthur's Landing or Port Arthur, *pp. 31-2, 74-5*]

Port Arthur Foundry

Messrs. Woodside Bros.[39] are just establishing themselves in the foundry industry. Hitherto there has been no means of obtaining anything
in the casting line, for which this mining country so often calls, without
transportation to the lower provinces, accompanied by no little vexatious
delay. The machine shops, 20 × 10, are now erected and the addition,
30 × 15, to contain the moulding and blacksmith shops, will be constructed with no loss of time.

Mr. Jas. H. Woodside is a very practical man, being a millwright and
pattern maker of twenty years experience. Mr. John Woodside is no less
practical than his brother, with over fifteen years experience as a moulder.

Mr. T.A. Woodside has charge of the machinery and engine department with the benefit of sixteen years practice in that particular branch
of the industry. It is thus readily seen that the firm is composed of all
practical business heads, whose combined knowledge is a sure indication
that all work will be personally looked after in every particular.

Their markets, in addition to the local needs, will extend throughout

---

[39]This new firm, established in 1883, was the joint enterprise of three of the sons
of Thomas Woodside, who had been resident in Prince Arthur's Landing from the
early 1870s. John and James Woodside had also been residents of the area for some
years, while Thomas A. moved to Thunder Bay to join his brothers in the new
business.

the North-West Territories. This industry means capital, push and enterprise, and a great boon to the young and growing city in which its interests are vested. The foundry occupies the corner of Manitou and Wellington streets, a very convenient location, and will prove a boon to the manufacturing classes of this country.

Elevator "A", Shuniah Dock and Forwarding Co. (Limited)

This company was organized in 1882, with a capital stock of $300,000. but have only recently received their charter, and are now prepared to push the work for which they were organized in legal shape. The officers and promoters of the company are Geo. H. Kennedy, President;[40] W.F. Davidson,[41] Vice-President; John T. MacKay, Secretary; A.W. Thompson, Treasurer;[42] and Robert Hoods, Dr. Smellie and Hugh Wilson of Mount Forest, all the above-named gentlemen form the board of directors. They own somewhat over four acres for use in the construction of docks, etc., all of which they propose to utilize. The width of projected dock is 145 feet, and will be extended out into the lake sufficient distance to give from 20 to 30 feet of water for boats. Warehouses, etc., will be built thereon, and all the modern machinery and appliances for the rapid transfer of freight will be put in use. The company have reserved the railway right of their water frontage, and can at no time be blocked by cars, etc., therefore as a local dock their property will also be valuable. The gentlemen composing this company are not only men of means but men of enterprise and push, and will spend a large amount of money during the coming winter in actual improvements.

Thunder Bay Dock Forwarding and Elevator Company

This company was organized in 1882 with a capital stock of $300,000, of which Mr. Thos. Marks is president and principal stock-holder, with Messrs. Geo. T. Marks,[43] F.S. Wiley, H.A. Wiley,[44] and W.C. Dobie as directors. The docks and improvements of this company will be seen from

[40]George H. Kennedy had been a resident of the Landing since 1875 and, although his early efforts at homesteading had not been productive, he had established himself as the successful head of the "Thunder Bay Stove and Tin Manufactory."

[41]W.F. Davidson had moved to the Landing in 1870, and had soon become local manager for steamship lines, first the Collingwood Line, then the Beatty Sarnia Line.

[42]A.W. Thompson was the local manager for Thompson Bros. & Forrest, a Winnipeg jewellery firm. He was also associated with James Conmee in the lumber business and in politics, and later became sheriff in Port Arthur.

[43]George Thomas Marks, the nephew of Thomas Marks, the first mayor of Port Arthur, had been a resident of the Landing since his return from college in 1874. By the early 1880s he had become a managing partner in the family enterprises. He was elected to the Council in 1885 and became Mayor, 1893–9. He became President of Canadian North West Steamships and a powerful figure in Thunder Bay's economic development.

[44]F.S. and H.A. Wiley, nephews of Thomas Marks, were associated with him in a number of business ventures. F.S. Wiley was at this time owner of the Queen's Hotel.

the following figures to be far the most extensive of any of the five docks at this place.[45] The dock is 1100 feet long by 100 feet wide with a lower railroad track in the centre and two enormous freight sheds built on either side. The shed on the eastern side is 45×500 feet giving 22,500 square feet of floor room, the western shed is 23×500 feet, and over 800 tons of freight has been handled in one day on this extensive transfer depot. The company have already spent $50,000 in improvements and construction, and will increase the facilities for handling goods with the growing demand. This dock has been leased by the Canadian Pacific Railway for the present season and is used exclusively by them. As is characteristic of Mr. Marks' business tact the enterprise has proved a financial success.

Lake Superior Dock, Forwarding and Elevator Company

This company was organized in 1882 and is the work of purely local enterprise and capital. The capital stock is $300,000[46] and over $25,000 has already been spent on improvements. A dock extending 800 feet into the bay, 48 feet wide, has been built, warehouses placed thereon, and a railway track laid, while they are now making extensive additions. Large quantities of freight is daily handled owing to the advantages offered for transfer.

The officers and principal stock-holders are N.K. Street, President; W.H. Carpenter, Vice-President; A.L. Russell, C. McKenzie, Directors; D.F. Burk, Secretary-Treasurer. The management of the dock, etc. is attended to by Mr. F. Davidson,[47] agent for the North-West Transportation Company. This Company, comprised as it is of capitalists who are deeply interested in the welfare and growth of the city, will soon begin the erection of elevators and warehouses, which are so necessary at a place where the railway terminates and the water route begins. The company have handled 600,000 feet of lumber over their dock this year so far and all local freight from Beatty's Sarnia Line.

I 19 S.J. DAWSON, M.P. FOR ALGOMA, UNDER ATTACK
[Port Arthur Weekly Herald, October 17, 1883]

Advices from Toronto and the eastern part of Algoma are to the effect that the Conservatives are endeavouring to explain away and excuse their recent defeat by throwing a large measure of the blame upon our fellow

---

[45]By 1889 there were seven docks at Port Arthur, totalling 7100 linear feet. All, except for the government dock, had been built by local individuals or groups.

[46]In 1889 the capital of this company was given as $100,000, but the coincidence of three new companies all beginning with precisely the same amount of capital raises the question of error in the 1883 pamphlet.

[47]The overlapping of interests among the three companies was notable. W.F. Davidson presumably planned to make use of the Lake Superior dock only until the new dock was constructed for the Elevator "A" ... Company of which he was Vice-President.

townsman, Mr. S.J. Dawson, M.P. They say that he has got to be far too heavy a load for them to carry any longer, that it was only by the most superhuman efforts and the wholesale fraudulent voting manipulated by Govt. timber pirates and railway contractors, that they managed to re-elect Dawson in 1882, and that his Parliamentary course since then has been such that the most ardent of his party associates decline to further follow him. Then too, the friends of Mr. Plummer at Sault Ste. Marie[48] and other portions of eastern Algoma expected, as they were promised by Mr. Dawson, a much larger vote for Mr. Plummer at Port Arthur and throughout the Thunder Bay District [in the 1883 provincial election]. They claim to have fulfilled all their promises as to what the east would do, just as they did when Mr. Dawson himself was a candidate; and they expected Mr. Dawson would return the compliment and fulfil his pledge, upon which Mr. Plummer was induced to become a candidate, by piling up a large majority for the latter in the recent contest. But they have been greviously disappointed. Instead of a majority of from three to five hundred in the west for Mr. Plummer, it is only about fifty. And at Mr. Dawson's own door, where he himself polled a very heavy vote last year and where he may be supposed to have special influence, that majority has dropped about 200 percent! Mr. Plummer and his friends in the east, who have always faithfully supported Mr. Dawson, naturally feel sore at such a result and are evidently inclined to look upon the matter in much the same way. So that our fellow townsman seems to have a somewhat unpleasant prospect before him to allay these party suspicions. And it looks as if all his cunning would be required to do it.

In justice, however, to our distinguished though somewhat erratic fellow-citizen and representative, we submit that too much blame for the Algoma disaster ought not to be laid at the door of Mr. Dawson. He probably did all for Mr. Plummer that, under the circumstances, he was able to do. But Mr. Dawson's past political course made him a singularly weak and ineffective opponent of the Mowat Government and its North Western policy. For years Mr. Dawson had sat in the Legislature as a warm supporter of that Government; upon his advice, to a considerable extent, the Government had relied and acted with reference to local and general matters affecting Algoma ... Hence it was that Mr. Dawson, despite his crafty persuading, and the exercise of unlimited official patronage from Ottawa, utterly failed to carry the Conservative electors of even his own town with him into opposition to the Mowat Government. The task was too heavy for him. That was all. But he ought not to be blamed further than this. He did his best; but his best could not save Mr. Plummer, nor will it save Mr. Dawson himself as a future candidate in Algoma.

[48]William Plummer, Conservative, polled 1511 votes in the constituency of Algoma in the Ontario election of 1883, to 1625 for the victor, Robert A. Lyon of Manitoulin Island. Before the next provincial election, the riding had been divided into East and West Algoma.

I 20 "As Late as Election Returns from
Algoma"[49]
[*Thunder Bay* Sentinel, *October 20, November 17, 1883*]

As soon as the crushing reactionary[50] result of the Provincial election
in February last was realized by the Mowat faction a determined and
daring scheme was propounded to retain the Algoma seat. The voice of
the country spoke with such force to the damaging policy of the Reform
party – their ranks had been so completely demoralized and decimated –
that it was at once considered necessary to hold, at all hazards, this important constituency. The first act was to delay the election as long as
possible, in order that the bitter feeling against the party might to some
extent subside, and in order that during the interim every available influence might be brought to bear upon the electors. Consequently nearly
two-thirds of a year was allowed to elapse before the election took place.
In the meantime, agents were sent, with pockets well lined, into every
part of the district under pretences at once ridiculous and fradulent. Newspapers were offered sums of money to change their political complexion –
at least two of which, in disgrace to the name of journalism, were bought
over[51] – men of cunning were authorized to pay with the public money
exorbitant prices for "exhibits" of all kinds for the Provincial exhibition
which correctly interpreted simply meant the wholesale purchase of
votes; road commissioners received definite instructions as to the fradulent course they were to pursue, and money was lavishly spent and promised in every direction. The Sheriff, in whom was vested the duties of
returning officer before it was seen how the elections had turned, was
robbed of his appointment and a strong partizan politician put in his
place,[52] and a hundred and one other gross irregularities and frauds prepared to fight the battle.

[49]It was the usual practice to carry on the slow Algoma vote well after the results
of the general election elsewhere were known. Opinions varied as to the effect of
this circumstance on voting patterns in Algoma. The Ontario 1883 election was an
extreme example of delay in completing the election returns.

[50]The *Sentinel*'s phrasing is obscure. The voters' reaction against the Liberal
government of the past years had been to return it with a somewhat reduced majority.
The Mowat government remained in power and, according to the *Sentinel*, was
conspiring to add one more seat in the late Algoma elections.

[51]The phrasing here seems to represent an attempt to attack the rival *Herald*
without risking a libel suit. The *Herald* had avowed its support for the Conservative
party when it began publication in April 1882, but by the end of the same year was
calling itself independent. During the election campaign of 1883 it was bitterly
critical of the actions of S.J. Dawson in campaigning for the Conservative candidate.
Before the next election it was firmly supporting Reform candidates.

[52]Both the Sheriff, John F. Clarke, and the man who displaced him as returning
officer and eventually succeeded him as Sheriff, A.W. Thompson, were supporters of
the Mowat government. The *Sentinel* was here attacking the honesty of individuals
rather than the partisan nature of the appointment.

Who has been elected member for Algoma? It is now nearly six weeks since the election took place, and the official returns have not been announced. The excuse was first made that the keys were not sent with the ballot boxes, but to get over this difficulty the returning officer broke them open. The count evidently did not appear satisfactory, and the officer above mentioned gave out that the returns would not be announced until such time as he could hear from the deputy returning officers at Algoma Mills and Rainy River. Communication from Algoma Mills should not take more than a week at the latest to reach Port Arthur, and the full particulars concerning the non-arrival of the ballot boxes at Rainy River – for which Providence was thanked – has been discussed by the press throughout the Dominion for the past three weeks. And still the result remains a secret. If the Ontario Government think to withold the official returns until the time for a protest to be put in has elapsed, they are mistaken, as the protest has been prepared and put in on chance against Mr. Lyon.[53]

I 21   DAWSON'S LAST ELECTION VICTORY
[*Fort William* Journal, *March 31, 1887*]

The anxiety and suspense attending the recent election in this district has received a quietus by the proclamation of returning officer Wilson of Sault Ste. Marie to the effect that Mr. S.J. Dawson was elected by a majority of eleven. The air is filled with rumours of a protest, and it is more than likely that vigorous effort will be made to unseat Mr. Dawson. It is claimed that some shady transactions were carried on during the campaign which, if carried into court, may have a very damaging effect. The official statement does not include Campbell or White River returns. Why these places were omitted can only be conjectured. Information received from private sources gave Mr. Burk a majority of seven at White River and two at Campbell.[54]

[53]Robert A. Lyon, a supporter of the Mowat government, had been elected to represent Algoma in the provincial Legislature after Simon Dawson resigned to contest the federal seat in 1878. Lyon continued to represent the riding until it was subdivided, and then the eastern part of it until 1890. His brother, W.D. Lyon, was at one time M.P.P. for Halton, then Stipendiary Magistrate in the early 1880s for what was then Thunder Bay West, with headquarters at Rat Portage (Kenora).

[54]In 1887 Dawson was challenged by D.F. Burk, running for the Liberals. A request for a recount was thrown out at Sault Ste Marie when Dawson's agent pointed out that the applicant had failed to post the necessary deposit. There were still rumours of a recount and on May 19 both Dawson and Burk filed their complaints against the other in Toronto. Both sets of charges were later dropped, amid speculation concerning the reasons, and Dawson continued to represent Algoma until 1891.

I 22   THE FIRST VESSELS REGISTERED AT
PORT ARTHUR
[*P.A.C., RG 12 A-1, Port Arthur Shipping Register*]

	Date of Registry	Tonnage	H.P.
1. Kakabeka[55]	1886	74.94	5.43
2. Butcher Boy[56]	1886	145.93	17.74
3. Ida[57]	1887	13.17	2.13
4. Richmond[58]	1889	9.74	1.63
5. Brothers[59]	1891	11.9	6
6. Zena[60]	1891	3.69	3
7. Algonquin[61]	1892	1172.02	150

I 23   "THE NORTHERN,[62] THE FINEST HOTEL IN
CANADA WEST OF TORONTO"
[*Roland*, Algoma West, *pp. 41–3*]

This location was well chosen, being on the corner of South Water and Park Streets [Port Arthur] with an abrupt fall to the water, thereby secur-

[55]The *Kakabeka* was the first entry in the Port Arthur Shipping Register – completed in Toronto, May 2, 1886, registered in Port Arthur two days later, Thomas Marks owner. It was later sold to the Servais brothers, Port Arthur fishermen, and remained in service on Thunder Bay until 1893.

[56]Built in Bay City, Michigan, in 1879, registered in Port Arthur, May 8, 1886, the *Butcher Boy* was owned by Aaron Squier, insurance agent, then George A. Graham, lumber merchant. It was sold to a Toronto, then a Barrie company, and was lost off the Christian Islands in 1890.

[57]The *Ida* was built in Port Arthur for Harry Servais. It was registered on May 19, 1887, and sold in 1890 to a group at Port Coldwell (at the eastern end of Lake Superior).

[58]The *Richmond* was also locally built and registered May 23, 1889. The original owner, Steven B. Richmond, sold the vessel in 1891 to Joseph Brinison, Port Arthur express agent. In 1893 the *Richmond* was transferred to Winnipeg and its local registration cancelled.

[59]The *Brothers* was built at Port Arthur and registered September 14, 1891, the property of Eli J. Nuttall, Port Arthur fisherman. It remained in service in the area until it sank in Black Bay in the early twentieth century. The registry was not closed until 1937, when the son of the former owner gave information to the Department of Transport.

[60]The *Zena*, built at Fort William, was registered September 14, 1891. Peter Nicholson was the original owner, and he sold the vessel to James Whalen, Port Arthur contractor, in 1892. It was lost in the Nipigon River, date unknown, but, as in the case of the *Brothers*, only an investigation in 1937 and information from the son of the former owner brought about cancellation of the registry.

[61]The *Algonquin* was by far the largest vessel registered at Port Arthur in these years. Built in Glasgow, it was registered in Port Arthur in the name of Thomas Marks, with John W. Plummer of Idaho (a son-in-law of John McIntyre) holding a mortgage. Marks sold the vessel to the Canadian Steel Barge Company, and it remained in service on the Great Lakes until 1916, when its registry was transferred to Pictou, Nova Scotia.

[62]The Northern Hotel was built by Thomas Marks and his associates, among them Harold A., M.N., and F.S. Wiley. The last named acted as manager of the hotel in 1887 when this description was written. In 1888 the hotel was bought by M.P.P. James Conmee.

ing one of the most essential points – good drainage. Facing a large open space of water, it commands a magnificent view of Thunder Bay, with the Cape and Welcome Islands in front and Isle Royale in the distance. To the right is Pie Island, and further south the majestic McKay Mountains, guarding as it were the mouth of the beautiful Kaministiquia. Where can be found a site to equal this panorama of scenery?

The architecture of the new building is modern *renaissance* of Queen Ann style, built with red brick. The front has large and elegantly finished verandahs to each floor, with communication with each other by means of iron steps in cases of urgent need. The lowest verandah is continued the entire length of the building on Park street, affording a splendid promenade. The space between the walls and woodwork has been ingeniously filled in with cross pieces, and in places necessary with brick and plaster, to prevent draught in case of fire. The main entrance is off Water street, a dozen wide steps leading into a large and finely constructed vestibule; thence into the main lobby where one is at once struck with the beauty of both the general finish and work in detail of the interior. To the left is the writing-room; on the opposite side the reading-room, facing which is the office, and in rear of that is the wash-room, finished with fine white marble, and a stairway leading to the basement into the water closets. To the front of the basement, and immediately under the reading-room is fitted up and used as a barber shop. Under the writing room and on the corner is situated the cigar and tobacco store, behind which are three large and airy sample rooms for the use of commercial men. The cellar commences here and runs almost the entire length of the building. In the office a large electric bell indicator has been placed in position, connecting with every room in the house. Opposite the office is the grand stairway, wide and built with low rises, the balustrade under the hand railing being composed of beautifully carved hard wood uprights. On reaching the first landing an immense stained glass window, facing on Park street, gives the surroundings a rich and elegant appearance. On gaining the first floor you turn to the right into the main drawing-room and parlor, 45 × 25, with entrances to the verandah. A fine marble mantle with open English fire place, gives it an air of comfort. A lobby leads to the hallway of the south wing; further to the north along the lobby the hallway of the wing commences, the rooms of which are all *en suite* in two and three; this is carried on throughout the whole of the first floor. On the second floor in front the rooms are also arranged *en suite*; are large and with fine transoms with patent attachments. There are 100 bed-rooms in all. A ladies' entrance with private stairway leads to every hall, and ladies' conservatories and bath-rooms are on each floor. Great attention has been given by the architect in following closely in his fine design, privacy for lady guests, which is very requisite for a summer hotel. A delightful view is obtained from the windows in front on the top floor facing the bay. A large water tank with a capacity of 5,000 gallons is on the top floor supplying water to the house, and connections are made with every floor, where a large amount of hose will be constantly on hand in case of fire. A back stairway in the south wing leads down to the culinary and kitchen department, the one in the north wing leading to the laundry; also two fire escapes on the outside reach from the top to the bottom of the building. The dining-room is on the ground floor, 25 feet wide, and extends from the office corridor 76 feet through the south wing. The billiard room and bar occupy the same space in the north wing, with ample room for six large billiard tables, at the back end of which is the bar, with more commercial rooms in the rear.

I 24 REPORT OF DR SMELLIE, NOVEMBER 15, 1887
[*Ontario*, Sessional Papers, *1888, Department of Health Report,
no 41, pp. 33–5*]

As required by law, I herewith present my health report of the town of Port Arthur for the portion of the year 1887 which has elapsed.

During the whole of the year there has been remarkable freedom from all varieties of disease. No epidemic has visited the town; we have had only one isolated case of diphtheria in ten months, one of typhoid fever, and two very slight cases of scarlatina.

There have been comparatively few cases of really serious illness, and the death-rate for the year, so far as it has gone, will be found to be un-usually small.

The causes leading up to such a satisfactory state of things as compared with two or three years ago, may be enumerated as follows:

(a) Better house accommodation and, in particular, the absence of overcrowding, which formerly caused so much of the sickness.

(b) The large fires of last winter, which destroyed four or five blocks of buildings right in the heart of the town and the centre of the over-crowded part.[63] These buildings have been replaced by much more spacious, healthy and handsome structures with all desirable conveni-ences; so that even if fully occupied in future, the occupants will find them-selves as residents under very much improved conditions. For the time being, too, the empty spaces formed by the fire gave lungs, so to speak, to the town and lessened the probabilities of disease.

(c) The better attention paid to the condition of the streets, drains, and yards. In the early part of the spring all householders were compelled to clean their yards, cellars, etc. An examination of all streets cellars, and drains, was also made by the Medical Health Officer, and a report thereon submitted to the Board, on which immediate action was taken. In almost every case the nuisance was promptly abated, either by the owner, or,

[63]The Cumberland Street fire of February 1887 burned a block of general stores, offices, and private dwellings as well as three hotels, the Bodega, the Brunswick, and the Ottawa. At the time of Dr Smellie's report, Oliver Daunais had plans for a new block to be built on the west side of Cumberland Street opposite the scene of the fire. He had acquired the property from S.J. Dawson for $10,000 and it was rumoured that he was prepared to invest another $75,000 in the project. The Daunais block, however, never proceeded further than architects' drawings.

when the matter had to be attended to by the town council, by that body. By the first of the warm weather, there was not a known nuisance existing in the town, and where such have arisen subsequently, they have been promptly attended to. In this connection, it may be proper to speak of the most efficient manner in which the Municipal Health Inspector has performed his duties, and to whom nearly the whole credit of the present condition of the town is due. In my opinion, Chief Nichols[64] has performed his duty in this respect in a most thorough and capable manner.

As yet the people of the town are drinking pretty much the same quality of water which they were using last year. But a good deal of quiet work has been done by the council in the way of providing a system of water-works; and though there may not yet be much to show as a result, it is well to hasten slowly in such matters, if the causes of delay be merely to ensure a cheap, plentiful and pure supply of drinking water, and to avoid the recurrence of costly and irremediable mistakes through the too hasty adoption of some imperfectly devised scheme ...

Up to the evening of November 15, 1887, sixty-one deaths have been registered at the office of the town clerk, and I have reason to believe that all deaths occurring during the year in the town have been faithfully recorded. But of this number more than one-third represent deaths which occurred outside the town, which were recorded here only for the purpose of burial. To represent fairly the health of the town, we should deduct the following deaths:

Deaths occuring at Rabbit Mountain		2
"	Beaver Mountain	3
"	in Oliver Township	2
"	at Fort William	1
"	Peninsula Harbor	1
"	Verte Island	1
"	on Canadian Pacific Railway	11
	Total	21

This leaves forty deaths as actually occurring during the time specified, and really occurring in the town, including also all deaths at the hospital. But a still further deduction may be made since two patients admitted during the year were moribund on their arrival, leaving the death toll at thirty-eight for the ten and a half months. Should the same ratio of deaths be maintained up to the end of the year, the death rate of the town for 1887 would be in the immediate neighbourhood of twelve-and-quarter to the thousand of population, which may be looked upon as an exceedingly low rate.

The total number of births cannot be accurately estimated; but it cannot fall short of one hundred for the portion of the year which has already elapsed.

[64]Richard Nichols had been on the Port Arthur police force since the town was incorporated, but had only been appointed Chief in 1886, replacing the controversial John Bourke, who then became a provincial constable.

I 25   THE LEADING INDUSTRIES OF FORT WILLIAM,
1887
[*Roland,* Algoma West, *pp. 75–7*]

The industries of Fort William lie principally in the lumber trade, of which she is probably the chief depot on the upper lakes. First, we have the establishment of Messrs. Graham, Horne & Co., who, if not the first pioneer lumber dealers of this section, are at least the oldest existing establishment of the kind. Their large planing mill has a capacity of 24,000 feet per diem, and their average sales of dressed lumber have amounted to better than 12,000,000 feet per annum. In addition to dealing in rough and dressed lumber, these gentlemen do quite a trade in coal, lime and salt. They also do a considerable shipping or forwarding business, being owners of the palace-steamer Ocean, the tug Salty Jack and the large schooner Sligo. The members of this firm, being shrewd business men, give prompt attention to all orders entrusted to their care, and generally try to make things pleasant for customers.

W.H. Carpenter comes next with a saw-mill capable of cutting 25,000 feet daily; the planer run in connection has a capacity of 12,000 feet per diem. Mr. Carpenter has 35 men in the woods this season, and will get out over a million feet of logs.

The Neebing Lumber Company, Charles Garner, Manager,[65] also has a considerable force of men and teams engaged in the woods getting out logs and shingle bolts, and a portable saw and shingle mill will shortly arrive for them to manufacture lumber and shingles ...

Messrs. Hammond and McDougall[66] give employment to a large number of men in the woods, their forte being ties and piles. They have large contracts with the Canadian Pacific Railway and do a good business in the lines mentioned.

The Fort William Brick Works, Messrs. Armstrong, proprietors,[67] come next in order. These gentlemen manufacture a really excellent quality of red and white re-pressed brick, which are fully equal to the St. Louis article – for proof of which see the "Northern" Hotel and the school-house, Port Arthur. While not at liberty to state the amount of business done last year, we are assured that Messrs. Armstrong realized their most sanguine expectations, and are now confident that the coming season will find them doing a much larger trade. They are quite capable of sup-plying the demand. The clay used contains neither lime nor alkali, and is found in almost unlimited quantities. As yet their trade is confined to sup-

[65]This Company's operations, like those of the Algoma Lumbering Company, which Roland reported as lying idle because of dissension among the proprietors, seems to have been of short duration. Later descriptions of the lumber industry at Fort William contain no mention of either firm.

[66]Hammond and McDougall were general contractors in the Town Plot of Fort William.

[67]The hopes of this firm do not appear to have been realized. Case's *Directory* of 1894 lists no Armstrong who were proprietors of brick works, and no brick works in either town.

plying the home market, but we are assured that the manufacturers purpose making a "big push" during the coming summer [1887] to place their
brick in the Winnipeg market, where we have no doubt it will give the best
of satisfaction and command a ready sale.

I 26 RÉSUMÉ OF SHIPPING–1889 SEASON
[P.A.C., RG 16 A 5-7, Port Arthur Customs Records, v. 2, p. 269]

		No. of Vessels	Tonnage	Tons Carried	Crew
Inwards	Canadian Steamers	230	200,191	79,303	8375
	Canadian Schooners	23	9,284	8,076	166
	American Steamers	142	62,436	59,241	1835
	American Schooners	35	16,444	30,301	135
	Totals	430	288,355	176,901	10,511
Outwards	Canadian Steamers	230	200,191	112,016	8375
	Canadian Schooners	23	9,284	2,885	166
	American Steamers	142	62,436	996	1835
	American Schooners	35	16,444	—	135
	Totals	430	288,355	115,897	10,511

I 27 STATEMENT OF IMPORTS AND EXPORTS, 1889–90
[P.A.C., RG 16 A 5-7, Port Arthur Customs Records, v. 2, pp. 407–8]

Statement showing value of Imported goods which were entered for consumption at the
Port of Port Arthur during fiscal year ending 30th June, 1890.

Dutiable		Free	
Coal	$206,891.00	Anthracite coal	$32,317.00
Meats etc.	17,844.00	Fishing Twines etc.	1,533.00
Coal oil	13,244.00	Eggs	402.00
Iron, Machinery etc.	6,515.00	Settler's Effects	1,190.00
Candles	1,989.00	Other	6,068.00
Gunpowder	5,233.00		
Other	17,154.00		
	$268,858.00		$41,509.00
Shipped from Great Britain	2,684.00		750.00
U.S.	264,962.00[68]		40,759.00
Other	1,212.00		—
	268,858.00		45,509.00

[68]The large dependence on American imports had been evident from the
beginning of Customs records. The 1884 list, for example, enumerated the value of
horned cattle, bacon and hams, beef, various types of cotton goods, and baking
powder (worth $720) imported from the United States and manifested from
Winnipeg to Port Arthur.

Statement showing value of Exports from Port of Port Arthur, Ontario, during fiscal
year ending June 30, 1890.

	Silver ore	$195,326.00
	Baryta ore	770.00
	Fresh fish	12,314.00
	Coin & bullion	4,984.00
	Sundries	6,062.00
		$219,456.00
Shipped to:	Great Britain	15,100.00
	U.S.	204,356.00
		$219,456.00

I 28   A POLITICAL MEETING IN OLIVER TOWNSHIP
[*Port Arthur* Weekly Herald, *June 3 1890*]

David Squier[69] occupied the chair and explained that Messrs. Gorham
and Burk could have *half an hour* between them and introduced a man
who was well known to them all.

Dr. Smellie, – who stated that he was not a public speaker and that he
did not pretend to know much about politics, but that he could tell them
that Oliver Mowat had done nothing right and he continued grumbling
for nearly an hour about the following matters: The temperance question
(he forgot to tell them he was a druggist and could sell liquor); the
murders that have been committed, which Mowat should not have allowed; John Bourke, constable, Kreissman, who is in South Africa; All
Four Thompsons; his own quarrelling; school teaching in Essex; dangling
offices before the electorate; Fish Inspector Dobie; what he knew about
his next door neighbour; who ought to have been jail surgeon, and a lot
more of the same kind.

Mr. Aaron Squier[70] then made a neat little speech, telling the electorate
how he had pulled off his coat, rolled up his sleeves, and farmed in Oliver
himself.

The opposition candidate [G.H. Macdonell] then introduced himself,
adjusted his spectacles and started off with his usual set speech, which he
had before him in a neat bundle of papers. Every few minutes Mr. Baxendale[71] asked him to go easy. He had an audience that could not be stuffed.

[69]David Squier of Ilderton had applied for land in Oliver Township in December
1877, and had located there soon afterwards. Two other Squiers, Thomas and
William, had located in Oliver even earlier and applied, in one case for the land
adjoining, at about the same time.
[70]Aaron Squier left York County for Oliver Township in 1877, but his name was
soon associated with business and municipal politics in Prince Arthur's Landing.
He was Mayor of Port Arthur in 1890.
[71]The Baxendale family was as well known in Oliver Township as the Squiers.
Three Baxendales, Charles, John, and Richard, applied for homesteads in the township in 1878 and 1879, and indicated on their applications that they were already
resident in the township at the time.

So he ordered Mr. Baxendale to shut up and dry up. After a while he brought out the Winnipeg Tribune, edited by a Mr. McIntyre,[72] who had for a long time been editor of the *Port Arthur Sentinel*, of which the speaker had been president and is now a director and endeavoured to prove that because that paper had an article in it praising up himself and his chances that the people of Oliver should believe the yarn. He wound up by telling the people that he was not buying votes, that we would not buy a vote if he could get it for five cents; in fact, he would not pay five cents for the whole Oliver vote.

The Chairman then read a note which had been handed up to him
To the Chairman

On behalf of Mr. Conmee, we submit that one half hour is not a fair allowance of time to us at this meeting, and not such as your people have been getting at our meetings. As it has been stated by some of your people that we are not giving you fair play, we hereby challenge you to meet Mr. Conmee hour about at Port Arthur on June 4th, when you will be allowed equal time with himself.

(Sgd.)   D.F. Burk
T.A. Gorham

To which the opposition candidate replied: I am just as good looking a man as Mr. Conmee; I am just as strong morally and physically. I am not afraid of him in any way, but I won't be buldozed. I will meet him if I want to and if I don't want to I won't. I am not going to be forced to talk to a lot of chairs in Port Arthur filled with morons and rowdies.

I 29 THUNDER BAY AND UNRESTRICTED RECIPROCITY[73]
[*Thunder Bay* Sentinel, *February 20, 1891*]

Fort William has grown greatly, and if its growth meets the most moderate expectations of the friends of [this] prosperous municipality, it has a great future before it and, let us hope, not so very far before it.

Mr. D.F. Burk has been over to the Fort to talk to the people there on the question of unrestricted reciprocity and he is reported to have raised up great hopes of what is to be when there is unrestricted reciprocity between Canada and the United States. Mr. Burk knows a great deal better than that, and if he does not know better the people of Fort William do.

---

[72]D.L. McIntyre had been managing director of the *Sentinel* from 1887 until 1889, when he had departed for Winnipeg.

[73]As the 1891 election approached and D.F. Burk was again campaigning for the Liberals, the *Sentinel* was quick to point out that the entire district, even including Fort William, had much to lose if unrestricted reciprocity should become government policy.

Ask anyone in Fort William this question: To what does Fort William owe its existence as a municipality, and to what does it owe its continuance? There can be only one answer. The c.p.r. Of that there is no sort of doubt.

Would the existence of the c.p.r. be possible without the trade of the North west? Not at all. Take away the trade of the Northwest and the c.p.r. would soon be two streaks of rust and the rising towns on Thunder Bay only recollections in men's minds.

Let no one delude you; even if it were admitted that unrestricted reciprocity would be good for Canada in general of its effects on Thunder Bay there is not the least room for speculation or doubt.

Duluth even now is making a big bid for the carrying trade of the Canadian Northwest, and the Duluth & Winnipeg road is being pushed through as fast as possible. With that road completed and unrestricted reciprocity then Fort William's doom is sounded.

I 30   JAMES CONMEE, M.P.P. FOR WEST ALGOMA
[*Thunder Bay* Sentinel, *April 1, 1892*]

It seems, from the reports of those who have come back to Port Arthur from Toronto, that the main obstacle to be overcome in Port Arthur getting from the Legislature what was applied for, was the opposition of Mr. Conmee. Mr. Conmee opposed and things were not got.

It is unfortunate that Mr. Conmee is concerned in so many projects which are, if not inimical, certainly opposed to the interests of the town.[74] When any of these are before the Legislature it places Mr. Conmee in a very awkward position.

I 31   THE POSSIBILITY OF A FEDERAL
CONSTITUENCY OF THUNDER BAY
[*Thunder Bay* Sentinel, *April 23, 1892*]

According to the *Empire* the Electoral District of Algoma will be divided and another member given it. We are not quite certain that this is an unmixed good. As Algoma now stands in the local house, the Western Division is almost entirely a c.p.r. consitituency. It is hopeless to elect anyone whom the c.p.r. has an interest in defeating. It may appear to the casual observer as though it would be almost impossible to elect Mr. Jas. Conmee, as he is not likely to be in the good graces of the c.p.r. But the

[74]The *Sentinel's* opposition to Conmee was of long standing. Its particular complaint against him on this occasion was that he had not been sufficiently energetic in pressing in the claims of the Port Arthur Street Railway which was attempting to extend its line into Fort William against the protests of at least some of the voters of Algoma.

fact of the matter is that Mr. Jas. Conmee is a supporter of the Ontario Government and it is the Government the c.p.r. looks at and not the individual.

This is shown in the result of the last elections. Mr. Macdonell was defeated by Mr. Conmee for the Local, while he defeated an immeasurably stronger man for the Dominion House.[75] The difference between success and defeat was just the difference between plus and minus c.p.r. influence.

I 32   A VIEW FROM THE WEST – A MANITOBAN
DESCRIBES THUNDER BAY[76]
[Woodside, H.J., "The Queen's Highway," in Dominion Illustrated Monthly, December 1892, pp. 691–2]

Fort William, on Lake Superior, is a place of no mushroom existence. For over a century, the Hudson's Bay Company have maintained a post there.[77] The importance of the post was attested by the fact that several severe struggles took place for its possession, between the retainers of the Northwest and Hudson's Bay Companies. The old post which has been swept away by the advance of civilization, was the scene of many a grand pow-wow with the Indians, of ceremonious receptions to distinguished visitors and wild dissipation, when trappers, couriers-du-bois and Indians made their annual pilgrimage to the "fort." Immense stores of supplies were received yearly and distributed over a vast region.

In the early seventies when the McKenzie Government began the construction of the Canadian Pacific Railway, the terminus of the Thunder Bay division was placed at a point four miles up the Kaministiqua River, and the new town was named Fort William, although it was more popularly known as the "Town Plot" ... or as it is now called "West Fort William," flourished in the possession of the round house and terminal buildings of the railway, until a couple of years ago, when the Canadian Pacific Railway Company having purchased the extensive tract of land owned by the Hudson's Bay Company, decided to remove the headquarters and staff of the Winnipeg, or Western division, to the new town site.[78]

The quaint and picturesque old fur traders' buildings, guarded by a

[75]Macdonnell won the federal seat in the 1891 election. His opponent was D.F. Burk.

[76]The author was Captain H.J. Woodside of Winnipeg, youngest son of the Thomas Woodside, Sr., who had settled in Prince Arthur's Landing more than twenty years earlier. Captain Woodside had attended school in the Landing at the height of the dispute with Fort William in the 1870s, and his brothers continued to live there through the more recent disputes.

[77]If the reference were intended to be to Hudson's Bay Company operations in Thunder Bay rather than at Fort William itself, the time was very little exaggerated.

[78]At the end of the 1880s Van Horne was alleged to have threatened Winnipeg (as well as Port Arthur) with the loss of c.p.r. business. When an extensive building operation began at Fort William in 1890, some assumed that this meant the phasing out of Winnipeg operations.

high stockade, became as a tale that was told, and in their places have risen mighty sky-scraping elevators, long wharves and coal docks. The ground once trodden by the Indian alone, is now laid out in streets and town lots.

Fine brick blocks have been built where the savage pitched his tent. Axe and fire are ravaging the tamarac swamp behind the town converting it into gardens and grass plots. A new town containing many pretentious business blocks and private residences has sprung up very rapidly at Fort William, and incorporation as a town has followed naturally the growth of the place in its march towards the goal of cityhood.

The Canadian Pacific Railway Company with that enterprise so characteristic of its history, has determined to handle the crops of Manitoba via Fort William, and has erected elevators "A", "B" and "C" in succession on the banks of the Kaministiquia. They are among the largest of their class on the continent. The capacity of Elevator "A" is one million bushels, Elevator "B" one and a quarter million bushels, and Elevator "C" one and a half million bushels of grain. In the year 1891 they handled over twelve million bushels of grain shipped east by water. Each elevator is fitted with the best machinery throughout, and fairly bristles with spouts and legs for the purpose of loading boats and unloading cars. The lower story of one of these giant elevators, with its massive timber supports, rows of boxed carriers and bin spouts, may well be likened to the dim vista of a pine forest where the giant trunks of trees and thick over-reaching branches shut out the clear light of heaven. As the grain trade increases the Canadian Pacific Railway Company will erect more elevators on Thunder Bay to meet the increase.

APPENDIX
ORIGINAL TEXTS OF DOCUMENTS

A 13   Père Frémiot à son Supérieur à New-York
[*Archives de la Société de Jésus du Canada Français (A.S.J.C.F.),
Nouvelles Missions, v. 1, pp. 448–53*]

[Fort William]
le 18 octobre, 1849

J'assistais aux séances comme simple spectateur, et j'acceptais l'office de M. Mackensie de partager le dîner de ces messieurs. Je suis donc, comme témoin oculaire, vous tracer fidèlement la physionomie de l'assemblée. M. Vidal occupe le fauteuil du milieu, et écrit tout ce qui se dit de part et l'autre. Le capitaine Anderson siège à sa droite. Il parle anglais, français, et sauvage, tandis que ses deux collègues ne parlent qu'anglais. C'est lui qui propose aux sauvages les questions du gouvernement, et interprète leurs réponses. Derrière lui se trouve un de ses rameurs, Peter Bell, jeune homme du Sault Ste. Marie, qu'il interroge lorsqu'il est dans la doute. M. Sommerville assis à la gauche de M. Vidal, a son bureau à part, et ne paraît guère s'occuper de la séance.

En face de ces messieurs, sur des chaises ou fauteuils, sont assis nos deux chefs. Joseph, La Peau de Chat, est à la première ligne. Il est habillé comme les blancs, ainsi que tous les sauvages. C'est un homme d'environ 40 ans, grand et bien fait de sa personne, à la voix vibrant et sonore. Sa fougue éloquente, sa véhemente impetuosité l'ont fait choisis pour chef par les sauvages. Il ne lui manque qu'une âme plus fortement trempée dans la vie et les vertus chrétiennes. L'autre chef est un vieillard septuagénaire qu'on appelle *L'illinois*. C'est tout simplement un de ces chefs de pelleteries établis par la Compagnie de la Baie d'Hudson. Il en reçoit tous les ans deux habits, dont l'un est rouge, galonné, et garni de boutons en métal. C'est-ce qui lui a fait donné le surnom de Miskouakkonaye (rouge habilé). Il y a un certain nombre d'années qu'un ministre Baptiste du Sault le plonger dans la rivière avec quelques membres de sa famille. C'est là tout ce qu'on lui appris de la religion, car il ne sait absolument rien. Ce vieillard que les sauvages veulent bien considérer comme chef, mais qui n'a pas la principale autorité, porte aujord'hui, comme bien vous le pensez, son habit d'ordonnance. M. Sommerville passe la première partie de la séance à le dessiner ce plaisant costume, rehaussé encore par son grand calumet qu'il repose sur la cuisse en le soutenant de la main. Pauvre calumet ! Que de mal n'eut-il pas à t'allumer ! Pendant plus d'un grand quart d'heure il fit jouer le briquet au muet sourire de l'assistance. Derrière les chefs, tout autour de la salle, les sauvages sont assis par terre, adossés contre le mur.

On commence par faire l'appel nominal, d'après une liste composée la veille par M. Mackensie. On passe les métis sous silence, car ils n'ont pas la parole dans ces sortes d'assemblées. Est-ce politique ? Et craindrait-on que, plus instruits que les sauvages, il ne sussent mieux défendre leurs droits ? ...

On commence la longue série de questions que les Messieurs viennent adressés aux sauvages de la part du gouvernement – « Quelle est votre origine ? votre nom ? sont-ces là vos chefs ? Lequel occupe le premier rang ? (Joseph, La Peau de Chat, répondent les sauvages) Quelle est la forme, l'étendue, la qualité de vos terres ? Quels sont les animaux que les habitent ? Voulez-vous vendre vos terres ? Quelle est l'estimation que vous en faites ? »

« Outre une réserve sur les deux bords de la rivière où nous habitons, nous demandons trente piastres par tête, y compris les femmes et les enfants, chaque année jusqu'à la fin du monde, et cela en argent, non en marchandises. De plus, nous demandons aux frais du Gouvernement un maître d'école, un médécin, un forgeron, un menuisier, un fermier, et un surintendant pour rendre la justice ».

Avant de clore cette première journée, le Capitaine Anderson dit aux sauvages. « Il est deux choses qui ne nous font pas plaisir, et qui ne verra pas non plus de bon œil, à ce que nous pensons, notre Père qui est à Montréal. La première, c'est qu'il ne connait point, c'est qu'il n'a pas approuvé celui des deux chefs auquel vous donnez la préférence. La seconde, c'est que vous demandez un trop haut prix pour vos terres. Voyez l'autre côté du Lac, ce que fait le Grand-Coteau. Les sauvages ne sont payés que pendant vingt-cinq ans et encore beaucoup moins chaque année que vous ne demandez vous-mêmes. Et vous, ce serait jusqu'à la fin du monde ! et trente piastres par tête ! De plus, le Grand-Coteau, une fois la terme de paiement expiré, chassera les sauvages au déla du Mississipi ; vous, au contraire, vous resterez ici à jamais, paisibles possesseurs de vos terres. Enfin, de l'argent vous serait plus nuisible qu'utile ; voyez ce qui se passe à La Pointe. Les sauvages donnent une piastre, même jusqu'à une couverture, pour un verre d'eau mélangée d'un peu de wiski ; le même chose arriverait ici. Il vous sera bien plus avantageux d'avoir des vêtements pour vous couvrir. Réfléchissez-donc cette nuit à ces deux points et si, demain, vous persistez dans les mêmes sentiments, cela sera écrit. Maintenant, c'est un conseil d'ami que nous vous donnons; car nous ne pensons pas que le Grand Chef qui est à Montréal vous accorde tout ce que vous avez demandé ».

Le lendemain, après la messe, Joseph La Peau de Chat vient me dire que l'Anglais le craint et veut le destituer, mais qu'il va de ce pas, faire rayer lui-même sont nom –

« Mon enfant, lui dis-je, l'anglais ne te craint pas ; l'anglais ne craint aucun sauvage. L'anglais ne veut pas, non plus il ne peut pas, te destituer. Ce sont les sauvages qui t'ont choisi pour chef, tu le seras tant qu'ils te maintiendront. S'ils répondent comme hier, ce sera une affaire finie, il n'en sera plus question. Seulement l'anglais n'a pas ta prière, l'Habit Rouge, lui, a la prière de l'anglais. Voila pourquoi l'anglais serait bien aise de le voir le premier chef. Ne crains donc rien, et garde-toi de faire rayer ton nom ;

tu perdrais tout. Si tu ne veux plus être chef, tu le diras plus tard, et les sauvages en choisiront un autre. Mais ce n'est pas aujourd'hui le moment ».

Les sauvages témoins de cette entrevue avaient pris leurs mesures pour élire un autre chef, en cas qu'il fit un coup de tête en pleine assemblée. Mais, apparemment, la réflexion le prit en chemin, car, sans parler de sa démission, il se contenta de dire fort sagement à ce suject : « Ni la Grand Chef qui est à Montréal, ni la Reine, ne prétendent rien changer aux élections des sauvages, ni influencer en rien leurs déliberations ». Cette déclaration etait écrite. Quant aux prix des terres, il n'en fut plus question ce jour-la ...

Lorsqu'on fut réuni de nouveau, l'Habit Rouge, ou le vieux chef, prit pour la première fois la parole. Il débuta en ces termes. « Mon Père, je ne sais ce que je veux dire ; je n'ai plus d'esprit, je te ressemble, je suis bien vieux ». Après cet exorde insinuant, notre Nestor sauvage remonte, je crois, jusqu'au déluge, out peut-être au déla, puis, descendant de proche en proche, il en vient à l'apparition des blancs sur cette terre, et aux choses merveilleuses que le sauvage vit alors pour la premiere fois. « Ce n'est pas toi, Anglais, qui vins le premier, on te connaît à peine ; nous l'appelons Ouemitikoje, Français, celui qui nous vista d'abord » Quant à la péroraison du discours, je vous avoue qu'elle s'est enfuie de ma mémoire ; je n'en retrouve que quelques fragments incomplets. Il était tard et les sauvages, dont l'appétit commençait à se faire sentir, s'ennuyaient de ces longueurs homériques. Un des gendres de l'orateur alla même jusqu'a lui dire « C'est assez, beau-père ». « Patience », répliqua l'autre, « je ne gâterai rien ». Enfin, un autre de ces gendres, assis à son côté, et qui parfois inspirait charitablement sa mémoire en défaut, lui coula doucement à l'oreille que c'était bien, et aussitôt le docile orateur, ayant prononcé la formule « C'est la tout ce que j'avais à dire » s'assit et se tut.

Alors le capitaine Anderson se lève a son tour pour faire le discours de clôture ... Il les exhorta fortement à embrasser la civilisation des blancs, à se vouer à l'agriculture... « Ecoutez votre Robe-noire ; ne faites pas tort à votre Bourgeois, car le Grand Esprit voit tout ; mais surtout méditez souvent la vie éternelle ».

Après cette édifiante péroraison, l'on se donna la poignée de main d'adieu, et l'on se quitta bon amis...

Tel est, mon Révérend Père, la récit de cet événement mémorable pour notre mission. Voilà donc nos pauvres sauvages à la veille de recevoir, non une fortune toute faite qui les dispense de travailler aussi quelqu'uns se l'imaginaient bonnement, mais quelques faibles secours qui, du moins, les aideront à s'habiller. Car, ici, la difficulté n'est pas de vivre, mais de se vêtir. La culture et la pêche fourniront une nourriture suffisante, mais le vêtement il en coûte davantage de procurer, par la raison que la Compagnie de Baie d'Hudson a jusqu'ici le monopole des fourrures, et par conséquent du commerce.

A 14   Peau de Chat à R. P. Choné, 1849
[A.S.J.C.F., A-16-1]

« D'où viens-tu, toi, qui habite ici ? »

« Du corps d'un homme, je suis né » lui ai-je dit, lui répondant. Sa question était ambiguë, ma réponse fut sans ombrages. Il ajoute « La terre est-elle bonne à Népigon, à l'intérieur des terres ? Penses-tu qu'on puisse vivre de culture ? »

« A coup sur lui » répondis-je.

« Quelles espèces d'arbres y-a-t-il ? Je lui numerai toutes les essences, sauf l'érable, le chêne rouge, le pin rouge, et le bois blanc.

Il ajoute « Quel est votre chef ? Quel est celui qui vous commande ? » Ils répondent « C'est Joseph ».

« Ce vieux, » ajoute-il, « quand l'avez-vous élu ? »

« Nous l'avons élu le dernier de tous ».

« C'est de vous qu'il tient son élection ; il n'est pas encore chef ! Il n'aura pas de pouvoir. Tout de même je le connais pour un homme sage ; je le connais parfaitement ». « Je te comprendre » lui dis-je et donc j'ajoute : « Je suis le chef des catholiques.. Tu veux m'arracher le pouvoir et le donner à un autre, si tu peux ; voila ton dessein. Tu as l'intention du faire chef un bête de sauvage. Tu te dis que tu t'empareras de notre territoire, tout simplement. Jamais la reine, no plus que le chef de Montreal, ne modifie ce qui les sauvages ont decrété ». Voila ce que j'ai dit à And...

Il me questionne sur la paie qu'on reçoit aux Etats-Unis. « Qu'est ce que tu veux savoir » (lui ai-je dit) serait-ce un pêche pour le Grand-Coteau de me payer ? Serait-ce un pêche pour les Anglais aussi de me payer ? »

« Au contrairie, c'est un devoir de me payer. Ta question est oiseuse ». N'est-ce pas ma terre à moi dont il s'agit dans ce marché ? La terre des Anglais. C'est aussi ma terre.

C 5   Contrat de Mariage entre Louis Bouchard et Charlotte Fainiant
[P.A.C., H.B. Co. Records, B-231-z, Fort William Miscellaneous Items]

Contrat de mariage fait et passé entre Louis Bouchard de la Paroisse de Maskinongé dans la province du bas Canada d'une part, et Charlotte Fainiant du Fort William de la province du haut Canada avec le consentement de ses parents, de l'autre part. Le dit Louis Bouchard volontairement s'oblige et promet fidèlement de prendre au presence de Dieu et en face de l'Eglise la dite Charlotte Fainiant comme sa femme legitime, de la proteger, la cherir, et de l'entretenir en santé comme autrement durant la terme de la vie naturelle et a la première bonne occasion de faire solemniser leur mariage selon l'usage des Pays civilizés et de plus le dit Louis

Bouchard en cas que la dite Charlotte Fainiant le survive volontairement s'oblige de ceder et laisser pour le seul profit, usage et benefice de la dite Charlotte Fainiant et ses enfans produit de son mariage tout l'argent au biens, soit en monnoyes, en meubles, ou autre choses que le dit Louis Bouchard pourra posseder a sa mort, et en cas que le did Louis Bouchard meurt au manque de remplir fidèlement les conventions et arrangements susdits auparavant de marier la dite Charlotte Fainiant il consent et volontairement s'oblige de laisser et de faire payer a la dite Charlotte Fainiant tout l'argent et monnaie qu'il a presentement ou qu'il pourra avoir entre les mains de l'honorable compagnie de la Baie d'Hudson et de ces argentes le dit Louis Bouchard consent aussi de quitter par chaque année entre les mains de la dite compagnie pendant les années qu'il continue en leur service la dixième part de ses Gages, expressement pour l'object de faire une petite provision pour la benefice de sa famille en cas de quelque casualité vient lui mourir.

Fait et passé au Fort William, District du Lac Supérieur, le dix-huit d'octobre, l'an mil huit cent vingt huit, après-midi, et ont signé a l'exception du dit Louis Bouchard, lequel ayant declaré ne savoir signer a fait sa marque ordinaire après l'écriture faite.

Témoines	Sa
Benj. McKenzie	Louis X Bouchard
Duncan Haggart	Marque

C 15   R.P. Choné à un Scolastique de la
Société de Jésus
[*A.S.J.C.F., Nouvelles Missions, v. 1, pp. 362–3*]

Manitoulin, le 24 fevrier, 1848

Figurez-vous que ces peuplades isolées, privées de commerce des autres nations, sans ressource pour l'intelligence, reserrées dans une circonférence peu étendue, toutes occupées de la vie présente, se sont crues longtemps les seuls habitants de la terre, ils n'ont pas par conséquent d'autres idées que les leurs, et pour se faire catholiques il doivent entrer dans une atmosphère tout à fait inconnue. Il faut que l'échange des pensées s'opère peu-à-peu, et pour l'obtenir cet effet il n'y a que la parole du missionaire lequel soit se borner longtemps à l'explication d'un petit nombre de verités. Point de terres, point de connaissances reçues par le commerce avec les peuples civilisés, peu de developpement d'intelligence. Ensuite difficulté pour le missionaire d'apprendre la langue, difficulté bien plus grande encore de faire passer dans cet idiome original les idées que lui sont étrangères – Aussi les sectes protestantes qui ont fait traduire leur bible par les métis du pays ont un ouvrage non seulement imparfait mais faux, avec les plus grossières erreurs.

C 18   R.P. Frémiot et les Indiens du lac Supérieure

[A.S.J.C.F., Nouvelles Missions, v. 1, p. 381; v. 2, pp. 1, 26, 105, 168, 195, 205]

Rivière aux Tourtes
le 24 juillet, 1848.

Vers midi nous entrons dans cet autre Jourdain qui arrose notre terre promise. Mais ici pas de Jébusen à combattre, personne pour vous en disputer la paisible possession. En effet nous mettons pied-à-terre et que voyons-nous ? Là et là quelques maisons inachevées... puis, sur un plateau central, au bord de la rivière une église en bois à laquelle il ne manque jadis la couverture, mais qui maintenant tombe pièce-à-pièce ; un peu plus loin une maison ou, si vous aimez mieux, une cabane qui se compose d'un seul appartement et qui laisse voir la ciel à travers les fentes de la toiture. C'est la maison que nous est destinée. Un missionaire, M. Pirse, la fit bâtir ainsi que l'Eglise il y a cinq ans ; puis effrayé des difficultés qu'offrait alors la mission, il l'abandonne pour aller au Sault Ste Marie ; il est aujourd'hui à l'Arbre Croche, mission d'Ottawas sur le lac Michigan.

Fort William
Janvier 1850

« Au lieu d'une petite chapelle d'écorce où le vent jouait à son aise, se riait d'une poële embrasé, nous en avous quelques semaines une fort grande en bois et du moins quelque peu confortable. Au lieu d'une petite croix en sapin, nous en avons une fort belle en fer supportée par une belle boule d'orée...

« Comment s'y prendre ? Point de briques, pas même de pierres, excepté les rochers ou les cailloux du rivage. On commence par planter en terre quatre perches de la hauteur de la cheminée ; car on a eu soin de laisser dans le toit une vide assez considérable qui ne sera rempli qu'après la cheminée faite, ces quatres perches souliées ensemble par des barres transversales distantes d'un demi-pied l'une de l'autre, ce qui forme une espèce l'échelle pyramidale. Tel est le squelette de la cheminée. Pour la garnir on enferme de la glaise mêlée de sable, dans un petit rouleau de foin, qu'on presse, qu'on manie jusqu'à ce que la glaise le compénètre et resorte par le bas. Un second, vient s'accoler au premier, puis un troisième au second, et ainsi toute la cheminée s'élève, unie, solide et compacte.

Fort William,
le 21 juin, 1850

La procession (le Fête-Dieu) fut renvoyée au dimanche, suivant à cause de mauvais temps. Ce jour-là deux reposoirs bien modestes furent dressés. Dix beaux sapins décoraient à l'intérieur la maison de la prière, d'autres ombrageaient la façade et bordaient la place qui est à l'entrée ainsi que les avenues qui conduisaient aux reposoirs. Comme presque aucun des assistants ne savait ce que c'était qu'une procession, ce ne fut pas sans peine que je parvins à organiser une marche un peu regulière, mais par la même raison, quelque modeste que fut cette fête religieux au milieu des forêts, c'était un spectacle magnifique pour les sauvages ; ils en furent tous dans l'admiration.

Sault Ste. Marie
le 2 février, 1851

Déjà ces riantes espérances commencent à se réaliser. L'été dernier deux familles de la *Rivière des Sauteux* dans le Michigan sont venues se fixer ici ; leur parens, au nombre de plus d'un cent, doivent venir les réjoindre le printemps prochain. Une autre circonstance à faire affluer ici à la même époque, un bien plus grand nombre de sauvages – c'est la mesure adoptée par le gouvernement américaine de refouler au delà du Mississipi tout ce qui reste encore de Sauteux à l'Est de ce fleuve. Cette immigration forcée doit avoir lieu l'été prochain, et c'est pour s'y soustraire, pour s'épargner les misères qu'elle entraînera infailliblement à sa suite, que les Sauvages de *La Pointe* et plusieurs de *Fond du Lac* veulent, eux aussi, venir se réfugier sur le territoire anglais. Mais d'après les clauses du traité que le gouvernement anglais vient de conclure avec les Sauteux de Haut-Canada rélativement à la vente de leurs terres, les émigrants ne pourrant se fixer d'une manière stable que dans les quelques Réserves concédées à perpetuité aux sauvages. Or *L'Immaculée Conception* est une des plus considérables et la seule à proximité des Etats-Unis à cette extremité du Lac. Tout ce monde va donc arriver par la force des circonstances, et l'on pourra, avec la grâce de Dieu, faire une bonne recrue pour grossir les rangs décimés de notre petit troupeau. Tout récemment, j'ai déjà baptisé les premiers de ces futurs néophytes de l'*Immaculée Conception* et le jour même du nouvel an, j'ouvrais l'année 1851 par le baptême d'une femme du Nipigon, poste de la compagnie de la Baie d'Hudson à six journées de marche au nord du F.-W. et d'où nous espérons aussi recueillir des brebis pour notre bercail.

Fort William,
le 3 décembre, 1851

La vie nomade – c'est là le grand obstacle qui empêche d'agir sur les masses du moins d'une manière constante. Ceci est vrai surtout pour les infidèles qui, sauf un mois ou deux, ou seulement huit ou quinze jours de l'année, apparaissent près des Forts, et le reste du temps vivent disseminés au milieu des forêts. Ceci est vrai encore jusqu'à un certain point pour les néophytes qui sont obligés de s'absenter une bonne partie de l'année... Il faut donc gagner et instruire ces pauvres gens, non seulement famille par famille, mais individu par individu, car l'indépendance ou l'égoisme sauvage est tel que les plus proches parents ne se donneront pas même un conseil en ce point et, d'un autre côté, cependant, le respect humain a tant d'empire que si le chef d'une famille est indifférent ou contraire à la religion, les autres membres n'oseront l'embrasser...

Un infidèle de Fort William, que je croyais le plus près de la verité et que je ne pensais plus d'âge à tenir à ses deux femmes, me fit bien voir que je me trompais. « Autrefois » dit-il, « un traiteur voulut m'engager à ne plus garder qu'une seule femme. Je lui répondis que les Peaux-Blanches avaient bien aussi plusieurs femmes en cachette et que je connaissais plus d'un traiteur dans ce cas ». Un autre infidèle de F.-W. avait déjà quatre femmes attitrées ; il en prit, en printemps, une cinquième venue du Lac de la Pluie et en revanche fut abandonné par une des anciennes qui se croyait méprise... Joignez à la polygamie l'adultère et tout les honteux attirail de la license, l'usage si commun des philtres des remèdes pour prévenir la conception ou en détruire l'effet...

Lorsque tous nos sauvages se sont rendus à l'Ile Royale pour la pêche ; à l'exception de quelques femmes et peut-être d'un homme, vous n'en trouverez pas un seul qui n'aît bu... Un sauvage a vendu son calumet pour une piastre et il s'est hâté d'en faire de l'eau de vie. Sans compter ce qui a été acheté frauduleusement sur les vaisseaux, deux Américains ont dépensé là, avec nos sauvages, dans l'espace de deux ou trois mois (le croirez-vous ?) par moins de deux barils d'eau de vie de 36 galons chacun.

Le Lac Nipigon
le 19 mars, 1852

C'est un catholique qui se trouve en ce moment à la tête du Poste, M. Louis Denis de Laronde, canadien de naissance, mais dont le père était français. Ses demoiselles qui parlent mieux la sauvage que le français et l'anglais qu'elles comprennent cependant sont d'un grand secours pour le chant des cantiques. Autre le commis il n'y a en tout que six engagés, deux écossais protestants et quatres catholiques, dont un canadien, un métis, et deux sauvages. Sur ces six hommes, trois catholiques seulement sont mariés, ce qui, avec la famille du commis, forme un total de 27 personnes dans le Fort. Joignez-y 7 adultes et trois enfants que la mort de deux chasseurs a plongé dans le veuvage ou rendus orphelins, et qui sont venus s'abriter près du fort.

Ile Royale
le 2 juillet, 1852

Quelques-uns des hommes du Fort ont soin de se rendre en quai pour recevoir les ballots de pelleteries qu'ils portent dans une salle destinée à la reception des Sauvages. On évite par là à ceux-ci la peine de monter les trente à quarante marches qui conduisent au Fort. Ils arrivent ensuite eux-mêmes sans avoir rien à porter que leur calumet ; ils sont généralement en grand tenue, ayant eu soin de faire toilette avant d'aborder.

La traiteur ou commis leur donne une poignée de main avec une torquete de tabac, puis, on compte en leur présence le fruit de leur courses et de leurs fatigues. Il en est quelquefois qui apportent trois ou quatre peaux d'ours, autant de renards, des loutres, des castors, des rats musqués etc. Telle est la monnaie avec laquelle ils achètent leur habillement et leur munition. Cependant, les femmes sont restées au bord de l'eau, et après avoir reçu les baisers de leurs commères, se sont mises en devoir de dresser la loge, ce ne sera que plus tard qu'elles iront au Fort si tant est qu'elles y paraissent.

C 23 R.P. POINT DE FORT WILLIAM, LE 15 SEPTEMBRE 1859

Le supérieur a d'excellentes qualités, volonté forte, cœur excellent, courage, ponctualité parfaite. Son caractère rigide pour lui-même et trop pour les autres, l'éprouve lui-même et surtout les autres. Son principe est toujours le zèle de l'ordre. Il ne sait pas assez fléchir, consoler, encourager... Il veut trop la pauvreté et l'économie, et même la mortification dans la vie commune. La fermeté, une certaine sévérité, est nécessaire avec les sauvages, mais il y en apparence de l'irritation nerveuse qui empêcha l'onction de sa parole. C'est la règne de la crainte plus que de l'amour, surtout dans ses instructions. Mais il aime sa vocation ; il aime ses sauvages. En particulier, il est patient, complaisant, charitable. Pour apprécier le père Choné, il faut le connaître à fond ; pour lui être utile il ne font pas exagérer ses torts et faut lui parler au cœur. Les reproches vifs et secs ne lui conviennent pas.

De son côté, le P. Ferrart a quelque chose de sec et de mordant. Nécessairement tous deux souffriront, l'un et l'autre. Heureusement, le P. Ferrart a deux missions à visiter ; il ne sera pas longtems à la résidence.

E 27 DE LA BAIE DU HÉRON À PORT ARTHUR
[*Daoust, Cent Vingt Jours de Service Actif, pp. 28–33*]

Enfin à six heures du matin le train arrêta à la Baie du Héron. En moins de cinq minutes tout le bataillon était descendu en ligne. Pour la première fois une pauvre ration de rhum fut donnée à chaque homme et sans rien exagérer elle avait été richement gagnée. Bientôt après on nous servit à déjeuner dans les chantiers du Pacifique...

Après un copieux déjeuner, le bataillon remonta à bord et l'on continua dans les mêmes chars jusqu'à Port Munroe, ou l'on arrivera vers neuf heures de l'avant midi. Ici, on laissa les chars et la marche à pied commença. Chaque soldat portait sur lui, outre sa carabine et ses munitions, toutes les parties de son accoutrement, havresac et autres. Après une aussi mauvais nuit, la marche de long de la rive nord du Lac Supérieur vingt-cinq milles, fait en moins de dix heures, tient du prodige.

Peu d'hommes, même de vieux militaires auraient pu résister aussi bravement à une aussi forte étape, et chose plus étonnante encore, pas un seul homme ne fut malade. Une seule halte fut faite pendant la marche à Little Peak, où l'on fit une distribution de rations, fromage et « hardtacks ». Si la fatigue fut grande, on eut une faible compensation par le magnifique coup d'œil présenté par le coucher du soleil sur le lac...

Vers huit heures du soir tout le bataillon était remonté dans les nouveaux chars, pires que ceux qu'on venait de laisser. Ceux-ci n'étaient formés que de plate-formes simples avec une planche chaque côté pour servir de garde-fou.

Sur les planches d'autres plus minces étaient posées aussi près que possible les unes des autres, et servaient de sièges aux soldats fatigués. L'on marcha ainsi tout le reste de la nuit et il était une heure du matin quand on descendit à Jackfish Syndicate.

A peine les soldats étaient-ils descendus des chars que la pluie commença à tomber. Malheureusement il n'y avait aucun abri pour recevoir tous les soldats et plusieurs compagnies attendirent, au-delà d'une demi-heure exposées à l'intempérie de la saison...

A deux heures du matin, après avoir bien mangés, les compagnies 2, 3, 4, 5 et 6 se retirèrent dans les hangars de la compagnie du Pacifique, tandis que les autres, 1, 7 et 8, remontèrent en chars et durent conduites au village de Jackfish, où un grand hangar avait été preparé pour elles. Un bon feu fut entretenu toute la nuite dans les deux poêles de l'habitation, et pour la première fois depuis leur départ de Montréal, les volontaires dormirent bien et se reposèrent...

Pendant l'après-midi, les volontaires se réfugièrent sous les tentes et l'on s'amusa à chanter pour passer le temps, car la pluie ne cessait pas. Quelques-uns se dirigèrent vers une vieille mâsure dont l'enseigne moins prétentieuse par la forme que par le nom qu'elle portait avait attiré leur attention. On vendait de la boisson dans ce chantier, la bière s'y debitait à 15 centins, et ce qu'on etait convenu d'appeler du « whiskey » a 25 centins le verre...

Des quatre heures le lendemain matin, les trois compagnies qui avaient passé la nuit au village se levèrent et les chars n'arrivant pas, elles se mirent en marche et traversèrent le lac à pied jusqu'au Syndicat.

Après une heure de marche, ces soldats n'eurent pour tout déjeuner qu'une tranche de lard entre deux morceaux de pain.

A huit heures a.m. les premiers traîneaux, chargés de soldats, se mirent en marche et les autres ne tardèrent pas à les suivre. Ce nouveau trajet le long du Lac Supérieur, malgré qu'il se fit en voiture, ne fut guère plus plaisant que le premier. Le froid était très grand et les soldats entassés dans les voitures furent souvent obligés de descendre pour ne pas geler des pieds. Enfin vers deux heures de l'après-midi, le premier traîneau entra dans une baie profonde dont on ne put connaître le nom. Après une halte d'une heure et demie en cet endroit, le bataillon remonta en chars plate-formes et continua jusqu'à McKay Harbour où il y avait un hôpital. Ici, on laissa notre invalide Boucher...

A sept heures et demie, les soldats durent traverser de nouveau à pied un longueur de onze milles sur la Baie du Tonnerre et arrivèrent à Red Rock à onze heures du soir.

Ici les chars à passagers attendaient le régiment et vers minuit le train partait.

Cette journée fut une des plus rudes pour les soldats. De quatre heures du matin à onze heures du soir, on n'avait pas cessé de marcher un seul moment. Quatorze milles à pied, vingt-deux en traîneaux et plus de cent milles en mauvais chars découverts et tout près de cent cinquante milles parcourus dans la journée.

Vers six heurs jeudi matin, l'on entra dans Port Arthur. Les soldats furent bientôt éveillés par les cris de la foule qui les attendait à la gare. Pendant que les compagnies s'éloignaient, chacune de son côté, pour déjeuner dans les différents hôtels de la ville, les officiers se rendirent à l'hotel Brunswick sur l'invitation du maire de la localité.

BIBLIOGRAPHY
AND
INDEX

BIBLIOGRAPHY

MANUSCRIPTS

CANADA

Public Archives of Canada (P.A.C.)
Algoma Silver Mining Company Papers, MG 28 III-19
American Fur Company Records, microfilm of originals in the possession of the New York Historical Society
Alexander Begg's Red River Journal, MG 29, F-3
James Bissett Diaries, MG 24, H 36
Sandford Fleming's C.P.R. Letterbooks, MG 29 A-8
RG 7 G-1, Despatches from Colonial Office to Governors-General
Hudson's Bay Company Records, 1821–70, microfilm of originals in Hudson's Bay House, London
Indian Affairs Department Letter Books, RG 10 C-3
Keefer Papers, MG 29 B-10
Lefroy Papers, MG 24 H-25
Lisgar Papers, MG 27 B-2
Lorne Letter Book, MG 27 I B-4
Macdonald Papers, MG 26 A
Macdonell of Collachie Papers, Allan Macdonell, Mining Papers, MG 24 I-8
McIntyre Papers, MG 29 D-10
Northwest Papers, Miscellaneous Correspondence 1797–1850, MG 19 A-30
Port Arthur Customs Records, 1874–91, RG 16 A 5–7
Port Arthur Shipping Register, 1886–1913, RG 12 A-1
Stephen Papers, MG 29 A-20
Van Horne Letter Books, typescripts from the originals in the possession of Canadian Pacific Railways, Montreal, MG 28 III-20
Map Division
Print Division

ONTARIO

Department of Public Records and Archives (P.A.O.)
Alexander Campbell Papers
Charles Clarke Papers
Colonization Roads Papers

Crown Lands Papers, Townships of McIntyre, Neebing, Oliver, and Paipoonge
Dawson Papers
Education Office, Incoming General Correspondence, 1870–
Irving Papers
Lands and Forests Department Papers –
  Applications for Timber Licences
  Ground Rent Journals
  Minutes, Association of Ontario Lumbermen, 1887–1905
  Western Timber District Licentiates
  Woods and Forest Branch Report Book
Miscellaneous Manuscripts
Strachan Papers
Surveyors' Accounts
Surveyors' Letters
David Thompson Journals, 1823–5
Map Division
Print Division

Corporation of the City of Fort William
Fort William Council Minutes, 1892–7

Lakehead University Library (L.U.L.)
D.F. Burk Papers
Documents dealing with the history of the Rescue Company
Early Lakehead newspapers
Silver Islet Papers
Hudson's Bay Company Letters

London, University of Western Ontario Library (U.W.O.)
Coyne Papers

Corporation of the City of Port Arthur
Port Arthur Council Minutes, 1884–92
Port Arthur Board of Health Minutes
Port Arthur City Files – Taxation

Metropolitan Toronto Central Library (M.T.C.L.)
Denison Papers, Frederick C. Denison Diaries
Roderick McLennan Papers

Archives of the United Church, Victoria University
McKerracher Diaries and Correspondence

Private Ownership
Dr P.M. Ballantyne, Thunder Bay, Petition drawn up by the Fort William Indians, 1886

Miss Joan Featherstonhaugh, Richmond Hill, Thomas G. Anderson
  Papers
Mrs Gordon McLaren, Paipoonge Township, Diary of Peter McKellar,
  1874–5

QUEBEC

Archives de la Société de Jésus du Canada Français (A.S.J.C.F.)
  Lettres des nouvelles missions du Canada, 1844–52
  Letters and reports by Father Choné, Father Point, and Father Jones

UNITED STATES

National Archives, Washington, D.C.
  Letters of Major Joseph Delafield

NEWSPAPERS AND PERIODICALS

Algoma Missionary News and Shingwauk Journal, 1877–80.
Fort William *Journal*, 1887–91, weekly; 1891–3, semi-weekly.
Toronto *Daily Globe*, 1858–95. On microfilm.
Toronto *Daily Mail*, 1872–95. On microfilm.
Thunder Bay *Sentinel*, 1875–95, weekly. On microfilm.
The Weekly Herald and Lake Superior Mining Journal, Port Arthur,
  1882–7. On microfilm.
The Weekly Herald and Algoma Miner, Port Arthur, 1887–95. On micro-
  film.

CONTEMPORARY WORKS, DESCRIPTIVE ACCOUNTS, AND TRAVELS

AGASSIZ, LOUIS, *Lake Superior, its physical character, vegetation, and
  animals compared with those of other and similar regions, with a nar-
  rative of the tour by J. Elliot Cabot* (Boston, 1850).
BALLANTYNE, R.M., *Hudson's Bay; or Every-day life in the wilds of
  North America, during six years' residence in the territory of the Hon.
  Hudson's bay company* (Boston, 1859).
BIGSBY, DR J.J., *By Shoe and Canoe; or Pictures of Travel in the Canadas*
  (2 vols., London, 1850).
CASS, LEWIS, *Remarks on the Policy and Practice of U.S. and Great
  Britain in the Treatment of the Indians*, reprinted from the *North
  American Review*, April 1827.
CUMBERLAND, F.B., ed., *The Northern Lakes of Canada; the Niagara
  River & Toronto, the Lakes of Muskoka, Lake Nipissing, Georgian
  Bay, Great Manitoulin Channel, Mackinac, Sault Ste. Marie, Lake
  Superior* (Toronto 1886).

DAOUST, C.R., *Cent Vingt Jours de Service Actif – récit historique très complet de la Compagne du 65ème au Nord Ouest* (Montreal, 1886).

DELAFIELD, JOSEPH, *The Unfortified Boundary: a diary of the first survey of the Canadian boundary line from St. Regis to the Lake of the Woods by Major Joseph Delafield, American agent under articles VI and VII of the Treaty of Ghent*, ed. Robert McElroy and Thomas Riggs (New York, 1943).

DUFFERIN and AVA, HARIOT GEORGINA HAMILTON-TEMPLE-BLACK-WOOD, MARCHIONESS OF, *My Canadian Journal, 1872–8; Extracts from my Letters Home, written when Lord Dufferin was Governor-General* (London 1891).

GARRY, NICHOLAS, "Diary of Nicholas Garry," ed. F.N.A. Garry, Royal Society of Canada, *Transactions*, 2nd series, 1900, v. 6, pp. 73–204.

GRANT, W.M., *Ocean to Ocean; Sandford Fleming's Expedition through Canada in 1872* (rev. ed., Toronto, 1925).

———— *Picturesque Canada: the Country as it Was and Is* (2 vols., Toronto, 1882).

HAMILTON, JAMES CLELAND, *The Prairie Provinces, sketches of travel from Lake Ontario to Lake Winnipeg* ... (Toronto, 1876).

HARGRAVE, JAMES, *The Hargrave Correspondence*, ed. G.P. deT. Glazebrook (Toronto, 1938).

HARGRAVE, LETITIA, *The Letters of Letitia Hargrave*, ed. Margaret A. MacLeod (Toronto, 1947).

HEWSON, M. BUTT, *Notes on the Canadian Pacific Railway* (Toronto 1879).

HIND, HENRY Y., *Narrative of the Canadian Red River exploring expedition of 1857 and the Assiniboine and Saskatchewan exploring expedition of 1858* (2 vols., London, 1860).

HUYSHE, G.L., *The Red River Expedition* (London, 1871).

JACOBS, PETER, *Journal of the Rev. Peter Jacobs, Indian Wesleyan Missionary from Rice Lake to the Hudson's Bay Territory and returning, commencing May, 1852* (Toronto, 1854).

KANE, PAUL, *Wanderings of an Artist among the Indians of North America*, ed. L.J. Burpee (Toronto, 1925).

LOGAN, W.E., *Remarks on the Mining Region of Lake Superior* (Montreal, 1847).

MACDONELL, ALLAN, "Observations upon the Construction of a Railroad from Lake Superior to the Pacific," in *Project for the Construction of a Railroad to the Pacific* (Toronto, 1852), pp. 5–36.

———— *The North-west Transportation, Navigation, and Railway Company: Its Objects* (Toronto, 1858).

McKENNEY, THOMAS L. and HALL, JAMES, *History of the Indian Tribes of North America, with biographical sketches and anecdotes of the principal chiefs* (2 vols., Philadelphia, 1836).

McLEAN, JOHN, *Notes of a Twenty-Five Years' Service in the Hudson's Bay Territory*, ed. W.S. Wallace (Toronto, 1932).

McLEOD, MARTIN, "The Diary of Martin McLeod," ed. Grace Lee Nute, *Minnesota History*, Nov. 1922, pp. 351–423.

Prince Arthur's Landing and the Terminus of the Canadian Pacific Railway (Toronto, 1878).

Prince Arthur's Landing or Port Arthur, Ontario, Canada, the "Silver Gate" and her Leading Industries (Winnipeg, 1883).

The Question of the Terminus of the Branch of the Pacific Railway North Shore of Lake Superior (Ottawa, 1874).

ROLAND, A.W., *Algoma West; its mines, scenery, and industrial resources* (Toronto, 1887).

—— *Port Arthur Illustrated* (Winnipeg, 1889).

RYERSON, JOHN, *Hudson's Bay; or a Missionary tour in the Territory of the Hon. Hudson's Bay Company* (Toronto, 1855).

SIMPSON, FRANCES (LADY), "Frances Simpson's 1830 Journal," ed. Grace Lee Nute, *Beaver*, March 1854, pp. 12–17.

SIMPSON, SIR GEORGE, *Narrative of a Journey round the World during the years 1841 and 1842* (2 vols., London, 1847).

WARREN, W.W., *The History of the Ojibway Nation* (Reprinted Minneapolis, 1957).

WOLSELEY, SIR GARNET, *Narrative of the Red River Expedition* (Reprinted from *Blackwood's Magazine*, Dec. 1870–Feb. 1871).

—— *A Soldier's Life* (2 vols., London, 1903).

WOODSIDE, HENRY J., "The Queen's Highway," in *Dominion Illustrated Monthly*, Dec. 1892, pp. 691–8.

The Woodstock Letters, a record of current events and historical notes connected with the colleges and missions of the Society of Jesus in North and South America (35 vols., New York, 1872–1906).

GOVERNMENT PUBLICATIONS, OFFICIAL REPORTS, DIRECTORIES, AND CALENDARS

ASSOCIATION OF LAND SURVEYORS, *Annual Report* (Toronto, 1886–).

BLUE, ARCHIBALD, "The Story of Silver Islet," Ontario Bureau of Mines, 6th *Report* (Toronto, 1896).

BORRON, E.B., *Reports of the Stipendiary Magistrates with respect to the Northerly and Westerly Parts of the Province of Ontario* (Toronto, 1880–4). Title varies.

CANADA (PROVINCE OF) Statutes, 1841–66.

—— Legislative Assembly, *Journals*, 1841–66.

—— Legislative Assembly, *Sessional Papers*, 1841–66.

—— Department of Crown Lands, *Report*, 1856–66.

—— Geological Survey, *Report of Progress*, 1843–66.

—— *Report of the Special Commissioners appointed on the 8th of September, 1856, to investigate Indian Affairs* (Toronto, 1858).

CANADA (DOMINION OF) *Statutes*, 1867–92.

———— Department of the Interior, *Report of International Boundary Commission* (Ottawa and Washington, 1931).

———— Geological Survey, *Report of Progress*, 1867–92.

———— House of Commons, *Debates*, 1867–92.

———— House of Commons, Select committee on the boundaries between the province of Ontario and the unorganized territories of the Dominion, *Report* (Ottawa, 1880).

———— Senate, *Journals*, 1867–92.

———— *Sessional Papers*, 1867–92.

Canadian Parliamentary Companion, 1862–95 (title varies, publisher varies).

CASE'S *Director of Fort William and Port Arthur and the district of Thunder Bay* (Fort William, 1894).

COTÉ, J.O., ed., *Political Appointments and Elections in the Province of Canada, 1841–1866* (Ottawa, 1866).

DAWSON, S.J., *Report on the Exploration of the Country between Lake Superior and the Red River Settlement* (Toronto 1859).

———— *Report on the Line of Route between Lake Superior and Red River Settlement* (Ottawa, 1868).

FLEMING, SANDFORD, *Progress Report on the Canadian Pacific Railway Exploratory Survey* (Ottawa, 1872).

———— *Report of Progress on the Explorations and Surveys* (Ottawa, 1874).

———— *Report and documents in reference to the location of the line and a western terminal harbour* (Ottawa, 1878).

———— *Report to the Minister of Public Works in reference to the Canadian Pacific Railway* (Ottawa, 1879).

———— *Report and Documents in reference to the Canadian Pacific Railway* (Ottawa, 1880).

GREAT BRITAIN, Parliament, *Correspondence relative to the Recent Expedition to the Red River Settlement with Journal of Operations* (London, 1871).

HIND, HENRY Y., *North-west Territory; Reports of Progress, together with a preliminary and general report on the Assiniboine and Saskatchewan exploring expedition, made under instructions from the provincial secretary* (Toronto, 1859).

INGALL, E.D., *Mines and Mining on Lake Superior*, Geological Survey of Canada Annual *Report*, 1887–8 (Montreal, 1888).

LEWIS, RODERICK, comp., *A Statistical History of all the Electoral Districts of Ontario since 1867* (Toronto, 196?).

LINDSEY, CHARLES, *A Report on the Boundaries of Ontario* (Toronto, 1873).

MILLS, DAVID, *A Report on the Boundaries of Ontario* (Toronto, 1873).

MONTREAL MINING COMPANY, *Rules and By-Laws* (Montreal, 1847).

———— *Annual Reports*, 1852, 1853, 1860.

MORRIS, ALEXANDER, *The Treaties of Canada with the Indians of Mani-*

toba and the North-West Territories (Toronto, 1880).

ONTARIO, DEPARTMENT OF CROWN LANDS, *Northern Districts of Ontario* (Toronto, 1899).

—— *Report*, 1867–92.

ONTARIO, BUREAU OF FORESTRY, "A History of Crown Timber Regulations from the Date of the French Occupation to the Present Time, Compiled with the Assistance of Mr. Aubrey White," Ontario, Bureau of Forestry, *Annual Report*, 1899, pp. 29–139.

ONTARIO, Legislative Assembly, *Journals*, 1867–92.

—— *Sessional Papers*, 1867–92.

—— *Statutes*, 1867–92.

—— *Statutes, Documents and Papers Bearing on the Discussion respecting the Northern and Western Boundaries of the Province of Ontario* (Toronto, 1878).

NUTE, GRACE LEE, ed., *The Papers of the American Fur Company* (American Historical Association *Report*, 1944, vols. 2 and 3).

QUEBEC AND LAKE SUPERIOR MINING ASSOCIATION, *Report to the Directors*, 1847–8 (n.p., 1847–8).

SHORTT, ADAM, and DOUGHTY, A.G., eds., *Documents Relating to the Constitutional History of Canada, 1759–1791* (2 vols., Ottawa, 1918).

THOMAS, L., *Fort William, Port Arthur, and Thunder Cape*, Memoir #167, Geological Survey, Department of Mines (Ottawa, 1931).

VOORHIS, ERNEST, *Historic Forts and Trading Posts*, Department of the Interior (Ottawa, 1930).

SELECTED SECONDARY WORKS AND REMINISCENCES

BERTRAND, J.P., *Highway of Destiny* (New York, 1959).

BOND, C.C.J., *Surveyors of Canada, 1867–1967* (Ottawa, 1966).

BOON, T.C., *The Anglican Church from the Bay to the Rockies* (Toronto, 1963).

DYKE, GERTRUDE H., *Historic Silver Islet* (Fort William, 1964).

Fort William – the Gateway to the Gold Fields (Fort William, 1898).

DE LA FOSSE, F.M., "Reminiscences of a Vagabond," in Thunder Bay Historical Society *Papers*, 1926–8, pp. 62–75.

FOUNTAIN, PAUL, *The Great Northwest and the Great Lakes Region* (London, 1904).

FREGEAU, F., "Reminiscences of Early Journalism in Fort William," in Thunder Bay Historical Society *Papers*, 1911–12, pp. 20–1.

GALBRAITH, JOHN S., *The Hudson's Bay Company as an Imperial Factor* (Toronto, 1957).

GILBERT, HEATHER, *Awakening Continent – the life of Lord Mount Stephen, 1829–1891* (Aberdeen, 1965).

HASTE, RICHARD A., "The Lost Mine of Silver Islet," in Thunder Bay Historical Society *Papers*, 1926–8, pp. 36–43.

Historic Fort William (Fort William, 1927).

INNIS, H.A., *A History of the Canadian Pacific Railway* (Toronto, 1923).
—— *The Fur Trade in Canada* (Toronto, 1930).

KING, JOHN, "C.P.R. Construction in Fort William in 1875," in Thunder Bay Historical Society *Papers*, 1926–8, pp. 44–52.

LEHMANN, JOSEPH, *All Sir Garnet* (London, 1964).

LIVINGSTONE, JANEY C., *Historic Silver Islet; the story of a drowned mine* (Fort William, n.d.).

LONGSTRETH, T.M., *Lake Superior Country* (Toronto, 1924).

LOWER, A.R.M., *Canadians in the Making* (Toronto, 1958).
—— *The North American Assault on the Canadian Forest: A History of the Lumber Trade between Canada and the United States* (Toronto, 1936).

MACFARLANE, THOMAS, "Silver Islet," a paper read in September 1879, parts of which were selected by W.J. Hamilton for publication in Thunder Bay Historical Society *Papers*, 1911–12, pp. 31–42.

MACGILLIVRAY, G.B., *A History of Fort William and Port Arthur Newspapers from 1875* (Fort William, 1968).

MACKAY, DOUGLAS, *The Honourable Company* (Toronto, 1936).

MACKENZIE, N.W.M.J., *Men of the Hudson's Bay Company* (Fort William, 1921).

MCINTYRE, ANNIE E., "John McIntyre," in Thunder Bay Historical Society *Papers*, 1926–8, pp. 76–9.

MCKELLAR, PETER, "How Nepigon Bay Lost the C.P.R. Shipping Port on the Great Lakes," in Thunder Bay Historical Society *Papers*, 1911–12, pp. 25–7.
—— "The Original Kaministiquia Club," in Thunder Bay Historical Society *Papers*, 1915, pp. 7–9.

MOBERLEY, H.J., *When Fur Was King*, in collaboration with W.B. Cameron (New York, 1929).

MORTON, A.S., *History of the Canadian West to 1871* (Toronto, 1939).

NORTON, SISTER MARY AQUINAS, *Catholic Missionary Activities in the Northwest, 1818–1864* (Washington, 1930).

NUTE, GRACE LEE, *Lake Superior* (New York, 1944).

PACKARD, PEARL, *The Reluctant Pioneer* (Montreal, 1968).

PIPER, W.S., *The Eagle of Thunder Cape* (Toronto, 1924).

REEVES, HELENA K., *In the Shadow of the Sleeping Giant* (Port Arthur, 1947).

RUSSELL, A.L., "Fort William in the XIX Century," in Thunder Bay Historical Society *Papers*, 1915, pp. 11–16.

RICH, E.E., *The History of the Hudson's Bay Company 1670–1870* (2 vols., London, 1958–9).

SPRY, IRENE M., *The Palliser Expedition* (Toronto, 1963).

THOMSON, DON W., *Men and Meridians – a History of Surveying and Mapping in Canada* (2 vols., Ottawa, 1966, 1968).

YOUNG, J.E., *Grain Elevator Construction and Shipping in the Lakehead Harbour since 1883* (Port Arthur–Fort William, 1964).

INDEX